The Multics System:

An Examination of Its Structure

The MIT Press
Cambridge, Massachusetts,
and London, England

The Multics System:

An Examination of Its Structure

Elliott I. Organick

This book was designed by the MIT Press Design Department.
It was set in IBM Press Roman
printed on 55# Mohawk Neotext Offset
by Vail-Ballou Press, Inc.
and bound
by Vail-Ballou Press, Inc.
in the United States of America.

Library of Congress Cataloging in Publication Data

Organick, Elliott Irving, 1925–
The Multics system.

Includes bibliographical references.
1. Multics (Electronic computer system)
I. Title.
QA76.5.073 001.6'4 78–157477
ISBN 0–262–15012–3

Contents

Foreword

The Multics project began at M.I.T. in the fall of 1964 and became, by early 1965, a cooperative effort involving the Bell Telephone Laboratories, the computer department of the General Electric Company,[1] and Project MAC of M.I.T.[2] The goals and aspirations of the project were comprehensively set out in a series of six papers presented at the 1965 Fall Joint Computer Conference.[3] The essence of these goals was to develop a working prototype of a computer utility embracing the whole complex of hardware, software, and users that would provide a desirable as well as a feasible model for other system designers to study. The system was offered for general use at M.I.T. in October 1969.

From the inception of the project, a principal objective has been the transmittal to others of the knowledge and understanding of system organization that would come out of the effort. As a first step in this direction two major policies were established from the beginning. The first policy declared that all program modules were to be designed and thoroughly specified before implementation; the second policy stated that all modules were to be programmed in the PL/I language[4] so that the design issues would be more lucidly expressed. It was recognized, however, that the system in the form of program modules and specification would never be self-explanatory. Clearly there would have to be a variety of other means employed to illuminate the system mechanisms. Most important, there would have to be comprehensive descriptions giving perspective to key ideas of the implementation.

Thus, the present book must be viewed as part of the task of transferring to others the knowledge embedded in the Multics implementation. The Multics project was most fortunate in being able to attract the interest of Professor Elliott Organick, whose previous works of technical exposition have received wide distribution. It is indeed seldom that a computer operating system has obtained such a competent external view even while it was under development. Many difficulties had to be overcome. Professor Organick had to learn about the system in periods of intense development and redesign, and

1. Now part of Honeywell Information Systems Incorporated.
2. The work done by Project MAC was sponsored by the Advanced Research Projects Agency, Department of Defense, under Office of Naval Research Contract Number N00014-70-A-0362-0001.
3. *AFIPS* [American Federation of Information Processing Societies] *Conference Proceedings, Volume 27, Part 1, 1965 Fall Joint Computer Conference* (Washington, D.C.: Spartan Books, 1965), pp. 185–247.
4. "PL/I as a Tool for System Programming," *Datamation* 15, no. 5 (1969): 68–76.

often he had to obtain key information by interviewing busy programmers or by reading hastily written memoranda. During these periods, his patience, tact, and open-mindedness were especially appreciated by the members of the development team.

The structure of this book is best understood from its origins. One of the goals that was set for the Multics system was that it should serve as a foundation upon which persons other than the system designers could build complicated and sophisticated software subsystems. If done well, such a foundation would remove many of the burdens and technical concerns that a subsystem designer might have. Nevertheless, it was realized that even the expert programmer would have to have a detailed understanding of the many mechanisms he was relying upon if he were to use the novel aspects of the system effectively. For this reason Professor Organick initially set out to write a guide for subsystem writers that would give them a better comprehension of the system mechanisms they were to depend on. It was soon apparent from the drafts of the first chapter that such a limited goal could not be achieved out of the context of a full integrated description of the system. Professor Organick then began a systematic study of the system from the ground up, beginning with the hardware modifications that transformed the GE 635 computer into the GE 645. He gradually developed chapter after chapter describing the fundamental structure of the system. It is a testimonial to his diligence and perseverence that the present work correctly describes the system up to the fall of 1970, even though both system and book have evolved in major ways since he started.

Today the Multics system is by most standards a large one involving about 1500 modules each averaging 200 typewritten lines; the full system compiles into about a million lines of code. Yet the system is probably one of the few in the world of such size that is well-suited for long-term evolution and that within a certain class of machines can be installed on new hardware foundations. But whether one is attempting to modify the system or to develop similar operating systems, one needs to have an understanding of the many ideas and internal strategies that must harmoniously and self-consistently work together. The listings of the system are far too detailed and frequently obscure the intentions of the programmer-designers who developed the modules. The original papers on Multics describing the goals and objectives are vague when it comes to specific details. The external specifications of how one uses the system do not attempt to describe with any depth the means by which the mechanisms are accomplished. In short this book fills a void by developing key expository paths through the system.

This book represents the first generally available comprehensive description of the Multics system that exposes the key mechanisms required for the computer utility goals. The approach taken parallels the system development and thereby ensures that each idea is built upon a firm description of the earlier ideas. This method of presentation has the advantage that the reader is able to climb upward from the foundations of the system, never having to doubt whether some major ideas or mechanisms have been glossed over. By contrast, many of the published papers on Multics have the quality of aerial photographs, where although it is clear that one has an excellent overview, one is not always certain what lies beneath the surface. The difficulty with the papers is that, even taken as a whole, they are still fragmentary and incomplete. Thus, the present book represents a major milestone in the descriptive history of the Multics system.

This foreword would not be complete without expressing the warm gratitude of the Multics development staff towards Professor Organick. For he brought to the effort, not only his expository talents, but a sustained enthusiasm that significantly contributed to the success of the Multics system development.

Finally, I would like to express my personal pleasure in having the privilege of working with Professor Organick during the development effort. His presence at M.I.T. as a colleague during 1968 to 1969 will be remembered, not only for his technical contributions, but also for those qualities of his spirit which mark a scholar, a gentleman, and a friend.

F. J. Corbató

Cambridge, Massachusetts
December 13, 1971

Preface

Multics and the Challenge to Describe It

In 1966 Multics was a plan for a computer and programming system environment that was new in concept, large in scope, and unique in its implementation relative to its predecessors. Its overall objectives were in harmony with what are now widely accepted goals for large-scale, time-shared, general-purpose utilitylike information systems. In a sentence, these objectives were and are to provide multiaccess computer use to a large community of individual problem solvers, teams of cooperating researchers, and/or (legitimately) competing entrepeneurs, by providing reliable processing power and storage that expands as required and in which information private to its users can be shared in a controlled manner.

In 1971 Multics is a reality and indeed has a growing community of such users. How should the structure and potential of such a system with its several important and innovative features be conveyed to its relatively sophisticated user community? That nontrivial challenge clearly had to be met. A number of key people within the Project MAC effort at M.I.T. realized this at an early date.

A system as large as Multics deserves several attempts at description, possibly from different levels of detail and from different points of view. This book is one of several, hopefully, complementary efforts.

The complement of this book that is currently most accessible from the standpoint of readability, accuracy, and usefulness is the "Multics Programmers' Manual," or MPM. It offers readers an opportunity to gain a rather quick overview of the structure and objectives of Multics from a top-down viewpoint. A significant amount of primer and reference material, including the descriptions of a large number of "commands," is also included in the MPM. Using it, beginners and more sophisticated users can teach themselves how to use the system.

Of course, sophisticated users can expect to make excellent use of the system almost from the start. However, many will find themselves needing or wanting to know more about Multics, especially *how it works*, in order to gain confidence that they are really able to exploit the system fully as they design increasingly larger programs and subsystems.

Anticipating the eventual and successful completion of Multics, the preparation of this book was undertaken to serve the expected needs of the subsystem designer.

The following two assumptions have been made about the reader. (1) He is a moderately well informed computer user (though perhaps not a "computer professional") accustomed to predecessor systems, either like CTSS, the first large time-sharing system at M.I.T., or like the still-prevalent batch-oriented compile-load-and-go services. (2) He has probably already read some of the overview literature of Multics, perhaps some of the published technical papers on Multics. Preferably, he has read the overview found in the "Multics Programmers' Manual." (A Multics bibliography appears at the end of this volume.)

The task of preparing this book had its obstacles, and these have certainly influenced the resulting product. First, the author's understanding of operating systems like Multics's immediate predecessors was at the outset rather limited. Second, the detailed design of Multics itself was then (in 1966) only just emerging from its first iteration. Though the Multics objectives and overview were published at an early date [FJCC '65 papers], it was at first difficult for the author, functioning mainly as an observer, to relate with ease the emerging design details to the objectives and overview. Possibly this difficulty could be explained by the fact that documentation of the former was available in a set of working papers that were sometimes too detailed, and sometimes not yet written. The collection of these papers, now rather complete, form what is called the "Multics System-Programmers' Manual" (or the MSPM).[1] This is an ambitious and well-structured, evolving documentation of the entire software and hardware structure of Multics. It is without question the principal source material for the present book. (To be sure, there were also countless discussions with the Multics designers and systems programmers that authored or edited the MSPM. These discussions, amounting mostly to tutoring the author, proved to be crucially valuable for gaining the needed understanding.)

As a way of extracting and abstracting the heart of this material and as a way of modeling the path of the author's progressive understanding, the approach taken here is to give a bottom-up view of Multics. Admittedly, the order of topics that proved helpful or revealing to the author may not at all seem appropriate for some readers. It is hoped that some of these will read patiently and find that the approach I have taken has some merit after all.

The bottom-up view of Multics begins by explaining the machine, that is, those hardware features of the GE 645[2] that seemed especially important or that lent themselves easily for implementing some of the critical functions and properties of Multics. The idea was that an understanding of this hard-

1. It is possible that these papers, which are rather voluminous (at last count over 3000 pages), may someday be edited and published.

2. Since this book was written the computer division of General Electric has been purchased by Honeywell. The GE 645 computer is now named the Honeywell 645.

ware, treated in Chapter 1, would provide a firm base for gaining a progressively stronger grasp of the large and essential concepts of Multics, such as the virtual memory, dynamic linking of (information) segments, process structure, storage management, and processor management. Roughly speaking, the chapter sequence was planned to build an understanding of increasingly larger entities in Multics, proceeding in turn from the segment to the process (in one protection ring), to the full multiringed (view of a) process that is able to interact with and take full advantage of the file system and other system-provided services. After the process, sets of coexisting and cooperating processes are considered, at last giving the reader the topmost view of Multics as an operating system that oversees the distribution and fair sharing of the available resources, for example, memory, processors, and input/output devices, as well as segments, to satisfy the needs of collections of coexisting processes.

First, segments and the addressing of segments are considered (Chapter 1). Then, the ways procedure segments may link dynamically to one another and to data segments are treated (Chapter 2) as well as how procedure segments may be shared and reentrant. Accepting the objective of dynamic linking led the system's designer to develop and implement the Multics virtual memory.

Next (Chapter 3), how Multics provides for the solution of problems in the communication among procedures (of a process) using standard call, save, and return instruction sequences is considered. These sequences, incidentally, permit every pure procedure to be recursively called. It is only later that the reader can appreciate that the powerful (modular) facilities for interprocedure communication and dynamic linking that are developed to this point are fully exploited in the design and implementation of the system software itself. Users (subsystem writers) as well as systems programmers have essentially equal opportunity to exploit these facilities in their creative endeavors.

By now a reader would be gaining a picture of what a process is, a locus of control or execution point that passes through a collection of mutually accessible segments, that is, one that forms an address space. The early chapters do touch on the concepts of making a segment known to a process, that is, adding a segment to the address space of a process; however, they do not fully consider the organization and design of the file system that exercises the address-space management functions on the user's behalf. Chapter 4 introduces part of the file-system organization and services—that part deals with access control and protection. Here in this chapter full consideration is also given to per-process compartmentalization in the form of a *ring structure* that divides the address space of a process into domains of access privileges. The Multics access control and ring structure details as described in Chapter 4 are intended to offer the reader a nearly complete view of the potential for achieving controlled sharing of information in and for the subsystems that designers may build in Multics.

Chapter 5 is somewhat of a digression. Here two mildly esoteric forms of interprocedure communication within a process are considered along with the mechanisms to achieve these forms of communication. These two forms are the *signaling* of *conditions*, that is, the invocation of selected code (handlers) upon subsequent recognition of certain previously defined conditions, and the execution of *abnormal returns*, that is, transfers to return points either in the calling program or in a dynamic antecedent of the calling program—all the while recognizing that the recursive and reentrant environment forces consideration of the individual activations of these dynamic antecedents. The reader will see how the introduction of the process's ring structure (Chapter 4) has contributed to the complexity of the mechanisms needed to solve the interprocedure communication problems treated in Chapter 5.

In Chapter 6 the segment management functions of the Multics file system and how the user may employ these facilities to advantage are considered, Here the reader adds further to his increasing view of the open-ended information storage that Multics structures hierarchically through a system of directories. He is shown how the system creates and deletes segments, how it alters the attributes of segments and directories, and how an executing process may identify the directories and segments that it needs to link to so as to establish the address space required.

Chapter 7 can be regarded as the climax of this upward climb toward a top-level view of Multics and how it works. Here the life of a process in coexistence (competition, and/or cooperation) with other processes is pictured. The first part of Chapter 7 surveys the concepts of processor- and core-resource management, the multiprogramming and time-sharing strategies and mechanisms employed within Multics. The aim of this survey is to understand the opportunities for interprocess communication offered by Multics, as described in the second half of Chapter 7. A service in Multics known as the Interprocess Process Communication Facility provides users a chance to build subsystems that consist of sets of processes that may communicate through shared data bases, synchronize their respective activities, serve notice one to another of observed events thought to be of interest, and so on. Thus we hope to suggest ways to model or construct, through the asynchronous tasking facilities implied here, subsystems that are far more complex than could otherwise have been implemented using predecessor computing facilities.

The concluding Chapter 8 surveys the simple and relatively noncentral input/output control system of Multics. This input/output system is remarkable in that on the one hand its role is peripheral to Multics, and on the other hand it is both powerful and flexible. It is hoped that this chapter will also show the power of the Multics design because the input/output system is largely an application of the more-central system facilities described in earlier chapters.

What topics have been left out of this book or not adequately treated? For better or worse, direct discussion of a number of topics that will be of importance to many readers has been omitted. The list is long, but a few of its items are

system initialization,

system control and administration over who may use the system, how the resources other than hardware processors and core memory are managed and allocated, and how to charge for services,

user control including the login and logout procedures,

process creation details,

the command loop including the command language interpreter (the listener) and the nuances and power of the command language itself, and

the absentee monitor system.

Most of these topics are treated in the MPM.

This book cannot be regarded in any sense as a definitive work describing Multics. For one thing, Multics is a living, changing system and no book once bound between its covers can remain for long a true snapshot of that which it describes. Nevertheless, it is hoped that much of the flavor, structure, and power of Multics will remain revealed here for some time. Certainly the book reflects Multics as it has been first implemented. Principally, this material must be regarded as a supplement to a small, though growing, collection of documents that describe Multics from different viewpoints, levels, and purposes. The "Multics Programmers' Manual" and the research/design papers that have appeared in ACM, AFIPS, other journals, and symposia, all contribute, in the author's opinion, to a total view of Multics.

Other books and papers are awaited and will be most welcome. Especially helpful will be papers and books contributed by the principal designers and implementers of Multics, who are most likely to provide the much-wanted insight that will be useful for the design of future systems. Readers are reminded of the reading list of the available papers that appears as a bibliography.

It is a pleasure to recognize a number of M.I.T. faculty and research associates whose encouragement, counsel, or technical assistance contributed significantly to the completion of this study-writing project. I give special thanks to Professors Robert M. Fano and Fernando J. Corbató, and to Mr. Robert C. Daley.

Professor Fano, while director of Project MAC, invited me to participate and contribute to the Multics documentation effort. Professor Corbató, one of the principal architects and director of the Multics project at M.I.T., has been encouraging and patient with the iterative approach that I employed in learning how Multics works. Under his direction Professor Corbató and a team of other Multics designers and implementers patiently read the several drafts of this material always offering excellent criticism. Mr. Daley patiently read and criticized the manuscript in its entirety and in detail during the last several iterations. If this book exhibits clarity, internal consistency, unity, and authenticity, then much credit for it should go to Mr. Daley.

The helpful guidance and criticisms of Professors A. Evans, Jr., R. M. Graham, and J. H. Saltzer are also sincerely acknowledged. Other good teachers were M. Thompson, D. Clark, C. Garman, K. Martin, C. Marceau, R. Rappaport, M. D. Schroeder, A. Bensoussan, M. J. Spier, B. A. Tague, and M. Padlipsky. I am sure I have omitted the names of several other friends on the Multics staff (M.I.T., G.E., or Bell Labs) whose ideas or suggestions I have attempted to incorporate directly or indirectly in this work. To all these mainly young men and women whose brilliance and *esprit de corps* have helped to make Multics a pioneering success and an inspiring reality, I happily and gratefully dedicate this book.

Elliott I. Organick
Professor of Computer Science
University of Utah

The Multics System:

An Examination of Its Structure

1 Segmentation and Address Formation in the GE 645

1.1 Introduction

Computer specialists that read overviews of systems like Multics are generally quick to grasp their aims and objectives, but some others may be slow to comprehend how they work. They then find a need to dig into the details, attempting to reach an ultimate understanding of the system by starting from the inside core and working outward toward a grasp of the whole.

What constitutes the "inside" of Multics? Until it is understood better, there will probably be differing opinions. I believe it to be the *virtual memory environment* that Multics manages to provide[1] with the aid of special features that are built into the hardware of the GE 645 computer. For this reason most of this chapter is devoted to a look at these new features.

A prime purpose of the Multics virtual memory is for achieving controlled sharing of information among the system's users.

Information that is stored on-line in large information utilities generally far exceeds the size of available core memory. At one time or another not only must it be possible to make any of this information directly accessible to the central processors (on behalf of users), but in the most general case, provision must be made to share this information among several users whose separate computations share the system's resources, such as memory, processors, and input/output devices, in some controlled fashion.

There are significant gains in efficiency and in reduction of program complexity to be achieved if all the (on-line) information in storage can be made *processor addressable.* Efficiency is improved by elimination of the need for copying information unnecessarily (i.e., duplication of procedures and data or portions thereof). The Multics virtual memory is designed to take maximum advantage of these gains. A Multics user program, operating as it does in the virtual memory environment provided by the hardware and software, can directly address any required programs or parts of programs that it needs. This makes unnecessary the loading and binding together of copies of procedures needing execution. A Multics user program can also directly address just those data items it needs from the extensive on-line data files, so that each reference to such data items can (in the logical sense at least) be a single-step operation. The actual reference need not first be preceded by an input/output system request to input a (partial copy of that) file, nor be followed by an

1. A valuable (and readable) description, some of whose introduction we have taken the liberty to paraphrase in this introduction, is given in "The Multics Virtual Memory," by A. Bensoussan, C. T. Clingen, and R. C. Daley, *Second Symposium on Operating Systems Principles, Princeton University, October 1969* (New York: Association for Computing Machinery, 1969), pp. 30–42.

input/output system request to output the altered information to its original location.

In traditional systems, by contrast, core copies of data and procedure files are loaded (and possibly interlinked) to form "core images" for execution. These copies must be created by explicit file-system action (e.g., by read-file operations). In some systems, the file copies lose their original identity in the systemwide sense when they become part of a user program's core image. Because of this, data files so copied cannot then be shared by programs of other users. To make them shareable once again, data file copies must be remapped into files by explicit action (e.g., by write-file operations) before they can again be shared on a system-wide basis.

Even if the file copied into a core image does not lose its identity and therefore can still be shared with other processes via interpretive (rather than direct) accessing, there remains intrinsic to such systems the added complexity that results from dealing with two classes of information (programs or program segments and files) rather than one class (segments only) and the need to repeatedly map from one regime to and from the other.

Since program addressability in Multics is happily extended to the entire information store of the utility, ways must be found to "limit or control access to this information so that a computation may be self-protected from its own mishaps and so that different computations that share the same physical facilities may be mutually protected."[2] In Multics this control is achieved by compartmentalizing all of the stored information into discrete packages called *segments*, each having associated with it a set of access attributes that, among other things, describe the fashion in which each user is permitted to reference the contained procedure(s) and/or data. Although the processor is capable of addressing items within any package, the access attributes for the referencing user must be (and, indeed, are) enforced by the processor on each reference (to any package).

The segment can also be thought of as an extension of the notion of *file* found in more traditional systems. Thus, the Multics segment, like the CTSS file, is the unit of sharing, carries a symbolic name (or names), has a set of associated attributes, is permitted to grow and shrink, and so on. The Multics segment is directly addressable in programs; the CTSS file is not.

The combination of direct addressability and ability to control access to individual segments of information according to permissions given to each user provides the basis for the controlled information in Multics.

2. Ibid.

Prior to Multics, several well-known computer systems offered pioneering implementations of large virtual memories, that is, memories that permit the execution of programs whose size exceeds that of available core memory. Among these the implementation achieved by *demand paging* in the Atlas computer[3] and the implementation achieved by *segmentation* in the B5000 computer[4] are noteworthy.

The Atlas *demand paging* scheme allows a program to be divided physically into pages such that only some of these need reside in core memory at any one time. Moreover, any page may be relocated into any available (equal-sized) block of core memory for its period of residence there.

The B5000 *segmentation* scheme allows a program to be divided logically into segments, each being distinguished by its name, size, and other attributes. Only some of the segments of the program need be in core at any one time. Segments may be relocated into any section of core memory independently of other segments. However, since the entire segment must be brought into core when any part of it is needed, a contiguous section of core large enough for the entire segment must be found or made available for each segment's stay in core.

1.1.1 Paging and Segmentation in Multics

As we shall see in the details that follow, the GE 645 hardware, like that of several other more recent systems,[5,6] provides a combination of features rather similar to, but by no means identical with, the Atlas paging and B5000 segmentation. The net result is that only a few pages of a few segments need be available in core while a program is running. Moreover, the Multics segment relates more strongly (than in the case of the B5000) to the properties and uses of files.

The paging features provide relocatability, that is, location independence, of programs and lead to efficient and simple core memory resource management. Thinking in terms of layered constructs, one may picture that the

3. J. Fotheringham, "Dynamic Storage Allocation in the Atlas Computer, Including an Automatic Use of a Backing Store," *Communications of the ACM* [Association for Computing Machinery] 4, no. 10(1961): 435–436.

4. The Burroughs Corporation, *The Descriptor–A Definition of the B5000 Information Processing System* (Detroit: The Burroughs Corp., 1961).

5. W. T. Comfort, "A Computing System Design for User Services," *AFIPS* [American Federation of Information Processing Societies] *Conference Proceedings, Volume 27, Part 1, 1965 Fall Joint Computer Conference* (Washington, D.C.: Spartan Books, 1965), pp. 619–628. (This concerns the IBM 360/67 system.)

6. S. Motobayashi, T. Masuda, and N. Takahashi, "The HITAC5020 Time Sharing System," *Proceedings of 24th National Conference–Association for Computing Machinery*, ACM Publication P-69(1969), pp. 419–429.

segmentation scheme is built "on top of" the "paged machine." At least, one can better cope with the complexity of the combination if one proceeds in this fashion. For this reason, details of paging will, to some extent, be taken for granted in the early discussions but given some attention later in this chapter.[7]

It is also true that a user of the Multics system may reach a point of considerable sophistication (as a user), while ignoring the very existence of the paging mechanisms. The Multics design, in fact, makes paging transparent to the user. Thus, a user cannot directly create or delete a page in any way, but he can create or delete a segment and/or manipulate its attributes. For instance, a user can create a segment by issuing a call to the system supervisor, giving as arguments the appropriate attributes such as symbolic segment name, name of each user allowed to access the segment with his respective access rights, and so forth.

It is helpful for the user to think of the Multics memory in its idealized form, that is, as a large number of independent linear core memories, each capable of "housing" a segment that he (or someone else) may create. Associated with each of these memories is a descriptor, a small piece of additional memory for the storage of a segment's attributes. Once a segment has been created (i.e., assigned to one of these linear memories and its attributes placed in the associated descriptor memory), any word of that segment may be referenced by addressing the respective word in the corresponding linear memory. Such an address is actually an ordered pair [name, i], where "name" is the symbolic name of the segment and "i" is the word number in the corresponding linear memory for that segment. Of course, any other user can also reference (or attempt to reference) word i of this same segment, also using the pair [name, i], but he can access that word only according to the access rights (if any) that he was given by the creator of that segment and that are recorded in its descriptor. Combinations of "read," "write," "execute," and "append" access rights are possible. The hardware support for access rights are described in this chapter, but the strategies for use of these rights (access control and protection) are discussed mainly in Chapters 4 and 6.

The next subsections explain how, at the hardware level, the addressing of

7. Details of paging are provided partly to satisfy the curious and partly to assist those who may eventually become concerned with understanding core resource management issues and how they are handled in Multics, a topic given further attention in Chapter 7.

items in segments is accomplished in a given user's computation. The reader should be prepared to shift into the "low gear," that is, be ready to read some material that is given in reference-manual style. Material in subsequent chapters will help the reader to see how the idealized memory just described is realized (simulated) with benefit of the hardware features described in the remainder of this chapter.

1.2 Some Definitions and Concepts

1.2.1 Processor

A computer processing unit as found on any familiar computer.

1.2.2 Process (Lay Definition)[8]

A set of related procedures and data undergoing execution and manipulation, respectively, by one of possibly several processors of a computer. (The notion of the Multics process is central to this book, and unfolds informally throughout Chapters 1, 2, 3, 4, 6, and 7.)

1.2.3 Segments

A segment of a process is a collection of information important enough to be given a name. A segment is a unit of sharing and has associated with it a collection of attributes including a unique identification.

Segments are, generally speaking, blocks of code (procedures) or blocks of data ranging in size from zero to 2^{16} words.[9] Each segment can be allowed to grow or shrink during execution of the process. A record of its size is kept in the "descriptor word" associated with the segment.

1.2.3.1 Pages

Unseen by the user, hardware mechanisms exist for subdividing a segment into smaller units called *pages*, each of which may be located in smaller, discontiguous blocks of core memory. All pages of a segment are of the same size and are 1024 words.[10] If a segment is so subdivided, it is said to be "paged." Every segment that a user will have any control over will be paged.

8. The following technical definition is given in J. B. Dennis and Earl C. Van Horn, "Programming Semantics for Multiprogrammed Computations," *Communications of the ACM* [Association for Computing Machinery] 3, no. 9(1966):143–155. "A process is a locus of control within an instruction sequence. That is, a process is that abstract entity which moves through the instructions of a procedure as the procedure is executed by a processor."

9. The GE 645 hardware allows for segments of up to 2^{18} words, however Multics arbitrarily restricts this limit to 2^{16} words.

10. The Ge 645 hardware allows for two page sizes, 1024 words and 64 words, but Multics permits only the former size to be used.

1.2.3.2 Page Table

For each paged segment, the supervisor creates a table called a *page table* that, when stored in core memory, will contain pointers to the individual pages of the segment that may also be currently stored in memory.

1.2.4 Descriptor Segment

A table of some of the facts concerning the segments of a given process, one entry per segment. These entries are called descriptor words (or segment descriptor words).

1.2.5 Descriptor Word

A single entry (36 bits) in the descriptor segment. Each entry contains a pointer to the page table of the segment, if the segment is known to be residing in core memory. Otherwise, an indication of the segment's absence from core is provided in the entry. Also contained in the entry is the size (or

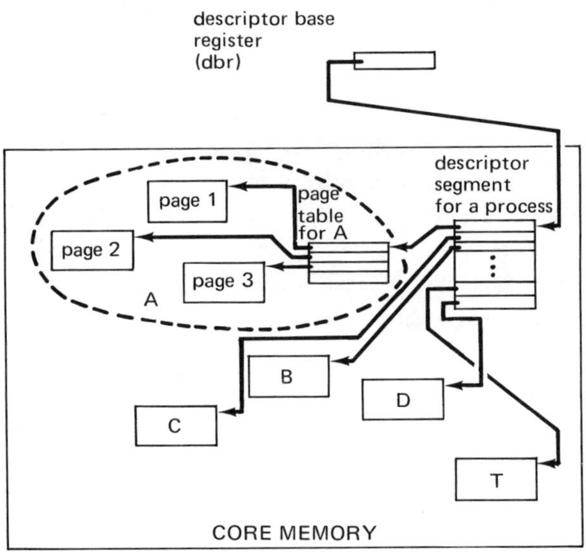

Figure 1.1. A process resident in core memory

The depicted process has a number of segments called (symbolically) "A", "C", "B", . . ., "T", "D". This is the order in which pointers to these segments happen to be listed in the process's descriptor segment. Note that the current contents of the descriptor base register (dbr) points to the head of the descriptor segment. The dbr is explained in Section 1.2.14.

(Each segment should, strictly speaking, be diagrammed with the detail shown for segment A. That is, first the page table and then the individual pages. To simplify the figures, I shall ordinarily avoid such detail and hope it will be inferred from the simplified, single-block pictures illustrated for segments C, B, etc.)

maximum allowable size) of the segment and a "descriptor" field (Figures 1.1 and 1.2).

1.2.6 Descriptor Field

This field is sometimes referred to as the *access-control* field. Bits in this field are set by the supervisor and interpreted by the hardware. (See Table 1.1, when details are wanted.) A segment exists in one of five classes defined by one subfield (bits 33–35). Another subfield defines the access rights to the segment of a currently executing segment, for example, permission to read and/or write in the segment. In the event the segment is not in core, the subfield defines the desired trap (hardware fault) to the supervisor. Other bits relate to details of the segment's further subdivision into pages—the level of detail that is curtained off from the eye of the user.

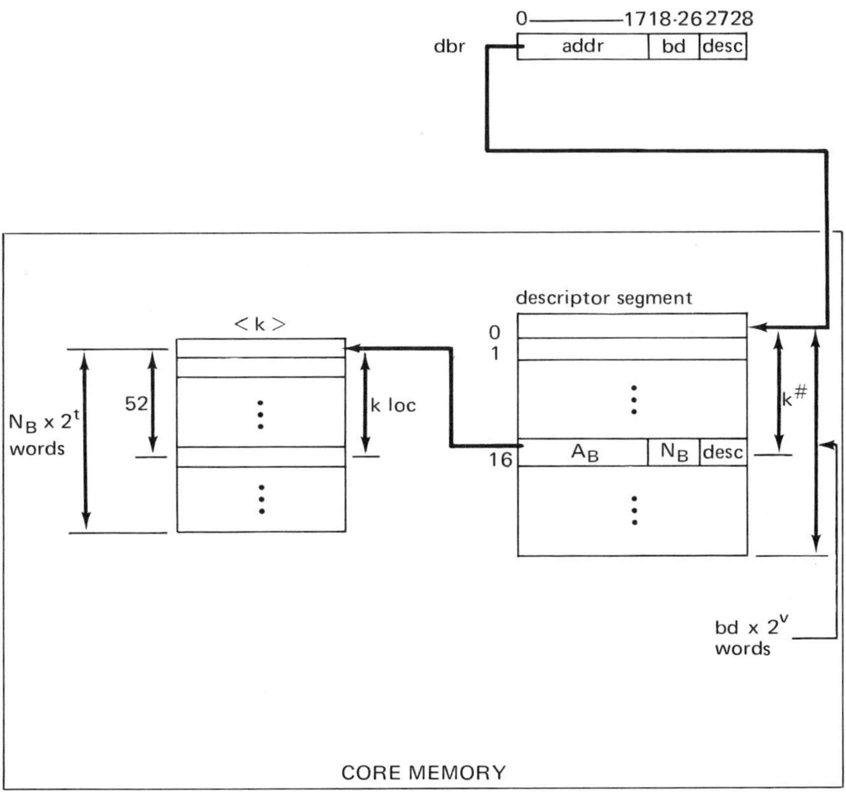

Figure 1.2. System of pointers to locate the core address of <k>|[kloc]

Table 1.1. Descriptor Field of the Segment Descriptor Word

Bit position

27	28	29	30	31	32	33	34	35
Page (block) size 1024 = 0 64 = 1	Paging for segment yes = 0 no = 1	Not used	Directed Fault 0 – 7, if segment class A; Write Permit MM = 0 only Slave = 1	Master Access MM = 0 only Slave = 1	otherwise bit 32 unused and bits 30 & 31 as shown	Segment Class A = segment missing (see bits 30–32) B = data C = procedure slave D = procedure execute only E = procedure master		

Note: Binary coding is used for the segment class subfield (bits 33–35) of the segment descriptor word; i.e., A = 000, B = 001, C = 010, D = 011, and E = 101. Binary coding is also used for the directed faults (bits 30–32).

1.2.7 Supervisor

A collection of segments made part of each user process that perform various process-management service functions. Thus, certain supervisor segments are responsible for core allocation; others are used for searching secondary storage for needed segments; and still others are used for the construction, loading, and maintaining of segment or page descriptor words. Some supervisor segments execute in slave mode and others operate in master mode.

1.2.8 Mode of Execution–Master/Slave

There are two modes of execution, master and slave. A procedure segment is classified as either master or slave by a bit set in its segment descriptor word. When the processor is executing in a *master* procedure segment, any one of the entire repertoire of GE 645 instructions may be executed. When the processor is executing in a *slave* procedure segment, certain instructions are "off limits." An attempt to execute one of these special instructions will cause a hardware fault that in turn causes a trap to one of the supervisory segments of the process.

1.2.9 Segment Class

The GE 645 hardware recognizes five classes for a segment as it attempts to reference that segment through its descriptor word. These classes, only three of which are of prime concern to the subsystem writer, are distinguished by virtue of a three-bit subfield of the descriptor field.

1.2.9.1 Class A–Segment Fault (Code is 000)

The code 000 causes a directed fault that the software interprets under the general "heading" of *segment is missing*. Attempted access of any word in this segment will cause this fault.[11]

1.2.9.2 Class B–Data Segment (Code is 001)

Segment is *data* (it may be read or written on only according to the setting of read and write permit bits of the descriptor field). It may never be executed; that is, information from this segment cannot be fetched as instructions during the instruction cycle of the GE 645.

1.2.9.3 Class C–Ordinary Slave-Mode Procedure Segment (Code is 010)

Segment is a *procedure*, garden variety. It is called ordinary slave ØS, the kind that any user can code. Normally, the descriptor for an ØS procedure has its read permit bit *on* so that data (constants) compiled into the procedure may

11. Up to eight separate interpretations are possible. This is because a three-bit subfield is also provided in the descriptor for indicating the kind of fault.

be read, but the write permit is usually *off*, so that the procedure may not be modified before, during, or after execution.

A procedure segment that is not modified in any way as a result of being executed is called a *pure* procedure. All others are regarded as *impure*.

Writing impure ∅S procedures (i.e., procedures that may be written into) is not recommended, since a single copy of an impure procedure cannot effectively be shared by two or more processes.

1.2.9.4 Classes D and E–Execute-Only and Master Procedure Segments

Execute-only procedure segments (Code 010) are not utilized in Multics for reasons that will not be discussed here, nor will the properties of such procedures be discussed. Master procedure segments (Code 100) execute in *master* rather than in slave mode and hence can execute the "privileged" instructions. Only a very few of the Multics supervisory procedures are coded as master-mode procedures. Since master procedures may not be compiled and executed on behalf of users, they will be of little or no interest to subsystem writers.

1.2.10 Segment Naming and Segment Numbering (Notation)

Multics has adopted a standard notation to refer to the name of (i.e., symbolic reference to) a segment and to its number (i.e., to the position of its descriptor word within the descriptor segment–see Figure 1.2).

Example: If the segment is the cosine routine, the segment name might be referred to as <cosine>, and its number is referred to as cosine#. In general, <seg> means that the name of the segment is seg, and seg# means the number of the segment whose name is <seg>.

1.2.11 Named Locations and Numeric Locations Internal to a Segment

At the assembly-language level of discourse, Multics has adopted a standard notation to refer to an "internal address," that is, to an address relative to the word zero of the segment. If the location is known symbolically, for example, via a name in the location field of the assembly-language coding, then this name is indicated by enclosing the name in brackets. Thus in <cosine>, if there is an instruction named "loop" then this name is referred to as [loop] and the symbol "<cosine>|[loop]" means location named "loop" within the segment named "cosine".

Note that the symbol "<cosine>|[loop]" is an example of what can be regarded as a generalized or virtual address. Such an address is an ordered pair or two-component address, the first component identifying the segment and the second component identifying an offset within that segment (i.e., relative to the zeroth word of the segment).

In the assembly-language form of the generalized address, the vertical bar always separates the segment name or segment number from the local, or internal, name.

Example:

<k>|[kloc]

means location "kloc" within segment "k".

To distinguish the internal symbol from its *value*, we simply remove the brackets when we want to speak of the *value* assigned to that symbol. Thus if [kloc] were assigned the value 52 within <k>, and if k# were 16, then

k#|kloc

would mean position 52 from the top of segment number 16. This pair of numbers determines the core-memory address of <k>|[kloc] during execution, once we determine the address of

k#|0

which is the address of word zero of <k>. For our example, the address of k#|0 is stored as a pointer in the 16th word of the descriptor segment. See Figure 1.2 for details.

The strategy in describing the details of the GE 645 address mapping will be first to mainly ignore the existence of the "paging" hardware so as to concentrate entirely on familiarizing ourselves with the "segmentation" hardware. Only then (Section 1.5) will we consider how the paging hardware works. And since the user actually never "sees" the paging activity, he may well wish to skip these details.

1.2.12 Core Address

A physical memory address in the GE 645 is 24 bits long. In forming this core address for a fetch or store of a word, or of a pair of adjacent even-odd words, the GE 645 employs address components that are stored as 18-bit fields (or less). To form a 24-bit core address, a left shift of six bit positions is performed on the value copied from the pointer in the descriptor word. If, for example, the pointer has the value X, then the core block to which it points is located at $X \times 2^6$. In Figure 1.2 and in succeeding representations of descriptor words, the pointer field is represented by the symbol A_B.

1.2.13 Address Bounds Field of the Descriptor

Each descriptor word (see Figure 1.2) contains an eight-bit field called N_B. This field reflects the size of the segment measured in blocks of 2^t words, where t identifies the page size.[12] The field N_B is also the number of words in the segment's page table. Each time a memory reference is made to a position within a segment <k>, say at <k>|kloc, the value of N_B is automatically employed by the hardware as a bounds check to be sure that <k>|kloc lies within <k>.

1.2.14 Descriptor Base Register (dbr)

This all-important register is 29 bits in length. (There is one dbr for each processor.) The register has only two fields of interest to us. They are called "addr" and "bd" in all the figures in which the content of the dbr is depicted. We pay no attention to the field marked "desc."[13] The field addr serves as a pointer to the head of the descriptor segment for the process *that is currently running on the processor* to which this dbr belongs. The field bd is a bounds value. It gives the size of the descriptor segment measured in blocks of 2^v descriptor words.[14]

1.2.15 Two or More Processes in Core Memory

In principle, a number of different processes may cohabit memory. (See Figure 1.3.) To switch a processor from process 1, say, to process 2, all that is required is to save the contents of the dbr and replace it with addr, bd, and desc fields appropriate to process 2. In simple terms, just make the dbr point at a different descriptor segment.

In actual fact, process switching in Multics is somewhat more complicated, as described in Chapter 7.

1.2.16 Common Segments

Figure 1.3 shows that two processes (residing in memory at the same time)

12. If the number of words in the segment is what is meant by size, then N_B is the integer ceiling of size/2^t. Bit 27 of the descriptor word determines t as follows:

t = 10 if bit 27 = 0, i.e., page size is 1024 words,
t = 6 if bit 27 = 1, i.e., page size is 64 words.

This means that a segment is allocated space in blocks of 1024 words (2^{10}) if bit 27 = 0. As far as the hardware is concerned, such a segment can never exceed $2^{8+10} = 2^{18}$ words even if core memory should grow beyond 2^{18}. Otherwise, if bit 27 of the descriptor word = 1, the segment is allocated space in blocks of 64 words; in which case the segment can never exceed $2^{8+6} = 2^{14}$ words.

13. This is a two-bit field that gives information as to whether and how the descriptor segment, pointed at by addr, is subdivided into pages. We will never, as users, have any control over these bits. Such control is a supervisory function, part of a collection of routines that manage core memory, a subject discussed partially in Chapter 7.

14. Here v = 10 or 6 in value depending on whether bit 27 of the dbr is set to 0 or 1, respectively. If the addressing mechanism (described in Figure 1.2) is ever used to access a word in the descriptor segment that lies beyond addr + bd x 2^v, then an automatic fault will be detected and control would be transferred to a master mode supervisory procedure segment. (Remember that the supervisory procedures are automatically made a part of every user process.)

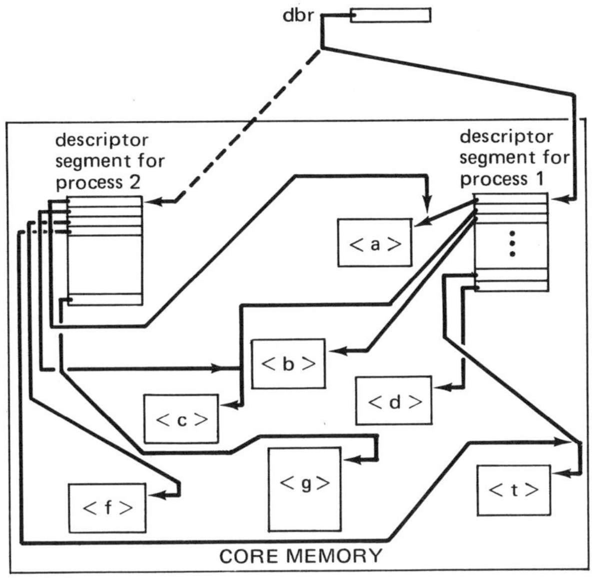

Figure 1.3. Two processes resident in memory
Process 1 consists of segments called <a>, <c>, <b>, . . ., <t>, <d>, in the order listed in the descriptor segment.
Process 2 consists of segments called <a>, <c>, <f>, <t>, . . ., <g>, in the order listed in the descriptor segment.

Note: Both processes share certain segments. Thus, segments <a> and <c> are identically numbered 1 and 2, respectively, in each process. But segment <t>, which is also a shared segment, has a different number in each process.

By the *number* of a segment in a process is meant simply:
A segment has the number *k* if it is pointed to by the *k*th word of the descriptor segment for the given process.

can *share* common data or procedure segments (and their respective page tables). There is a good deal of this sharing in Multics. Every process has certain key segments that are supervisory procedures provided by the system. Some are called "hard-core," some "administrative," routines. Certain of these procedures are automatically made part of every Multics user process. These are generally the lowest numbered segments in the process. Moreover, a few of the segments, such as those employed for process switching, are given the same numbers respectively in each process (like segments <a> and <c>). Other segments may be common, but they need not be numbered identically in each process.

1.3 Core-Address Formation

I will now explain how core addresses are formed for purposes of fetching instructions and data during the execution of a user's process.

Conceptually, every memory reference is to a particular location within a particular segment. This is sometimes referred to as "two-component" addressing, because one component may be thought of as the segment number, an offset within the descriptor segment that determines the desired segment, and another component is the offset within the desired segment. For this chapter, the first component is sometimes called the "effective pointer" and sometimes called the "external base," while the second component is often called the "internal base" or "internal address."

1.3.1 Fetching Instructions

In a conventional computer like the IBM 7094, addressing is with one component. The instruction counter ic holds the absolute location of the instruction to be fetched. In the GE 645, the ic merely holds the value of the second component, that is, the relative location within the desired procedure segment. The value for the first component is the segment number for the currently executing procedure. This number, held in a separate register discussed below, points to the desired descriptor word, which in turn contains the pointer A_B to word zero of the desired segment. Construction of the actual core address that is finally referenced is as follows:

core address for the fetched instruction = core address of desired segment + (ic)

If a procedure segment is executing a sequence of instructions that lie entirely within the segment, the value A_B remains stationary. Only the ic changes in value, increasing by one for sequentially executed instructions, or replaced by new values in the case of a successful transfer instruction to some arbitrary point within the same segment.

How, then, is A_B established? If one is talking about segment <k>, then clearly some available register could be designated to serve as a pointer to the proper descriptor word that holds A_B for <k>. In the GE 645, a special 18-bit register has been provided for this purpose, and it is called the "pbr", or *procedure base register.* The value of k# must be established and held in the pbr as long as procedure <k> is executing. Figure 1.4 gives an illustration of this instruction address determination.

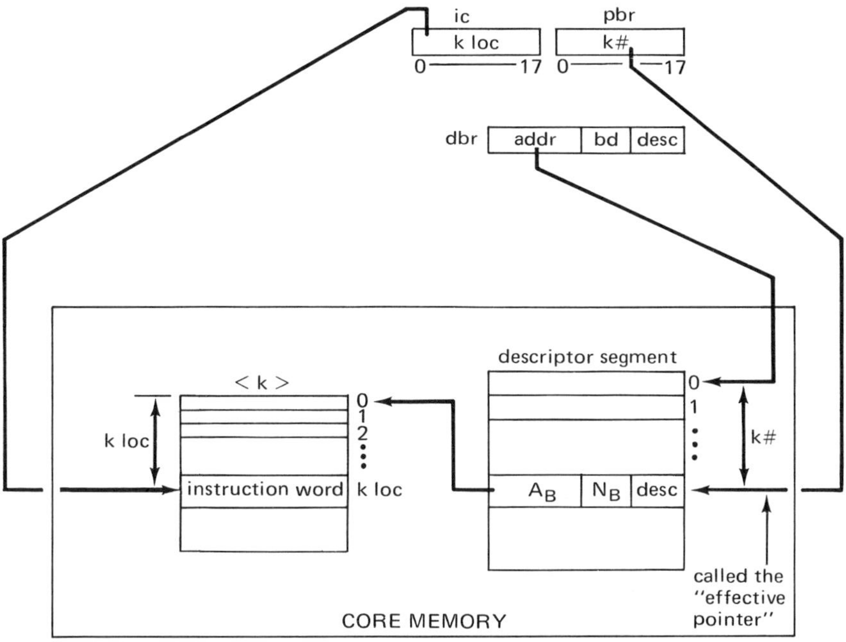

Figure 1.4. Address formation to *fetch an instruction* at <k>|[kloc]
The actual core address is $A_B \times 2^6$ + kloc. The value of A_B is found after setting a pointer value k# in the pbr. The dbr points at the base of the descriptor segment, and the pbr provides the necessary offset to get at A_B.

1.3.2 Fetching or Storing Data

Most procedures in Multics will be *pure*, so the alterable data associated with the procedure are almost certain to be located in some other segment (or segments) of the same process. Hence, to form the address of a word in the data segment, it is necessary to point within the descriptor segment to a different descriptor word than the one currently pointed at by the pbr. If one is going to hold a value in the pbr as an *instruction* pointer for a series of instruction-fetch cycles, one will need another register for use as a *data* pointer during a series of execute (data-fetch) cycles. In this way the computer can alternate between instruction and execute cycles without having repeatedly to reset the pbr's pointer value. The special 18-bit register used in the GE 645 for the execute-cycle address formation is the "tbr", or *temporary base register*. On each execute cycle the tbr holds the value for the first component of the two-component data address.

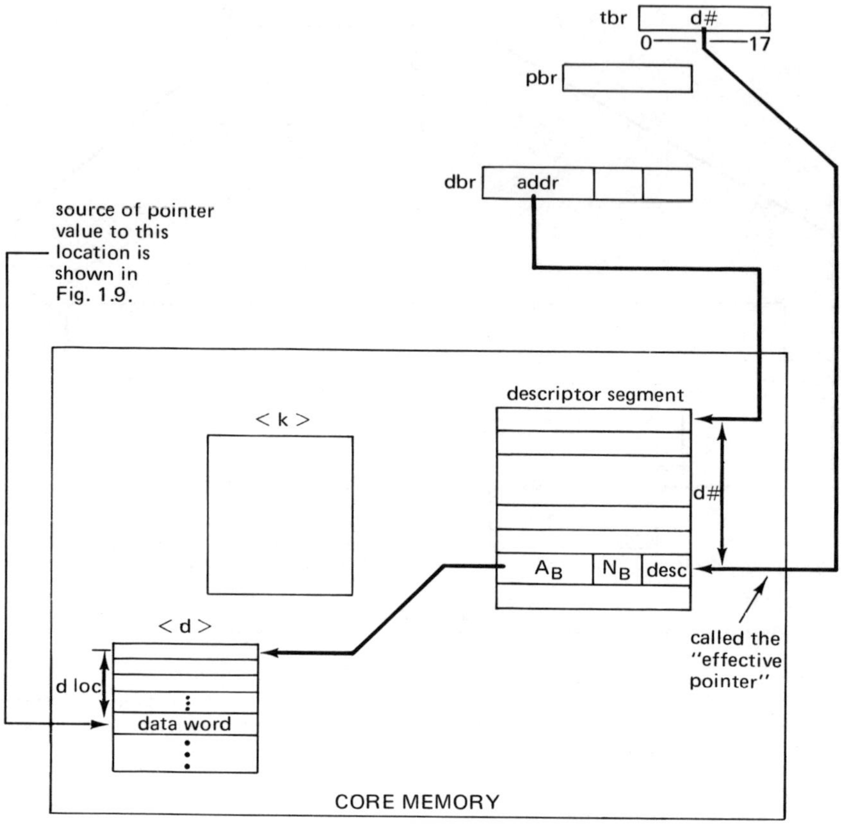

Figure 1.5. Partial address formation during an execute cycle to obtain a data word at <d>|[dloc]
The tbr points at the d#th descriptor word, which in turn points at <d>.

Figure 1.5 illustrates the partial determination of the core address for a data word located symbolically at

<d>$_{l}$ [dloc]

In this figure it is shown how the address of <d> is determined (although it has not yet been shown where the value to put in the tbr comes from). It remains now to show how the relative location within <d>, that is, dloc, is determined.

1.3.3 Computing the Effective Internal Address

The full answer to the question, How is the effective internal address dloc (i.e., the address within <d>) determined? will have to be approached in stages.

There are two characteristic formats for a GE 645 instruction as shown in Figure 1.6. (Instructions of type 1 are recognized by virtue of bit position 29 = 1, while instructions of type 0 are recognized by a 0 in bit 29.)

Type-0 instructions are used for referencing *data or instructions within the segment currently being executed*, while type-1 instructions may reference data or instruction in *any* segment. Because there *appears* to be something inherently more general about type-1 instructions (and for no other reason), these will be discussed first, and type-0 instructions will be treated later (in Section 1.3.8).

For a type-1 instruction, the effective internal address is made up of three parts. The three fields *y*, *tag*, and *segment tag* of the instruction, either directly or indirectly, determine these parts.

The *address field y* is a signed 14-bit quantity (i.e., an address that ranges over values from -2^{14} to $+2^{14}$).

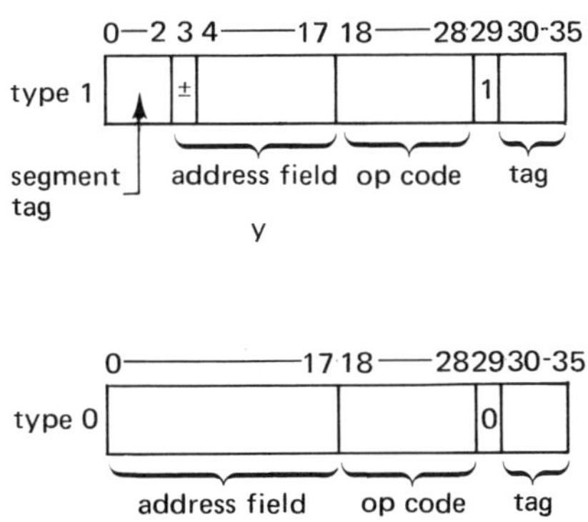

Figure 1.6. Formats of typical GE 645 instructions

Table 1.2 Tag-Field Details for Indexing and Indirect Addressing

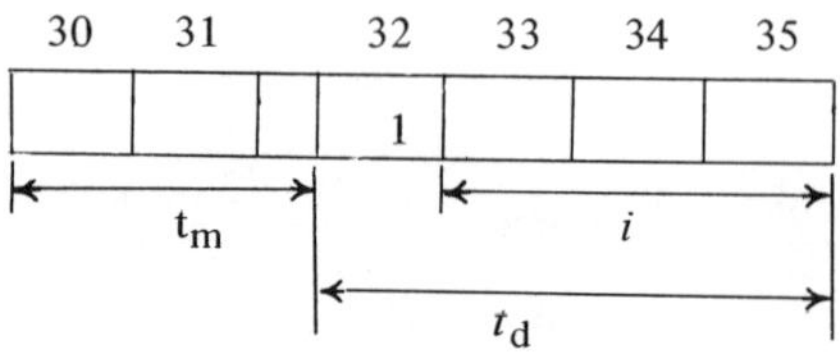

There are two main subfields, called t_d and t_m. Subfield t_d, provided bit 32 = 1, designates index register i in bits 33–35. Subfield t_m designates the type of indirect addressing, if any. Several types of indirect addressing are available; however, only one, type RI, is of immediate interest.

t_m	635 Parlance	Interpretation
00	R-type	no indirect addressing
01	RI-type	multilevel indexed indirect addressing
11	IR	not discussed in this book. See GE 635 Reference Manuals for details.
10	IT	

The tag field is a fairly complicated 6-bit field. Some details can be found in Table 1.2. For the present the following simplification can be made.

1. Three of these bits designate one of the eight 18-bit index registers (0–7).
2. Two bits specify the type of indirect addressing, if any, for this instruction.

The *segment tag field* points to one of eight so-called address base registers.

1.3.4 The Eight Address Base Registers

There are eight address base registers (abr's). Any one of these may, in principle at least, be pointed at by the segment tag of a type-1 instruction. Historically, the purpose of the address base register was to be a convenient place to store effective pointers, that is, segment numbers of data or procedure segments other than the one currently executing. As the hardware developed further, another possible use was developed for these registers, namely, as a convenient place to store the effective internal address or a component of it. The designers then decided to permit each abr to serve either purpose, that is to say, it was allowed either to hold the effective pointer to a descriptor word (in which case it would be referred to as an "external base") or to hold a

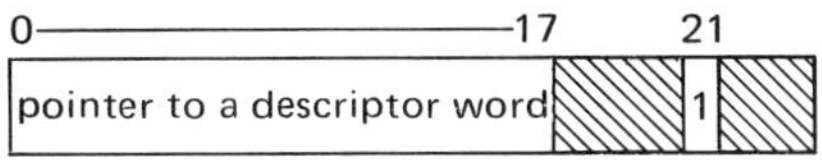

a. as an *external* base

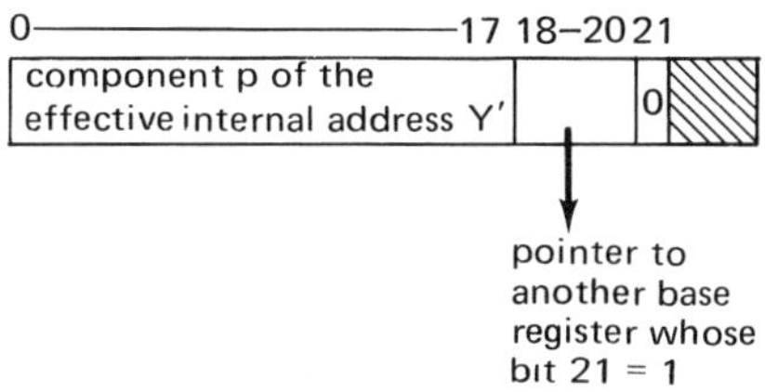

b. as a component of the effective *internal* address with a pointer to an external base

Figure 1.7. Two ways for an address base register to function

component of the effective internal address (in which case it would be called an "internal base"). As an internal base the abr can act like a second index register, but if so, it must also point to another abr holding an external base. Each abr has 24 bits, sufficient to hold both an 18-bit address field and a control field with which to identify the function of the first field as external or internal. This is illustrated in Figure 1.7.

There is an interesting capability, fully exploited in Multics, for pairing the abr's. If bit 21 is a 0, then bits 0–17 serve as an internal base. It serves as the so-called p component of the effective internal address. Moreover, three other bits in the same register (bits 18–20) are interpreted as a pointer to another abr whose bits 0–17 are then taken as the external base or effective pointer.

In short, by properly presetting the control bits in the abr, the segment tag of a type-1 instruction can point not to one, but to a pair of abr's. The first will contain a component part of the internal address, and the second will contain the effective pointer.

In Multics operation, the eight registers are paired by presetting the control bits (18–21) in the registers so that they may always act *effectively* as four pairs of base registers (18 bits per register), as shown in Figure 1.8. To address a particular pair of these registers in a type-1 instruction, one needs

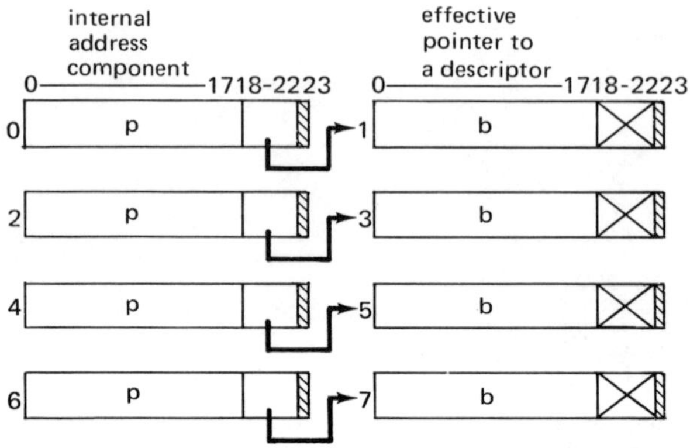

Figure 1.8. Multics standard pairings of the eight address base registers (For more details on bits 18–23 in each register, see Table 1.3.)

to give as the segment tag the address of the internal base, that is, 0, 2, 4, or 6.[15]

The reader is now ready to follow the rest of the explanation of how to determine the core address for the data word <d>|[dloc]. The internal effective address, dloc, in this case is formed from three components y, (i), and p;

dloc = y + (i) + p,

where y is the signed 14-bit value in the address field of the instruction, (i) is the contents of the index register pointed at by the tag field of the instruction, and p is the contents of the internal address base register pointed at by the segment tag field of the instruction.

Moreover, since the internal base register is *coupled* to an external base register, the contents of the coupled external base serves as the value d#, destined to be copied into the tbr. All this is illustrated in Figure 1.9.

Before attempting to summarize the discussion to this point, one further pictorial technique is offered to help in the condensation of future diagrams. In the future the group of eight address base registers will be depicted and named as shown in Figure 1.10.

15. In writing instructions in a Multics assembly language, standard two-letter names are used in place of the numeric values. These are the following:
ap for address base register 0,
bp for address base register 2,
lp for address base register 4,
sp for address base register 6.

Table 1.3 Normal Control Field of the Address Base Registers

Register: Multics Name	Register: Number	Bit No. 18 (Specifies register that is external if this one is internal)	19	20	21 (Int = 0, Ext = 1)	22 (Lock Base[a])	23	Remarks
ap	0	0	0	1	0	0	Not used	internal
ab	1	Not used			1	0	Not used	external
bp	2	0	1	1	0	0	Not used	internal
bb	3	Not used			1	0	Not used	external
lp	4	1	0	1	0	0	Not used	internal
lb	5	Not used			1	0	Not used	external
sp	6	1	1	1	0	0	Not used	internal
sb	7	Not used			1	1	Not used	external

[a]Lock Base = 0 means that the first 18-bit field of this register may be loaded in slave mode. All abr's except sb are set = 0 by the Multics supervisor.
Lock Base = 1 means this register is locked against change in slave mode. This means a user will never be able to destroy the current value in sb.
To alter any of the control field bits in an abr requires a privileged (master mode only) instruction, so the user will never be able to alter these bits.

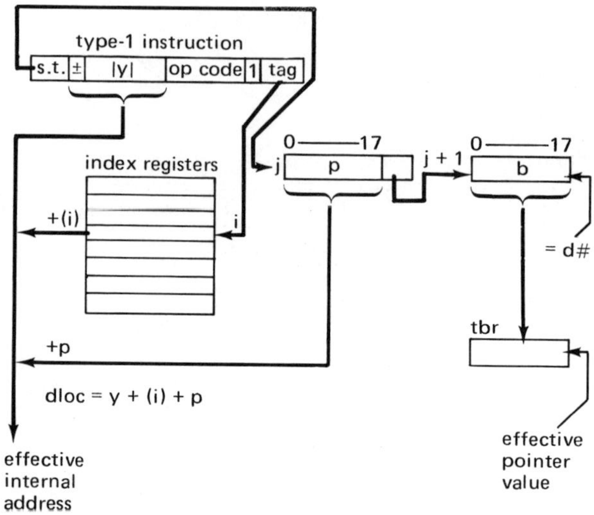

Figure 1.9. Effective internal address formation from a type-1 instruction

The *tag* is assumed to indicate *direct* addressing rather than indirect addressing and points to index register i. The value of the segment tag is j where j = 0, 2, 4, or 6 in normal Multics operation. The current value of the coupled base register j + 1 is assumed to have been preset to equal d#.

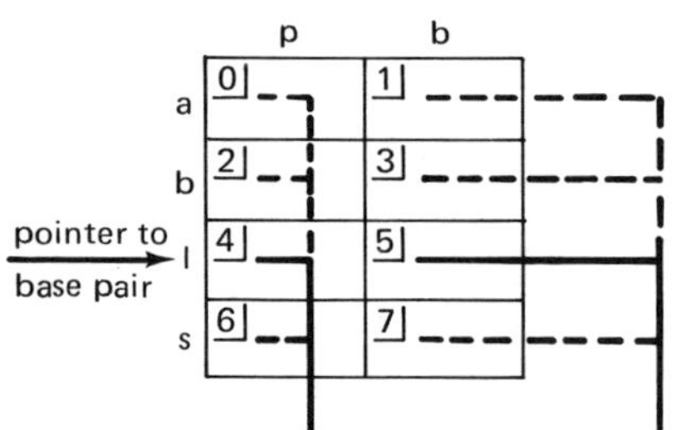

Figure 1.10. Eight base registers
The four coupled registers or "base pairs" are

Numbers	Coupling Notation Used in Multics
0, 1	ab ← ap
2, 3	bb ← bp
4, 5	lb ← lp
6, 7	sb ← sp

The array representation of the eight registers suggests that--

1. each row is a coupled base pair;
2. the register in column 1 is the internal base or p-type and the register in column 2 is the external base or b-type.

The Multics names given to the 4 pairs are

a for *a*rgument-list pointer,
b for general *b*ase,
l for *l*inkage-segment pointer,
and
s for *s*tack-segment pointer.

Some preliminary motivation for these names is attempted in Section 1.3.5. You can skip over this for the present if you want to get on with the details of address formation.

1.3.5 Address-Formation Strategy

A typical process will involve a large number of segments. Many of these segments are part of the system supervisor. Entries for these segments are automatically (templatewise) added to the descriptor segment of each process. Apart from these segments, each process will generally have one or more procedure segments, one or more *data* segments, a *stack* segment, and a *linkage* segment for each procedure segment. (Stack and linkage segments are motivated in the following discussion.)

Let us suppose the process involves a typical FORTRAN job. There would be a procedure segment for the main program, one for each separately compiled subprogram, and perhaps one for each library program.

Suppose the FORTRAN compiler is written to structure object code in such a way that variables local to each of the FORTRAN procedures (and for that matter possibly those in COMMON as well) are allocated storage in a single data segment. Let us suppose the name of this segment is <stat_>, for static storage.

A process may also refer to other data banks such as publicly available tables of read-only data, or perhaps an input-buffer or an output-buffer area. Such data areas, because they might have different access controls associated with them, will normally be stored in independent data segments.

Each time one procedure calls on another (including recursively called procedures) data and machine conditions such as contents of index registers must be saved. These are stored in the segment called <stack>. In general, the stack segment temporarily holds data values that apply to each separate activation of each and every procedure that is called for a single process. The planned use of <stack> is thoroughly discussed in Chapter 3.

The *linkage* segment contains certain vital symbolic data, descriptive information, pointers, and instructions that are needed for the linking of procedures in each process. In general, the linkage segment will hold data that are "static," which means that they apply for *all* activations of the same procedure for a single process. Much more will be said about the linkage segment in Chapter 2.

Most of the data segments (other than <stack>) that a procedure needs to refer to are referenced *indirectly* via special intersegment pointers placed in the *linkage* segment. These pointers are called "its" or "itb" pairs and are discussed in Section 1.3.9. Basically, they permit formation of a final effective address for the desired data element without further need of the base address pairs.

The tentative conclusion one can make here is that a typical process, grinding away on a processor under the plan for the Multics system, will find itself making direct references to data and instructions from a relatively small number of different segments over relatively large time spans. These segments are

1. one or more independent data segments,
2. the *procedure* segment currently being executed,
3. the *linkage* segment for the procedure currently being executed,
4. the one *stack* segment for the process containing the disposable (and hence perishable) data of the process.

Now one begins to see how the paired address base registers are typically employed. By controlling their contents, pointers may be set to four different entries in the descriptor segment besides the currently executing procedure segment that is pointed at by the pbr. During the execution of one procedure, the frequency with which it will be necessary to reset any of these four paired "base" pointers may be low.

1.3.6 Summarizing Direct Address Formation

All of the discussions on address formation so far are now summarized. Note the following points:

1. To fetch an instruction (instruction cycle), the contents of the pbr become the effective pointer. From this the address of the desired procedure segment is obtained. To this address are added the contents of the ic to obtain the address of the particular instruction.
2. To fetch a data word (execute cycle of a type-1 instruction), as illustrated

in Figure 1.11a, the effective pointer to the required descriptor word is obtained from the tbr. The value of the tbr is *copied* from the current contents of one of the base registers ab, bb, lb, or sb, depending on the value of the segment tag in the current instruction, being 0, 2, 4, or 6, respectively. The effective internal address, hereafter called Y′, is formed as

$$Y' = y + (i) + p$$

where p is the current contents of ap, bp, lp, or sp, according to whether the segment tag has the value 0, 2, 4, or 6, respectively.
3. The dashed line indicating actual *data flow* from the tbr to the pbr will be explained in the following discussion.

1.3.7 Transferring Control to Another Procedure Segment

How a transfer instruction to a another procedure segment using a type-1 instruction is accomplished is considered here. If a new procedure segment is to be executed, there must be a new setting for the pbr so that hereafter it points to the new procedure segment. Let us consider what happens when procedure segment <a> executes any successful transfer instruction (of type 1). The effective address of a tra type instruction in most early computers like the IBM 7094 simply replaces the value currently in the ic. In the GE 645, two things happen. (1) The effective internal address Y′ = y + (i) + p replaces the contents of the ic, and (2) at the same time the effective pointer b, which is brought to the tbr, is then copied into the pbr. In other words,

$$\text{ic} \leftarrow y + (i) + p \qquad (1)$$

and

$$\text{tbr} \leftarrow b \qquad (2a)$$

$$\text{pbr} \leftarrow b \qquad (2b)$$

Now then, if b points to the descriptor word for <a>, a tra *within the same segment* will be achieved. But, if b points to a different descriptor word, say for segment <t>, then the transfer to <t> is automatically achieved, because t#, which is really what b then amounts to, will have been placed in the pbr.

The next instruction executed will then be fetched from <t> at location of word zero of <t> + (ic), by virtue of having altered the contents of the pbr.

1.3.8 Address Formation for Type-0 Instructions

Any time an executing procedure segment attempts to make a *self-reference*, formation of the data address can be greatly simplified, since the effective

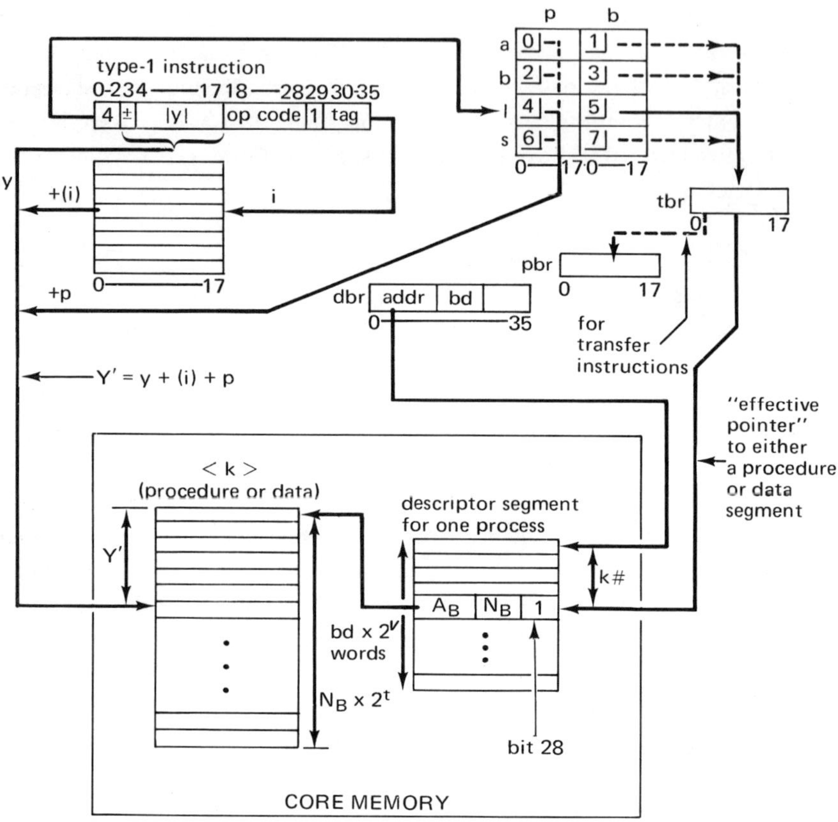

Figure 1.11a. Address formation in the execute cycle of type-1 instructions
(For simplicity imagine that segment <k> is not paged. This would be reflected in the fact that bit 28 of the descriptor word for <k> = 1.)

pointer is already known to be in the pbr. To make it possible for the computer to recognize this simple case, a type-0 instruction[16] is used. When such an instruction is being analyzed for execution, recognition is made by virtue of bit 29 = 0.

The effective pointer is copied into the tbr from the pbr, that is,

$$\text{tbr} \leftarrow (\text{pbr})$$

The effective internal address is made up of only two components. (You should review Figure 1.6.) The two components are $\tilde{y}$ and (i), where $\tilde{y}$ represents the 18-bit address field (bits 0–17) of the instruction.

$$Y' = \tilde{y} + (i)$$

This type of address formation is shown in Figure 1.11b.

If the type-0 instruction is a *transfer* instruction, the net effect is

$$\text{ic} \leftarrow \tilde{y} + (i) \qquad (1)$$

and

no change in the contents of the pbr. (2)

1.3.9 Multilevel Indirect Addressing (RI-type) and Its Restrictions

The basic form of indirect addressing in the GE 645 is inherited from the GE 635 circuitry. This is indirect addressing via the type-RI tag, which is sometimes called multilevel indexed indirect addressing. This is very similar to that of, say, the IBM 7094, except that in the case of the GE 645 indirect referencing continues to any number of levels instead of halting after two memory references.

When a data word or transfer address is being fetched via a chain of one or more indirect words, the core address of each new indirect word, as well as

16. If you were coding in a symbolic assembly language, the distinction between a type-1 and a type-0 instruction would be purely syntactical. For example, in the assembly language of Multics, ALM, the variable field for a type-1 instruction always begins with a segment name or abr name followed by a vertical bar. For a type-0 instruction, this component is missing.
Thus,

```
lda bp|6
```

is automatically recognized by the assembler as a type-1 instruction. It means load the accumulator with the data word located from a segment whose effective pointer is bb and whose effective internal address is 6 + bp.
The instruction

```
lda 6
```

on the other hand, is recognized by the assembler as a type-0 instruction. It means load the accumulator with the data word found in location 6 of *this procedure segment*.

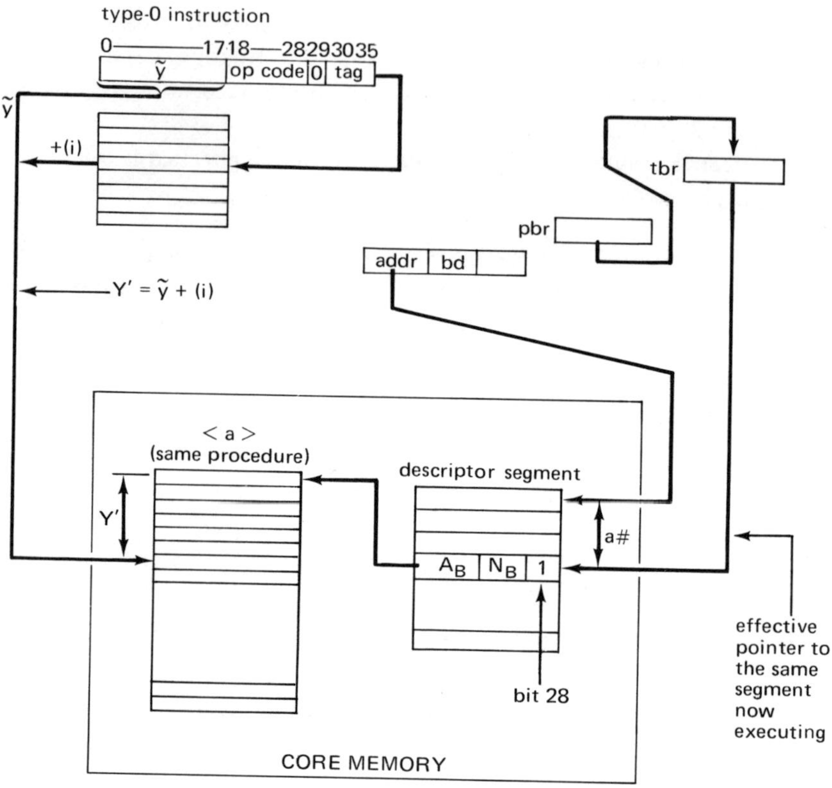

Figure 1.11b. Address formation in the execute cycle of type-0 instructions
(For simplicity it is still imagined that segment <a> is not paged. This would be reflected in the fact that bit 28 of the descriptor word for <a> = 1.)

the final effective address, is determined in essentially the same fashion as given in Figure 1.11 b. In particular, only two fields of each indirect word are brought out of memory to be examined. These are the address field $\tilde{y}$ (bits 0–17), and the modifier field (bits 30–35). To form the intended two-dimensional address that is coded in this indirect word, the effective pointer held in the tbr remains unchanged from its preceding value. The effective internal address is

$$Y' = \tilde{y} + (i).$$

In other words, the address formation for the coding in an indirect word is handled much like that of a type-0 instruction in spite of the fact that the originating instruction may have been a type-1 instruction. The net effect is that no matter how many indexed indirect addresses are formed in one chain, the second and all succeeding addresses are treated as belonging to the segment pointed at by the *first* address in the chain. For example, if the originating instruction has an RI tag and if its external base points to segment <b>, then the effective pointer for the next indirect word (and all others, if more than one) in the chain will remain *internal* to <b>. Figure 1.12 illustrates the two possible cases that can arise.[17]

For fully general intersegment programming, it would be *ideal* if the indirect addressing mechanism at our disposal were such that one could cross from one segment to another in going from one indirect word to the next. This capability is provided in GE 645 hardware as described in the next paragraphs.

1.3.10 Indirect Word Pairs or Generalized Addresses

The GE 645 hardware facility described here allows fully general indirect addressing. For example, starting from segment <a>, if the indirect target in, say, segment <b> is a special hardware detectable *pair* of indirect words (called either an "its" or an "itb" pair), the content of this word pair then designates the address for a point within an arbitrary segment. Hardware recognition of its or itb pairs is explained in the next subsection.

Understanding the role of the its pair will be critically important to most subsystem writers. Occasional but important use may also be found for itb pairs. Details of the its or itb pair will be described shortly. The essential point to note here is that such a pair designates for the GE 645 a two-component virtual address, that is, the address of an *arbitrary* segment and internal address within that segment. Moreover, this word pair may also indicate further indirection. In short, use of an its pair allows us to "travel" from one segment, through a second one, to a third segment, say <c>, and so on. This feature is illustrated schematically in Figure 1.13a. As a special case, an its or itb pair can also refer to the containing segment as suggested in Figure 1.13b. As a further special case, of perhaps lesser interest, if the fetched

17. The MPM referred to in Figure 1.12 and in many other places is the following loose-leaf document: Project MAC, "The Multiplexed Information and Computing Service: Programmers' Manual," Preliminary Edition, Revision 7, April 5, 1971, Massachusetts Institute of Technology, Cambridge, Massachusetts. It is currently being extensively revised. It is available at a cost of $12 from the Publications Office of the M.I.T. Information Processing Center.

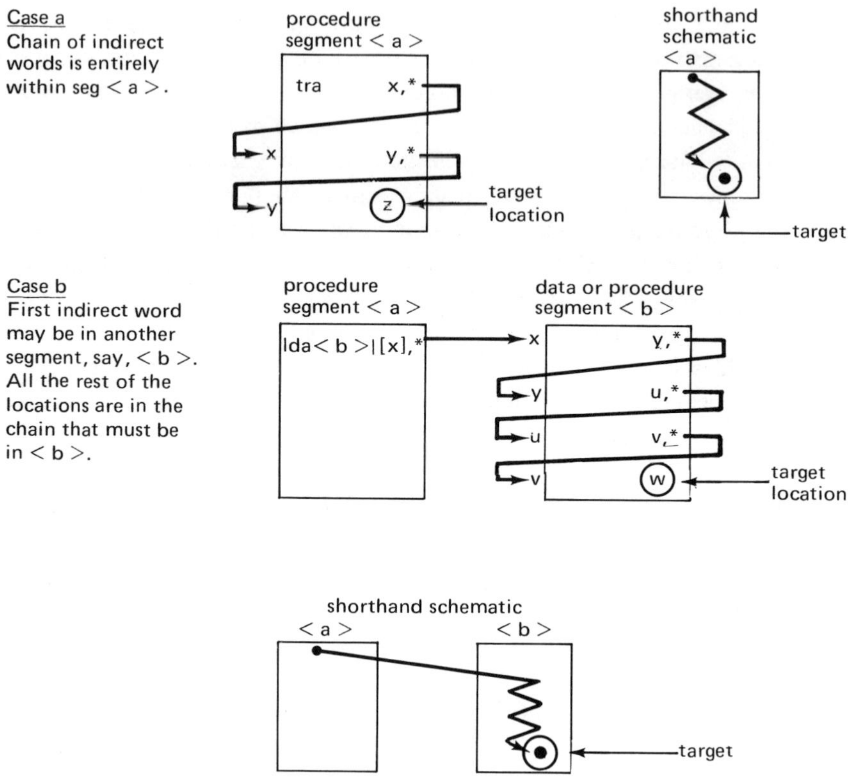

Figure 1.12. Two cases of multilevel intrasegment indirect addressing (RI-type)

The notation "tra x, *" and "lda <b>|[x], *", etc., is GE 645 assembly language (ALM) notation. (See the MPM, Reference Data section on linkage formats, for further illustrations.)

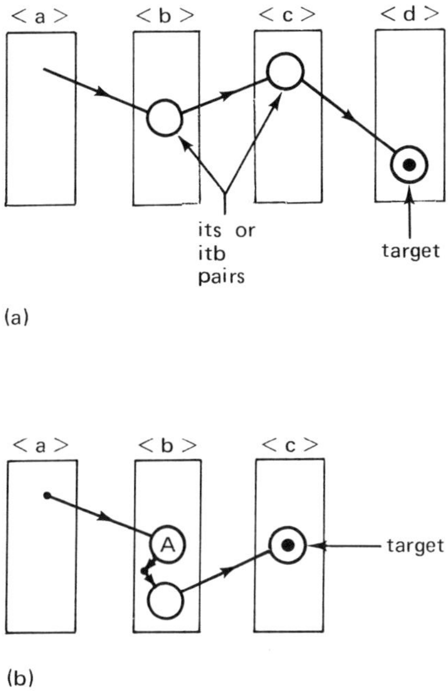

Figure 1.13. Multilevel intersegment indirect addressing
(a) Use of its or itb pairs.
(b) An illustration of how its or itb pairs may refer to the same segment. The its pair marked A is an example.

indirect word or word pair is not an its or itb type but does suggest further indirect addressing, then such addressing continues within the segment established from the preceding fetch. This is illustrated in Figure 1.14.

1.3.11 Details of its and itb Pairs

The format of its and itb pairs is displayed and interpreted as shown in Figure 1.15. There are four fields of interest in each its or itb pair. Hardware recognition of its and itb pairs comes about in the following way.

When the address of an indirect word is *even*, the computer always fetches a pair of words. Whenever a pair of indirect words is fetched such that *the second field of the first word*, a six-bit identification code, has the octal value of 43 (its) or the octal value of 41 (itb), the computer recognizes the containing word as the first word of an indirect word pair.

The second field of the second word is the standard GE 635/645 modifier or tag field, as exhibited in Table 1.2. In the examples for this field, an index

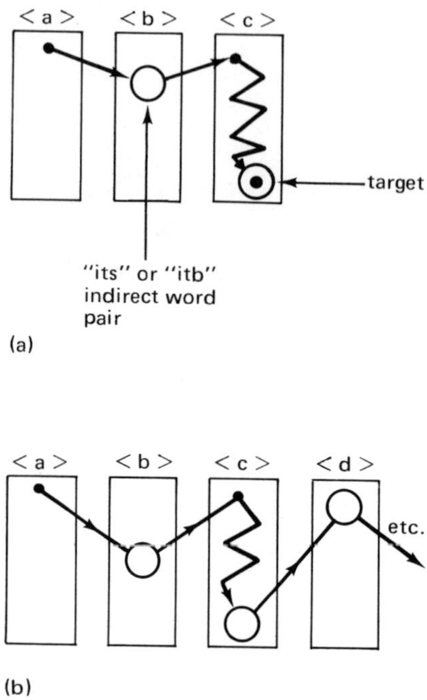

Figure 1.14. Continuing the indirect intersegment chain
(a) Indirection may continue inside a third segment to the desired target without further use of its or itb pairs.
(b) It is quite permissible to keep the intersegment chain going if each its or itb pair points to an ordinary indirect word of the RI type. One of these can then point to another its or itb within the same segment. This its or itb could then allow a "leap" out to still another segment, etc.

register and, if indirect, a "*" are shown following the register number. The full range of possible modifiers is available.

The first field of the first word is either the effective pointer to the desired segment (for an its pair), or the *external* base register number that has been preset to hold the effective pointer to the desired segment (for an itb pair).

The first field of the second word is the 18-bit internal address within the desired segment that is designated in the first word.

Figure 1.16 illustrates how address formation continues for an indirect its word pair. Figure 1.17 shows address formation for an itb word pair.

By way of summary five types of address formation that have been dis-

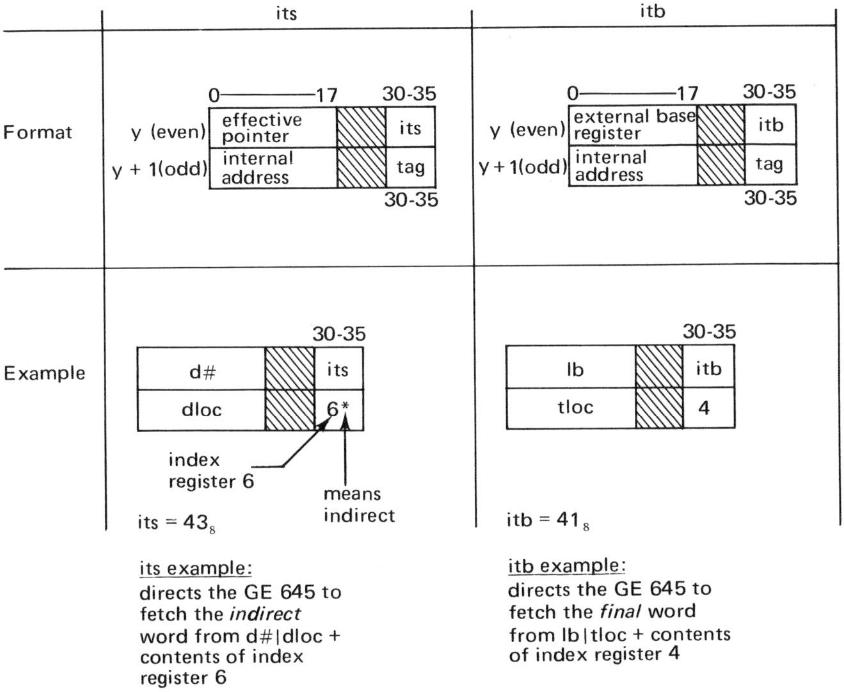

Figure 1.15. Format of its and itb indirect word pairs

cussed to this point and the figures where these have been illustrated are listed here.

Type	**Illustration**
1. Instruction cycle	Figure 1.4
Execute cycle	
2. Type-1 instruction	Figure 1.11a
3. Type-0 instruction	Figure 1.11b
Indirect word pair	
4. its	Figure 1.16
5. itb	Figure 1.17

Figure 1.18 is an attempt to create a composite view of three of these, types 1, 2, and 4, in order to see in one frame how each of the important registers plays its role. It may be worthwhile for the reader to superimpose the details of types 3 and 5 also. Different colors are recommended.

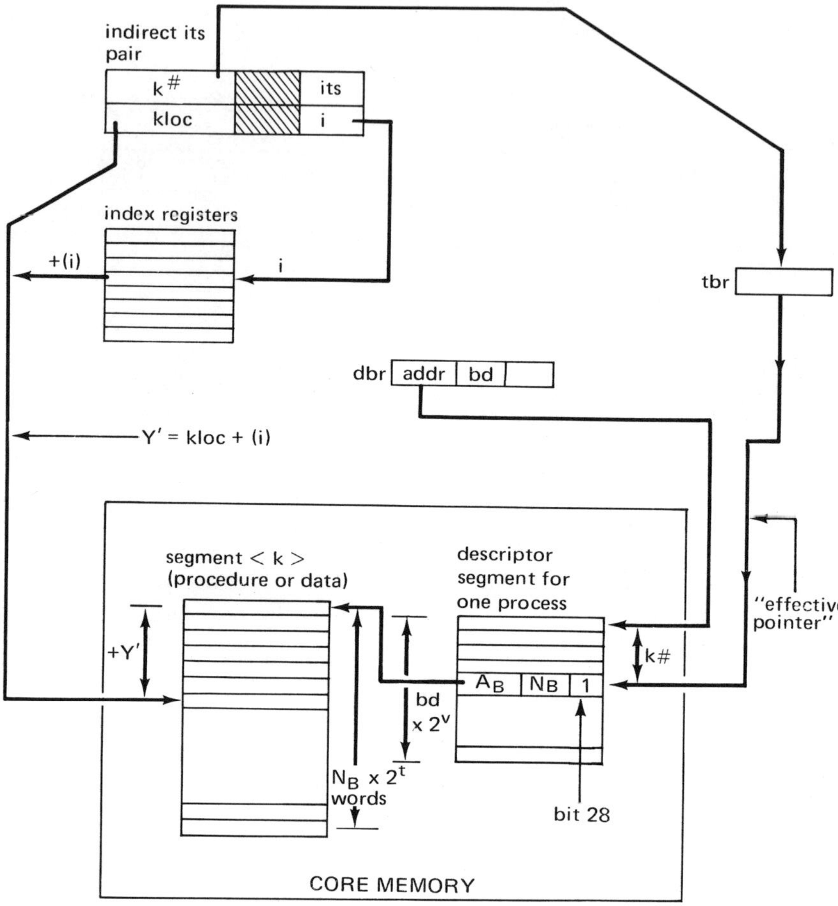

Figure 1.16. Address formation for its pairs

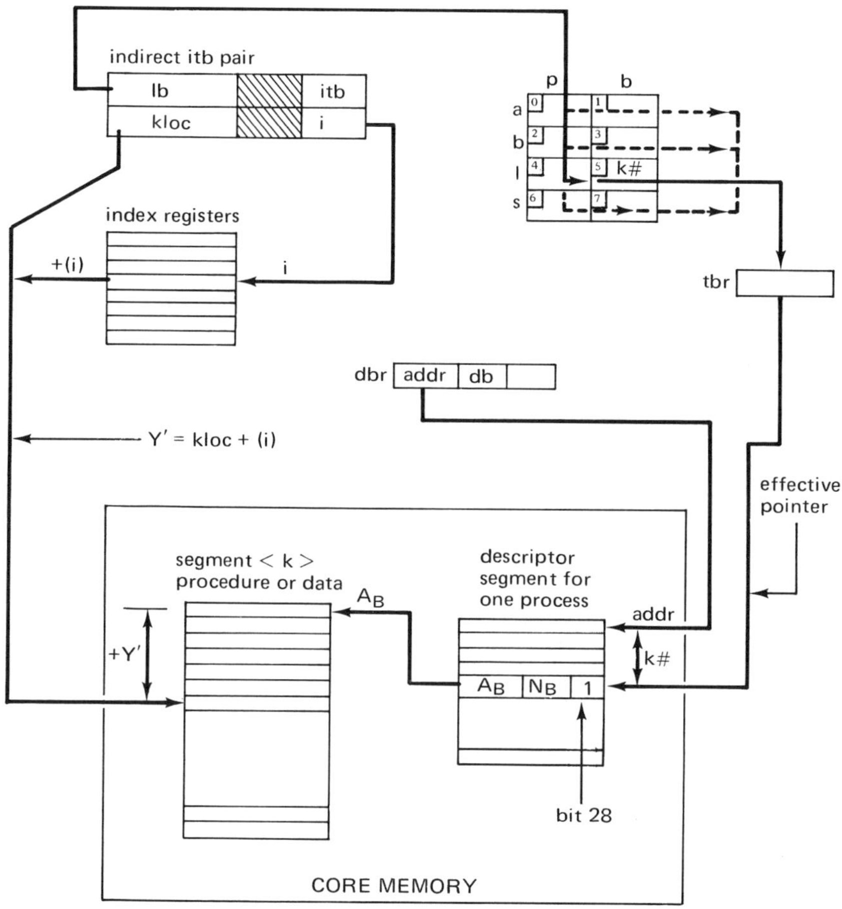

Figure 1.17. Address formation for itb pairs

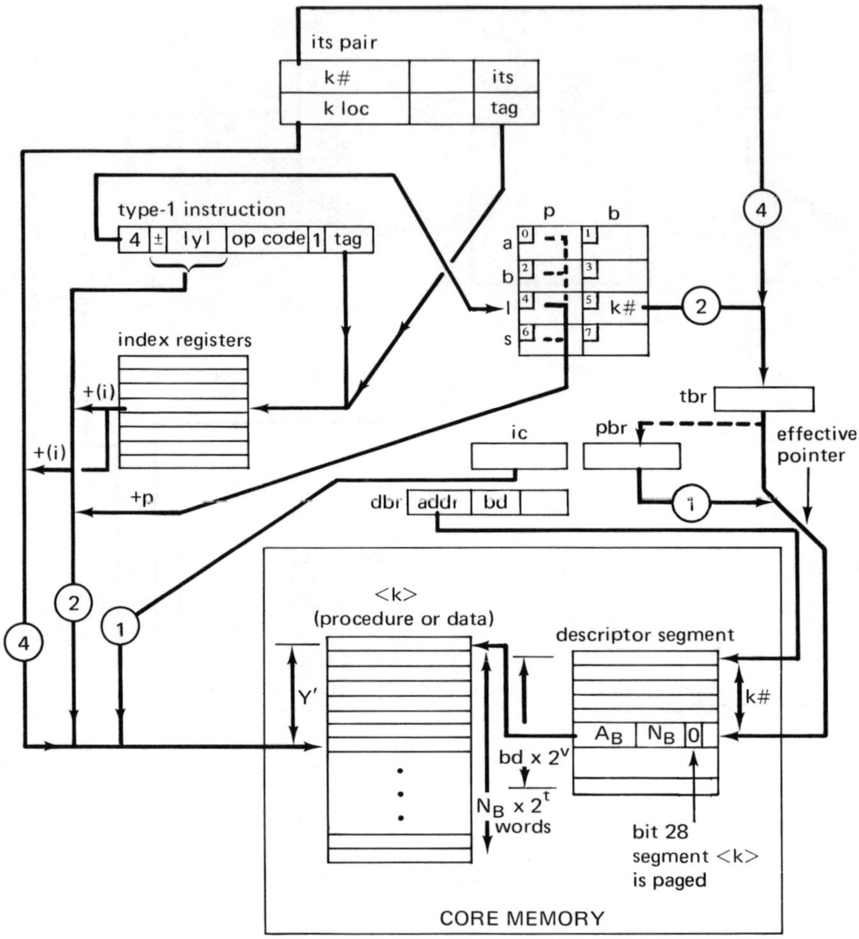

1 instruction cycle
2 execute cycle — type-1 instruction
4 execute cycle — its pair

Figure 1.18. Composite view of three types of address formation

1.4 Special Instructions to Manipulate Address Base Registers

Easy manipulation of the contents of the eight address base registers in the GE 645 has thus far been implied. Here some of the powerful instructions that are available to a subsystems writer to do the job are enumerated. The most important ones are the eap and stp instructions.

	Symbol	Instruction
(1)	eapi	*effective address to pair i* i = 0, 2, 4, or 6.

This *very important* instruction sets a pair of coupled base registers specified by i. In Multics assembly language you actually use one of four symbolic (pseudo) op codes. You use

eapap instead of eap0
eapbp instead of eap2,
eaplp instead of eap4,
or
eapsp instead of eap6.

The internal base is set from the effective internal address of the instruction (i.e., $Y' = y + (i) + p$). The external base is set from the effective pointer of the instruction.

The eapi instructions are especially useful in developing efficient code for the innermost loops of highly repetitive computations where one wishes to avoid indirect addressing. This concept will be further explored in the chapter on intersegment linking.

	Symbol	Instruction
(2)	stpi	*store pair i*, meaning, store the contents of the ith pair of registers (p and b) into a pair of memory words beginning at the specified core address that must be an *even* address. The format of the stored pair is

Y (even)	b	0	its
Y + 1 (odd)	p	0	0

In Multics assembly language, you actually use one of four symbolic op codes. You use

stpap instead of stp0,
stpbp instead of stp2,

stplp instead of stp4,

or

stpsp instead of stp6.

The eapi and stpi instructions are generally used in pairs. For example, to store and later restore the current values of the ab←ap pair, you might write in assembly language

stpap hold + 6, 4

.

.

.

.

eapap hold + 6, 4*

Several applications illustrating the use of these instructions will be found in Chapters 2 and 3.

	Symbol	Instruction action	
(3)	lbri	*load base register i* from specified core address.	i = 0(1)7
(4)	sbri	*store base register i* into specified core address.	i = 0(1)7
(5)	eabi	*effective internal address to base register i.* The effective internal address of this instruction is assigned to address base register i.	
(6)	adbi	*add to base register i* from the specified address, which is the effective internal address, (i.e., from y + (i) + p). In slave mode, i may be any register except sb.	
(7)	ldb	in master mode, *load all eight base registers* from eight successive memory words beginning at a specified core address, which is (=0 modulo 8). In slave mode, load seven base registers (i.e., all but sb) from eight successive memory words beginning at the specified core address.	
(8)	stb	*store all eight base registers* into eight successive memory words, beginning at a specified core address, which is (=0 modulo 8).	

The stb and ldb instructions are especially useful in *call* and *return* sequences (as described in Chapter 3), because contents of the eight bases along with the contents of the eight index registers and other machine conditions (the pbr and the indicators) must be saved and restored in transferring to and returning from another procedure segment.

A user is free to store the contents of all address base registers and is free to alter all but the sb base register, as previously suggested in Table 1.3. Only the supervisor needs to be able to set the sb register.

1.5 Notes on Paging in the GE 645

As mentioned earlier, in Multics, user segments are in fact always paged, that is, further subdivided into divisions called pages. The pages of all segments[18] are stored in blocks of memory, 1024 words each, wherever room can be found. Allocation of core blocks for the purpose of "paging" is done by a supervisory routine called Page Control.[19] In normal programming, even at the assembly-language level, the user will not be concerned with (or aware of) paging. Moreover, there is no direct way that a user can detect paging.

In spite of this preamble on why the mechanics of paging need not be paid attention to, no red-blooded assembly-language programmer will remain uncurious forever. For the reader that must "have a look," therefore, some figures are offered here that may help to picture address formation for a paged segment. These are Figures 1.19, 1.20, and 1.21, which are roughly the counterparts of Figures 1.11a, 1.16, and 1.18, respectively.

Comparing these figures, a segment descriptor word, or SDW, is now seen to point, not to word zero of the segment, but to *word zero of the page table for that segment.*

Each word of the page table serves as a page descriptor word, or PDW, as follows:

1. If the associated page has been loaded in memory, the PDW contains a pointer A_p to word zero of that page.
2. If the page is not present in memory, bits are set in the descriptor field of the PDW to indicate that the page is missing.
3. Access rights and use bits are also stored in the descriptor field, but only the use bits are of interest (as explained in Chapter 7).

The detailed use of the page table and its control information is a supervisory function and should not concern us here. But the net effect is important. In particular, only those pages of a segment that are actually required during execution will be loaded. If a page is missing when referenced, a

18. Strictly speaking, there are certain system-maintained segments not directly accessible to user-written procedures that are paged into 64-word blocks. Among these is the segment that contains the page tables for all other segments.
19. Management of core resources is discussed in Chapter 7.

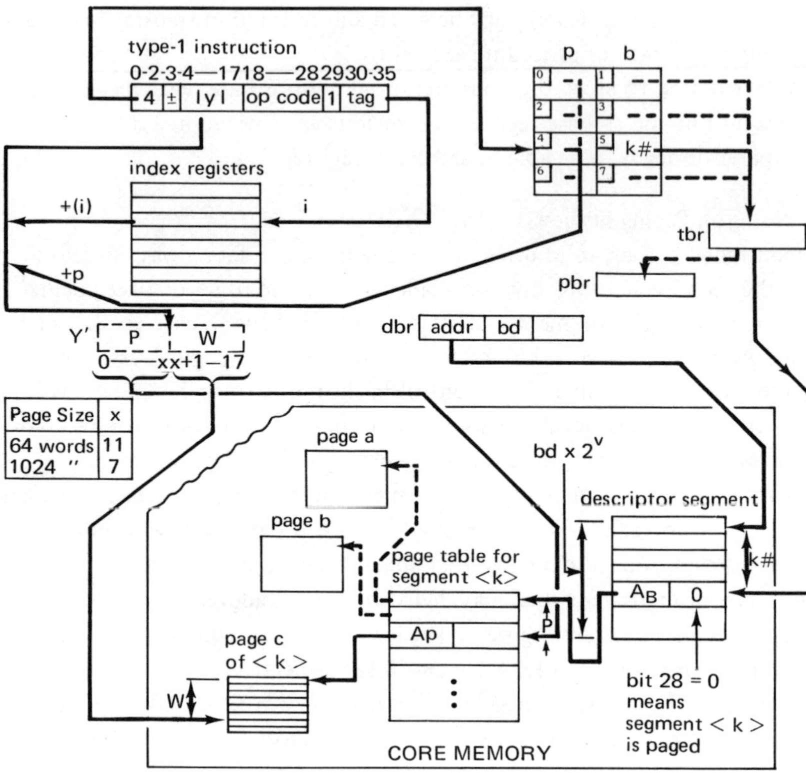

Figure 1.19. Address formation for type-1 instructions (paged mode)
Key to new notation:

P means page number
W means word number within the page
A_p is address (times 2^{-6}) of the page

missing-page fault will occur that will invoke a supervisory program that will create the missing page or load it from secondary storage.

In Figure 1.19 one sees that the effective internal address, when formed, is split into two parts. The high-order part serves as the *page number*, that is, as an offset P within the page table. The low order part serves as the word number within the page, that is, the offset W.

In Figure 1.20 one sees how the internal component of the its pair is also split into the two parts P and W. Finally, in the composite. Figure 1.21, note that the (ic) is also split the same way.

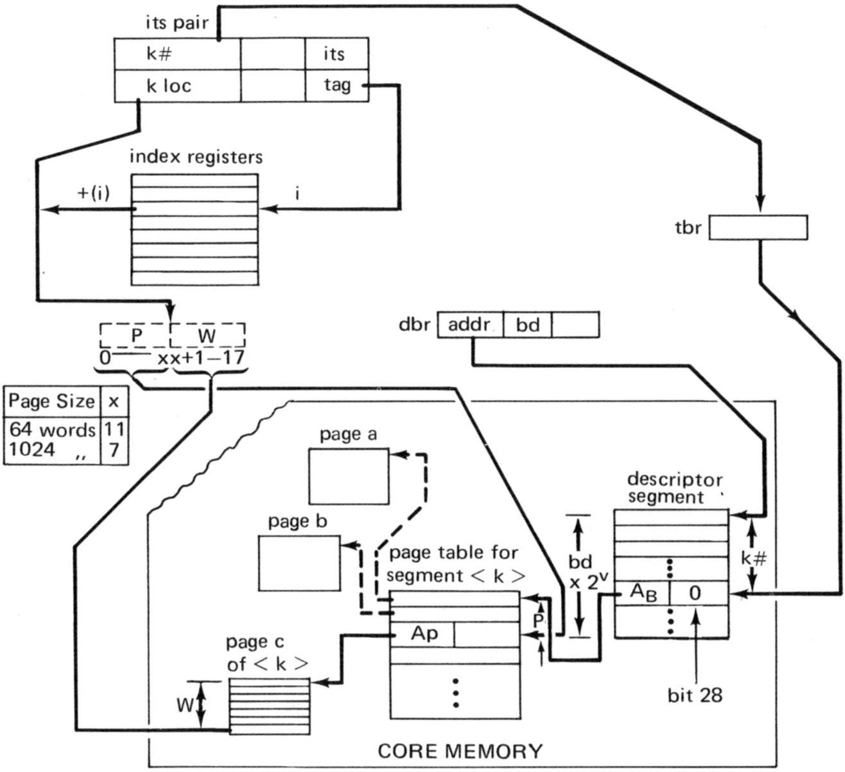

Figure 1.20. Address formation for its pairs (paged mode)

1.6 Notes on the Associative-Memory Addressing Facility

The elaborate address-formation schemes thus far discussed, or (in the case of paging) alluded to, are implemented efficiently in the GE 645 processor hardware with the aid of a small associative memory (AM). This is a slave memory of 16 words. The operational details of the associative memory to speed up the address-formation (and bounds-checking) operations is, like paging, something that subsystem writers will never need to know about. Nevertheless, because it is new (and because it is complicated and a small challenge to understand), a red-blooded programmer will at one time or another take up the mountain climber's rallying cry, "Because it's there!" and make the assault.

To help satisfy the too-early too-curious, first the important concepts will

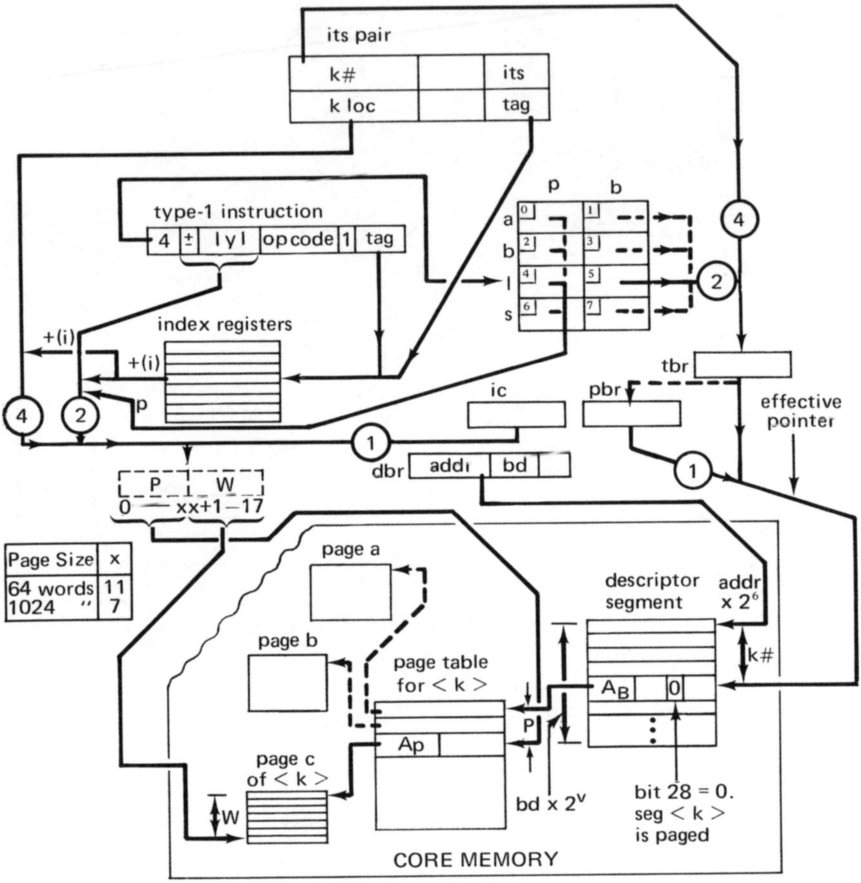

1 instruction cycle
2 execute cycle – type-1 instruction
4 execute cycle – its pair

Figure 1.21. Composite view of address formation (paged mode)

be summarized, and then some of the details will be presented using several figures and a very brief verbal description.

Every hardware reference to a target in core memory requires the use of either a segment descriptor word (an SDW) if the target lies in a nonpaged segment, or both an SDW and a page descriptor word (a PDW) if the target lies in a paged segment. Each time one of these descriptor words is needed, a copy is stored in the associative memory. Stored with each SDW or PDW will be the associated segment number. Naturally, since the AM is small, each new descriptor word that is entered calls for the discarding, by destructive read-in, of one already-resident descriptor word. An "lru" (least recently used) discipline is employed in the hardware for deciding which word is discarded. How this is done will be described momentarily.

Basically, there are two possible "hits" that can occur in the search of the AM. Either the desired SDW is found (and for a nonpaged segment this will be sufficient) or the PDW is found. Bear in mind that information must be extracted from the SDW to determine if the segment is paged (bit 28) so as to decide if a PDW is needed. If it is needed, the SDW also provides (bit 27) the page size information necessary to determine the page number P from the effective internal address. As you will see, the hardware needs to know P as an additional input argument for the associative lookup of the PDW in the AM. If the SDW is not found, or if the SDW is found but the PDW is not, part or all of the "normal" address formation as described in earlier sections of the chapter apply. That is, the necessary memory cycles must be taken to fetch first the SDW (to produce the pointer A_B) and then the PDW (to produce the pointer A_p). Of course, the hardware avoids taking the first of these memory cycles if the SDW was forthcoming from the AM and avoids taking both cycles when the PDW "emerges" from the AM.

Figure 1.22 suggests in a simplified way the functional value of the associative memory. Figure 1.23 shows the format of the 59-bit words in the associative memory, and Figure 1.24 is a logic flow chart to suggest how the searching of the AM is done.

It has been mentioned that when a segment is not paged, the AM is searched only once (one pass). However, when a segment *is* paged, the associative memory is searched at least once but, in fact, as many as *three* times (though this more elaborate search is still loosely called the "two-pass search"). Figure 1.24 and the subsequent discussion of it will explain when the third search is needed. This figure and the discussion in the next section

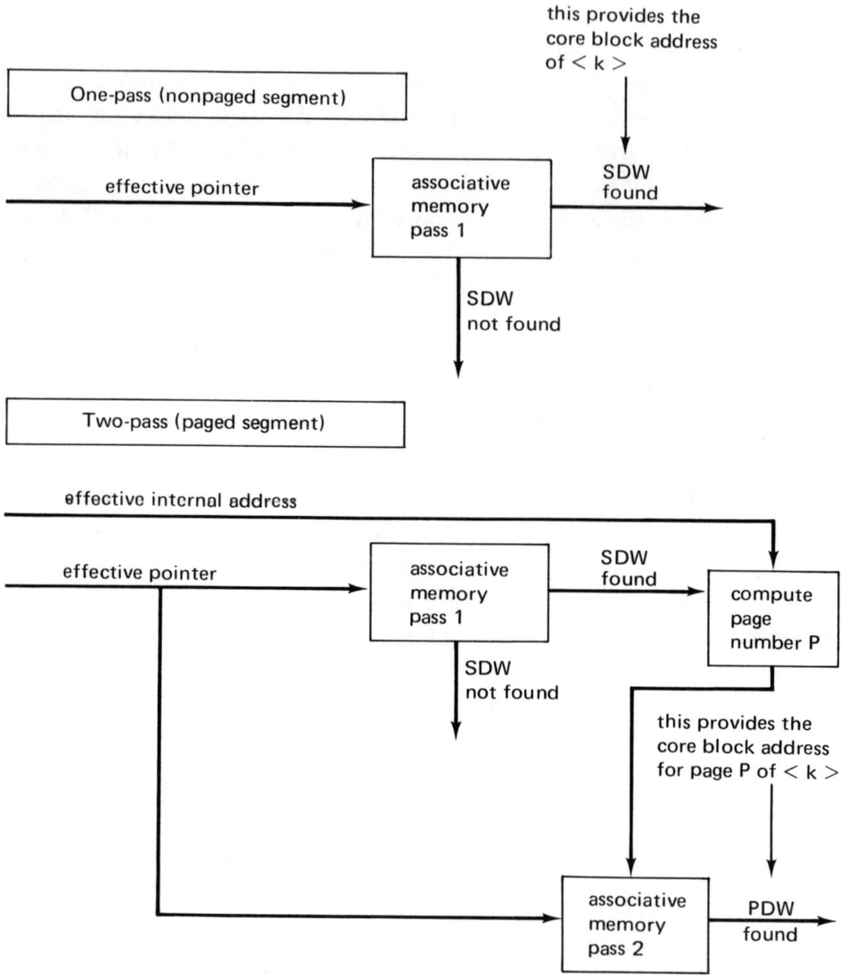

Figure 1.22. Functional overview of the associative memory

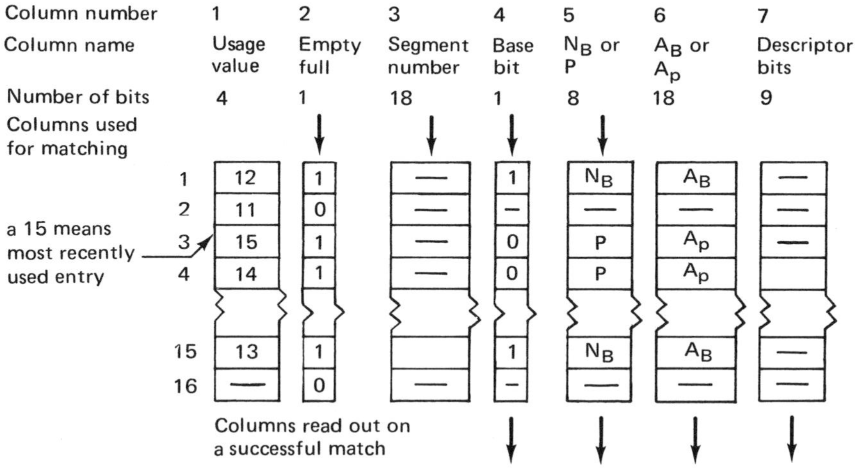

Figure 1.23. Format of the 16 associative memory entries
Notes: There are 59 bits per entry.

$$\text{Base bit} = \begin{cases} 1 \text{ if SDW in this entry} \\ 0 \text{ if PDW in this entry.} \end{cases}$$

make reference to Figures 1.25 and 1.26. The latter two figures are the counterparts of Figures 1.18 and 1.21, respectively.

1.6.1 A "Walk" through the Associative Memory

In the following discussion, *column numbers* refer to those in Figure 1.23, and *box numbers* refer to the flow chart in Figure 1.24.

Pass 1: Locate an entry that satisfies the following two conditions (box 1).

1. The content of column 2 is a 1.
2. The content of column 3 matches the given effective pointer.

A failure signifies that no pertinent descriptor word resides in the AM. Route 3 (Figure 1.26) must therefore be taken. That is, the required descriptor words must be fetched either from the descriptor segment alone (if the fetched descriptor word indicates no paging) or from both the descriptor segment and the page table (if the fetched segment descriptor word shows the segment to be paged). *Each fetched descriptor word is then inserted in the associative memory.*

1.6.2 Inserting Descriptor Words into the Associative Memory

We digress momentarily for an explanation of the rules for inserting descriptor words into the associative memory. Each inserted descriptor word replaces the one word whose usage value in column 1 equals zero. Bits of the

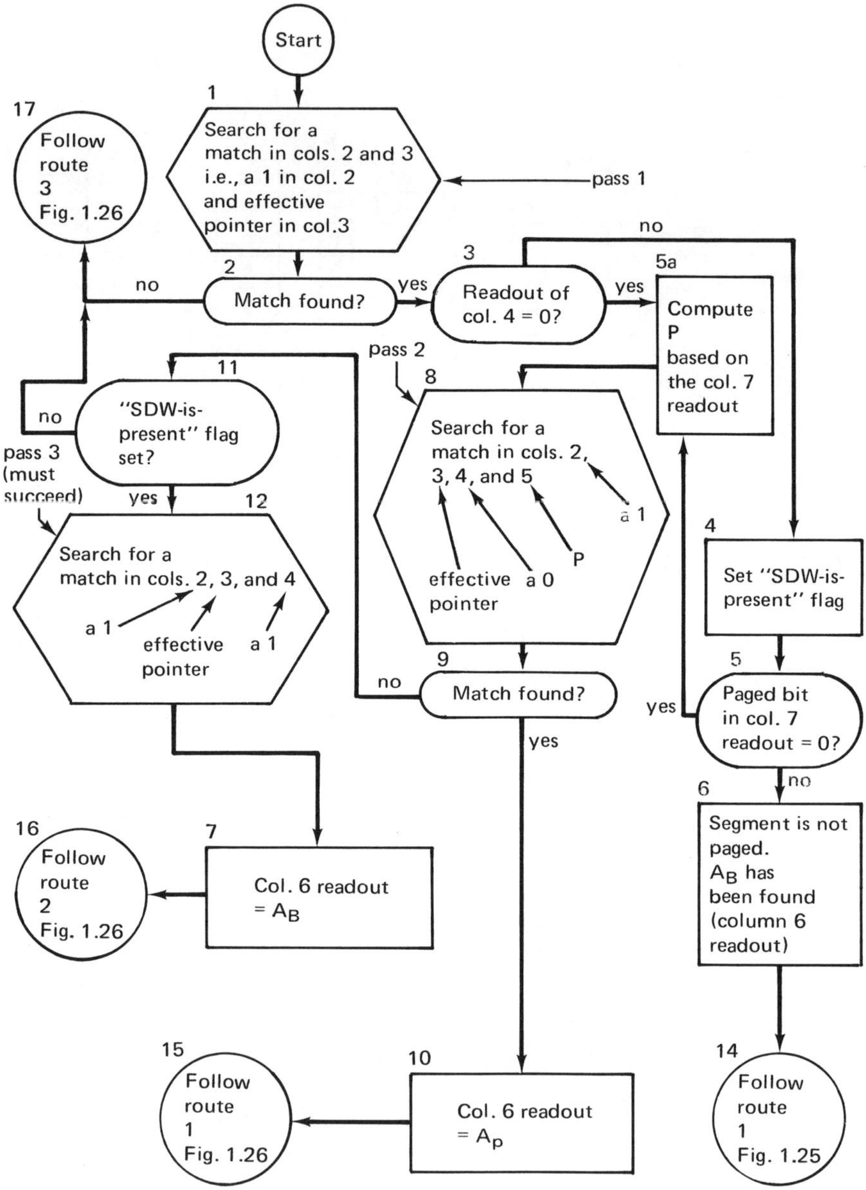

Figure 1.24. Detailed flow chart showing associative-memory action
Note: When routes 2 or 3 are followed, there is a simultaneous (asynchronous task) adjustment of the associative memory to include an entry corresponding to the one not found in the pass that just failed.

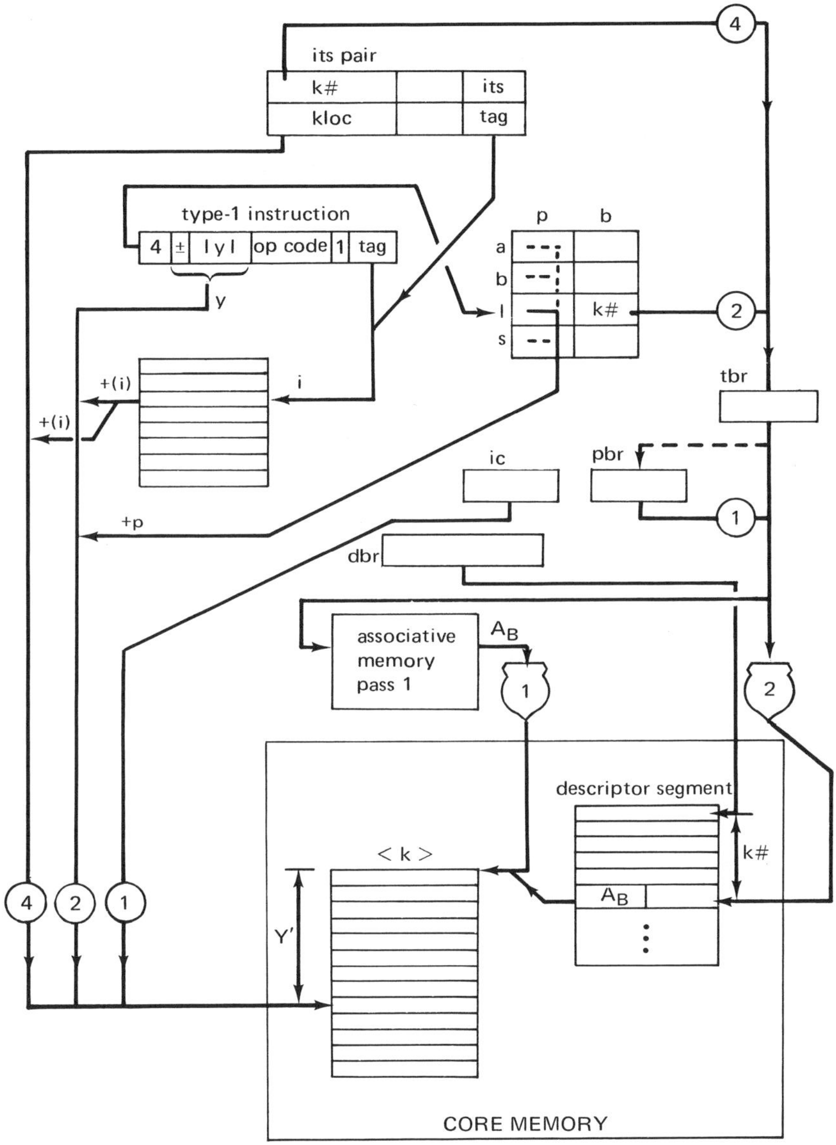

Figure 1.25. Composite view of three types of address formation (nonpaged case) This shows two routes to the block address of segment <k>. Route 1 through associative memory (Figure 1.22), and route 2 through the descriptor-segment mechanism.

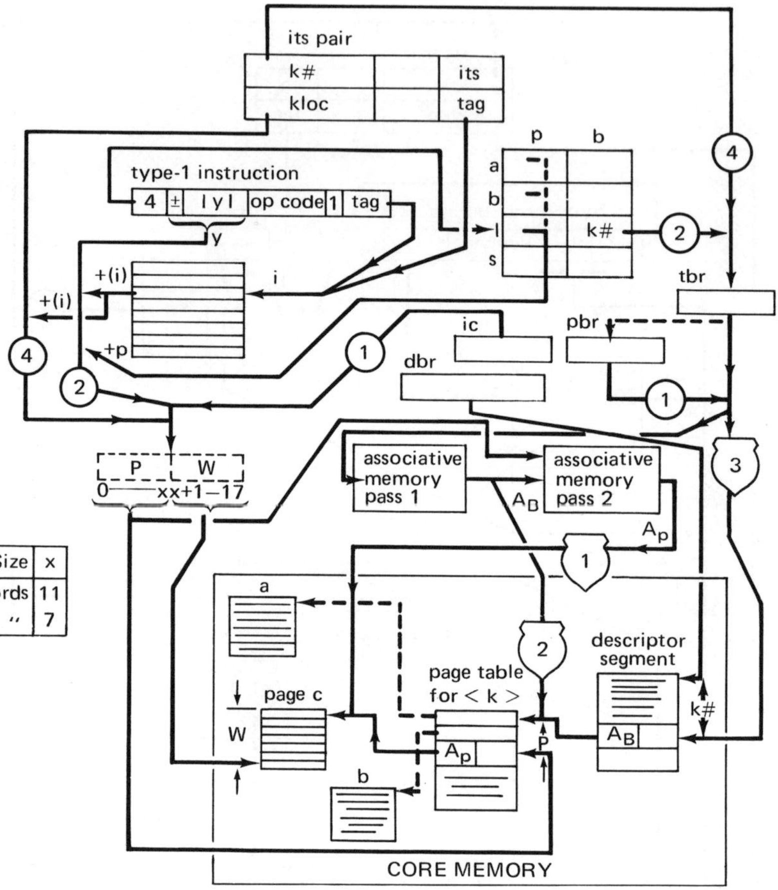

Page Size	x
64 words	11
1024 "	7

Figure 1.26. Composite view of three types of address formation (paged case)
Two primary routes to the block address of page c of segment <k> are shown. Route 1 is through the two-stage associative-memory mechanism. Route 3 is through the descriptor-segment mechanism. Route 2 is an intermediate route; i.e., via the one-stage associative memory to the page table for segment <k>.

inserted descriptor word are placed into columns (fields) 5, 6, and 7. The base bit (column 4) is set to 1 if an SDW (a segment descriptor word) is being inserted, and is set to 0 if a PDW (a page descriptor word) is being added. The empty/full bit (column 2) is set to 1, and column 3 is set to the segment number associated with the inserted descriptor word. Finally, the usage value for this word (column 2) is set to 15, and the usage value of every other word in the associative memory is decreased by 1. This last ritual guarantees the AM's least recently used discipline. That is to say, each new insertion is made at the expense of the *oldest resident.*

1.6.3 A Continuation of the "Walk"

A success (in pass 1) causes a "readout" of the information in columns 4, 5, 6, and 7 of the matching entry. The descriptor word just found may be an entry for another page of the same segment; it may be for the wanted PDW, it may be the SDW for the referenced segment, or it may be the OR'ed value of several of these. The first step to resolve this multiway ambiguity is to decide whether the matched entry (or entries) includes the SDW (or consists only of one or more PDWs). This is done by checking the value of the column 4 readout (box 3). If only PDWs have been found, that is, if the readout is zero, we know the segment under consideration must be paged, so we now "gamble" and make a second search of the AM looking to see if the desired page-table word is present (box 8). This thread will be pursued at the paragraph marked Pass 2. If on the other hand an SDW was found, progress has been made for one of two reasons. Either the readout of column 7 will show the target segment to be nonpaged, in which case the desired SDW has been found (leading to an exit via box 14), or we are certain to find the SDW of the target segment in the AM, if needed, during a third-pass search (box 12). For this latter reason, an "SDW-is-present" flag is set in box 4.

Next we check to see if the descriptor bits of the discovered SDW indicate that the segment is paged (box 5). A *no* means one type of success (box 6). We've found in *one pass* the desired value of A_B, which locates the desired nonpaged segment. We now follow route 1 of Figure 1.25. A *yes* means the segment *is* paged, so another search of the associative memory should be made in hopes of finding the desired PDW (box 8). First, of course, the page number P is computed (box 5a) from a knowledge of the page size (also indicated in the column 7 readout) and the effective internal address.

Pass 2: For this search we input both the effective pointer *and* the page number P. We actually try for a match on columns 2, 3, 4, and 5. That is we look for an entry that is "full" (column 2 = 1), that represents a PDW (column 4 = 0), and that has the desired segment number (column 3) *and* page number (column 5).

Success on this second search means the desired page address A_p is the column 6 readout (box 10). We now follow route 1 of Figure 1.26.

Failure on this second search prompts us to check if the "SDW-is-present" flag was set earlier (box 11).

If *yes*, then a third and final search is called for to locate the desired SDW that is now known to be present in the AM. On this search, we look for a match on a "full" entry that has its base bit (column 4) equal to 1, signifying that we will this time restrict the search to SDW's only. The input for this search (box 12) is the effective pointer to be matched by the contents of column 3. This search must perforce be successful, yielding A_B as the readout of column 6 and allowing us to follow routc 2, Figurc 1.26.

If *no*, then we've learned that the AM contains neither the desired PDW nor the desired SDW. We follow route 3 of Figure 1.26.

The reader may be wondering if simplifications in the logic design might eventually reduce the number of required passes through the associative memory to one or, at most, two passes for all cases and hence achieve some speedup in address formation. Follow-on versions of the GE 645 may well produce such speedups. Several alternative strategies have been considered, and these are mentioned briefly in the remainder of this discussion.

1. This strategy aims at a one-pass AM. Its basis is an agreement to restrict the system to the use of a single page size. With just one page size it would never be necessary to keep SDWs for paged segments in the associative memory. Hence, one pass of the AM would either find the wanted PDW for a paged segment or the wanted SDW for a nonpaged segment.
2. This strategy aims at a two-pass (maximum) AM in which the first pass is done early and looks only for an SDW match. This search is made as soon as the segment number is known, which is long before the internal address may be known. The first pass would essentially be "free" when it typically overlaps computation of the second address component. For paged segments the second pass would search for the wanted PDW. If more than one page size is permitted, as indicated by a set flip-flop, the page size would be determined from (successful) output of the first pass; otherwise the second-pass search would be automatic.
3. This strategy is based on splitting the AM into two parts, one holding

SDWs only and the other holding PDWs only. Searching of the duplicate AMs could proceed in parallel if the page size is known in advance (true for the one-page-size case).

Strategy 2 is attractive because it is adaptable to the use of multiple page sizes. Strategy 3 may be conceptually the "cleanest" but is likely to be the most expensive to implement.

2 Intersegment Linking

2.1 Virtual Memory and Address Space

In Chapter 1 the grand plan for the Multics virtual memory was identified. Then much of the hardware that would be needed to effect that plan was described in detail. This description created a conceptual gap, because, on the one hand, memory was pictured as an open-ended collection of segments, each with its set of attributes including the access rights for possibly several users. On the other hand, when the hardware address formation was focused on, the discussion concerned the reference to segments that belong to a specific computation or process, where that process normally relates to a single user. Thus, the descriptors that are arrayed in the descriptor segment of that one process refer merely to some subset of the segments extant in the system's virtual memory. Moreover, for any given segment in the process, the coded set of attributes that is kept in the descriptor word for that segment is itself a subset of the set of attributes for the segment, that is, the access of the user associated with the specific computation. The identification and creation of these subsets (of segments and their attributes), one per process, is an essential function of the system's supervisor.

There is a collection of supervisory modules that goes under the umbrella name of *file system*. This set of modules has the responsibility for mapping the selected segments of the Multics virtual memory (together, of course, with subsets of their attributes) into what we might picture as per-process virtual memories.

Merely to avoid confusion, I shall always refer to the per-process virtual memory as the *address space* of the process. The term *address space* is intended to refer to that collection of segments (space of addresses), each having a unique identification and size, that the program, aided by a combination of the GE 645 hardware and the Multics software, can address.

I shall now try to show, without getting too involved in detail just yet, why it is that the set of segment descriptor words arrayed in a descriptor segment for a particular process does in effect represent the address space of that process.

Picture first the extreme and totally unlikely case that every SDW in a descriptor segment points to in-core information. That is, suppose that page tables for every listed segment are in core and that each page listed in each page table is also in core. Were this situation to occur, there can be no question, based on the hardware facts presented in Chapter 1, that the descriptor segment represents the address space of the process. We, of course, bear in mind that pointers, size parameters, and access-rights parameters in the segment descriptor words determine, via the page-table descriptor, all valid core addresses, as well as the type of access permitted.

Two more likely cases must be considered. First, what if some page of some segment is missing from core? Second, what if some entire segment, that is, its page table, is missing from core? How is the address space of a process affected by such "missing" information? In other words, to what extent, if any, is program addressing affected? Not at all! Of course, hardware faults are incurred upon recognition of the missing information, but user's object code is compiled so that its execution *need not anticipate such faults.* The file system is invoked on a "page fault" or a "segment fault," respectively, and its job is to "repair" the fault by employing data available to it that is kept in per-system and/or per-process tables. I do not intend to burden the reader with details but shall provide a "flavor" of this detail here so that a conceptual model may begin to form in the reader's mind concerning the handling of such faults. Thus, for each potentially missing page of a page table, the system keeps an auxiliary table of pointers (called a "segment map") to the secondary-storage addresses from which such pages may be retrieved. For each potentially missing page table of a segment, file-system modules will access a per-process table in which may be found for each *known* segment of the process the unique identification of that segment necessary for retrieval of file-system information to construct the missing page table and segment map in core. The objective of sharing segments among processes adds additional complexity to the handling of segment and page faults, but this matter need not be considered here.[1]

The dynamics of a Multics process is mirrored in the evolution of its descriptor segment. At the outset of a process, its descriptor segment is endowed with segment descriptor words for certain shared segments of supervisor procedures and their data bases. But there are no SDWs for the user's segments yet appended. These SDWs are constructed and added to the descriptor segment as needed by modules of the file system that are automatically invoked for this purpose. The activity of appending SDWs to a descriptor segment is related to *making segments known* to a process. The important observation to be made here is that the address space of a process grows as more segments are made known and as any one known segment grows in size, and it is independent of the physical location of pages of these segments. [An address space may, of course, also shrink as segments shrink in size (or are *deleted* from the process, thereby causing their respective SDWs to be deleted

1. Such problems are considered in Chapters 6 and 7.

from the descriptor segment).] Segments are caused to grow (or shrink) in size or are caused to be made known to (or unknown to, i.e., deleted from) a process by execution of calls to (i.e., use of special entry points into) the file system.[2] Users will occasionally write code that executes such calls either as library subroutine calls or as commands,[3] but most of the time these calls are issued implicitly or indirectly, frequently as a result of faults that induce calls to these file-system procedures.

The foregoing introduction to the address space of a Multics process, though admittedly quite sketchy, is sufficient to provide a picture of the environment for a detailed study of intersegment linking within a process, the principal objective of this chapter.

2.2 Linking and Loading

One of the key problems needing solution in any programming system is this: Given two segments <a> and <b> of a process, suppose <a> is a procedure that needs to fetch from, store into, transfer control to, or return from <b>. How is <a> "told" where <b> is located in memory so that executable code for such inter-segment references can be written and then executed?

In a conventional batch operating system, all segments of a process (in common FORTRAN parlance, for instance, these would be the main program and separately compiled subprograms) are declared in advance in some way. Segments are then loaded for execution and, in the loading process, their physical locations are determined so that each procedure segment may then be "told," such as by establishing its transfer vector, where each of the other segments it needs to know about is located. This "telling" is known as "linking." Note that linking, the construction of executable instructions that achieve references to external objects (or segments), is in this type of system inextricably keyed to the loading process. If a new loading involving the same set of programs were ever required, a complete relinking might also be required, unless all programs were restored to their original positions or unless a sufficient number of relocation registers were available.

In Multics, by happy contrast, loading and linking are entirely separate and independent activities. A target segment need only be *known* to be addressable at run time; the physical location of the target is always immaterial.

2. Only the file system can perform these actions, because, by careful system design, only file-system modules are privileged to alter a segment's attributes (e.g., change its size) or to write in a descriptor segment of a process.

3. For example, the initiate command causes a designated segment to be made known. Chapter 6 discusses the "initiation" of segments in some detail.

Also, by contrast, every segment remains fully identified, that is, has lost none of its properties, such as its ability to be shared with other processes, by virtue of having been made known to this process.

Linking involves altering the code related to a procedure so that the references to its external targets are expressed as addresses of those targets. In Multics, naturally, the [segment number, offset] address pair for a target cannot be determined before the target segment is itself made known (because only then will its segment number be established). In theory anyway linking to a target <t> can be achieved at the earliest whenever it becomes feasible to make <t> known. It is, in fact, even more interesting to consider until how *late* linking can be postponed. In a Multics process, making a segment known and linking to it can be postponed until the actual reference is executed. This flexibility is available because of the ingenious use of the link-fault-inducing capability of the GE 645 hardware—about which I will have more to say later. In brief, however, a reference to an external target can, if desired, be compiled into the form of a fault-inducing, indirectly referenced word pair, which, upon use for the first time, induces a fault. The faulting word pair is in turn converted into an its pair that effectively serves as the desired link to the target—no small feat, mind you.

When linking is done in this wait-to-the-last-possible-moment-to-do-it fashion, it is known as *dynamic linking*. This type of linking is the normal mode of linking in Multics.

The establishing of links at reference time on an as-needed basis is a fundamental service of Multics. Note that the inducing of a special link fault will bring into play all the power of the Multics supervisor as needed. If the target segment is not yet known, necessary steps are taken to *make* that segment *known* (if at all possible) or *create* it, or both, as found necessary, so that the segment number of the target may be determined and employed in creating the link. Bear in mind, too, that the ordinary user will be completely unaware that this interplay between his procedures and the supervisor is going on. One should note, in completing these introductory remarks, that the Multics dynamic-linking service for the creation of intersegment references builds nicely on top of (and not interdependently with) the virtual-memory machine that we have already accepted as having been constructed in the "basement layers" of the GE 645 system. We are reminded that (hardware/software) paging mechanisms, the lowest layer, provide for the automatic relocation of pages and page tables, and that (hardware/software) segmentation features, the next layer, complete the location independence of information by providing a way of making direct access to a segment, knowing only its name, and thus leading to mechanisms for the controlled sharing of segments. The remaining two paragraphs of this subsection merely reinforce, with an example, the notion of location independence that is produced through paging and segmentation mechanisms. (The services described below, it should be remembered, are functions of the file system upon which the linking mechanisms are built.)

Multics manages to develop and retain a fixed pairing of s# with <s> in a very simple way. The very first time the need for <s> is recognized, <s> must be established as a member of the set of segments *known* to the process. Once a segment is made known to a process, the system can construct and append a segment descriptor word for that segment to the descriptor segment. Picture that the descriptor word is "tacked on to" the current end of the descriptor segment, say at position 56. This means that s# = 56. If the page table for <s> is ever removed from core memory temporarily, certain bits of the descriptor word of <s> (see Table 1.1) are automatically reset to indicate the segment is *absent*. Any future attempt to address a word in this segment will incur a "directed fault" during the formation of this address. Of course, the details of how the GE 645 and the Multics software handle this fault are skipped over here, and only the resulting effect is looked at. As a result of this fault, the page table for <s> will be reloaded into core memory, this time probably into some other core location. When reloading is completed, instead of adding a *new* descriptor word for <s>, <s>'s old descriptor word (number 56) is adjusted to reflect the new core address of <s> (i.e., the "A_B" field). Also, the segment-missing bits are reset to (a) designate that the segment is again present and (b) denote the segment class. (Review Section 1.2.9 for an explanation of segment class.) Address formation, interrupted by recognition of the directed fault, is now allowed to go to completion as if the fault had not occurred at all.

In summary, the important concept to take note of is that addresses for instructions of a segment <a> that refer to locations within another segment <s> need not be changed after the first change is made to reflect a known value of s#. Each such address is established by determining two values that, generally speaking, are s# and sloc. The location sloc is an offset from word zero of <s>. Neither of these values will have changed in spite of the fact that the absolute core location for <s>|0 may have changed. Even if the segment is removed from core, the value s# and sloc still apply.

2.2.1 Segment Binding

Dynamic linking is the default mode for establishing intersegment references in Multics, but it is by no means the only way to achieve this objective. I shall offer additional motivation for dynamic linking in Section 2.2.3, but, before doing so, I give brief attention to an attractive alternative called *segment binding*. Suppose a programmer has coded, compiled, and debugged m highly interrelated procedures, <S1>, <S2>, . . . , <S*m*>. Further suppose that in each of the m procedures there are on the average n intersegment references to the $m - 1$ other segments. Compilation must generate at least $m \times n$ separate links in producing the target code for these procedures. If recompilation is expected to be infrequent, if $m \times n$ is large, and/or if the set of m procedures is to be used in many processes, the default mode of dynamic linking may prove an expensive form of linking for some applications.[4] Assuming this may be the case, users are provided with a system command [5] that, when executed, packages sets of already compiled individual procedures into a single segment, thus binding into a single segment a set of previously compiled "object" segments. This process converts what were intersegment (and indirect) references among the set of segments being bound into internal (direct) references, thereby reducing the subsequent execution overhead of the bound package.

To more fully appreciate the trade-off between segment binding (i.e., prelinking), and dynamic linking (i.e., postponed linking), the reader may want to study much of what is covered in this chapter. The following philosophy has guided the Multics designers in their use of the binding feature (and subsytem designers may wish to take note).

1. In most circumstances system modules should be bound to improve performance–after they have been fully checked out. But, binding should be postponed as long as it is feasible, because premature binding causes a loss of flexibility that often complicates debugging. Good judgment is obviously needed in deciding when the time for binding has arrived.
2. When binding segments, one should group them on the basis of most *locality of reference* rather than on the basis of their functional similarity.

4. The reader has not yet learned enough about how Multics works to appreciate the cost of establishing an intersegment link by the fault-inducing approach that was overviewed in the preceding subsection. So, here just assume that the per-link cost of dynamic linking is high in some relative sense.

5. See the command entitled bind that is described in the Commands and Active Functions section of the MPM.

The term locality of reference refers to the likelihood that one component of the group being bound will, during typical execution, reference (or be referenced by) another component within the same group.

2.2.2 The Need to Share Procedures

The objective of sharing certain procedures among two or more processes necessarily adds to the complexity of intersegment linking. To a large extent this added complexity is independent of the decision to use the prelinking or postponed linking alternatives discussed above. The following paragraph introduces the complicating issue that sharing raises.

Certain procedure segments will be shared as part of many user processes. Among these are a group of supervisory routines, library subroutines, compilers, and assemblers. It should be possible for several processes to share the same in-core copy of a procedure in order to conserve memory space and reduce unnecessary core-to-secondary-storage transfers. A first prerequisite for such shared procedures is that they necessarily be pure procedures. A pure procedure has been defined as one that does not change (not one bit of it) as a result of being used; that is, it has no moving or replaceable parts. However, the data with which, or on which, such a shared procedure operates will necessarily be different for each process that the shared procedure is attempting to serve. Consequently, the targets of data references given in the source text of the procedure must somehow change each time the procedure finds itself serving in a different process. This implies that the links used by the shared procedure <seg> when executing in process A must be physically different links from those used when executing in process B. A Multics mechanism has been developed to achieve this capability at an overall minimum cost in execution time or storage requirements.

2.2.3 Additional Motivation for Dynamic Linking

There is a cost, the cost of making a segment known, associated with addition of each new segment to a process—quite apart from the space occupied by the segment descriptor words in a descriptor segment. When a process begins functioning, it should not have to find and make known any more of its segments than is absolutely necessary to begin running. As the process executes, segments should be made known on an as-needed basis. The mere presence of a reference to an external segment in a segment's text is no guarantee that the flow of control will "touch" this reference. In fact, in a real sense, dynamic linking allows the running of incomplete programs.

Therefore, there is little point to undertake the "expense" of finding a

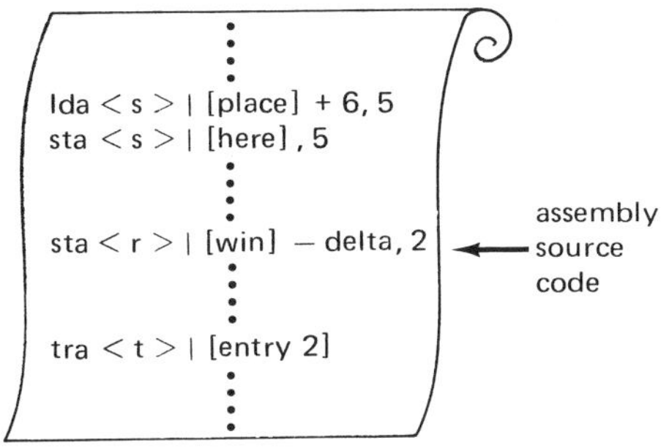

Figure 2.1. Procedure segment <a> with four instructions making intersegment references

segment and making it known unless there is some significant expectation that that segment will be referenced during the time, frame, or "quantum," allotted to that process.

Moreover–and more striking–some segments of a process cannot conceivably be known about in advance without following all links and making the corresponding segments known, a practice that is possible but hardly desirable. Thus, a user may type at the console the name of a segment as part of a command. Only at that point can it be learned that the named segment is related to the user's process. So, when I speak about a segment brought in *as needed*, I mean no earlier than at the time of the first executed reference. Let us, for example, see what this means for a procedure segment <a> that refers to places in two different data segments <r> and <s> and to an entry in one procedure <t>. Figure 2.1 shows a schematic of <a> showing four different instructions as they are likely to be written by the programmer in some symbolic language–I have selected the ALM assembly language,[6] but I could have also illustrated with a PL/I or FORTRAN segment.

Figure 2.1 tells us that <a> might at some time need to know s#, r#, and t#. But, we certainly can't say, at the time <a> is made known, when (during the execution of <a>) or in what order <a> will need to know these segment numbers. Depending on the detailed logic in <a> it is possible that none of these four intersegment instructions will be needed for some run of the process that <a> is serving. It is in this sense that we speak of making

6. Described in *EPLBSA Programmers' Reference Handbook*, by D. J. Riesenberg, it is the only currently available assembly language for the GE 645 computer. The initialism EPLBSA is the earlier name used for the Multics assembly language (ALM).

segments known on an as-needed basis. Thus, if in attempting to execute the instruction in <a>

lda <s>|[place] + 6, 5

a Multics process discovers that the pointer to <s> doesn't exist in its descriptor segment, then and only then will <s> need to be made known and, of course, the pointer to <s> (i.e., an SDW for <s>) placed in the descriptor segment. With respect to the particular example of the lda instruction, we must bear in mind that at the time <a> is assembled, no one can in general know any of the following vital facts.

1. What value will have been given to s# in the process of which we are speaking—that is to say, where in the descriptor segment a pointer to the core location for <s> will eventually be placed. (Recall that segment numbers are awarded on a per-process basis and assigned as needed in a process.)

2. Where, relative to the first word of <s>, may [place] be found, that is, the value of place. The programmer of <a> in general does not even want to be able to know this information about <s>. He only wants to be able to know and be able to use a character string that is the symbolic location for said position internal to <s>.

What mechanism can be employed to complete such an intersegment reference at execution time? The Multics mechanism for dynamic linking, though complex in detail, has already been overviewed in concept. A few more details will be added in the next paragraphs.

First, I draw on the reader's familiarity with the apparatus known as a *symbol table*. Any Multics segment that has locations within it that have symbolic names will have associated with it a table of "external" symbols. Normally, this table is prepared automatically by the assembler or compiler from the source-language representation of the segment. This table has a standard format, hence it can be searched in a predetermined way. A successful search of it will locate the numerical (location) equivalent of any locally defined symbol that may have been referred to by another segment. In the example, I would say that associated with <s> is a symbol table that can be searched for the locally unique symbol "place" and its corresponding numerical equivalent.

The linking mechanism can now be seen conceptually as following these basic steps relative to the example

lda <s>|[place] + 6, 5

1. If <s> is not already known to this process, then find it and make it known.

If <s> is known, then s# can be found in a data base called the Known Segment Table (KST), which is kept for every process. The KST is in essence a convenient association list that associates segment names and segment numbers. Associative lookup in this table finds s# (if <s> is already known). Finding <s> to make it known means to invoke a file-system search for <s>, searching for it by its unique name. The search is conducted in the tree-structured set of *directories* that is called the Multics *hierarchy*. [File-system modules (and only file-system modules) may search these directories.] The actual act of making <s> known amounts to creating an entry for it in the KST. By design, s# turns out to be the index of the newly formed KST entry. The attributes for the found segment, including information leading to the actual physical location of the segment, its size, access rights for this user, and other information describing the segment, are copied over into the newly formed KST entry. This saved information is employed later when the system constructs and appends an SDW for <s> in the descriptor segment at the offset = s#.

2. Determine the value of [place].

This can now be done because once <s> is known, it can be referenced by the supervisory modules, which can search <s>'s table of external symbols on behalf of the user to find [place] and thence find its numerical value.

Having determined s# and place, we can see how it would be possible to complete the process of generating the required machine code and use it to replace the equivalent symbolic form of the instruction

```
lda <s>|[place] + 6, 5
```

which was encountered when executing in <a>.

Examine the instruction

```
sta <s>|[here], 5
```

found in Figure 2.1, which is pictured as immediately following the lda instruction. When the latter is executed for the first time, the linkage mechanism as it has just been described will have resulted in making <s> known. So, when the computer next attempts to execute the sta instruction, the job of completing the machine code equivalent of the sta instruction is now quite a bit shorter. The segment number s# is determined simply by searching for and finding it in the Known Segment Table belonging to the given process, because there is now an entry for <s> in this table. The value of [here] is determined by searching for it, as for the value of [place], in the symbol table that is part of <s>.

2.3 Linking Details

Needless to say, a great deal of detail has been skirted in the mechanism just described. Some subsystem writers may need to understand this process in some detail in order to provide Multics with the data it needs in the proper format so that this automatic linking process can be achieved. The subsystem writer that may especially need to know these details is the one that will be building his own language processor, like an ALGOL or MAD compiler or an assembler, which will output target code *directly*—that is, one that does not output code or data in the syntax of a standard Multics-provided language like PL/I or ALM (assembly language).

The account will proceed by considering the linking details that are made necessary to meet the Multics objectives stated in the introductory discussion. Table 2.1 lists, as cross-references, sections of the MPM in which additional material on linking can be found.

2.4 Processes Sharing Procedure Segments

In preceding discussions the specific details of the original symbolic reference <s>|[place] as it is found in <a> at the time <a> is originally loaded were not actually given. Nor was the actual format of the numerical equivalent shown when that numerical equivalent of <s>|[place] was determined.

In this section the development of these details, which are somewhat complex, will begin. Strong motivation for the complexity comes from insisting that it should in principle be possible for any procedure to be (simultaneously) *shared* by two or more processes (access permitting).

Begin by examining Figure 2.2. Here one is reminded that a single GE 645

Table 2.1 References on Intersegment Linking in the "Multics Programmers' Manual" (MPM)

Title	Remarks
Intersegment Linking and Addressing	General and introductory
Segment Formats	Layout of object code for procedures
Standard Object Segment	The principal technical reference for this chapter

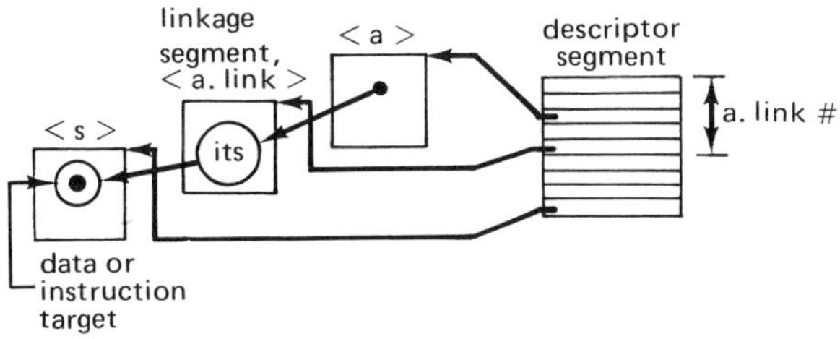

Figure 2.2. Referencing <s> from <a> via an intermediate linkage segment called <a.link>. Paging details are omitted to simplify the diagram.

instruction in one procedure segment can indirectly reference a location within another segment via a point within an intermediate segment containing an its indirect word pair. Shortly, the reader will see why it is a good idea to call this intermediate data base a "linkage section" or "linkage segment." In particular, a single instruction in segment <a> can make a data reference or an instruction reference (transfer or return) to any point within segment <s> via an intermediate linkage segment. In Multics, every procedure segment can make such cross-references, because it has an associated linkage segment. This segment[7] is copied from an appropriate template-linkage section that is produced and placed in the text segment, that is, in the object code, by the compiler or assembler. Generally speaking, segment <a> has associated with it a linkage segment called <a.link>. (Thus, if the name of the procedure segment is "cosine" then the name of its linkage segment is "cosine.link".) Note, too, that the notation for segment numbers naturally leads to interpreting a.link# as the segment number of <a.link>.

Initially it is hard to see why one needs to bother going to the trouble of making the reference from <a> to <s> through the intermediate segment <a.link>. As was suggested in Figure 1.12b, it would be possible to place the needed its pair in <a>. In the next paragraphs I hope to provide the why of the linkage segment. *Without doubt, there are few concepts more crucial to the power of Multics than that of the linkage segment.*

In Figure 2.3, segment <a> is a procedure segment that is currently shared by two processes. For illustrative purposes, let us imagine that <a> is an assembler or a compiler. An assembler that is being shared by two active

7. For the sake of efficiency, i.e., to save system overhead and core space, the individual linkage sections of many segments are in practice automatically combined by the system into a single *combined linkage segment*. However, for most discussions the reader will find it useful to think of the linkage section as a single and separate segment.

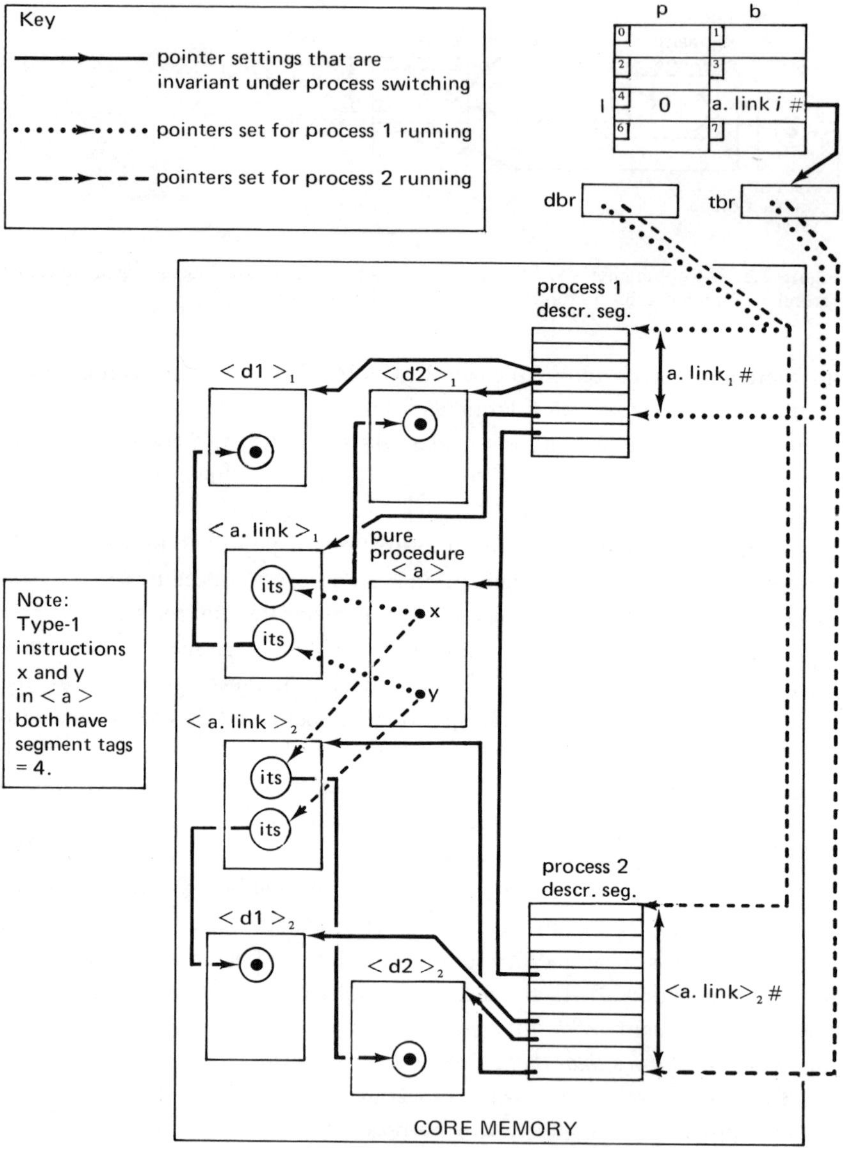

Figure 2.3. Two processes sharing a common reference procedure
Processes (i = 1, 2) share a common procedure <a> that makes data references to <d1>$_1$ and <d2>$_1$ when functioning for process 1 but makes data references to <d1>$_2$ and <d2>$_2$ when functioning for process 2. Each time process i takes charge, the lb base register is set to a. link$_i$#. Solid lines represent pointers that do *not* change as a resuit of process switching.

processes[8] may have to deal with two completely different sets of data stored in core memory at the same time.

It is highly desirable that <a> be a pure procedure. If so, then, as "ownership" of the processor is switched back and forth between two (or more) processes, the one copy of <a> can function effectively on the two different source-language programs that <a> treats as data.

For the assembler to be pure, all data on which it operates, for example, source-language program, symbol tables that are being constructed or being sorted, switch settings, and so on, must be maintained in one or more separate segments. Moreover, there must be a different set of such separate data segments for *each process* that the assembler currently serves. How, then, can the procedure <a> point to different data segments, depending on which process it happens to be "serving," and still be pure? The separate per-process linkage segment for <a> provides an attractive solution.

Connection to the data segments is made indirectly via the linkage segment of the procedure being executed. It is important to bear in mind that the linkage segment <a.link> is (and must be) generated by the assembler or compiler while it is generating <a>. During execution, the linkage segment is reached from <a> in a standard fashion; namely, one pair of base registers, in particular the lb ← lp pair, is *always* set to point at the associated linkage segment. (For example, if process 1 is in control, then at the time <a> is called, imagine that lb ← lp is then set to point at the <a.link> in that process. For process 1 I shall call the linkage segment <a.link>$_1$ and its segment number a.link$_1$#.)

Located within <a.link> will be found the its pairs, one for every unique symbolic intersegment data (or procedure) reference that appears in the programmer's source code for <a>. But, make a mental note of this fact: the compiler or assembler that is generating <a> and <a.link> cannot produce the desired its pairs, because it does not have all the necessary information. It does, however, produce equivalent word pairs that can eventually be transformed into the needed its pairs.

I'll now sketch how this linking mechanism works in one simple case (and describe the actual detail much more closely in the next section). Suppose an instruction in <a> originally appeared in source language as

8. "Active process" is a technical term. Its specific meaning is given in Chapter 7. A semitechnical definition would be that the supervisory system of Multics knows this process by virtue of knowing about its descriptor segment and by having the "name" of the process entered on a list of processes that are currently in one of three active states (running, ready, or blocked).

lda <a>|[place] + 6, 5

The assembled instruction would turn out to be an indirectly addressed lda instruction to a location in <a.link>. The assembled binary machine instruction would, if "unassembled," have the form

lda lp | k, *

Its meaning is as follows:

The segment tag of this instruction is 4. It points to the lb ← lp pair. So, the effective pointer is the contents of the lb base register, which presumably has been set previously to a.link#.

The effective internal address is k + (contents of the lp base register). To keep things simple, I have shown in Figure 2.3 that the contents of lp is zero. Here, k is a number determined by the assembler while assembling <a> to point to a strategically located pair of indirect words (i.e., a "link pair") within <a.link>. This indirect pair will ultimately have the its pair appearance

s#	0	its
place + 6	0	5

a completed "link"

when linking is completed.

The format of the linkage segment is the subject of the next section of this chapter, so we need not go into it in any detail here. You will see there how the constant k used in the lda instruction above is determined so that we are sure to address the right link pair in <a.link>. Also, you'll see just what the link pair looks like before it gets converted to the desired its pair. You will also see *how* it gets converted to the desired its pair.

To take stock—after our short look ahead into the next section—what has been said to this point can be summarized as follows: While operating in process 1, each time an intersegment reference must be made from <a> to some data or procedure segment, an indirect reference is used that employs an its pair located in <a.link>$_1$. All external references from <a>, regardless of the destination segment, are routed via its (or itb) pairs located in <a.link>$_1$. This linkage segment acts as a big switch box. Its purpose is eventually to hold its (or itb) pairs that will provide the generalized address, that is, segment number, offset (or base, offset) corresponding to each distinct external (symbolic) data and instruction reference that is given in the original source-language coding of <a>.

An interesting observation can now be made. When the processor is switched to process 2, <a> is immediately ready to serve in this process, provided there has been made known in it an appropriate linkage segment <a.link>$_2$ to act in a fashion similar to <a.link>$_1$.

How about the problem of being sure lb ← lp points to the right a.link#? Even this is handled automatically if, for example, we are switching back and forth between two processes that are both busy executing in <a>. Here is how. Suppose we are switching out of process 2 while executing in <a>. In this case the value in lb is currently set to a.link$_2$#. (It was set to this value automatically at the time some other procedure in process 2 called <a>.) Now, if and when process 2 is interrupted so that process 1 can take over, the software in Multics for process switching automatically saves all machine conditions, including the contents of all base registers. (These data are saved in a data base known as the "process stack" whose detailed format need not now concern us.) When ownership of the process is later regained by process 2, the lb ← lp pair, among other registers, will have its values properly restored. Thus, execution in <a> is resumed, and any intersegment references proceed as before—via <a.link>$_2$.

I observe in passing that there is fortunately no change required in the linkage segments of either process as a consequence of switching back and forth between processes, because the address-mapping hardware guarantees location independence of segments within a process.

2.5 The Format of the Linkage Segment

2.5.1 The Combining of Separate Linkage Segments

To this point it has been assumed that all procedures must have companion linkage segments to execute properly. This turns out to be an unnecessary but convenient oversimplification. For the sake of storage efficiency, the Multics supervisor can and does "splice together" what would otherwise be the many separate linkage segments of each process into a small number of what are called "combined linkage segments." But these are implementation details that are transparent to the user and that need not even concern the subsystem writer who must design the compiler or assembler that generates the per-procedure linkage "sections."[9]

The only point a compiler writer need note at this time is that the object

9. Compiler writers will see at the end of this chapter how the linkage section is designed to be self-relocatable, and hence how the system is able to take a copy of the linkage section that the compiler generates and combine it in any order with other such linkage sections into one combined linkage segment. Additional discussion on this topic can be found in the MPM section on the "standard object segment."

form of compiled procedure segments will contain a template of the linkage section. The system will make a copy of this template when the segment is first referenced via a link in a process, and that copy will be added to a combined linkage segment.

For the sake of simplicity, therefore, in the remainder of this chapter and, for that matter, for the remainder of this book, I shall frequently refer to linkage information as if it were compiled and executed as separate segments.

2.5.2 What If We Didn't Have Linkage Segments?

The following paragraphs are offered for those "from Missouri" that are not yet ready to accept the need for the <a. link> type of switch box. Others can skip over the following arguments as they see fit.

Suppose a shared assembler <a> were to use a more direct form of inter-segment addressing (à la Figure 1.12) in referring to the information in data segments. Suppose process 1 is currently employing <a>.

Now if the processor is switched to process 2, what guarantee do we have that data-referencing instructions, possibly established while using process 1, will now be applicable for referencing the corresponding data segments of process 2? As a matter of fact, even if corresponding data segments have the same names, like <d1> in process 1 and <d1> in process 2, is there any way to guarantee that their corresponding segment numbers will coincide with their respective descriptor segments? Quite the contrary, since segments normally become known to a process on an as-needed basis, the segment numbers that are assigned to these segments are also set on a first come, first served basis; hence, there is only a small chance for such a coincidence to occur.

It would, therefore, seem fairly clear that to avoid a linkage segment implies the need to change, within the shared segment, <a>, the data-referencing instructions each time <a> receives a new "employer." This contradicts the assumption that <a> might remain a pure procedure.

Suppose we agree that <a> must lose its purity. Let us set about *trying* to pay the price, hoping it won't loom as large as the apparently costly business of maintaining separate linkage segments in each process for each procedure segment, like <a>. A further question immediately arises. Who alters these instructions in <a> for each process switch, and how and when should it be done? It is fairly clear that another procedure, private to each process, would then be needed to properly alter <a>. This auxiliary procedure then serves <a> much like a prologue in a subroutine that is generated by a conventional MAD or FORTRAN compiler on a computer like the IBM 7094. A MAD prologue, for example, fetches each argument in the subroutine call and uses it to "set" or complete every instruction that involves the corresponding subroutine parameter. Unlike some subroutines, however, execution of this kind of prologue could never be avoided. It would have to be executed for process 1 each time process 1 obtains control of the processor. The cost of storing and repeatedly executing this prologue could be prohibitive if process switching frequency is high. What is worse, there would have to be a prologue executed for every *shared* procedure of a process, and *all such* prologues would have to be reexecuted each time the process gets hold of the processor! Worse yet, this solution breaks apart for a system of more than one processor unless a shared program is executed by one processor at a time.

The foregoing nightmare clearly suggests why impure procedures shouldn't be shared, and this observation would lead us to abandon the idea of sharing <a>, forcing us to award a full copy of <a> to each process that uses it. Giving up the sharing of procedures would in turn tend to "load up" system resources excessively. To wake up from this bad dream it is only necessary to remember that our trouble started with the suggestion that more direct inter-segment addressing of data segments might be worth a try.

2.5.3 Avoiding the Extra Memory Cycle in an Intersegment Data Reference[10]

Use of the linkage segment would seem to imply that every data reference (outside the procedure's segment) must be indirect and therefore must involve an extra memory cycle. Conceivably, this requirement could prove costly, for example, in executing the innermost loop of a highly repetitive procedure like a matrix multiply or, for example, where the innermost loop develops an inner product of two vectors. When execution efficiency is really needed, special assembly-level coding may reduce or in some cases even eliminate these inner-loop indirect memory cycles.

A coding technique that offers promise and that takes full advantage of the abr pairs of the GE 645 would be something like the following:

1. Load into available abr pairs from its pairs the generalized addresses of data variables that appear in the inner loop. (If the data variable is an array variable, then the its pair loaded into the abr pair would represent a base location in preparation for a "march" through one of the subscript ranges of the array variable.)
2. When inside the loop, reference the data, but via the abr pair for each desired datum. This is a *direct* reference in the sense that no extra memory cycle would be needed.

10. This section can be skipped during a first reading without loss of continuity.

I illustrate this by a hand-coded computation of a simple inner product in the segment <t>, which in PL/I might be written as follows:

```
innerprod = 0;
loop: do j = 1 to m; innerprod = innerprod + a(j)* b(j); endloop;
```

A possible hand coding (using integer arithmetic) would be

```
        eapap   <stat_>|[a]     put stat_#| a in ab ← ap.<stat_>
                                is the segment containing the data.
        eapbp   <stat_>|[b]     put stat_#| b in bb ← bp
        ldxj    =1              index reg j ← 1
        stz     innerprod       innerprod ← 0
loop:   ldq     ap|0, j         direct addressing used in formation
        mpy     bp|0, j         of aj x bj
        add     innerprod
        sto     innerprod
        tix     loop, n, j      some kind of an increment, test and
                                branch instruction like the IBM
                                7090 TIX.
```

Note that the first two instructions would be assembled in the form

```
eapap lp|k,*
eapbp lp|k + 2,*
```

These would refer to locations in <t.link> containing generated fault pairs. By "fault pair" I mean a pair of words that, when fetched and sensed by the hardware during an indirect memory cycle, trigger a recognizable fault. (That is to say, the first time the eapap and eapbp instructions are executed the corresponding fault pairs in <t.link> would be converted to the its pairs shown below.) The ldq and mpy instructions that form $a_j \times b_j$ are, as desired, *directly* addressed rather than indirectly addressed.

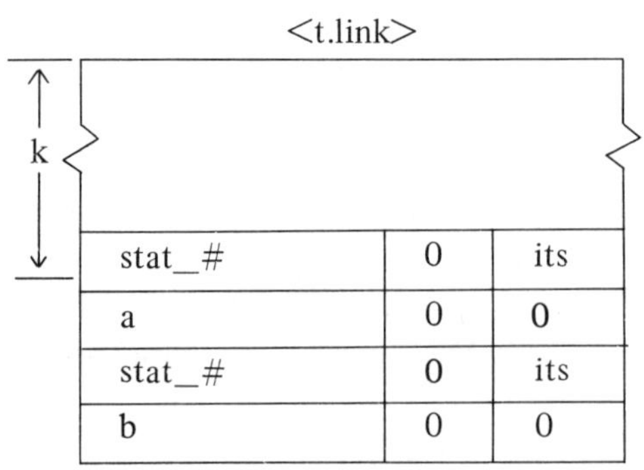

2.6 Establishing Links at Execution Time

We are now ready to examine many of the remaining details of linking. These are the details that are related to the fact that segments (and linkage segments) are "added" to the process on an *as-needed* basis, making it necessary that the conversion of symbolic intersegment references to numeric references be made at the last possible moment (i.e., at the time the first use of that symbolic reference is made).

Figures 2.4 and 2.5 are used as vehicles for motivating the detail in the remainder of this chapter. The subject of the illustrations is the intersegment linking implied by the instruction

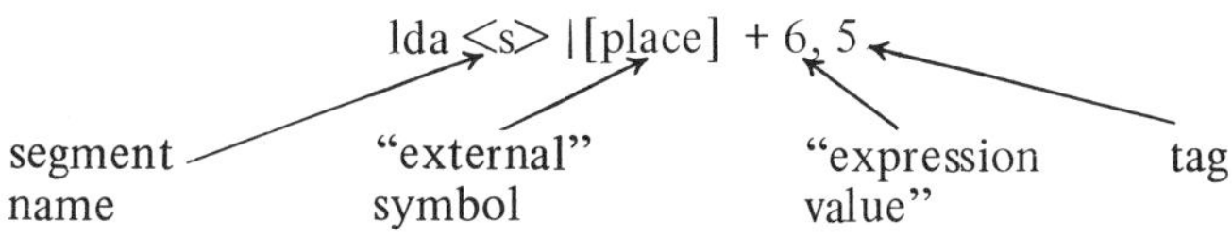

As suggested in the preceding section, the assembler translates this instruction into two parts.

a. A single, normally-never-altered,[11] instruction word whose binary form is equivalent to

lda lp|k,*

This instruction is made part of the object code for <a>.

b. A pair of pointers stored in the format of an ft2 word pair. This word pair is placed in <a.link> at a point k locations from word zero of <a.link>.

The symbol k represents a number generated by the assembler. Each time the assembler encounters an instruction with a distinct intersegment reference, it generates another fault pair for <a.link>. These pairs are ordered in some fashion relative to a.link #|0.

The ft2 fault pair contains pointers to all the remaining information embedded within the original symbolic instruction

lda <s>|[place] + 6, 5

11. Alteration would occur only in cases where the object code for <a> is *bound* together with that of other segments, including the target of the intersegment reference, that is, <t> in this case. The algorithm for binding <a> and <t> resolves the references between <a> and <t> so that an indirect instruction of the form: op lp|k,* to the offset [place] + 6,5 may be replaced in <t> by a direct, intrasegment reference of the form op m,5 where in this case, m is the offset that corresponds to [place] + 6 in <t>. Note, too, the link pair in the linkage section would then be discarded.

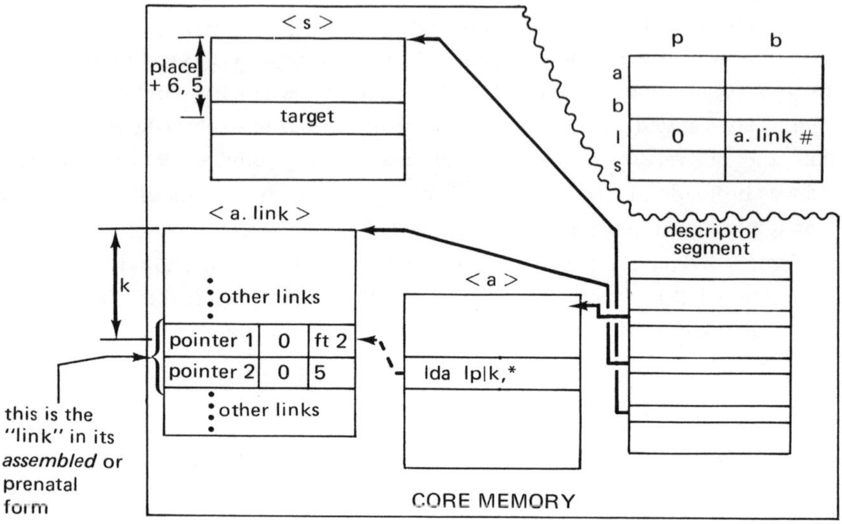

Figure 2.4. Assembling and storing a symbolic instruction
Symbolic instruction

lda <s>|[place] + 6, 5

is assembled and stored in <a> as the numeric (binary equivalent) of

lda lp|k.*

This instruction points at <a. link>|k, which is the first word of a pair of indirect words. In its initial state, that is, never-before referenced, it is a link in prenatal form. It contains a special tag ft2 in the first word to designate a fault. It also contains a pair of pointers that lead to symbols <s> and [place] and to the value for the remainder of the expression, that is, the value 6 in this case. The fault pair also contains a tag for index register 5.

2.6.1 The Linker—Phase One

In executing

lda lp|k,*

the GE 645 retrieves the ft2 pair as an indirect word pair found at location a.link# | k. This word pair is shown in Figure 2.4. When the special bit pattern denoted by ft2 is sensed, the GE 645 traps to a special memory location in what is known as the "fault vector." A short program called the "Fault Interceptor" takes over and saves saves all machine conditions on a stack. Next, the Fault Interceptor causes a special procedure to be invoked known as the "Linker." In the process of giving control to the Linker, the location of the offending ft2 pair is saved. The two pointers that were stored in the ft2 pair

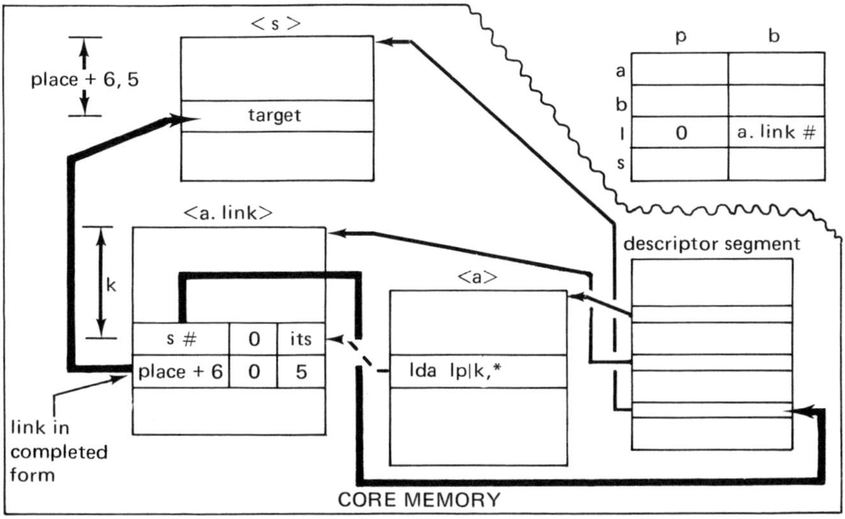

Figure 2.5. A completed its-pair link
This shows the link in the form of an its pair, as completed by the Linker procedure. This its pair replaces the ft2 pair. The its pair points at the desired target word.

are now employed by the Linker to retrieve vital information that is stored in a special list structure known as a *link definition.* As you might guess, the assembler generates a link definition to go with each ft2 pair. None of the information in a link definition is subject to change. Hence all link definitions are packaged as a single "table." For this the name "outsymbol table" will be used. This table is stored at the tail end of <a> itself, as suggested in Figure 2.6.

The orientation that explains the use of the term "outsymbol table" is this: We associate ourselves with the segment (<a> in this case) that is making an outbound reference to another segment (<s> in this case). It is as if we were standing inside <a> and looking outward. With respect to <a> the symbols in its outsymbol table are "outsiders."

2.6.2 Link-Definition Structure (Outsymbol Table)

Each definition begins with a header word that is referred to as the "expression word." Figure 2.7 shows the particular storage structure of the link definition for our example.[12] If the use of pointer1 and pointer 2 of the ft2

12. Depending on who writes the assembler or compiler that generates the outsymbol table, packaging can be more or less efficient. For the Multics assembler, efficiency is achieved by avoiding duplication of symbol strings. Thus, if two or more link definitions refer to the same segment-name string or external-symbol string, only one copy of the string is kept in the table.

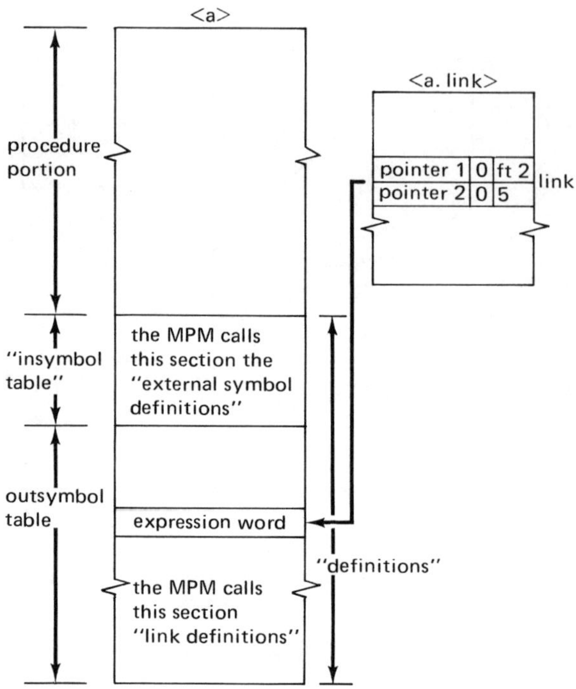

Figure 2.6. Schematic of an ft2 pair pointing at the head of its associated link definition that is located within a portion of <a> known as the "definitions" section

pair allows the Linker to locate the right expression word, it is a simple matter then for the Linker to extract the strings "s" and "place", and the value 6. (Since the ft2 word has a pointer to the outsymbol table, no searching is required.)

There is more to be said about the *general* structure of a link definition. We have only looked at one type; in particular we have seen a "type 4" link definition. There are several others, and some of these will be examined after the current example has been pursued to its conclusion, that is, after completion of the narrative on how the Linker constructs the desired its pair

s#	0	its
place + 6	0	5

which must replace the ft2 pair.

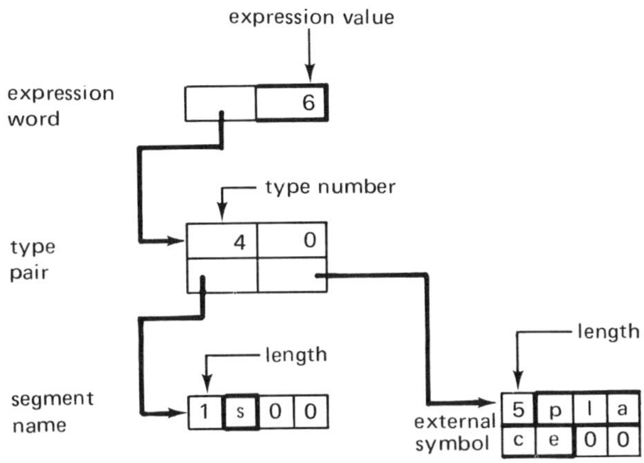

Figure 2.7. Data structure for the link definition stored in <a>
This structure is for the expression

<s>|[place] + 6

Note: Character strings are stored nine bits per character (seven-bit ASCII, right justified in a nine-bit field), four characters per word. Consecutively addressed words are used for strings of length $l \geq 4$ characters. The length l is coded in the first 9 bits of the first word used for the string. (Maximum length for such strings is seen to be $2^9 - 1$ or 511 characters.) The unused portions of a word containing the end of a string are shown as filled with zeros.

2.6.3 The Linker—Phase Two

The second phase of the Linker's activity is to determine s# from <s>, determine place from [place], and then form and store the desired its pair. To get s# the Linker calls on a module of the file system that is designed for this important and oft-recurring task. This module performs an associative lookup of the Known Segment Table (KST) that is kept for this process. If <s> is already known, the file-system module returns s# directly. If not known, additional machinery of the file system is invoked to search for and make known <s>. I have already touched on this activity in the introduction to this chapter and will make further remarks about it in Chapter 6, so not much more need be said about it here; some details are given in footnotes if the reader chooses to examine them.[13]

13. When a segment <s> is made known to a process by s#, its attributes are not immediately placed in word s# of the descriptor segment. This word has been initialized with the missing-segment bit on, so the first reference to <s> in this process by s# will cause the processor to generate a missing-segment fault and thereby induce the construction of the desired segment descriptor word.

Now that the Linker knows s#, its next job is to search a symbol table in <s>[14] for [place] in order to find the corresponding value assigned to it by the assembler or compiler that made <s>. When the table entry for [place] is found, the corresponding value for [place] (i.e., place) will also be found.

If <s> cannot be found (to make it known), recovery is possible at the console. Thus, the console message informing the user that <s> cannot be found may amount to giving the person at the console the opportunity to remedy the situation by creating the missing segment—on the spot.

2.6.4 External Symbol Definitions (Insymbol Table)

To this point the concept of linkage sections has been associated entirely with procedure segments, not with data segments. In the following paragraphs the astute reader will notice that for the first time a reason why certain data segments might also require a corresponding linkage segment is suggested.

The table that is to be searched is described in the Multics reference literature[15] under the name "external symbol definitions." I am going to rename it the "insymbol table" (and the reader should not confuse this table with the more-elaborate so-called segment symbol table.[16]

The orientation that explains the term insymbol table is consistent with the "outsymbol" terminology. A segment cannot only make outward references but can also receive references to it, that is, inward references. Thus, the symbols in the insymbol table for <a> are all those symbols, locally defined in <a>, which may be referred to from another segment.

The programmer, writing the source code for a given data or procedure segment "marks," via special pseudooperations or other declarations, those symbols whose values he wishes to make known (somehow) to other segments. The assembler or compiler then creates an entry in the insymbol table for each of these marked symbols (and their corresponding values).

Each entry has the format shown in Figure 2.8, and the structure for the entire table is pictured in Figure 2.9.

In most instances, the insymbol table for a segment <s> is invariant under execution, so it can be stored in <s>.[17] This idea was suggested in Figure 2.6

14. Of course, if <s> had just been made known, lookup of [place] in <s> would in fact constitute the first actual reference of <s> (preceding that which the user is "conscious" of). This Linker's reference to <s> will incur the missing-segment fault described in the preceding footnote.

15. See the MPM, Reference Data section on linkage formats.

16. The segment symbol table that may be generated by a compiler for a procedure segment associates with each symbol lists of attributes and other information valuable for debugging aids, data directed I/O, etc.—in addition to the address of the symbol. This

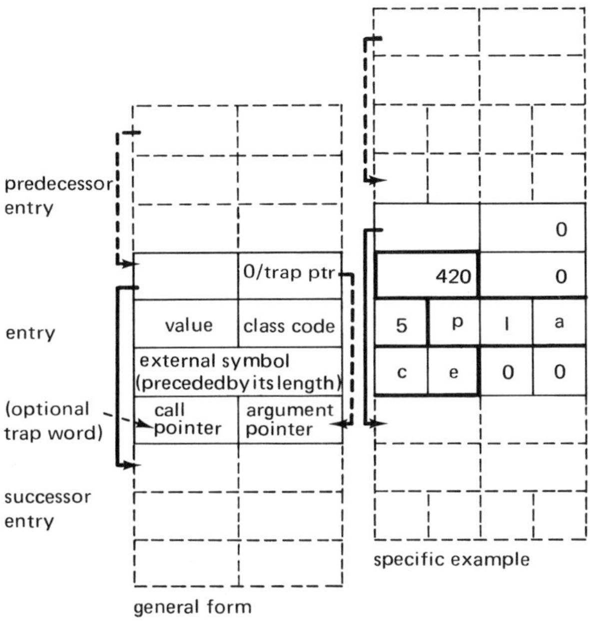

Figure 2.8. Insymbol table entries
In the specific example, the symbol is "place" (of length 5). Its *value* is imagined here to be 420. Assuming this entry is in the insymbol table of <s>, we see that the sought-after value of [place], which we have been previously denoting symbolically as place, is actually 420. The class code is 0 in this example, which means that place (=420) is an offset within <s> (rather than within <s. link>). (The optional trap word and the pointer to it refer to the trap-before-definition mechanism that is discussed in footnote 17.)

---

table is also stored in the object segment. (See the MPM, section on the standard object segment.)

17. A definition that holds a trap pointer, called a trap-before-definition pointer would be an exception. These definitions would be employed in special situations where a trap to a special procedure is desired at the time the Linker searches for this symbol the first time. In the initial implementation of Multics there is no support for this feature. I mention it here only to suggest that in principle a very sophisticated user might occasionally wish to employ this feature, taking care, of course, to substitute his own version of the Linker in place of the one provided by the system.

The trap-before-definition mechanism would be identical with the trap-before-link mechanism that is described in some detail in Section 2.8. Upon return from a trap procedure the Linker would reset this pointer and hence an insymbol table containing such definitions would have to be stored in the linkage segment. Users might note the careful design philosophy that is employed here. The existence of an option to trap, whether *before definition* or *before link* (as described in Section 2.8), costs the user nothing. The cost is incurred only if the option is exercised.

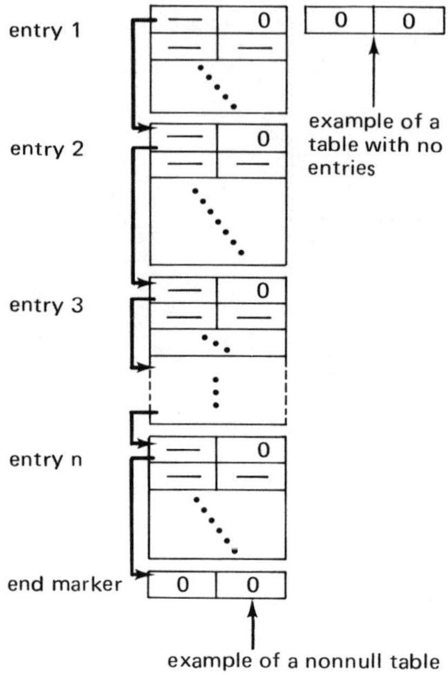

Figure 2.9. Format of the insymbol table

where the insymbol table was shown placed immediately following the executable code of the segment. The insymbol table always precedes the outsymbol table, by convention.

Each symbol entered in the insymbol table for <seg> is assigned a class code. The class code is used mainly to designate to which segment (i.e., <seg>, or <seg. link>) the particular symbol and its value refer. A class code of zero refers to <seg>, while a code of one refers to <seg. link>. I will have more to say about the class code when I speak about entry-point references in Section 2.9.

2.6.5 The Linker–Phase Three

When the value of [place] has been obtained, the Linker is now close to finishing its job by completing and storing the link and resuming execution. It has determined s# and place. Now it generates the its pair you saw in Figure 2.5 and stores this in place of the fault pair. (Remember, the location of the fault pair was stored as part of the trapping action.) Now the Linker returns to the "Fault Interceptor" that called it. The Fault Interceptor restores all machine conditions that existed at the time of the fault (popped from a special stack), but now corrected to reflect a stored its pair, and the GE 645 processor then resumes the execution of the lda instruction that caused the fault.

2.7 More on the Structure of Link Definitions

There are five *types* of symbolic intersegment reference one can make in assembly-language source code. For each type, there is a different structure generated for the link definitions, and a different type of link is generated. We have already looked at one of these types. It is called a "type 4" reference. Types 2, 3, and 4 are listed and illustrated in Figure 2.10.[18]

The link ultimately generated in a type-2 reference is necessarily an itb pair, while those generated for other types are its pairs.

Type No.	Source Code Examples	Syntactical Form of Intersegment Reference	Ultimate Form of Generated Link	
2	bp | [blue] + x − 6, 7* means segment tag = 2 We shall assume x = 2012 as set by the assembler	base | [ext]+ exp, m	base x 2^{15} | 0 | itb exp | 0 | m	general form
			2×2^{15} | 0 | itb blue+2006 | 0 | 7*	specific example
3	<weight> | mid + 50 We shall assume the assembler makes mid = 3422	< seg > | exp, m	seg # | 0 | its exp | 0 | m	general form
			weight # | 0 | its 3472 | 0 | 0	specific example
4	<s> | [place] , 3	<seg> | [ext] + exp, m	seg # | 0 | its ext + exp | 0 | m	general form
			s # | 0 | its place | 0 | 3	example 1
	<s> | [place] + key − 6 We shall assume the assembler defines key = 100		s # | 0 | its place + 94 | 0 | 0	example 2

Figure 2.10. External references–types 2, 3, and 4

Key:

base means register number
m means modifier
exp means expression
ext means external symbol

Note that either exp, or m, or both may be omitted without altering the type number.

18. Types 1 and 5, not shown in Figure 2.10, are special-purpose variations of types 3 and 4, reserved for self-references, i.e., references to the executing procedure, or to its linkage segment. More details may be found in the MPM, Reference Data section on linkage formats.

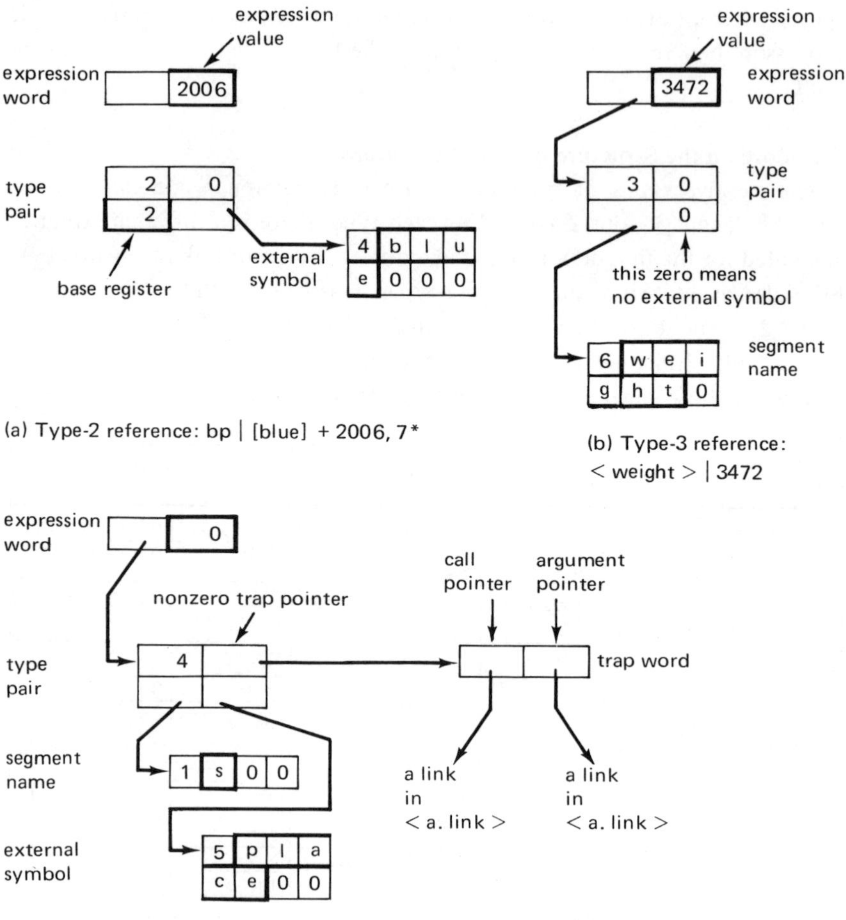

(a) Type-2 reference: bp | [blue] + 2006, 7*

(b) Type-3 reference: < weight > | 3472

(c) Type-4 reference with the trap feature invoked. < s > | [place], 3

Figure 2.11. Structure of link definitions
Normally, the right half of the first word of the "type pair" is zero. In case c, however, it contains a so-called *trap pointer* that leads to a pair of other pointers used by the Linker to generate a call on an arbitrary, user-specified procedure.

Figure 2.11 shows the storage structure for the link definitions that go with each of the three types of reference.

It is true that the storage structure for a type-4 link definition has been illustrated already in Figure 2.7. Nevertheless, a second example is given in Figure 2.11c to illustrate the important "trap-before-link feature" of the Multics linkage mechanism.

2.8 The Trap-before-Link Feature

2.8.1 Why Have It?

The trap feature has been incorporated in Multics for the benefit of some subsystem writers who must have the object programs that are produced by their subsystem, like PL/I or FORTRAN, automatically perform certain special storage-management tasks at the time certain segments are first referred to. For example, by inserting this trap feature in certain link definitions, the object program can create or grow segments as allocation for variables that, in PL/I terminology, are referred to as static-storage variables. For variables of either static storage or automatic storage, the trap procedure can also allocate space and assign initial values for those variables that are declared to have the *initial* attribute, that is, at the time the space for such variables is being created.[19] In other instances, it is conceivable that the trap procedure could be used to monitor (gather statistics) on segment usage for a set of object programs. It is likely that the subsystem writer will discover many applications for this feature (but he can also leave it alone). There will be no penalty paid for having the feature available and not using it.

2.8.2 What Is It and How Does It Work?

Suppose a user wishes to gain control (i.e., intercede) just before the link for some intersegment reference is completed. For example, let the instruction be

19. At the time the data space is allocated for a static variable, the compiler must create and add an entry to the insymbol table for the data segment. This table entry will provide the *value* of the symbol, that is, a pointer to the allocated slot in the data segment so that other links to this same location can be completed. These other links may be required for references to the same data location, either from the same procedure segment that makes the initial reference, or, if the variable is static *external* (like COMMON or PROGRAM COMMON in FORTRAN or MAD), from other procedure segments. Unlike insymbol tables for procedure segments, which are kept in the procedure itself, the insymbol table for a data segment is normally kept in the linkage segment associated with the data segment. In this way the data segment can grow as repeated allocations are made, and at the same time the corresponding insymbol table can also grow independently. Adding an insymbol table entry, extending the length of a data segment, and possibly assigning initial values must be "standard apparatus" for a compiler in Multics. For more details see the sections of the MPM that describe the PL/I implementation.

lda <s> | [place] , 3

Let the procedure that is to be executed before establishing the link to <s> | [place] , 3 be

<proced> | [begin]

Also, let the argument list for this procedure be located at <param> | 0.

When the Linker is busy searching through the link definition for the reference

<s> | [place] , 3

as shown in Figure 2.11c, it will discover a nonzero value in the right half of the type pair. A nonzero value will be interpreted as a trap pointer and this will immediately cause the Linker to digress for the purpose of executing the trap feature. By working its way over to the links that contain the name of the procedure and the information about the argument list, the Linker is able to generate and execute the call that executes the desired "trap" procedure. More details are given in the MPM, Reference Data section on linkage formats. Suffice it to say, that upon return from the trap procedure the Linker will again have control, so it can now complete the link that it started out to build. In this case it is, of course,

s#	0	its
place	0	3

2.9 Transfer to a Procedure Entry Point

Let us go back to Figure 2.1 and consider the linking process that is involved in executing the transfer instruction

tra <t> | [entry 2]

Such an instruction would normally appear in a program as a result of issuing any procedure call. In assembly language, for instance, the use of the "call" macro generates a stereotyped (but critically important) sequence of instructions called the call sequence, and this topic will be treated thoroughly in Chapter 3.

In transferring control from <a> to a point within another procedure segment <t> the linkage is necessarily more complex because, before beginning to execute in <t>, we want to load the lb ← lp base pair so that it points at <t.link> instead of <a.link>. Unfortunately, no special GE 645 hardware is available to accomplish the change in lb ← lp base-register values automatically. It can only be done by having the assembler convert the tra instruction into a short sequence of several instructions that does the job whenever executed.

You will see that the resulting code may force the Linker to do *double duty*. The "solution" presented here may not reflect the efficiency achieved by code generated by some language processors currently in use but should serve as a "primer" for understanding how entry sequences must work, in general, for Multics procedures. Section 2.12, prefaced by certain other details given in Section 2.11, explains how entry sequences are currently being generated by ALM and PL/I. The following account is a condensed sketch of the steps involved. (To make this sketch come alive, a "motion picture" illustration is given in Figures 2.12a, 2.12b, 2.12c, and 2.12d.)

1. In <a>: execute an instruction of the form

tra lp | k,*

which is a transfer through an indirect word pair found in <a.link>.

2. In <a.link>: the indirect word pair, pointed at by

lp | k

will be the link

t. link#	0	its
number 1	0	0

When this link has been completed after invoking the Linker, we now have a transfer from <a>, through <a.link>, to <t.link> | [number1].

3. In <t.link>: a quartet of instruction words and a related ft2 indirect word pair are provided. The instructions are located at <t.link> | [number1] through <t.link> | [number1] + 3.

The first of these is an eaplp instruction whose main purpose is to load the lb base register with t.link#. (More precisely, the eaplp instruction effectively causes the lb ← lp pair to be loaded as follows:

(lb) = t.link#

(lp) = offset of the beginning of the linkage information in <t.link>.)

The third instruction is an indirect transfer (through the above word pair) to <t>|[entry]. The indirect transfer is accomplished by using an ft2 fault

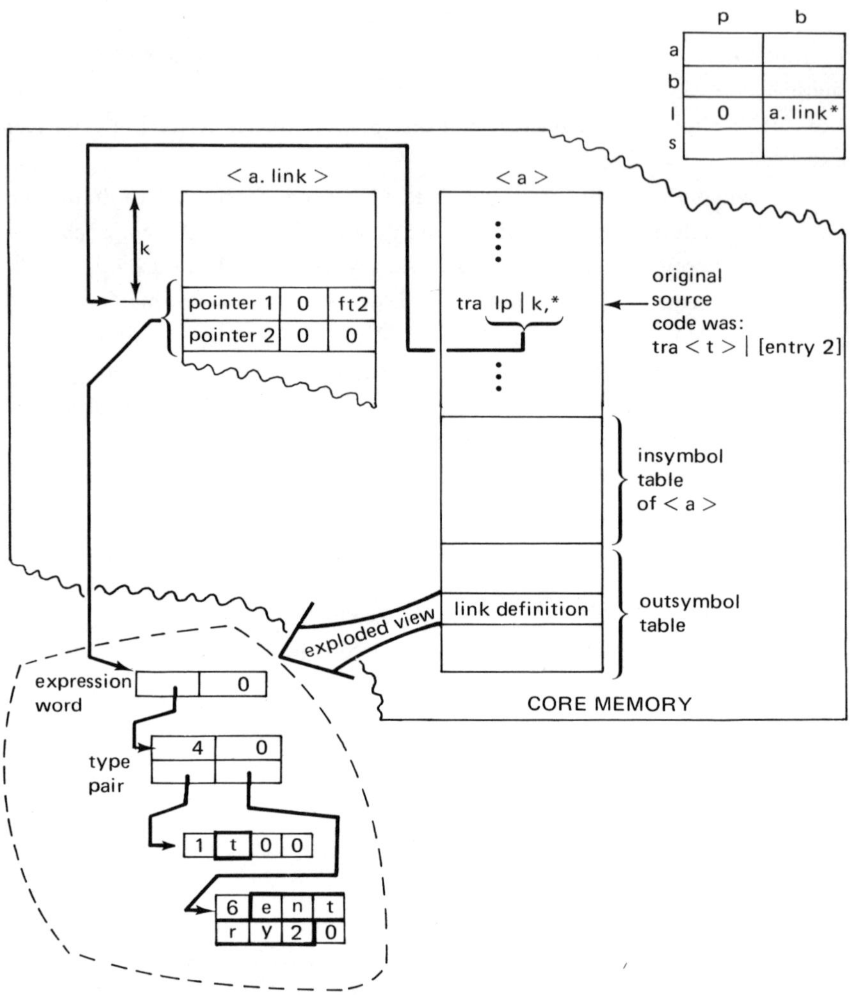

Figure 2.12a. Developing the first link (phase 1)
Searching the link definition in <a>.

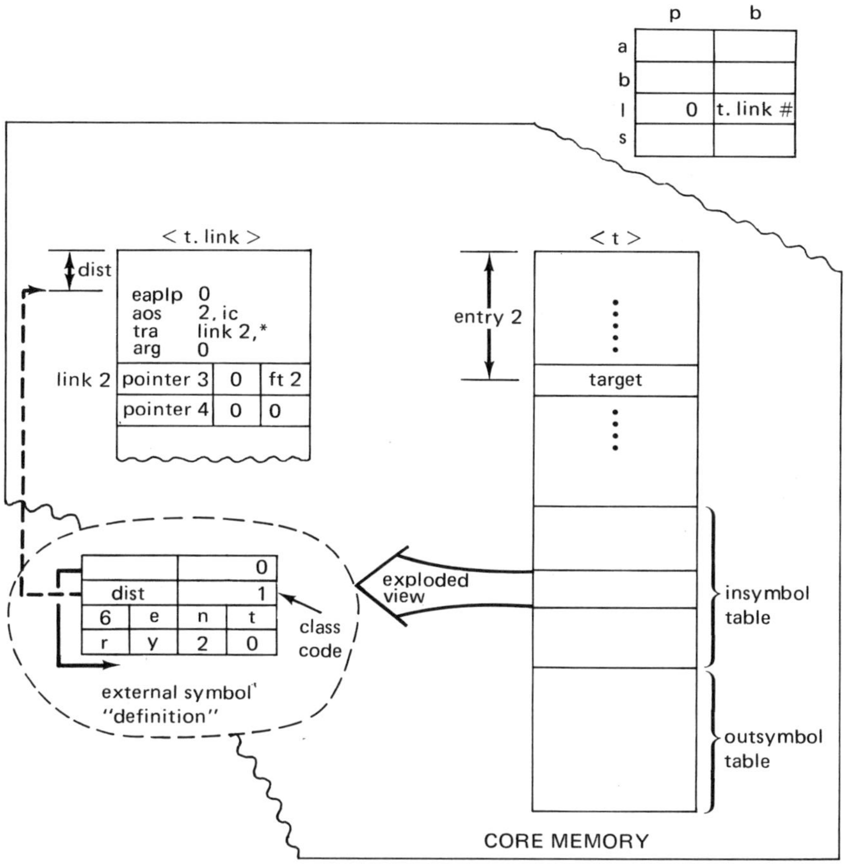

Figure 2.12b. Developing the first link (phase 2)
Searching the insymbol table in <t> for [entry2], and discovery that it is a class-1 symbol–which means that its value is relative to <t. link> and not to <t>.

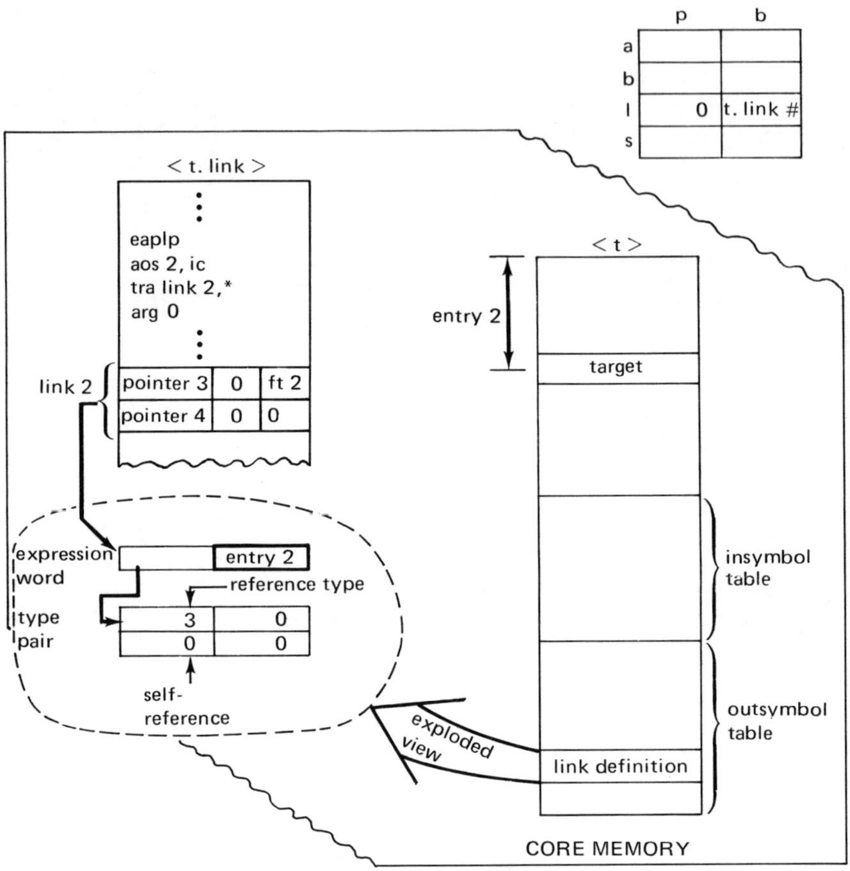

Figure 2.12c. Developing the second link (phase 1)
Searching the outsymbol table of <t>. Here the Linker discovers that the link is a type-3 reference, and moreover it is a *self-reference*. Consequently, the Linker accepts the value of the expression (stored in the right half of the expression word and shown as entry2) as the effective internal address within <t>! That is to say, no phase 2 is needed. The second link can now be generated as shown in Figure 2.12d.

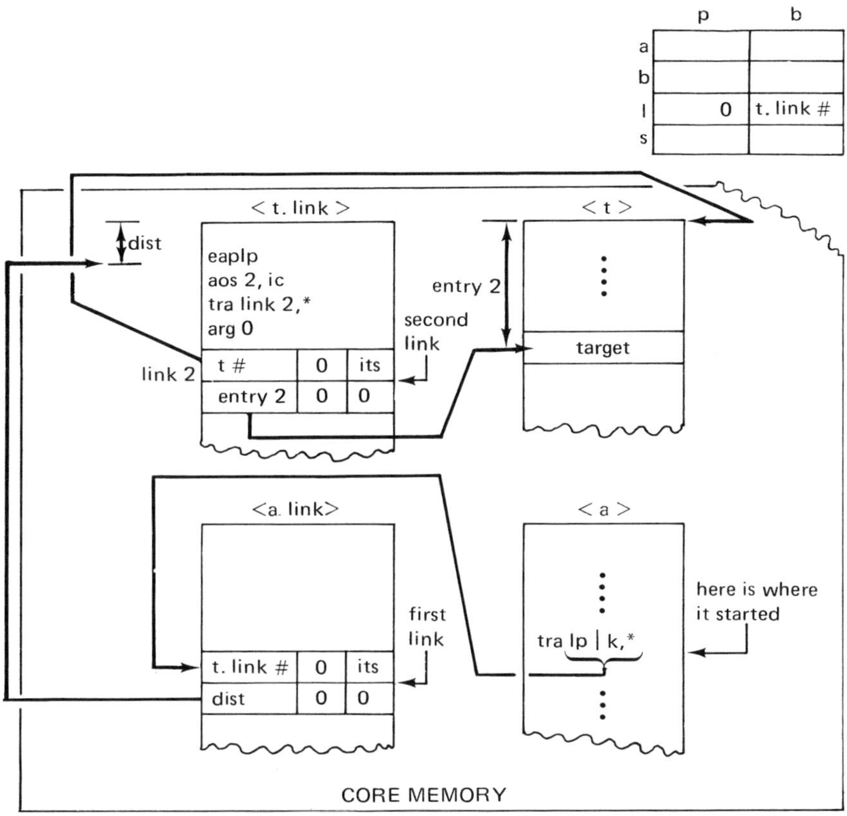

Figure 2.12d. A composite of both links completed for the intersegment transfer from <a> to <t>

pair. So, the Linker must again be invoked to convert this ft2 pair to a proper link. This time the completed link will look like

t#	0	its
entry2	0	0

And this last step completes the linking for the intersegment transfer.[20]

In order to complete this second link, the Linker first searches a link definition that is found within the outsymbol table of <t>. Here it discovers that the segment being referred to is <t> itself, that is, it is a *self-reference.* Moreover, since the link definition shows a type-3 reference, there is no external symbol whose value needs to be determined. The value has been preset by the assembler and placed in the right half of the expression word. So, the insymbol table for <t> need not be searched. A self-reference is discovered by the Linker whenever that pointer in a link definition, which ordinarily points at the character string for the segment name, turns out to be zero.

In summary, the work involved in an intersegment transfer is seen to be

1. Execute an indirect transfer from <a>, through <a.link> to <t.link>. In doing so, invoke the Linker (first time only, of course).
2. Execute an eaplp instruction in <t.link> to set lb ← lp for t.link#.
3. Execute an indirect transfer from <t.link>, through <t.link>, to <t>. In doing so, invoke the Linker again (first time only, of course).

Figures 2.12a–2.12d display core-memory representations for parts of <a>, <a.link> <t>, and <t.link> during the course of establishing the two links.

You might already be wondering why one transfers first to <t.link>. Why not go to <t> directly? The answers are these:

a. Loading the lb ← lp pair with t.link# takes only one (eaplp) instruction when executed from <t.link>. To accomplish the same task from <t> is practically impossible. The footnote explains why.[21]

b. We are going to need <t.link> in memory anyhow, in order to execute in <t>.

20. The second and fourth instruction words are of lesser interest. The fourth word serves as a usage counter, and the second word is the instruction that causes this counter to be incremented each time control passes through this entry. Periodic examination of the usage counter can provide the subsystem writer with helpful information. There is no obligation, however, on the part of the user to ever interrogate these counters.

21. If one transferred to <t> directly, how would <t> know the value of t.link# to use in loading the lb ← lp? One approach might be to have <t> call on a supervisory

Next you may have wondered by what magic was it possible to establish the first link as

t.link#	0	its
number1	0	0

instead of as

t#		its
number1	0	0

After all, the original instruction read

tra <t> | [entry2]

and not

tra <t.link> | [entry 22]

To answer this I call your attention to Figure 2.12b, where you see that, in searching the insymbol table of <t> for [entry2], it is found to be *a class-1* symbol. You will recall from Section 2.6.4 that a class-1 symbol is interpreted to mean that the proper segment number to use with the value of [entry2] is t.link# rather than t#.

2.10 Format of Linkage Sections

In preceding discussions I have implied that the Linker is able to use the pair of pointers that it finds in the ft2 fault pair to locate the expression word in

---

procedure to determine t.link# from a search of the KST. This would involve executing a large number of instructions. But wait a minute! How can <t> call on *any* procedure to help to find t.link#? Calling on another procedure implies that an instruction of the form

op code lp|k,*

can be executed, where lb ← lp contains t.link#. But, of course, if we had t.link# loaded into lb ← lp we wouldn't need to call on a supervisory procedure for help. It is clear, therefore, that transferring to <t> before loading lb ← lp with t.link# would have the effect of hopelessly isolating <t> from any communication with the rest of the system. In other words, a transfer to <t> in this way would result in a dead end with no way to return, except to the segment that called it. Clearly, this could not be a generally useful approach.

A second approach would be to design Multics so that there is always a predetermined relationship between t# and t.link# such that instructions executed in <t> could evaluate t.link# and then load it into lb ← lp.

the link definition. For example, in Figure 2.12a the fault pair

pointer1	0	ft2
pointer2	0	0

was shown in <a.link>, and it was suggested that the Linker employs pointer1 and pointer2 to locate the proper link definition in <a>. To explain how these pointers are used, it is helpful to digress for a look at the underlying format given to each linkage section as it should be produced by a compiler or assembler.

A design objective of Multics is that there be a capability of easily combining or binding together into one segment the separate linkage sections of two or more data or procedure segments. Suffice it to say that, in the interests of efficiency, certain groups of supervisory procedures have their linkage information bound into a single segment. To make it convenient to bind such information, each linkage section is structured so that it can become one block of a two-way linked list of blocks. The remainder of this section provides the details.

Every linkage section, when first generated, consists of an eight-word block header, followed by a "body" made up of entries and links belonging to this block and/or insymbol-table entries (for data segments). The block header contains three pairs of words (which are pointers) plus the length of the block. The eighth word is unused. The second and third word pairs are preset to zero and remain zero as long as the block is a "loner," that is, is not two-way linked to any other block. (The second and third word pairs of each block header are provided so that they can be made into its pairs and serve as "forward" and "backward" pointers to other block headers in a list of such blocks.)

The first word pair of the block header is used in one of two ways, depending on the nature of the linkage segment.

1. A linkage section for a procedure segment uses this first word pair as an its pair that points to the beginning of the (insymbol and outsymbol) definitions within the procedure segment.

2. A linkage section for a data segment uses only the first word of the first word pair as a single indirect word pointer to the beginning of the data segment's insymbol-table definitions, which are stored within the linkage segment itself.

Figure 2.13 illustrates the important connections for a single-block linkage

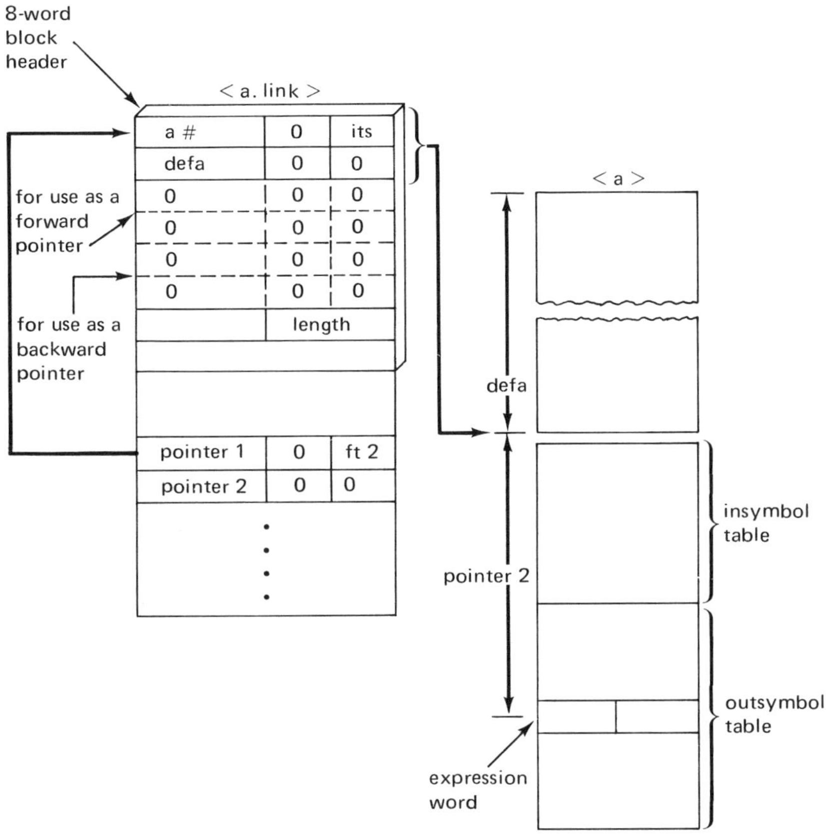

Figure 2.13. Single-block linkage section
This illustrates the pointer system from an <a.link> ft2 pair to the expression word in <a>.

section that refers to the procedure segment <a>. Note in this figure the following points:

1. Pointer1 of the ft2 pair is "self-relative" to the top of the block header where you see an its pair that points to

a# | defa

This is the beginning of the definitions section within <a>.

2. The assembler that generates <a.link> cannot, of course, know a# but it can and does know defa, so the as-generated (initial) condition of the first its pair in the block header is really set as

0	0	its
defa	0	0

At the time <a> is made known and gets a segment number assigned to it, the Linker will be invoked (automatically) to complete this its pair as you see it in Figure 2.13.

For a more specific example, suppose we consider the link called "link2" that is shown in Figure 2.12c. If this link is located 50 words from the top of <t.link>, then the value generated for pointer3 will be −50. (See Figure 2.14a.) The pointer in the first word of an ft2 pair is called the "head pointer." It is self-relative, pointing to the first word of the block header. The its pair located there points in turn to the top of the definitions section in <t>. It is called the "definitions pointer."

Suppose the expression word of the desired link definition is 80 words down from the top of the definitions section in <t>. Then the value generated for the second pointer of the ft2 pair will be 80. This pointer is called the "expression pointer."

Since the Linker is handed the core location of the ft2 pair, it can determine the location of the definitions pointer by the following relation:

location of definitions pointer = location of ft2 pair + head pointer

The pointer found here, together with the expression pointer, is then used to construct the location of the expression word, which in this example is

t# | 250 + 80

Figure 2.14a shows the details of this example. Figure 2.14b is a slight generalization using the terminology just introduced.[22]

22. This terminology is used in the MPM, Reference Data section on linkage formats.

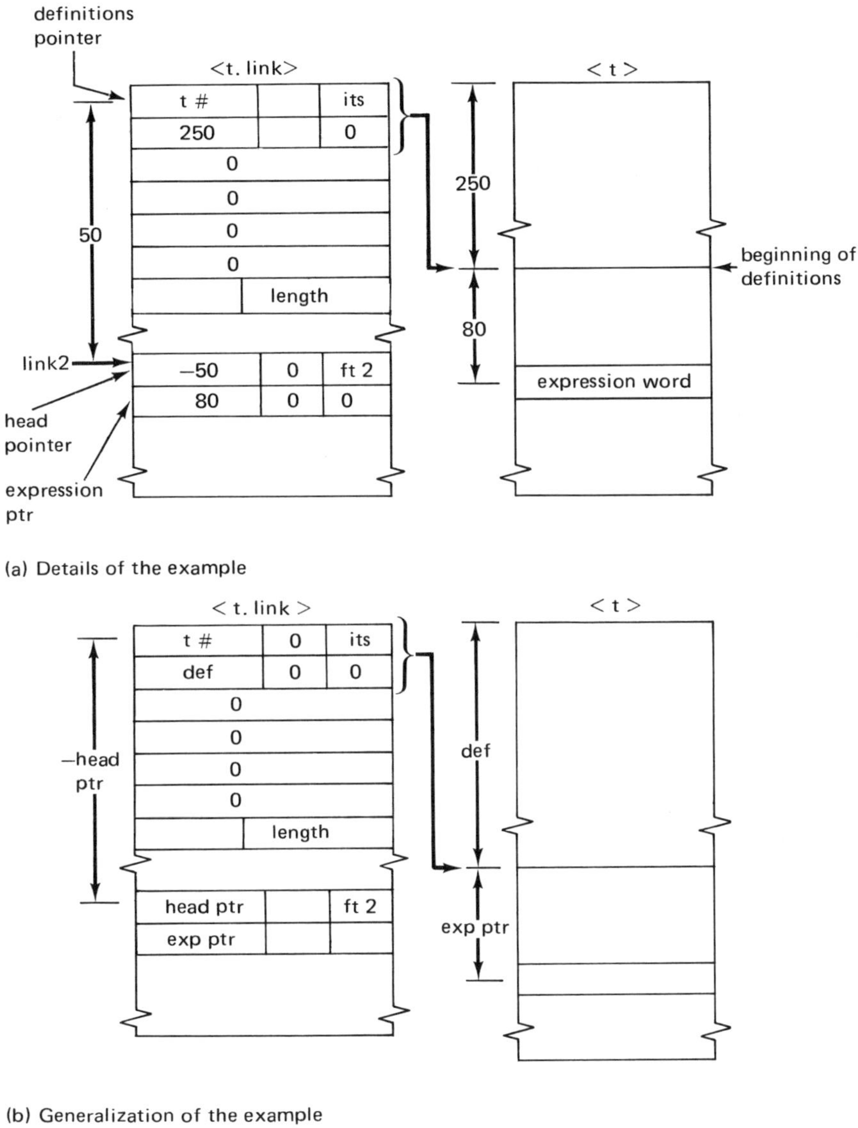

Figure 2.14. Single-block linkage section for link2

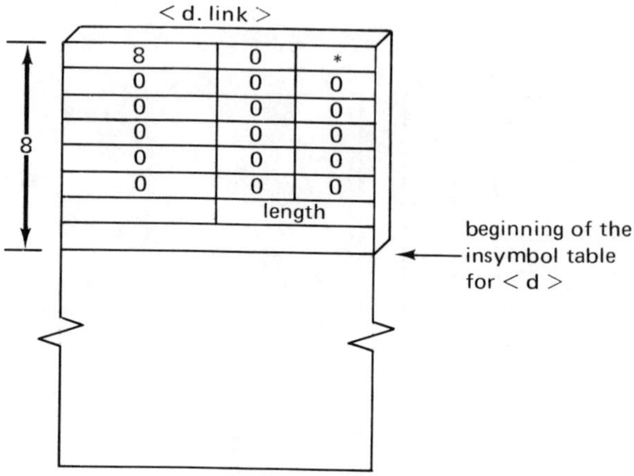

Figure 2.15. Intrasegment pointer in <d.link>
The first word of <d.link> is an intrasegment pointer (single indirect word) to the beginning of the insymbol table entries for the data segment <d>.

Figure 2.15 shows the appearance of a linkage section for a data segment <d> containing only insymbol-table definitions. The first word of the header provides an indirect word whose address is that of the body of this block. Figure 2.16 shows the appearance of a linkage section for an impure procedure <impa>. Imagine that this linkage section has two blocks. The first block would consist primarily of the information generated by the assembler of <impa>. It is x words in length. The second block linked to it could contain new insymbol table definitions that refer to locations named during execution. The user can add a block of such definitions using library procedure calls. The first word of the second block would contain the effective internal address $x + 8$, which locates the definitions in this block.

2.11 Self-Relative Addressing Used for the Entry Sequences of Linkage Blocks

Since linkage blocks can be added to form a chain of such blocks in one segment, there is a need to observe one oversimplification made in an earlier discussion that can now be removed. The point I am about to make is a subtle one and need not be considered on first reading.

Note the four instructions at <t.link> | dist in Figure 2.12d, and observe that in using these instructions we have assumed that the linkage block shown there begins at word zero of <t.link>. Suppose for reasons of efficiency we

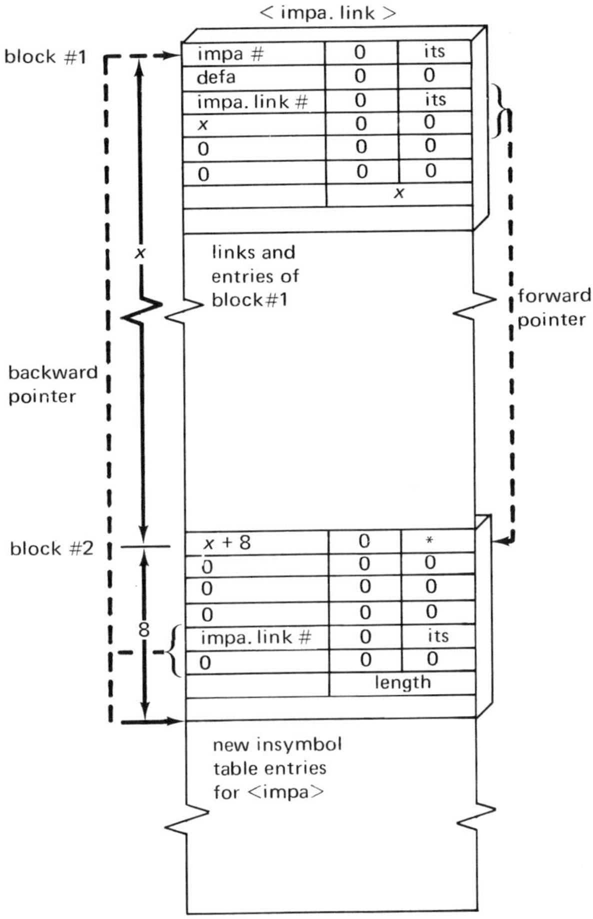

Figure 2.16. A second block added to <impa.link>

would like to bind several procedure segments (and their corresponding linkage segments).[23] It might happen that the <t.link> block shown in Figure 2.12d would now be appended to the end of another block in a newly formed, composite linkage segment. Now the entry sequence,

```
dist:   eaplp   0
        aos     2,ic
        tra     link2,*
        arg     0
```

no longer does the job. It is necessary in practice (and in fact it is a Multics standard) to use the following types of instructions to achieve self-relative addressing:

```
dist:   eaplp   -*,ic
        aos     2,ic
        tra     link2-*,ic*
        arg     0
```

Here the modifier "ic" means add the current contents of the instruction counter to the address value designated in the address field of the instruction. Thus,

```
dist:   eaplp   -*,ic
```

means establish in lb ← lp the values

lb ← segment number of executing procedure
lp ← (ic) − dist

this is the address of word zero of the containing linkage block for the eaplp instruction regardless of whether the block itself begins at word zero of the segment in which it's embedded.

When referring to these "entry" instructions in the future, as in Chapter 3, I shall illustrate with the standard forms introduced in this section, rather than the simplified versions previously shown.

2.12 Entry Sequences Generated by ALM and PL/I

The current ALM assembler and PL/I compiler generate procedure entry sequences that result in some streamlining that is worth knowing about, espe-

23. For more details on binding, see MPM, section on the standard object segment and Reference Data section on binding.

cially if the reader may have occasion to write his own assembler or compiler, or if he expects to read target code generated by the mentioned language processors. These entry sequences are designed to take advantage of the high likelihood that the procedure being translated from source code has multiple entry points, say $m(\gg 1)$ such entry points. Every one of the m entry sequences that is generated employs a common "inbound" link that need be "snapped," that is, converted to an its pair, only once. [Moreover, there also results some saving in the space needed in the linkage section ($m - 2$ words).]

For example, the coding now generated by ALM is

```
eaplp   -*,ic
aos     3,ic
eax7    entrypoint
tra     common_link,*
arg     0
```

The common link is generated having the form

common_link:

pointer3	0	ft2
pointer4	0	7

When referenced, the Linker will convert it to

common link:

t#		its
first_word		7

The eax7 instruction loads index register 7 with the offset of the given entry point (relative to first_word), then transfers indirect to common_link. If the common ft2 fault pair has already been converted to the intended its pair, no link fault will occur, even though a transfer to a perhaps not-previously used entry point is being effected. Note that the contents of index register 7 always add to first_word (normally zero). Since the assembler knows the offset value for each entry point in the target procedure, it can generate the constant values that must be referenced by the eax7 instruction in each such sequence.

The rest of the coding in the "standard" entry sequence should offer the reader no trouble, as it is similar to that discussed in the preceding subsection. The corresponding coding generated by the PL/I compiler is quite similar to that generated by ALM.

3 Interprocedure Communication

3.1 Introduction

Call, save, and return sequences are short sequences of instructions whose execution constitutes the standard way for one procedure segment to communicate with (i.e., transfer to, pass information to, and return from) another procedure segment.

The instructions in these sequences involve the management of the stack segment used by the procedures of a given process. Executing the standard call, save, and return sequences also ensures that *all* pure procedures are automatically *recursive* (and also shareable), a deliberately planned by-product. Nonstandard methods of communication, whose use in special cases may improve efficiency, are by no means ruled out in Multics. One such approach, known as the "short call," is discussed briefly at the end of this chapter. Such techniques may be used with care by the advanced subsystem writer when appropriate.[1] The successful execution of any process depends upon flawless management of the stack; hence, (independent) translators, including assemblers, which produce target code are responsible for automatically generating call, save, and return sequences. As a result the ordinary user is liberated from what might otherwise be an awesome task. In addition to user procedures, essentially all others, including those of the supervisor, the public library, and commands, employ the same intercommunication sequences. A subsystem writer that is going to produce an independent translator must become thoroughly familiar with the details of this chapter and with all the pertinent reference literature. The prime reference at this time is the Reference Data section on the standard subroutine calling sequence in the MPM. However, it would seem that any subsystem writer would need to become somewhat familiar with the role of the stack and its management.

This chapter begins with a discussion of the stack and the call, save, and normal return sequences for procedures. Argument lists, their structure and creation, are then treated. There is a brief summary of the storage structures for several types of arguments and a separate discussion for function-name arguments. Argument lists for calls to internal procedures are considered next. Talk about generation of argument lists for calls on procedures in outer protection rings (outward calls) is postponed. Chapter 4 will discuss protection rings.

1. A process may contain one or more groups of related procedure segments, so designed by a subsystem writer that intragroup communication is achieved *without* the standard call, save, and return sequences. While executing *within* a group, shortcuts can result in improved efficiency. At some point, however, such a group of segments must interface with system-designed procedures, and here the method of communication must be standard.

3.2 The Stack

The key to understanding the effectiveness of call, save, and return sequences is first to understand the concept of the stack segment. There is a stack segment created for each process.[2] Each time one segment transfers or returns control to another segment, a frame of data consisting of key information, such as index register contents, A and Q register contents, base register contents, and other pointers, is either saved in the stack segment or retrieved or released from it. Moreover, while a procedure segment <b> is in execution, space for all its temporary storage is allocated in the stack segment. When <b> returns to the program that called it, this temporary storage is automatically released by adjusting the stack pointer. The stack is used as a pushdown store by carefully maintaining a current stack pointer. This pointer is kept in the sb←sp base pair. The sb holds the effective pointer, that is, to word zero of the stack segment, and the sp holds the relative position within the stack segment (current pointer) of word zero for the latest frame of data added to the stack.

Figure 3.1 shows the layout of a typical stack frame. Each frame consists of a header (32 words) and a body. The header for the current frame on the stack is used to save the contents of registers, pointers, and so forth, that are meaningful to the currently executing procedure at the time it prepares to call on another procedure. The four words whose use is not specified should be considered as reserved for the use of future system services. The body of the frame is of variable length and provides the temporary storage required by the currently executing procedure. For PL/I procedures, for example, space for all variables having the *automatic* attribute is allocated in the body of a stack frame[3] as soon as execution of the procedure commences.

Normally, the amount of space required for the body of the frame will be determined by the compiler or assembler.[4] Therefore, at the time the frame is created, all the space required for the body can be allocated at one time, (Allocation is in units of eight words so that the immediately following frame header will begin at an internal address that is congruent to zero [mod 8].)

Figure 3.2 suggests how the stack grows frame by frame as execution moves from <alpha> to <beta>, then to <gamma>.

2. Strictly speaking, there is actually a stack segment created for every "ring of protection" within the process. The notion of rings and multiple stacks and descriptor segments is purposely delayed until Chapter 4.

3. Also, the "descriptors" for some types of PL/I arguments are kept in the stack frame. See the MPM, Reference Data section on standard data types, for more details.

4. Exceptions arise when the stack frame must be extended during execution of the procedure, as discussed in Section 3.4.

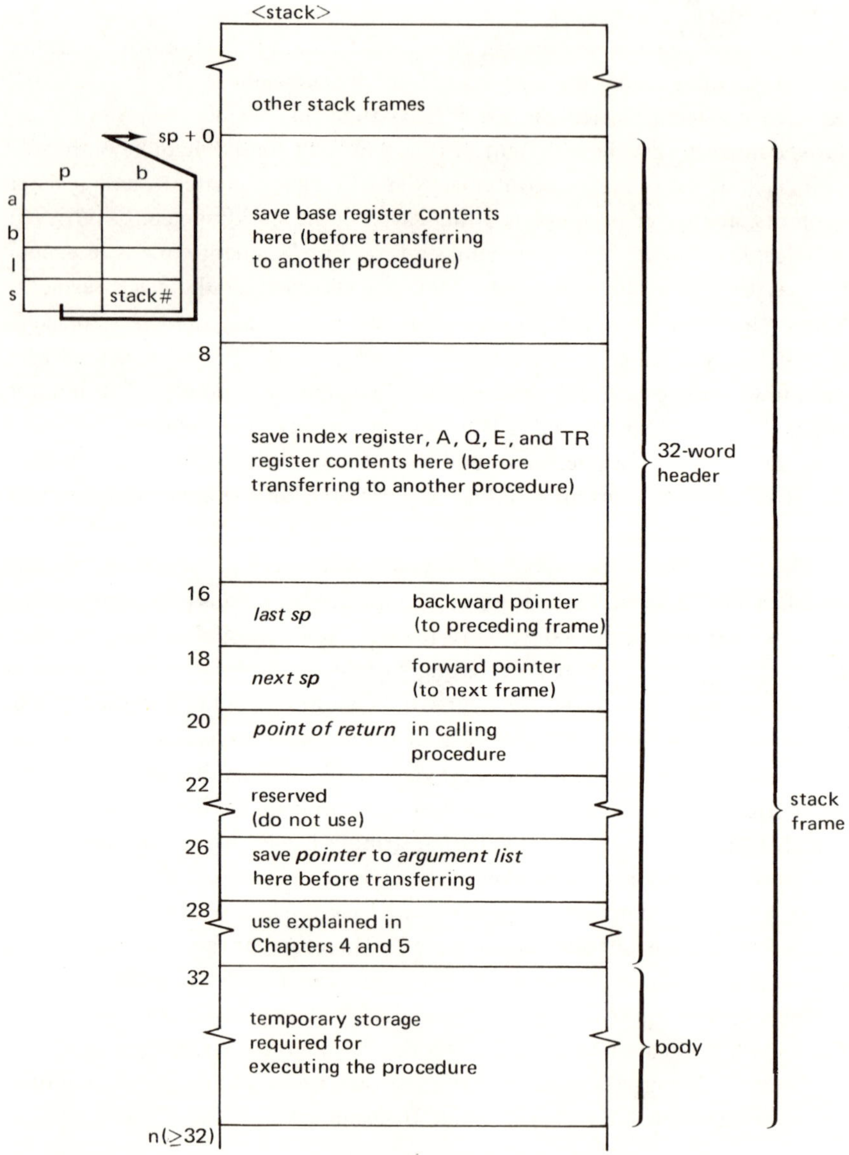

Figure 3.1 Layout of a typical stack frame

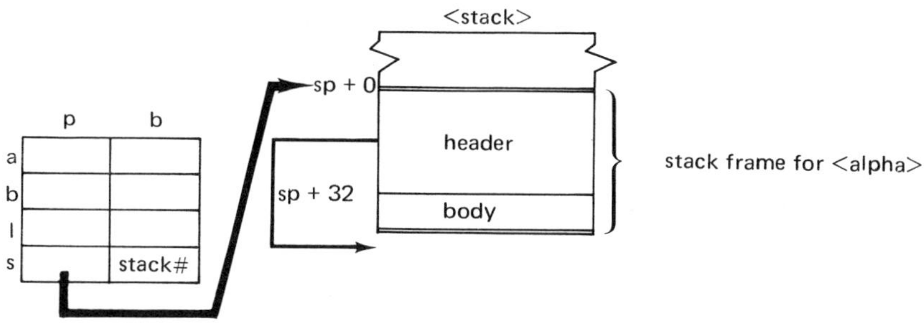

(a) <alpha> is being executed

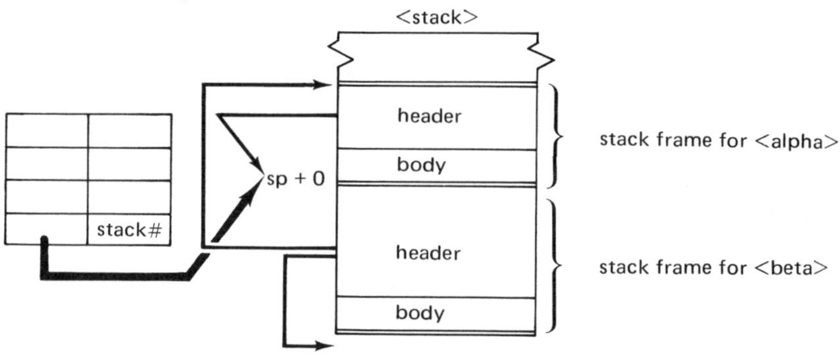

(b) <beta> is being executed after a call from <alpha>

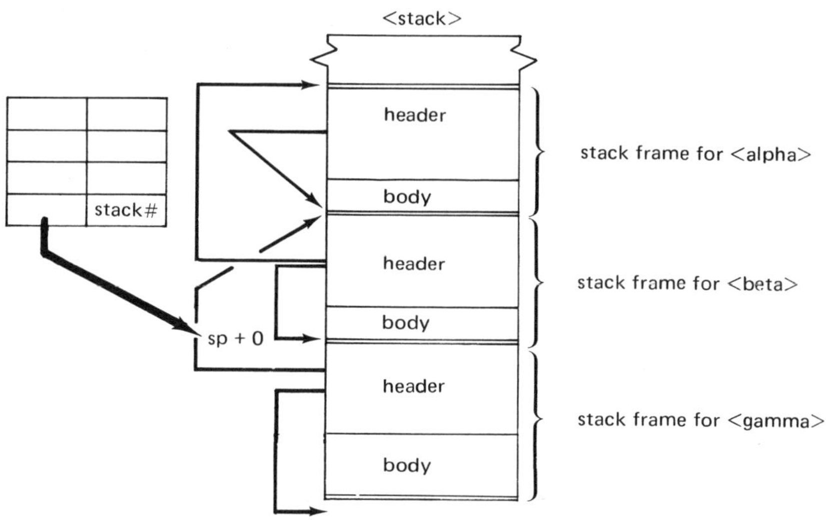

(c) <gamma> is being executed after a call from <beta>

Figure 3.2. Development of <stack> during a chain of calls

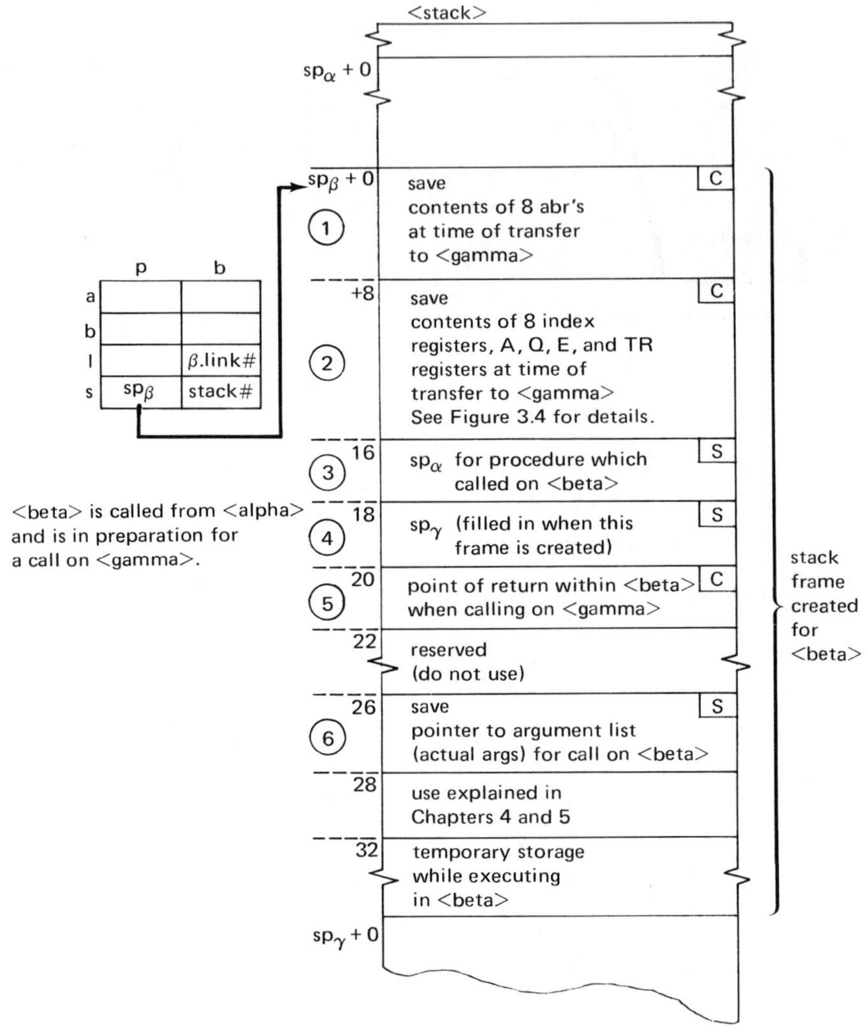

Figure 3.3. Appearance of a stack frame when executing in <beta>

5. A review of the instructions described in Section 1.4 may prove helpful in examining the coding sequences given in this chapter.

Figure 3.3 gives a closer look at the frame developed for and during execution in <beta>. It is convenient to think of the frame header as consisting of six items, so marked in the figure. Each header item is marked in its upper right corner to denote which sequence, that is, call (C) or save (S), is responsible for placing the item in the header. (The item numbers used in Figure 3.3 are used repeatedly in subsequent discussions.)

3.3 The Call Sequence

Whenever we wish to transfer from one procedure to the next, we would issue what amounts to a standard macro call. For example, the *call* macro in ALM has the form

call entrypoint (arglist)

Here entrypoint is the entry point of the procedure being called (any type of address may be used for entrypoint), and arglist is the location of the argument list. (Any type of address may be used for arglist, but I shall assume throughout this chapter that argument lists are always kept in the stack.)

For example, if the ALM assembler encounters

call<gamma>|[entry2] (sp|arglist)
(<gamma>|[entry2] = entrypoint; (sp|arglist) = arglist)

in processing the code for <beta>, then the expanded sequence will be[5]

1	stb	sp|0	Save contents of the 8 abr's in sp+0 thru sp+7. Item 1.
2	sreg	sp|8	Save contents of the 8 index registers, A, Q, E, and TR registers in sp+8 thru sp+15. Item 2. See Figure 3.4.
3	eapap	sp|arglist	Place the pointer to the argument list in ab←ap for use by <gamma>. The argument list is kept in temporary storage.
4	stcd	sp|20	Save the point of return to <beta> i.e., (ic)+2, and (pbr), and (indicators) in sp+20 and sp+21. Item 5.
5	tra	<gamma>|[entry2]	Transfer to called procedure (via the mechanism described in Figure 2.13).

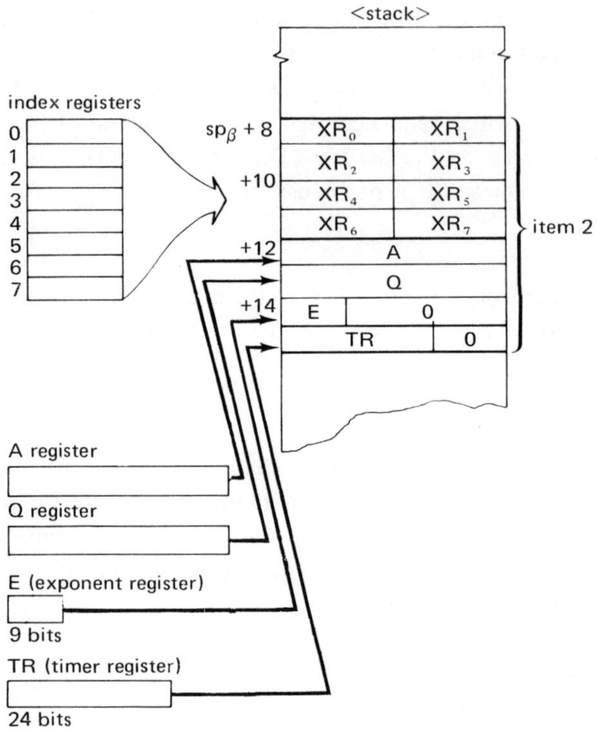

Figure 3.4. Saving the index registers and the A, Q, E, and TR registers upon execution of sreg sp|8

The first, second, and fourth instructions store items 1, 2, and 5 in the frame header. If we ever return to <beta> and at some later time issue a new call, possibly to some other procedure, new values for items 1, 2, and 5 would be stored in this header.

Item 5 has the format of an its pair

0——17	18——28	29–35
(pbr)	0	its
(ic)+2	(indicators)	0

The tra instruction of the call sequence will be assembled as

tra lp|k, *

The symbol "k" represents an offset within <beta.link>. The ft2 pair at this location is converted by the Linker (as explained in Section 2.9) to the its pair

k			
	gamma.link#	0	its
	dist	0	0

The set of instructions found at gamma.link#| dist, you will recall, is for the purpose of (1) loading gamma link# into the lb base register (and normally a zero into lp) and (2) transferring (via another its pair) to gamma#| entry2. If you have forgotten how this mechanism works, you should review the diagrams given in Figure 2.12.

3.4 The Save Sequence

The purpose of the save sequence is to (1) generate a new stack frame of 32 or more words for the just-called procedure and (2) supply values for items 3, 4, and 6 in the header of the *newly formed* frame.

Before explaining the details of the save sequence, I make the following general observation. If we continue following the example of <beta> calling on <gamma> (as we shall here), then items 3, 4, and 6 about to be established will be those of the <gamma> frame. To show how the corresponding items would have been established in the <beta> frame that is given in Figure 3.3, I would have to shift the reference point of the example to that of <alpha> calling on <beta>. I prefer instead to continue the "walk" through one complete call, save, and return cycle that starts with *call.*

The save sequence for <gamma> is actually stored in two parts. *Part 1* consists of the eaplp, aos, tra, arg quadruplet and the link, which are kept in <gamma.link>.

```
dist:     eaplp     -*,ic
          aos       2,ic
          tra       link2-,*ic*
          arg       0
```

link2:			
	gamma #	0	its
	entry2	0	0

The effect is to establish the lb←lp pair for pointing to <gamma.link> and transferring to <gamma>. *Part 2* of the save sequence is kept in <gamma> proper, beginning at entry2. This part has the job of creating the new stack frame of size tnew and storing item 6 (the argument-list pointer) into it. A new stack frame is said to be created when—

a. the new frame contains a backward pointer (item 3),
b. the new frame contains a forward pointer to the *next* frame (item 4), and
c. the sb←sp pair is reset to point to the beginning of the new frame.

A crucial Multics requirement is that during the course of executing instructions to create a new frame, there must never be an instant when the beginning of the next frame (i.e., the frame beyond the last fully created one) is *undecidable.* The reason is simple: The Multics supervisor may use the same stack to store the stateword of this process (i.e., register contents, etc.) in the event of a hardware fault or interrupt. If such an interrupt occurs during creation of a new stack frame there must be a completely safe way to identify the beginning of the *next* frame for use in handling the interrupt. The interrupt handler always locates safe-to-use storage at a point in the stack beginning at 32 words beyond the beginning of this frame.

The save sequence instructions of Part 2, on the facing page, are especially designed to meet this objective.

Note that at any given instant the frame pointed at by the sb←bp pair is the last fully created frame. Upon completion of the fifth instruction in the sequence (eabsp bp|−tnew) the new frame has been fully created. Interrupts occurring any time before or after this instant are treated as shown in Figure 3.5.

The particular instructions used in this sequence depend on the size, tnew, of the frame being created. The value of tnew[6] can ordinarily be determined by the assembler or compiler.

In short, upon completion of the save sequence in <gamma>, the sb←sp base registers have been set to point to the beginning of the new frame of

6. The maximum value that can be used for tnew in the type-1 instructions of the save sequence is 2^{14}. If a frame having a size in excess of 2^{14} words is to be allocated, two additional instructions may be generated at the end of the sequence:

```
eabbp    bp|excess    | Add excess to a copy of item 4, and–
stpbp    sp|18        | Store as the revised value for item 4.
```

This works if excess is itself $\leq 2^{14}$. A somewhat slower-to-execute sequence would be needed in building frames whose length ranges up to 2^{16} words. One such sequence might be

```
adbbp    excess, du   | Type-0 instruction: add excess to current contents of bp.
                      | The du, or direct upper modifier, indicates the value of excess
                      | is in the address field of this instruction.
stpbp    sp|18        | Store as revised value for item 4.
```

	Label	Instruction	Operand	Comment
1	entry2:	eapbp	sp|18,*	Save item 4 of the current frame temporarily in bb←bp. That is to say, let bp temporarily become the stack pointer for the new frame.
2		stpsp	bp|16	Store the current sp value (i.e., sp_β) as item 3 of the new frame.
3		eapbp	bp|tnew	Create item 4 for the new frame in bb←bp by adding tnew to what is already in bb←bp. (Item 4 is a pointer to the frame following the one currently being created.)
4		stpbp	bp|18–tnew	Store item 4 for the new frame in position 18 of the new frame. (It's stored in sp_γ+tnew+18–tnew or sp_γ +18.)
5		eabsp	bp|–tnew	Form a new stack pointer, i.e., sp_γ in sb←sp, by setting the sp part of sb←sp to point to the beginning of the frame for gamma (i.e., the bp part of bb←bp minus the length of the new frame).
6		stpap	sp|26	Save item 6. That is, save the argument-list pointer that was left in ab←ap by <beta>.

tnew words. Item 3 (sp+16) has been set to point backward to the beginning of the preceding frame for <beta>. Item 4 points forward to the beginning of the next frame, and item 6 holds a copy of the pointer to the argument list of the call to <gamma>. If, during execution in <gamma>, additional amounts of temporary stack storage are required, more space may be allocated to the frame simply by altering item 4.[7]

7. To give you some idea where stack extension might be used, you should note that in the original EPL implementation, temporary arrays that are *adjustable* are allocated space (when their space requirements become known) as an extension of the current stack frame. (The initialism EPL is the name given to an early subset of PL/I in which most of Multics was first coded and compiled.)

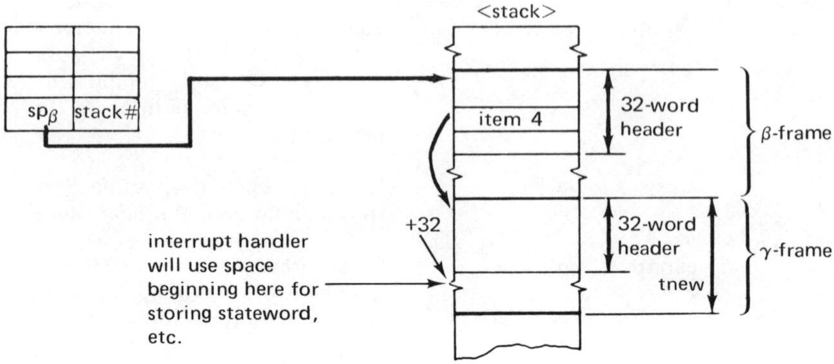

Case (a) If interrupt occurs before 5th instruction of save sequence

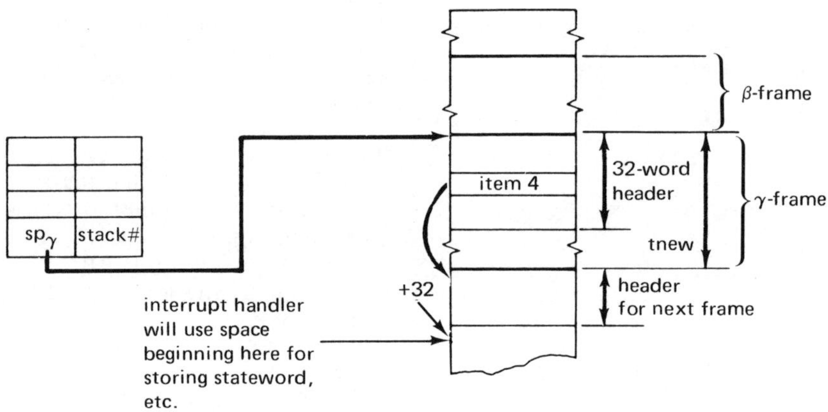

Case (b) If interrupt occurs after execution of 5th instruction of the save sequence

Figure 3.5. Handling interrupts before and after 5th instruction of the save sequence

The instructions

eapbp	sp|18,*	Get the current value in item 4.
eabbp	bp|extra	Increment by extra (which should be a number that is congruent to 0 (mod 8) and $\leqslant 2^{14}$).
stpbp	sp|18	Store the new value of item 4.

would do the job.

Also, by way of summary, the following is the condition of the abr's upon completion of the save sequence in <gamma>:

	p	b
a	sp_β+arglist	stack#
b	sp_γ+tnew	stack#
l	0 (normally)	gamma.link#
s	sp_γ	stack#

(← row b) bb←bp temporarily holds a pointer to the first word in <stack> beyond the <gamma> frame

3.5 Return Sequences

There are two types of return sequences that can be executed, the *normal* (or *standard*) *return* to the point of call and an *abnormal return*, that is, a return to a program point within an arbitrary procedure (the program point having been supplied as an argument). Only the normal return will be discussed here. Use of abnormal returns should normally be avoided, as there is a significant overhead attached. Chapter 5 provides a full discussion of abnormal returns.

3.6 The Normal Return Sequence

If you have followed what is required in the call and save sequences, the normal return sequence is quite simple to understand. All that is needed for <gamma> to return to <beta> is to

1. reload the base registers and index registers, and so on, (all but the TR register) whose values were saved in the <beta> frame during <beta>'s call on <gamma> and

2. restore the ic and pbr (and indicators) registers to the values tucked away as item 5 in <beta>'s frame.

Only three GE 645 instructions are actually required. The ALM macro call, return

expands to

ldb	sp|16,*	Reload 8 base registers.
lreg	sp|8	Reload 8 index registers and the A, Q, and E registers.
rtcd	sp|20	"Restore control word double."

The first of these instructions loads the eight base registers from the location pointed to by the contents of sp|16, which is item 3 of the <gamma> frame. Item 3 is the backward pointer to the top of the <beta> frame. The net effect is to reload the base registers stored in the <beta> frame. As a consequence, the sb←sp pair will now point to the beginning of the <beta> frame instead of the <gamma> frame.

The second instruction in the return sequence will reload all eight index registers and the A, Q, and E registers using the *direct* address

sp|8

since sb←sp now holds the desired pointer. Finally, the third instruction

rtcd sp|20

recovers all other machine conditions, that is, (ic)+2, (pbr), and (indicators), which were safe-stored as item 5 in the <beta> frame at the time <beta> called <gamma>. The effect of the rtcd instruction, a very "rich" transfer instruction, is to resume execution at a place two words beyond the stcd instruction in the calling sequence to <gamma>.

3.7 Basic Storage Structure for an Argument List

All compilers and assemblers operating in the Multics environment must produce lists of calling arguments that fall into certain standard patterns. Every operating system requires such standard patterns. In the familiar batch operating system on conventional computers, the argument list is usually supplied as a set of pointers or values immediately following the transfer and save (ic) instructions (e.g., TSX in the IBM 7094). The Multics argument list, however,

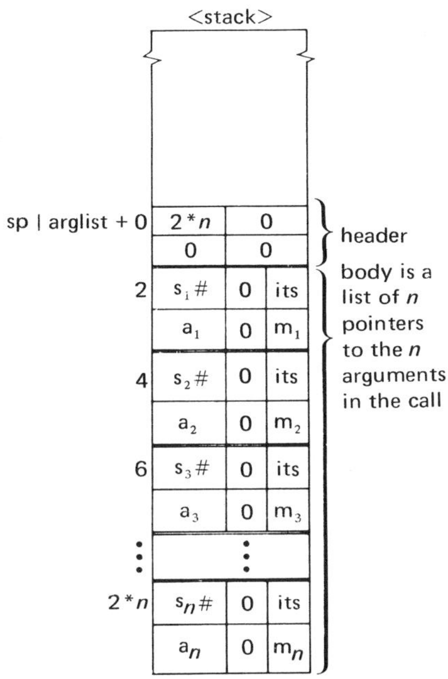

Figure 3.6. Basic storage structure of an argument list
This structure is for a call to an n-argument procedure segment. The m_i are modifiers that are normally 0 but that may be * (indirect).

may be stored in an arbitrary location, but it is generally kept in the stack in order to keep the procedure pure and to guarantee that it is recursive.[8] Moreover, the list consists only of pointers. No actual values are stored in the list.

Figure 3.6 shows the "basic" storage structure used for an argument list.[9] It consists of a two-word header followed by a body composed of n pointers (its pairs). The body length, 2 x n words, is given in the header whose address is sp|arglist.

8. An argument list must be generated and stored in the stack if at least one of the datum values it points to must be kept in the stack. This means that several copies of the argument list, each pointing to different "generations" of arguments, can be stacked at the same time. By a datum value I mean, for example, a variable, label, or procedure entry point.
9. This form must be embellished in one of two ways to achieve "special effects." One of the embellished forms is discussed in Section 3.11, the other in Chapter 4.

Each its pair can point independently, either directly or indirectly, to a corresponding argument. The its pair normally has a zero modifier, that is, it is direct, when the argument is local to the calling procedure. Indirect modifiers (*) are useful when the argument is externally defined, as will be explained in a later paragraph.

3.8 Putting its-Pair Pointers into an Argument List

The creation of its pairs for an argument list and the insertion of them in that list requires one of several coding techniques, depending on the kind of argument in the call. Three kinds are recognized here:

a. argument is *locally defined* within the calling procedure;

b. argument is a *parameter* of the procedure, that is, passed along as an argument by a procedure that called the currently executing procedure;

c. argument is *an external symbol.*

The different coding techniques are alluded to in the MPM, Reference Data section on the standard subroutine calling sequence, under "Notes and Comments." In the remainder of this section a small amount of elaboration is given. Feel free to skip over these details during the first reading. It may be that more detail is needed for subsystem writers that will be writing compilers or assemblers.

I shall sketch how each of the three kinds of argument pointers might be formed by basing examples on the following hypothetical situation. Imagine source code that shows <a> calling on <b>, which in turn calls on <c>. Then focus on the job of the compiler that must construct the code to generate an argument list for a call within <b> on <c>. Further suppose in all instances that this list is to be located at sp|arglistb. Let the *i*th argument in the call on <c> be given the name xb.

a. Argument xb is *locally defined* within <b>, and hence its value resides in the stack frame associated with <b>, say at some offset xxb from word zero of the frame. This offset is computable by the compiler. Suitable code to create and store the desired its pair pointer in this case would be

```
eapbp     sp|xxb                    Form address of argument.
stpbp     sp|arglistb+2*i           Store as ith its pair in arglistb.
```

b. Argument xb is a *parameter*, say the *j*th parameter of <b>. In calling on <b> we know that the procedure <a> has provided an argument list with an its pair pointer to this *j*th argument. Suitable code to form the *i*th its pair pointer for xb would be

```
ldaq    ap|2*j
staq    sp|arglistb+2*i
```

The ldaq instruction copies the its pair from the argument list supplied by <b> and the staq stores this copy in the argument list being constructed at sp|arglistb.

Notice that it would be a mistake to use code such as

```
eapbp    ap|2*j
stpbp    sp|arglistb+2*i
```

because this instruction pair would store a pointer to the pointer in <a>'s arglist, that is, the its pair

No good	(ab)	0	its	pointer to the arglist pointer
	arglista+2*j	0	0	

where (ab) means the contents of the ab base register.

c. The *i*th argument is *an external symbol*. In this case, the its pair that must be created and put in the argument list includes a segment number and an external symbol, values for which are not known to the compiler at the time it is generating the code that creates this argument list.

For example, suppose the *i*th argument is to be <data>|[x]. Source code like

```
eapbp    <data>|[x]
stpbp    sp|arglistb+2*i
```

would, when executed, certainly create the desired its pair, but in so doing it would force an ft2 fault to the Linker that must determine data# and x. This is because the generated code will be of the form

```
eapbp    lp|k,*
stpbp    sp|arglistb+2*i
```

The trouble with this approach is that it forces linking at too early a stage. After all, we don't really know if the called program <c> will ever use this argument. So, why link to it during the process of calling <c>? If <c> never uses this argument, the early linking could be a costly strategy.

A way to postpone this early linking is to create an *indirect* its pair pointer for the argument list.

Coding that could be generated to do this job might look like

eapbp	lp|k	Form address of the ft2 pair for <data>|[x] in base pair.
stpbp	sp|arglistb+2*i	Store the address (i.e., lb||lp+k) as an its pair.
lda	16,dl	Put an indirect code, which is decimal 16, into lower part of accumulator; dl means "direct lower."
orsa	sp|arglistb+2*i+1	OR the accumulator to storage to form an indirect modifier in the second word of the its pair.

An its pointer will then be constructed in sp|arglistb+2*i of the form

(lb)		its	indirect
(lp)+k		*	

where (lb) and (lp) represent the contents of the lb and lp base registers at the time the eapbp instruction is executed. For a more complete discussion on how to handle such arguments, see the appropriate section of the MPM.

3.9 Storage Structures for Different Types of Data

Thus far we have been discussing lists of pointers to the arguments of a procedure, but we haven't been paying attention to what the arguments themselves look like. Some types of arguments, for example, integer and real variables, are sufficiently simple so that their data values are pointed to directly by the pointers in the argument list. Other data types are so complex in structure that the argument pointers don't point to data values but, alas, to pointers that are part of the storage structure of the individual arguments. The subsystem writer must, of course, keep this in mind in instances where code is being constructed to fetch or store data values via argument-list pointers.

At least some of the procedures of every subsystem must interface with Multics system modules. Arguments passed to or from a subsystem procedure and a Multics system module must employ standard formats. Because the system modules are coded in PL/I, the Multics standard formats for data types are identical with those of (the Multics) PL/I.[10]

10. In the initial versions of Multics, where system modules were compiled in an early subset of PL/I (EPL), the standard data types were correspondingly restricted to those of

These standardized storage representations (structures) are definitively described in the MPM, Reference Data section on the standard subroutine calling sequence. Only a few of these types are redescribed in this book. Table 3.1 gives the full list of these data types (and the type codes by which they are known technically), and Table 3.2 gives schematics of storage structure for those data types that are of especial interest here. In each case the graphic form (P)→ denotes the item of the argument pointed to by the pointer in the argument list.

The full collection of data types, as given in the MPM section cited above, should also be of interest, but for somewhat different reasons. Thus a subsystem writer who is developing a new language processor, for example, MAD or ALGOL, may benefit by seeing the way $n(\geqslant 2)$-dimensional arrays are structured in the Multics PL/I. While these are perhaps not the best or only methods for representing such data types, two things are worth considering seriously.

1. These structures are tested and have proven practicable.
2. Multics will eventually provide an extensive library of subroutines written in PL/I. A subsystem writer that chooses PL/I storage structures can have the automatic by-product of being able to have his subsystem interface easily with (i.e., call directly on) a growing library supported by the Multics staff and the PL/I community. Enough said.

3.10 Function-Name Arguments, Ordinary Case

A procedure <p> may call on another procedure <r>, passing to it an argument that is a procedure entry. Suppose the argument passed to <r> is the procedure entry <q>|[entry3], in a call equivalent to

call<r>|[entry](arglist1)

EPL. Only the following data types could be passed for EPL-compiled routines.
a. All scalars:

arithmetic	integer real complex
strings	bit character
labels	(including procedure entry points)
pointers	

b. Any one-dimensional array of the above.

Table 3.1 The Multics Standard (and PL/I) Data Types

	type code
Single precision real fixed-point	1
Double precision real fixed-point	2
Single precision real floating-point	3
Double precision real floating-point	4
Single-word integer complex	5
Double-word integer complex	6
Single-word floating-point complex	7
Double-word floating-point complex	8
Pointer data	13
Offset data	14
Label data	15
Entry data	16
Arrays of types 1–4	17–20
Arrays of types 13–15	29–31
Structure	514
Area	518
Bit string	519
Character string	520
Varying bit string	521
Varying character string	522
Array of structures	523
Array of areas	524
Array of bit strings	525
Array of character strings	526
Array of varying bit strings	527
Array of varying character strings	528

Table 3.2 Types of Arguments and Their Storage Structures–Systemwide Standards

Type No.	Argument Type	Storage Structure
1	Single precision real fixed-point	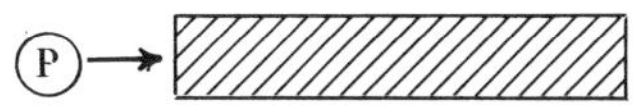
2	Double precision real fixed-point	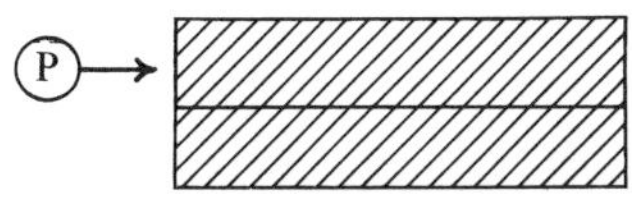
3	Single precision real floating-point	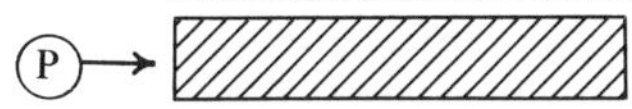
4	Double precision real floating-point	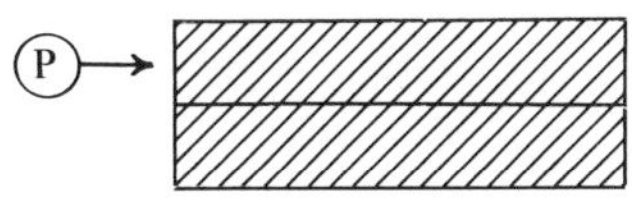
13	Pointer	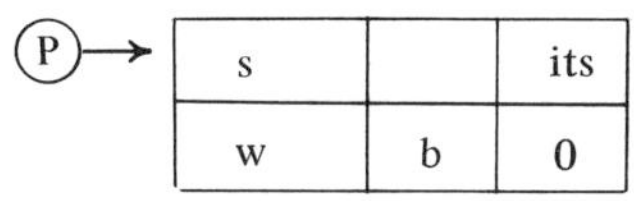 s = segment number (bits 0–17, first word) w = word offset (bits 0–17, second word) b = bit offset into the word addressed by w (bits 18–29, second word) (For "aligned" data being pointed to, b = 0. In general, 0⩽b⩽36.)
14	Offset (one word)	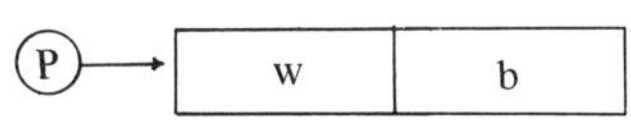 w = word offset (bits 0–17) b = bit offset into the word addressed by w (bits 18–35) (0⩽b⩽36).
15	Label } same storage structure	
16	Entry } same storage structure	

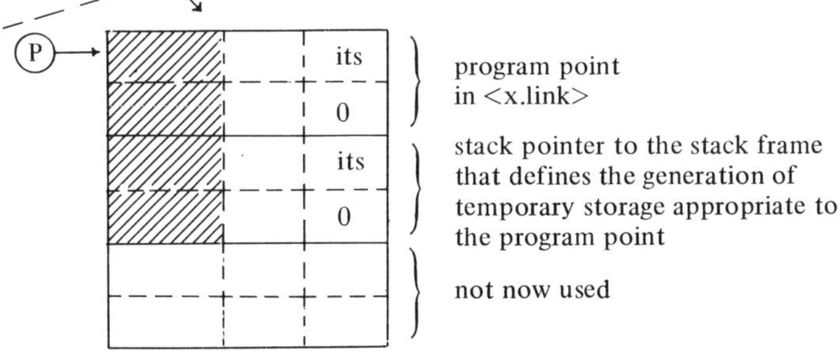

In this case the argument list contains a pointer to the entry datum that has a pointer to <q>|[entry3]. Some time later, while executing in <r>, we can have a call on <q> by referring to a parameter, say t, that corresponds to <q>. Such a call might have the appearance

call t(arglist2)

where t is declared to be the dummy procedure name, and the arguments x, y, and z of arglist2 are recognized as external symbols for (say floating-point) variables located in the segment <data>. A corresponding sketch is shown in Figure 3.7 using PL/I terminology.

The argument list generated in the call to <r> will have the appearance

arglist1

2	0	
0	0	
(sb)	0	its
(sp)+arg	0	0

The argument itself is supposed to be located at sp|arg. It has the format

entry datum

sp|arg+0

q.link#	0	its	
entrypair	0	0	
			normally zero (used only for internal functions)
			unspecified error check information

The first its pair points to an offset within <q.link> at which we can expect to find the quadruplet

```
entrypair:    eaplp    -*,ic
              aos      2,ic
              tra      link-*,ic*
              arg      0
```

whose execution basically results in the transfer to <q>|[entry3]. Ordinarily the second pair of words in the entry datum is zero. In certain cases, however, as will soon be explained, it will be used for holding a stack-pointer value. The third pair is to be used for as yet unspecified error-checking information.

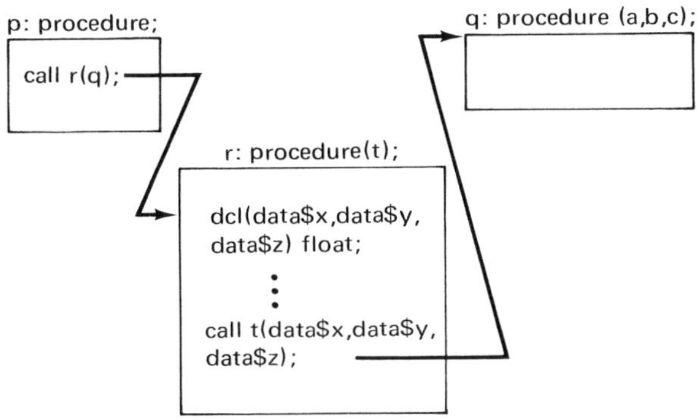

Figure 3.7. Calling an external procedure whose name (q) has been passed as an argument

To generate the call on the dummy t while executing in <r>, the last instruction in the call sequence might be preceded by the instruction

eapbp ap|2,*

to put the address of the function-name argument in bb←bp. The standard call sequence would follow, ending with the instruction

tra bp|0

which would cause the transfer to the address found in the first its pair of the function-name argument, that is, ultimately to the desired entry point in <q>.

The argument list that goes with this call on <q> would appear as

arglist2+0	6		0
	0		0
	data#	0	its
	x	0	0
	data#	0	its
	y	0	0
	data#	0	its
	z	0	0

3.11 Function-Name Arguments, Special Case

Suppose, again, the procedure <p> calls on <r>, passing to it as an argument an entry point in q. But this time, suppose q is a procedure that is *internally* defined within <p>. Figure 3.8 illustrates this case using PL/I terminology. We will imagine that the entry point is located at q+entry3 within <p>. Because q is an internal procedure, it may, whenever it is executed, require data values that have been allocated temporary storage in a stack frame created earlier by the containing procedure <p>. Somehow q will have to know how to reach this stack frame. This section explains the Multics conventions that are designed to aid subsystem writers in solving communications problems of this type. Such problems, of course, will occur in subsystems that permit the embedding and/or the nesting of internal procedures or blocks within procedure segments.

To continue with the example, suppose, then, that <p> calls <q> with a call equivalent to

call <r>|[entry1] (arglist1)

The argument list at arglist1 looks just like the one shown in the preceding discussion. However, the argument itself must now include a stack-pointer value for reasons that I shall be developing in the next paragraphs. Thus, the argument at sp|arg would now appear as

entry datum

sp arg+0	p.link#	0	its
	entrypair	0	0
	(sb)	0	its
	(sp)	0	0

Each call sequence that sends control from <p> to <r> must be immediately preceded by code that creates an argument in the form just exhibited.

The first its pair points to the entry instructions within <p.link> whose execution would result in a transfer to <p>|q+entry3. The expressions (sb) and (sp) refer to values of the sb←sp base pair extant immediately prior to the call. Code to generate the first two of these its pairs could be

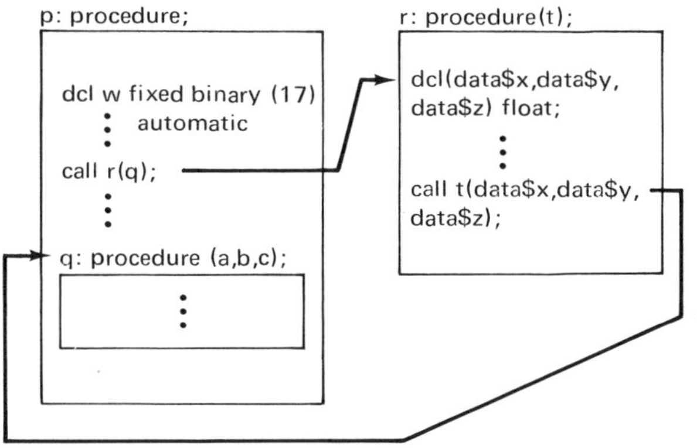

Figure 3.8. Calling an internal procedure whose name (q) has been passed as an argument

eapbp	1p|entrypair	Form the address p.link#|entrypair.
stpbp	sp|arg	Store as the first its pair in the function-name argument.
stpsp	sp|arg+2	Store the stack-pointer value as the second its pair.

Proceeding further with the example of Figure 3.8, suppose now that, while executing in <r> at some point, we wish to execute a call on q via reference to the corresponding parameter t, for example,

call t (arglist2)

Here, again, t is the dummy procedure name. The arguments x, y, and z of arglist2 happen to be externally defined within <data>.

Once the call sequence in <r> to p#|q+entry3 has been completed, it must be possible for the computation of q(x,y,z) to proceed successfully. But, suppose that while executing in q it becomes necessary to refer to a previously stacked data value, such as w, that was assigned during prior execution in <p>. Remember that the compiler does not and cannot furnish addresses that are relative to the beginning of the stack *segment*. It only furnishes addresses relative to the beginning of a stack *frame*. Therefore, q must know the stack-frame pointer that was in use at the time <p> called <r>. Note this is the pointer that would be made a part of the function-name argument to be "passed" to <r>. Obviously <r> itself has no need for this stack pointer, but notice that when <r> calls on q, <r> can pass this pointer back to q as an argument. In a sense, the stack pointer must make a "round trip" from <p> to <r> and back to <p>. The reader should now see why a function-name argument (entry datum) that refers to an internal procedure is designed to include the current stack-pointer value.

In just a moment, we will examine the structural form of the argument list that must be used in calling on q. Before doing so, several questions could be asked: What sort of call sequence should be used in calling an internal procedure? Should the standard call sequence be used? In any case, how should execution proceed in an internal procedure like q once it is called? Should there be a save sequence executed to create a separate stack frame for execution of q? Anyone writing a compiler for a language that has an ALGOL-like block structure, for example, one that permits the nesting of internal procedures and/or PL/I-like begin blocks, must provide his own answers to these questions.

Mechanisms have been developed by the EPL compiler writers for dealing with these problems. They are well documented in the MSPM. Other compiler writers may choose to adopt these techniques. If so, they will find the MSPM notes very helpful. Compiler writers should keep in mind, however, that the implementation described there is regarded by its developers as somewhat clumsy and subject to improvement.[11]

We are now ready to discuss the structure of the argument list that is used for calling on an internal procedure. This Multics "standard" takes the form

11. Those notes suggest one mechanism for handling the general problem that arises when the called procedure or block may be nested at any depth within a containing external procedure. The bookkeeping becomes more complicated, because successful execution of the called procedure may require knowledge of a (different) stack pointer for *each* of the "containing" procedures or blocks. That is to say, a mechanism is developed for knowing, when executing within a procedure or block that is nested at level i, where to find stacked data that was generated by containing procedures or blocks at various "shallower" levels $k<i$. In the EPL implementation, begin blocks are treated indistinguishably from internal procedures. To enter a block, one issues a standard call sequence, as if it were a procedure. Once called, the internal procedure executes the standard save sequence to create its own stack frame. Among other things that can be stored in this frame is the (set of) stack pointer(s) to the frame(s) for any outer-level procedures that the called procedure needs to refer to. This set of stack pointers is referred to as the "display," apparently after the plan described by Brian Randell and L. J. Russell in *ALGOL 60 Implementation* (New York: Academic Press, 1964).
The cost associated with a call to a nested procedure or block in the EPL mechanism unfortunately increases with increase in the depth of nesting. This objection is serious enough that work continues in quest of improved techniques whose calling costs are independent of nesting depth.

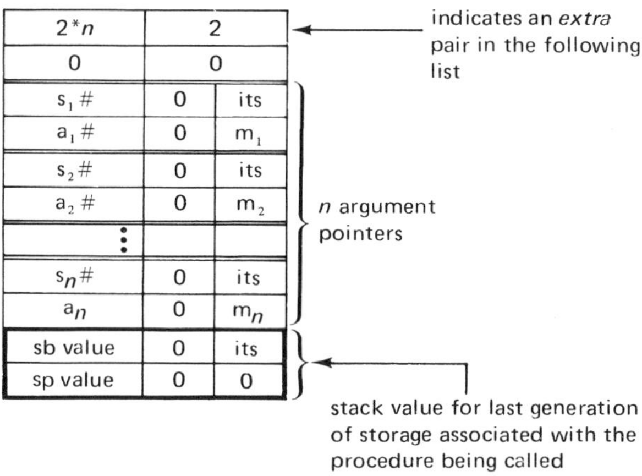

Figure 3.9. Structure for an argument list. This structure is used when calling on an *n*-argument internal procedure whose name was previously passed as an argument

of a simple embellishment to the structure of an ordinary argument list. The extended form is shown in Figure 3.9.

In our particular example we see that the PL/I statement

call t (data$x, data$y, data$z);

corresponds at assembly level to

call t(arglist2)

with an associated argument list that would look like

arglist2+0		6		2
		0		0
	+2	data#	0	its
		x	0	0
	+4	data#	0	its
		y	0	0
	+6	data#	0	its
		z	0	0
copied here from ap|2	⟶ +8	(sb)	0	its
		(sp)	0	0

In point of fact, ALM does not automatically generate the code to construct the argument list in the expansion of the call macro, although an assembler with a more advanced macro capability could be expected to do so. This means that any compiler designed to generate ALM code as output must bear the full responsibility for generating code to form the argument list *before generating the call macro.*

If we were to imagine the use of a more advanced assembler, then conceivably, a source statement like

call t(<data>|[x], <data>|[y], <data>|[z])

could be recognized. The assembler would then generate—

1. the code to form the complete argument list,
2. the call sequence.

Such an assembler would have to automatically recognize that t is a dummy representing an internal procedure in order that it (the assembler) could know to generate code for forming the n + 1st its pair of the argument list. A sophisticated assembler could recognize that t is an internal procedure in the following way.

Since t is a parameter, the assembler must generate code that, *when executed*, determines if the entry point that corresponds to t is internal or external. If external there is of course no need to add the n + 1st pointer. The distinction can be achieved by inspecting the second its pair in the entry datum. If it is zero, the entry must be external, because otherwise this pair would hold a stack pointer. Code like that which follows would, if generated, perform this discrimination during execution, add the its pair as needed, and so on.

	eapbp	ap|2*i,*	Establish a pointer to the function name arg, assuming it is the *i*th argument.
	ldaq	bp|2	Pick up (sb) and (sp) from the second its pair of this arg.
	tze	skip	Bypass.[12]
	staq	sp|arglist2+2*n+2	Store the stack-pointer value as the n + 1st argument in the call on q.
	⋮		Adjust word zero of the argument list.
skip:			

Once inside the called internal procedure, any reference to a local (automatic) variable in the containing procedure <p> must be accomplished via the stack-pointer argument. In the particular example, a reference to the variable w by the procedure q might be coded something like

```
eapbp     ap|8,*
lda       bp|w
```

3.12 The Short Call

Readers may well have wondered if any shortcut calling sequences are feasible as more efficient (and shorter) forms of the standard call, save, and return sequences described in this chapter. Shorter sequences would be especially welcome for calls to very short routines. A long call, save, return sequence to a subroutine that executes only a few instructions is truly an expensive proposition. One very short call sequence is described fully (with all its limitations) in the MPM, Reference Data section on the short calling sequence.

This *short call* sequence is simply

[eapap arglist]	Optional loading of an argument-list pointer.
tsbbp callee	Transfer to the callee, the return address being set in the bb←bp base pair.

Note that no registers or bases are saved and the contents of the bb←bp pair (and the ab←ap pair, if used) are lost.

The *short save* sequence is empty! The address *callee* in the tsbbp instruction is the actual entry point in the target procedure and not in the target's linkage section as in the standard call. In short, the target procedure must be (short enough to be) able to execute without its own linkage section or stack frame!

The *short return* sequence is simply

<table><tr><td>tra bp|0</td><td>Returns control to the instruction immediately following the tsbbp instruction, without restoring bb←bp (or ab←ap).</td></tr></table>

12. In the GE 645, execution of the ldaq instruction causes the zero indicator to be turned on when the loaded double word is zero.

A person reading the MPM reference section cited earlier will note that a number of warning flags are run up lest the subsystem writer pursue the use of the short call without fully appreciating its limitations. As an exercise, the interested reader can test his grasp of the material in this chapter by first enumerating as many limitations as he can think of and then comparing these with those listed in the cited MPM section.

4

Access Control and Protection

4.1 Introduction

In this chapter and its successor, I want to review the picture of interprocedure communication with a more realistic orientation. I want the reader to understand this communication as one going on in the multiaccess environment of Multics, where different processes coexist, undoubtedly involving a number of different users, each with separate objectives (and skills). The users often compete for the computer's resources. They "play" against each other in one way or another, fair or foul. Fair play, as in a management-decision game with several players, is to be encouraged. Foul play, as for instance one user inadvertently or deliberately destroying the data or procedures of another user or of the system itself, is to be more than merely minimized, discouraged, or outlawed. It is to be prevented in toto! Multics is designed so that a large measure of fair play can be achieved by cooperating users, while at the same time every type of foul play that can be anticipated is prevented.

This ambitious design objective is actually now nearing achievement in spite of the fact that encouraging fair play—that is, permitted cooperation between users—almost inevitably invites accidents, that is, suggests chances for damaging interaction between users or between a user and the supervisor—or so it would seem. A primary goal of Chapter 4 and, to some extent, Chapters 5, 6, and 7 is to explain how these two objectives are, in fact, achieved. Secondarily, I hope the reader of this chapter will gain confidence that Multics will indeed protect him from the inept practice or foul play of others that share the computer with him. He will also see that to a significant extent Multics can help to protect the user from himself as well.

4.1.1 Compartmentalization—General Concepts

One natural question a subsystem designer might ask is, How does a large process ever get debugged? What helpful provisions are there in Multics to effectively isolate (and insulate) procedure and data segments (or groups of them) from one another? Could one, in principle at least, test isolated parts and be sure that when tested parts are put together, undesirable interaction of the parts can be avoided or at least controlled? This principle of compartmentalization probably goes back to the early days of debugging, which, in turn, certainly dates from the first computers.[1]

Even on these simple, stand-alone computers where a user literally "owned" the entire machine while in execution, ideas of protection began to

1. Professor Maurice Wilkes, of Cambridge University, reports that his laboratory "discovered" debugging the first day the EDSAC became operational while attempting to execute a simple program for generating a table of prime numbers.

emerge. To increase the reliability of a program, ways were sought to safeguard data areas; procedures (subroutines) were invented to subdivide large programs, and attempts were made to limit the scope of procedures so that no one procedure would be allowed to access any more data than needed. Near the beginning, interpreters were invented as one of the software schemes to help achieve these measures of protection. Much later, hardware innovations provided alternative possibilities.

When batch monitor operating systems were introduced there were new problems of protection. Without benefit of hands-on control a sophisticated user had all the more reason to design large processes in a compartmentalized manner to achieve internal protection of his programs and data; But, in addition, as a consideration to other users in the batch, both ahead of him (on the output tape) and behind him, the isolation of the "supervisor" became critically important. In the batch system an executing process could be thought of as having two distinct domains: the supervisory programs and their data bases (S) and the user programs and their data bases (U). To act as a "protected supervisor" in any meaningful sense, it was essential that certain procedures in S have access to the programs and data of U. On the other hand, it became apparent that programs of U should be allowed no direct access to data in S and should be capable of only certain kinds of controlled access (e.g., "trapped" calls to the input/output (I/O) supervisor) to certain of the programs in S.

The latter distinction accords with the idea that only supervisory programs may execute I/O and other privileged instructions. Hardware developments have made it possible to facilitate this distinction. In many computer operating systems operating under batch monitors, "master mode," which permits execution of the full instruction repertoire, is reserved for supervisory programs. A user program can effect a transit into the master mode only by temporarily *giving up direct control*, such as by executing an instruction that traps his program to a master-mode fault handler.

Given this type of protection of S and given S's greater freedom to interact with U, we see that–

a. if S malfunctions, it can destroy both S and U;

b. if U malfunctions, at worst it can only destroy U, leaving S free to load and execute tasks for other users, for example, for U_1, U_2, and so on.

When we now consider an environment like Multics where we have a collection of user domains, U_1, U_2, . . . , U_n, and a common supervisor S, all our earlier incentives for isolating key compartments of a process remain. The consequences of not having adequate protection of S, however, are much worse. We must bear in mind that process 1 consists of U_1 and S; process 2 consists of U_2 and S, and so forth. Any time supervisory procedures in S are executing, they are maintaining data bases in S that pertain to the entire group of active user processes. If these tables are inadvertently or deliberately tampered with by U_1 (executing in process 1) or U_2 (executing in process 2), and so forth, not only would S be damaged, but one or more *other* user processes are likely to be defeated *at the same time*. (Destruction of processes can now occur en masse rather than, as typical in the batch system, merely invoking a delay in use of the system by users waiting in the queue.)

There are, of course, new kinds of problems that need to be considered in a multiprogrammed environment that were less serious in the batch system. One of these is the matter of privacy or, more generally speaking, control over the "sharing" of segments. If a general mechanism is to be provided for allowing two or more running processes to share the same segments, there must also be a complementary capability for preventing certain segments of one user's process from being shared, peeked at, or written in by procedures of another process. Thus to ensure that U_1 cannot interact with U_2, for example, by "peeking," we must rely on a carefully conceived scheme of *access control* for each segment used in each process. Moreover, the actuating of these access controls must be a function confined to the supervisory procedures in S, using data bases in S.

One begins to see how really critical the design of a "foolproof," "vandal proof," and "burglar proof" protection mechanism is, if any large, general-purpose, multiuser, multiprogrammed environment is to endure. The Multics design for access control and protection is intended to be "airtight." In this chapter we hope to describe a major part of this plan.

4.1.2 Compartmentalization–As Achieved in Multics

In Multics compartmentalization is achieved through two primary mechanisms, one supplementing the other.

a. Per-Segment Access Control

This is a means of denoting and controlling the type of access, to a particular shared segment, which may be accorded to an individual user. A segment may be shared by two or more processes, but the person that creates the segment and that "grants" permission for its shared use is able to specify the type of access accorded to each grantee.

By giving to each file's author the privilege of specifying the users that shall have access to it, Multics guarantees that a user is able to safeguard the information he creates and files away for future use. It is true that Multics permits the coexistence of many processes, each of which competes for the system's physical resources and employs the same file-system hierarchy. Nevertheless, sharp divisions may be maintained between the processes with respect to the information each may acquire in its address space and how such information may be used. Furthermore, the control rests where it may be most meaningfully exercised—with the user. Per-segment access control may therefore be viewed as a form of interprocess protection. Concepts of access control are introduced in Section 4.2 (and are further elaborated upon in Chapter 6).

b. Concentric Rings of Protection

The ring mechanism, by contrast, offers intraprocess protection of segments. The concentric-ring concept is essentially a generalization of the S and U (supervisor and user) domains. The segments of any one process are associated with a set of generally two, but possibly more, concentric rings. If a process has only two concentric rings, then the inner ring corresponds to S and the outer ring to U. But, provision has been built into the Multics design so that the subsystem writer may add (as justified) additional rings. In such applications, segments of the subsystem would be associated with the most appropriate ring (category) vis-à-vis privilege and protection. In this way a designer, say when developing a teacher-student subsystem, may establish one or more extra "lines of defense." These can result in increased protection of the key parts of the subsystem (e.g., teacher-written programs) from damage or misuse by other users of the subsystem (e.g., student-written progams).

Basically, a procedure that is assigned the category of ring *r* is privileged during its execution to call (or to reference) any procedure (or data) segment in ring *r* or in any ring peripheral to, that is, "outside of," ring *r*. Conversely, a procedure of ring *r* is *prevented* from referencing data segments in a more "privileged," that is, "inner" ring and is permitted call access to more privileged procedures only through specially controlled entry points called "gates."

The controlled entry via gates is into procedures that may reside in any one of several inner rings. This amounts to a software-augmented generalization of the call trapping capability that is employed in conventional batch monitor systems. In those systems, the caller traps, when permitted to do so, to procedures that have full privilege, often master mode. In Multics, the caller can, in effect, trap into procedures that have intermediate degrees of privilege, as deemed appropriate by the subsystem designer. (Even when trapping into procedures of the innermost ring, master-mode privilege is hardly ever required or employed.)

The set of supervisory segments, when viewed as a subsystem can, in principle, also benefit through subdivision into rings. Two rings were originally thought to be desirable; the first was variously referred to as ring 0, or the hard-core ring; the second, ring 1, was also called the administrative ring.[2] Experience in checking out the earliest versions of Multics indicated, however, that the cost (both in space and time) for maintaining two supervisory rings continually, that is, with a high frequency of interaction, was not justified. As currently implemented, the Multics supervisor resides essentially in one ring (ring 0). The logical structure to support a multiring supervisor has been carefully retained. So, a multiring supervisor can be readily employed whenever hardware improvements allow it to be justified. For this reason our discussions in this chapter will retain a generality, wherever appropriate, that presumes the existence of a multiring supervisor.

Here the motivation for multiple rings for supervisor and/or user is summarized.

By subsetting the segments of a process into rings and by effectively controlling interactions and communication between segments of different rings (supervisory or userlike), Multics provides the potential to isolate trouble and limit damage in the system. Different rings, in a way, may be equated to different levels of damage, that is, to the system, to the subsystem, to the subsystem user, and so forth, depending on the frame of reference. Greater damage to the total system operation would, in general, result from a malfunction of or damage to a segment, the closer its ring is to the hard core or "nerve center" of the system. Conversely, damage that occurs to a segment in an outlying user ring, would affect only the user's process or at worst those of other users that happen to share the affected nonsupervisory segments. In the minimal case the damage might be confined to the outermost ring of the process. Assuming good design in this case, the process (like a natural organism) might even be able to recover well enough to continue executing effectively, except in the damaged region.

2. Generally speaking, ring-0 segments were those most crucial to the operation of Multics. In this category fell certain key tables and vital procedures, which, for instance, govern the multiplexing of the core memory, of the processors, and of other key resources among the processes. A small portion of the ring-0 segments remain resident in core at all times. Such segments are referred to as "wired down" and their absolute addresses in memory are known to other ring-0 procedures. Ring-1 segments were, generally speaking, those more numerous and less vital supervisory segments that could more readily be debugged while the system was in full operation.

One would correctly intuit that there are nontrivial overhead costs incurred in implementing rings and the implied controls. For instance, extra execution time required to cross from one ring to another during a procedure call or a normal return is of the order of two to three milliseconds (round trip). (This is the cost using the current GE 645 hardware together with the software described in this chapter. Follow-on versions of the GE 645 may well implement improvements that eliminate most of this overhead.[3] The notes in Sections 4.2 and 4.3 will provide insight into the costs involved, so that you will be able to assess the trade-offs among subsystem designs employing alternative ring structures. One type of "ring" overhead is alluded to in the next two paragraphs.

4.1.3 Alteration of the Per-Process Stack Model

The per-process stack model that was developed in Chapter 3 must undergo an extension to be compatible with the concept of a process that is subdivided in the two-or-more-ring sense. We can no longer continue to think of a single (common) stack that can be employed by (i.e., be read-write accessible to) all procedures in one process. For, were this the case, the hoped-for isolation between rings would be easily circumvented. Any (offending) procedure could copy information from the stack or possibly destroy information (including instructions) in it that was stored there by supervisory ("superior" in the inner-ring sense) procedures. Security and protection of information vital to the functioning of a supervisory procedure would thereby be nullified. The Multics solution is to give procedures in each ring of a process a separate stack segment. Of course, all legal communication between procedures of different rings then becomes clerically (though not necessarily conceptually) more complicated than first described in Chapter 3.

It is hoped that readers can gain a full overview of all these new ideas by studying Section 4.2 and optionally proceed to Section 4.3 for still further details. Protection problems also arise in connection with other types of interprocedure communication, specifically condition handling and abnormal returns. A discussion of these problems and the solutions to these as developed in Multics, is the subject of Chapter 5. The MSPM documentation on which most of this "protection" material is based contains additional details, while the excellent paper by Graham [4] is a more succinct overview of the same subject.

3. For example, the S.M. Thesis by M. D. Schroeder, "Classroom Model of an Information and Computing Service," M.I.T., Department of Electrical Engineering, 1969, provides a design in which inward ring crossings are handled entirely in the hardware.

4.2 Access Control and Ring-Bracket Protection

In this section some basic details are provided on the two types of isolation techniques, access control and ring brackets,[5] which, in proper combination, are fundamental to the system of protection and to the controlled sharing of data and procedures in Multics.

It has already been suggested why segments within a process should be subdivided into rings and why there should be a separate stack segment for each ring. It is proper to remark here that ring compartmentalization is carried out with some hardware aid. Multics exploits special GE 645 fault-detection hardware to detect and trap a process whenever it attempts to make a cross-ring reference, in order to invoke the intervention of supervisory software.

Before we can proceed further with the details of the ring mechanism, it is necessary to acquire a clear understanding of the, perhaps more fundamental, per-segment access-control provisions of the Basic File System.

4.2.1 Per-Segment Access Control[6]

What follows assumes you have, at sometime in the past, read one of the several available Multics overviews on the Basic File System and, in particular, the directory structure of the file-system hierarchy.[7] A review of these topics may not be necessary now. I will assume that you have a general knowledge of the "file structure" and the terminology or jargon that has grown up with it: namely,

1. that it consists of a tree of directory and nondirectory files (really segments);
2. that among other things, a directory contains a set of entries called *branches*[8] each of which points directly to and describes a file (segment) in some detail (either a directory segment, i.e., another directory, or a nondirectory segment, i.e., a block of data or a procedure). A branch is, properly speaking, the set of attributes for a segment. Each branch includes the segment's unique identification. There is a one-to-one correspondence between

4. R. M. Graham, "Protection in an Information Processing Utility," *Communications of the ACM* [Association for Computing Machinery] 11, no.5 (1968): 365–369.

5. The notion of a ring *bracket* to be developed in this section is a slight extension of the ring concept already introduced.

6. Principal MSPM references are those that give an overview of the Basic File System, and of access control. Auxiliary MSPM references are those that discuss Segment Control, the directory data base, Directory Control, and the file-system commands. The file-system commands are also given in the MPM.

7. For instance, the overview given in the MPM, Chapter II.

8. Another type of entry, called a *link*, is discussed in Chapter 6.

the branches and the segments of the system's information storage; and
3. that branches, which are also termed "file descriptions," are specified either explicitly or by default rules at the time a segment is created. Each branch (or "file branch") includes a "permission list" that names each user who is to have access to the segment and that specifies the types of permitted access for each listed user. Of course, the creator of a segment (file) is automatically listed as a permitted user in the branch for that segment.

Figure 4.1 is a schematic of the directory structure. At the time he acquires "user status," each user usually has assigned to him a uniquely named "user directory" whose file branch is located in a project-maintained directory. Once a user begins executing processes in his own name, he may create new segments and add these to the Multics tree. The new segments will normally have their corresponding branches in the user's user directory.

A user is free to create either nondirectory or directory segments. The ability to add directories implies that a user, if he chooses, can add to the overall system hierarchy a subtree of arbitrary depth whose root is his own user directory.

When a process calls for the creation of a new segment, a name is specified,

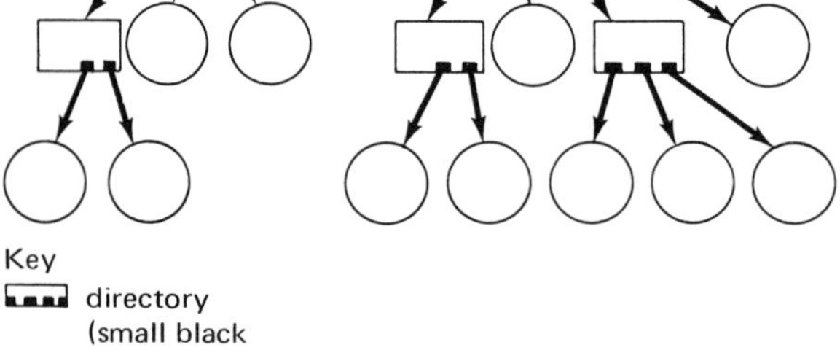

Key
directory (small black squares represent individual branches)
nondirectory

Figure 4.1. Schematic of directory structure of the file system
Each directory contains a set of "branches" (which point either to other directory or nondirectory segments).

together with other descriptors (attributes). These are employed by the Basic File System to construct and attach a branch to that segment in the appropriate directory.

A process will frequently make indirect attempts to access an existing segment, usually by making symbolic reference to it via the linkage mechanism. The Basic File System (BFS), which is invoked while handling the linkage fault to a heretofore unknown segment, will attempt to make the wanted segment known to the faulting process. Making the segment known (upon first reference to it), you will recall, involves associating with it a segment number and obtaining the information that is needed to form the appropriate segment descriptor word (SDW).

The Directory Control Module of the BFS will locate and then examine the particular directory [9] that holds the branch pointing to the desired segment. The "access-control information" found in this branch's "permission list" provides the wanted information. If, in the course of searching for the branch, it is discovered that the user lacks search rights to the directory that holds this branch, the Linker, so informed, will give up its attempt to establish the desired link, and transmit its failure to the Fault Interceptor.[10] The latter will now signal its failure to achieve the desired link, so that, at least in some subsystems, corrective action may possibly be taken by the user. (The technical meaning of signaling will be discussed in Chapter 5.)

If, as is normally the case, Directory Control locates the desired branch in the user's behalf, the segment will be made known in the user's process, whatever the access rights the user may have to it, including none at all. Subsequent reference to the target, as, for instance, through a constructed link pair, will trigger construction of the SDW with the appropriate access rights encoded therein. [Note that in the interim between make-known time and the first executed reference (through the constructed SDW) to the target, the user's access rights may well change (for better or for worse). For this reason, access faulting is delayed until the point in time of actual reference. This delay (of binding) is built in to the design at no cost to the user and can be taken advantage of by sophisticated users, who may, for example, initiate segments (cause segments to be made known, not through link faults, but rather via explicit calls to the BFS), interrogate their current access rights to

9. The mechanics of searching and locating the desired directory are examined in Chapter 6.
10. For a refresher on the role of the Fault Interceptor, refer back to Section 2.6.5. The design of this module is also detailed in the MSPM.

the target, and, if not suitable, take steps to avoid executing a reference that would result in an access fault. Chapter 6 discusses the explicit initiation of segments in some detail.]

4.2.2 Some Details on Access-Control Information

Now, to the details of access-control information. Begin by looking at a schematic of the data structure for a directory, Figure 4.2. A directory (for our purposes here) is thought of chiefly as a list of branches. Each branch is, in turn, conceptually divided into two parts, a permission list, hereafter called an access-control list (ACL), and a block of other information specific to the data of the branch, for example, where the file is located in secondary storage, its size, and so forth. A schematic of these lists is displayed in part (b) of Figure 4.2. The actual storage structure is documented in the MSPM but is of little interest to users, since their programs cannot directly access directories.

Associated with each listed user or class name [11] is information that denotes the *mode of access*, that is, read and/or write, and so on, and a *ring bracket.* The latter identifies the ring(s) from which the specified access mode is permitted. Access-control information may be altered only by the process(es) that enjoys write access privilege (W) in the directory that contains the branch to the file in question. Normally, this process is the one that has responsibility for creating the segment. A subsystem writer ssw will typically designate his own user directory as the one to hold branches for segments that he would let others have access to. Subsequently, only processes executed by ssw (or by anyone to whom ssw has given the W attribute to this segment) would have the write access mode necessary to alter branches to such segments.

Strictly speaking, a name on an access-control list in a branch is what is called a "user_id." When a user logs in, the process that is created for him and any others that may be subsequently spawned for him during the same console session are registered under a common user_id. The user_id is a concatenation of several components, the user's name, his project name, and an "instance tag" (i.e., a letter that indicates the particular incarnation of the process).

If a user is to have any access at all to a given file (segment), his user_id or a class name that includes the user_id must appear in an entry in the appropriate branch's ACL (access-control list). A search will be initiated at the

11. Access-control lists either name individual users (user_id) or *classes* of users. The coding schemes for naming classes of users is explained in the MPM, Chapter II.

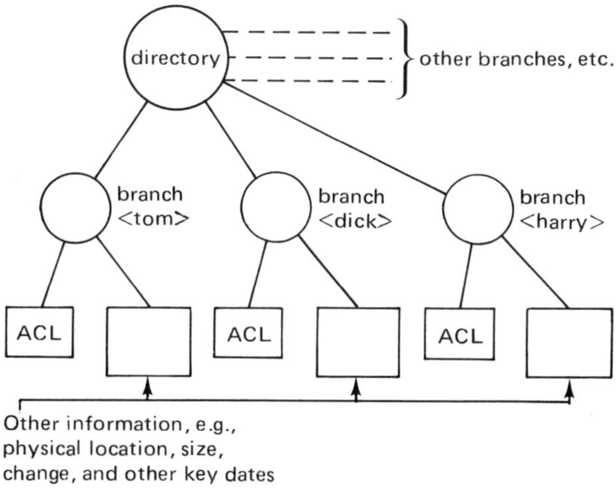

Key
ACL = access-control list for a particular branch

(a) Partial view of data structure for a directory

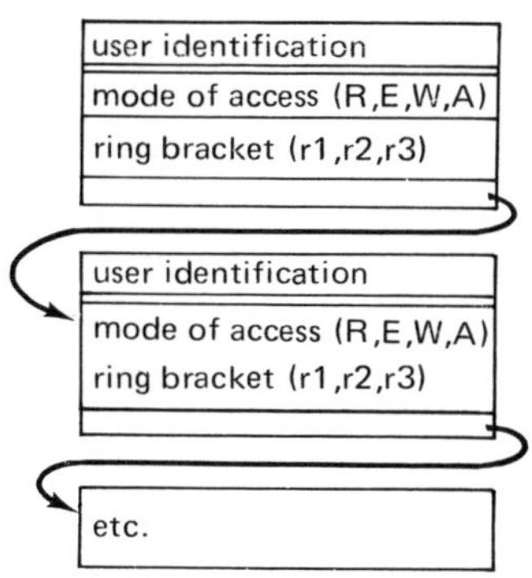

(b) Data structure of an access-control list (ACL) for an individual branch

Figure 4.2. Schematic of the directory data structure

request of the Linker in behalf of a given process with user_id as one of the arguments.

Specifically, if the search for the segment, say<tom> leads to the branch pictured in part (a) of Figure 4.2, then access will be permitted if and only if an acceptable match can be made between user_id and a corresponding user identification in an entry of the ACL for<tom>.

Usage Attributes

Codes defining the modes of access are found in the matched ACL entry. These codes, called usage attributes, determine the kind of access to be permitted this user. A module of the Basic File System called Segment Control will employ this information in setting the descriptor field when preparing the descriptor word for the segment being acquired. Segment Control is invoked in an appropriate manner when its services are needed, for example, by the Linker.

There are four usage attributes, each coded as an on-off switch. The switches are named R (for read), E (for execute), W (for write), and A (for append). Table 4.1 gives the *on* interpretation of the REWA switches in the typical case where the branch refers to a nondirectory file (as opposed to a directory file).[12] These four attributes define the so-called *effective mode* of the segment.

The important observation to make here, if you are a subsystem writer, is that two or more users may have entries on the same ACL with different effective modes. This can lead to a situation where, for example, the same unique copy of a data segment is acquired by two processes (active at the same time). One process is given read and write privileges to the segment, while the other is given only read privileges. This capability for the sharing of segments means it will be possible for certain key data and procedure segments of a subsystem to be under development (full access) by a subsystem writer while continuing to permit users of this system the appropriate, but

12. Interpretation of the switches for a *directory* file is discussed briefly in the MPM, Chapter II. Briefly: The *read* attribute must be *on* if a user wishes to examine the contents of a particular branch, e.g., to see if he is on the ACL for that branch and, if so, the type of access he has been granted.

The *execute* attribute must be *on* if a user wishes to search a directory to locate a particular named branch and if found to use the file to which it points.

The *write* attribute must be *on* if a user wishes to alter a branch, e.g., change access-control list information, or to delete the branch entirely (and its corresponding file).

The *append* attribute must be *on* if a user wishes to add a new branch to the directory (without altering existing branches).

Table 4.1 *On* Interpretation for the Four Usage Attributes in Nondirectory Files

Attribute	Code Letter	Type of Segment Implied	Type of Permission
Read	R	Data or procedure	Can read the contents
Execute	E	Procedure	Can execute as a procedure
Write	W	Normally data, occasionally procedure	Can truncate or rewrite existing contents (without increasing the length)
Append	A	Data	Can add to the segment *without* changing its current contents (Should be accompanied by the write attribute)[a]

[a] Ideally the concept of the A attribute for a data or procedure segment should be fully independent of the other attributes. Thus, to be meaningful, an A attribute should carry with it an implied write privilege in the section of the segment that is appended. The GE 645 has no hardware to support this independence. As a result, the A attribute by itself does not carry with it any write permission. For this reason, if the A attribute is given to a user of a segment, he should also be given the W attribute as well. Of course, this means that write permission is then given for the entire segment, not just for the append portion.

limited access to such segments (e.g., read only for the data and read, execute for the procedure segments).

Notice, also, that a user can have more than one process because he can have multiple project names. This means he has the possibility of giving one of his files, say segment <a>, different effective modes for his different processes, for example, under different project names, thus offering the possibility where necessary of a user "protecting himself from himself."

Recall from Chapter 1, that the GE 645 address-formation hardware has been especially designed to permit this "simultaneous" multitype use of a segment. Access to a segment is not a function of the physical location of the segment in core, but is a function of the descriptor bits set in the segment descriptor word (SDW) of the particular requesting process. These bits are, of course, independent of the segment's location. Each process sharing a given segment would have an SDW pointing at the (same) page table and each of these SDW's may be set with similar or different descriptor bits.

In summary, access-control list entries may be added, deleted, or altered by any user that is privileged to write in the directory containing the branch to a given segment. Thus, the subsystem writer that creates segments will be able to select the set of valid users for each of his segments and the type of access to be accorded each. The calls and the corresponding commands to the Basic File System for performing these ACL operations are described in the MPM in the section entitled "Standard Service System (SSS)."

4.2.3 Rings and Ring Brackets

The ring bracket found in each access-control list (ACL) entry defines the ring or bracket of rings to which the segment will belong in the process acquiring it. We initiate our discussion by considering the simple case where, for purposes of access, a segment is associated with a single ring, deferring discussion of the perhaps more general case where a bracket of rings is involved.

Figure 4.3 reviews the ring concept for grouping the segments of a process, suggesting the idea of a set of concentric rings, each ring being identified by a number, beginning with 0. Each segment of a process, data or procedure, can now be characterized by a ring number. The set of numbers 0 through 3, shown in Figure 4.3, is suggestive only. In its initial conception, there was provision in Multics for up to 32 rings for characterizing systems programs,

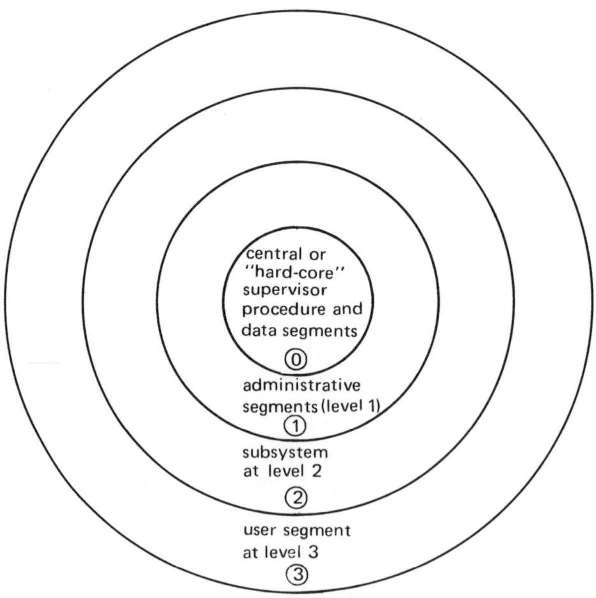

Figure 4.3. Segment groups illustrated as corresponding to a set of concentric rings

for example, central supervisor (ring 0), administrative segments (ring 1), and so on, and up to 32 rings for characterizing user-provided subsystems and other user programs and data, that is, rings 32 through 63.

The fact that up to 32 rings are available to user-designed subsystems is hardly to be construed as an urgent invitation to use them. The use of each additional ring in a subsystem can of course add to the cost of programming and execution. On the other hand, the multiring capability is available when it is needed.

Adding additional rings has the effect of creating additional segments to the process, for example, additional descriptor segments, combined linkage segments, and stack segments. Significant costs to the user will not be incurred in creating these segments. Costs will, however, mount if the required access to many of these segments is of high frequency, for example, if a short computation loop references or passes through many rings during each transit. Such costs relate to resource allocation for the "working set" of a process, a topic treated in Chapter 7 in some detail. As long as a user takes care in the design of his computation so that most of the time only two rings of the process are used, there is minimal overhead incurred.

4.2.3.1 Special Note

As actually implemented a total of only eight rings are employed. They are as follows: Rings 0 through 3 are used for supervisor and administrative segments. Rings 4 through 7 are the user rings. No special ring is needed for the exclusive use of the system library segments. These now "reside" in ring 4 along with user-created segments.

A typical user process executes in only two rings (rings 0 and 4). Some occasionally used administrative procedures execute in ring 1, and ring 3 finds occasional use to support the implementation of special subsystems. The user (e.g., subsystem designer) is free to add other rings, that is, rings 5, 6, and 7 (to his process), as he chooses.

In the remainder of this chapter the ring system is discussed as if it were used as initially conceived: namely, user segments reside only in rings $r \geqslant 32$. There is, of course, no loss in generality resulting from this (editorial) decision.

4.2.3.2 Student-Teacher Subsystem Example

When more than one user ring is needed, two rings will usually suffice. As an example, a student-teacher subsystem, such as the one mentioned in Section 4.1.2, would probably require no more than two user rings.

A number of teacher-student schemes can be devised. Here is one relatively simple kind that might be used for grading of student-prepared procedures. Let us suppose teacher X has assigned the students in his math class the task of programming a certain subroutine called <sub_stu_id>, where stu_id is any unique character string mutually agreed to by teacher and student.

Imagine that prior to the due date for this homework assignment, each student will have placed a tested version of <sub_stu_id> in X's user directory, ready to be graded. After the due date, X's grading program would systematically execute calls to each of the various <sub_stu_id>s found in X's user directory. The teacher program would somehow compare observed performance, for example, computed results, run time, and so forth, with certain preestablished norms as a means of evaluating the student's work.

If <sub_stu_id> and the teacher's grading program belong to the same ring, there is no foolproof way to prevent the student's procedure from damaging the teacher's segments. In this situation, a clever student might be able to help himself to an A! Thus, upon being called, <sub_stu_id> might be so written as to inspect the stack frame of the caller (the teacher) and from this information figure out a way to call on the caller, that is, study the teacher's grading program, and determine what the right answer should be.

Here is one of several ways to prevent costly damage to the teacher's subsystem. Assume that teacher X has previously "paved the way" for each student in the class to move his <sub_stu_id> to X's user directory. To get his homework graded, each student will move his own tested version of <sub_stu_id> into X's user directory on or before the due date. Before grading each <sub_stu_id>, now in X's own directory, the teacher's program makes two crucial alterations to the branch for each student's <sub_stu_id>, via the setacl command. (The teacher can do this, since he has write access to his own directory.)

1. In every ACL entry he deletes write access (so that neither the student author nor any "friend" of his can sneak in a change to the program after the due date and before the work is graded).
2. He creates an ACL entry for himself (teacher_id) with read, execute access rights and—here is the crucial point—with a number 33 as the ring number for this segment. When the teacher program later executes <sub_stu_id> in performing the grading, it will execute as a ring-33 procedure. In this way <sub_stu_id> would not be able to gain illegal control of or inspect the teacher's segment.

Here are two details omitted in the foregoing description:

1. The teacher "paves the way" for the student to move his <sub_stu_id>

by using the file-system command

create (See the MPM, Standard Service System, for details.)

2. The student moves his files when he chooses to by using the file-system command

moveb (See the MPM, Standard Service System, for details.)

These two steps must occur in sequence. Unless the teacher has created a properly named branch for each <sub_stu_id> (which, incidentally, he can do), a student may find he cannot successfully execute the moveb command.

4.2.4 A Guide to the Ring Assignment of Segments

Two general principles should be kept in mind when deciding on the appropriate ring(s) for the key segments of a process.

1. The Need to Know

A procedure <a> should have access only to those procedures and data segments necessary for <a> to do its task. Moreover, <a> should only have the mode of access to these same segments that is actually required (e.g., read, but not write, read-write, but not append, etc.). Graham's paper draws the analogy with a military system of clearance. The higher the clearance (the lower the ring number) the more documents one may have access to—and the fewer the number of individuals (segments) that are to be afforded such clearance.

2. Degrees of Likely Damage

If the segments of a subsystem can be effectively segregated according to the damage that may be wrought when these segments are misused, there may be good reason for compartmentalizing the segments into two or more rings. Those segments whose misuse is likely to cause the greatest damage would be accorded the lower ring numbers. The advantage gained by placing a procedure in an inner ring is easily nullified however, if insufficient care is given to the coding of it. A procedure that can cause extensive damage when improperly called can accomplish comparable damage if it malfunctions of "its own accord." For this reason one sometimes speaks about inner-ring procedures as needing to be more *trustworthy*. As a matter of fact, they aren't going to be more trustworthy simply by assigning them a low ring number, I'll attempt to explain what is meant by trustworthiness. In one subsystem we are given two procedures, <a32>[13] in ring 32 and <b33> in ring 33. We hope that the

13. By this unofficial naming scheme I hope to simplify the discussions. By appending "32" to "a" I hope unambiguously to suggest "<a> in ring 32."

likelihood that <a32> will misbehave by improperly calling a procedure in ring 33 *is less* than the likelihood that <b33> will improperly call on a procedure in ring 32. To the extent that this relationship is true (and is significant), we can say that <a32> is more trustworthy than <b33> and that one is justified in making the ring separations (and incurring some ring-crossing overhead) to protect a (debugged) <a32> from improper calls from <b33>. If damage does result from an improper call, we prefer that it happen in an outer ring where the damaged segments will affect the fortunes of fewer users or user groups. Note that if the tables were turned and the less trustworthy (poorly debugged) program were given a lower ring number, the purpose of the ring structure would be defeated altogether, and the user would merely inherit extra overhead for his troubles.

By the same reasoning, a more trustworthy low-ring-number procedure is less likely to misuse a given data segment to which it makes reference (read, write, or append) than will a higher ring-number procedure. The lower the ring number of a referenced data segment, the more universal is the damage likely to be when it is misused.

For the benefit of those who might be designing a multiring subsystem, our discussion thus far can be summarized by three rules (essentially axioms) that are enforced by the system. I preface these rules with the following remark:

I shall often speak of a procedure as "residing in ring *j*," or as "executing in ring *j*." What I have in mind is the notion that every executing process has a state variable known as the *current ring number*. Conceivably, this variable could be implemented as a special hardware register. If, for instance, the procedure <s33> were to transfer control (call or return) to <t32>, the "ring register" that holds the current ring number is pictured as being updated from 33 to 32. Prior to the transfer <s33> resides (or executes) in ring 33. After the transfer, <t32> resides in ring 32.

Rule 1. A procedure "residing" in ring number *j* should have the liberty to call any procedure segment residing in ring number *j* or in any ring number greater than *j*. The same procedure should also be permitted to make references to data segments (read, write, or append), as permitted by the effective mode of the particular data segment, provided the ring number of the data segment is *j* or greater.[14] The data and procedure segments in rings *j*,

14. The damage caused by misuse of a data segment is apt to be more localized the higher the ring number of that data segment. Note that if a procedure can be trusted to use a data segment in its own ring *j*, it can certainly be allowed to make references to data segments in rings higher than *j*.

$j + 1 \ldots$, are said to be the *domain of access* for a procedure segment in ring j.

Rule 2. A procedure residing in ring j should either be denied the privilege of calling a procedure in a ring numbered i less than j (inward call), or else this access should be limited, that is, controlled in some careful way.

Rule 3. The same procedure residing in ring j should never be given access to data segments having ring numbers less than j.

4.2.5 Ways to Recognize an Attempted Ring Crossing

If the ring model is to be implemented, it must be possible to detect and control each ring crossing that represents an inward call. In Section 4.3 you will see that other types of legal ring crossings must also be detected and controlled, for example, *outward calls*, to make inner arguments accessible to called procedures in outer rings, *inward returns* from outward calls, for similar reasons, and even *outward returns*.

From a design point of view, we would like all of this detection mechanism to occur "under the surface." At least the unsophisticated user should not need to be aware of the mechanism that causes the combined hardware and supervisory software intervention at ring crossings. Certainly no special coding should be required when he, for example, executes a call to a system or subsystem procedure that happens to reside in an inner ring.

Ways could possibly be found by software alone to check for ring crossings on all calls and returns. Thus, the system could operate entirely in the interpretive mode. This plan has been rejected as being too expensive as a general solution. Alternatively, the standard call and return sequences could be expanded by introducing additional ring-related arguments. This would prove costly enough in execution-time overhead. But, how would other, strictly illegal inter-ring references be prevented by software alone?

The use of special hardware facilities that could detect all cross-ring activities as faults and that would then trap to a special supervisory routine, is the only feasible approach. This is the approach used in Multics. The routine to which trapping is accomplished is called the Gatekeeper.

4.2.6 Two Hardware Approaches That Have Been Designed

Using current GE 645 hardware, the protection mechanism is achieved by having the supervisor maintain separate copies of the descriptor segment *for each ring used*. The per-ring descriptor segments differ only in the access-control bits of corresponding segment descriptor words. If we were to look, say, at the descriptor segment for ring j, we would see that special fault-inducing access-control bits are *preset* (by the Basic File System) in SDWs that point to segments of other rings $k \neq j$. One type of fault "detects" cross-ring references to procedure and data segments of *inner* rings. Another type of fault detects references to procedures residing in *outer* rings.

A more efficient scheme has been proposed for a future implementation of Multics wherein the need for multiple copies of the descriptor segment and the need for wall-crossing faults on inner-ring calls would be eliminated. Part of the proposal depends on altering the GE 645 hardware in the following way: First, a (six-bit) ring register would be added to the set of registers (on each processor) referred to as the "machine conditions." The ring register would at all times hold the ring number for the currently executing procedure segment. Next, the format of the segment descriptor word (SDW) would then be revised (or augmented) to include ring-number identification for the segment coded in the SDW. A new type of hardware faulting would occur when the address-formation mechanism, upon reaching the SDW, detects certain kinds of ring crossing based on a comparison between the contents of the ring register and the coded ring number in the SDW.

Section 4.3 gives a more detailed explanation of ring-crossing detection. The discussion is based entirely on current hardware.

4.2.7 Access and Call Brackets—Motivation

The simple ring model so far described is fine for protection, but it is, in fact, too good! The model implies that every segment of a process be associated with a single and fixed ring number. Two consequences of this simplicity turn out to be too restrictive. In order to circumvent each of these restrictions, when necessary, the Multics ring model has been made a bit more complicated.

4.2.7.1 The First Restriction

Consider a service routine that would be made available for use by ordinary user and supervisor alike. Suppose a single ring number is assigned to this routine. It would appear that either the supervisor or the user would invoke a ring-crossing fault[15] in calling this service routine, even if the model used only two rings. Now, whatever overhead is involved in executing this ring crossing (and these details are explained in Section 4.3) seems unnecessary. A service routine (or at least *some* service routines) can certainly be designed to take calls from segments in a wide class of rings, because it can be written as a pure procedure, that is, with write access to it prohibited. Hence, there is no

15. Strictly speaking, it is also possible to avoid these ring crossings by making multiple copies of each service routine, one copy assigned to each ring in which a call to that routine is made. This approach has not been taken in Multics.

reason why such a routine should be subject to damage or should cause any damage during its normal use. Extension of the model to three or more rings only strengthens the argument. It would, therefore, seem worthwhile if use of such service routines could be "exempt" from the ring-crossing overhead. The solution arrived at in Multics is to let each segment be optionally characterized by an *access bracket* instead of a single ring. The bracket constitutes a *band* of rings such that when a reference is made to one of these segments (data or procedure) from a procedure whose ring number is *within* the access bracket, no ring crossing faults are invoked (manifesting the fact that no protection is needed). A procedure called in this way will *execute in the ring of its caller*. All PL/I library routines are of this type, for example.

4.2.7.2 The Second Restriction

It is easy enough to prevent outright any outer-ring procedure from calling any inner-ring procedure, since a ring-crossing fault will be induced in the attempt, and the fault handler can then declare the caller "guilty." The real challenge is to provide a suitable screening methodology so that some inward crossings can be regarded as legal, possibly subject to some further checks, while other inward crossing attempts can be rejected as truly illegal. This type of control, for example, may be found necessary in the design of subsystems that have two or more classes of users, each being forced to write code that, when compiled, is executed in a distinct ring. Class A users, for example, whose associated ring number is r_A, might be permitted controlled access to a certain set of subsystem procedures via inward wall crossings, while Class B users whose associated ring number is $r_B > r_A$ would be prevented any access (at all) to the same set of procedures. To achieve this level of control over inward calls in Multics, it is possible to associate with any procedure, when needed, a *call bracket*, representing a band of rings immediately outside the access bracket. The call bracket of a segment <a> would identify the rings from which a calling procedure <b> is permitted to call <a> via an inward ring crossing. If <b> executes in a ring outside the call bracket, the fault handler rejects the call as illegal. If <b> executes in a ring within the call bracket, the fault handler will consider the call to be potentially OK and will then, before accepting the call as legal, perform a further check to be sure the target address is a specially declared entry point in <a>, called a *gate*. The concept of gates will be discussed in Section 4.3.

Figure 4.4 summarizes the foregoing ring-bracket concepts. The hypothetical case is considered for a target procedure <a> whose access bracket is rings 32, 33 and whose call bracket is rings 34, 35.

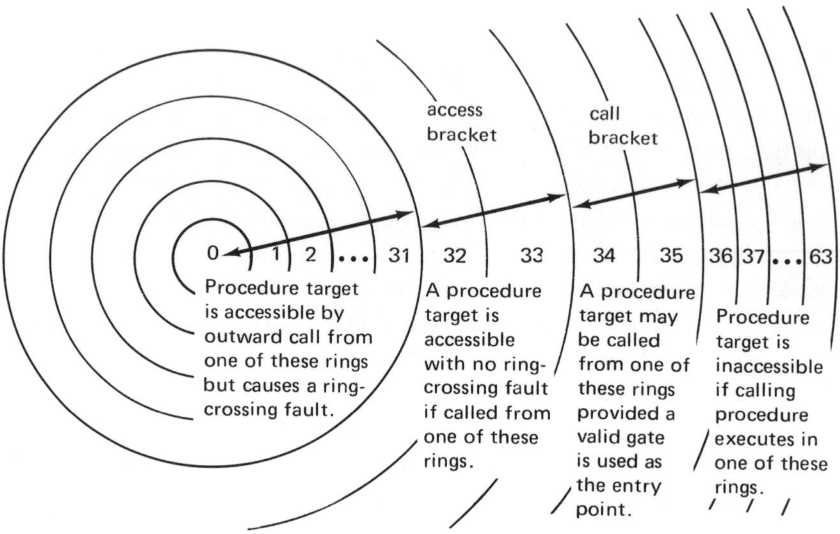

Figure 4.4. Access to a procedure target <a>. The target's access bracket is (32, 33), and call bracket is (34, 35)

4.2.7.3 Access Bracket–Details

In place of a single ring k, any data or procedure segment may be optionally characterized by the band of rings from k to l, where $0 \leqslant k \leqslant l \leqslant 63$. The band is represented by the pair (k, l), and is called the access bracket. Ring-crossing faults occur only when the ring of the executing procedure lies outside the access bracket of the target segment. The intended access discipline, (a) for procedure targets and (b) for data targets, is spelled out below and summarized in Table 4.2. For this discussion imagine that some procedure, whose ring number is r, is making an attempted reference to a target segment. One speaks of the referencing procedure as *executing in ring r*.

(a) For target procedure segments characterized by the access bracket (k, l), and having no call bracket the following is to be true:

1. A referencing procedure executing in a ring $r \leqslant l$ has what can be called "ring access" to the target. This means that actual access is governed by the effective mode of the particular target. Cross-ring (outward) faults are induced and detected in these instances only when $r < k$.

2. Access to the target is completely denied to any procedure whose ring lies outside the access bracket of the target, that is, which has ring number $r > l$.

Table 4.2 Access Discipline for Procedure and Data Targets
Key:
Referencing procedure executes in ring r
Target has effective mode = REWA
access bracket = (k, l)

Target Type	$r < k$	$r = k$	$k + 1 \leqslant r \leqslant l$	$r > l$
Procedure	REWA (but ring-crossing fault is induced)	REWA	REWA	~~REWA~~ (all access denied; segment fault is induced)
Data	REWA	REWA	RE~~WA~~ (write access denied)	~~REWA~~ (all access denied; segment fault is induced)

Directed faults, interpreted as *all access denied*, are detected in all instances where $r > l$.

(b) For target data segments having an access bracket (k, l), the interpretation is quite different:

1. A referencing procedure executing in a ring $r \leqslant k$ will have access to the target governed entirely by the target's effective mode. No ring-crossing faults will be induced during an outward data reference from a ring $r < k$.

2. Procedures referencing the target from rings $k + 1, k + 2, \ldots, l - 1, l$ will have access restricted. No writing in this segment will be allowed by the executing procedure even if the W bit in the effective mode is *on*.

3. Procedures attempting to make data reference to the target from rings $l + 1, l + 2, \ldots, 63$ will be denied all access. Directed faults are detected in all instances where $r > l$. For example, if <data> has the access bracket (35, 38), and if the effective mode for <data> is RW (i.e., read and write), procedures executing in rings with $r \leqslant 35$ will be permitted to read and write in <data>, procedures executing in rings 36, 37, and 38 will be permitted read-only privileges in <data>, while all access to <data> will be denied to any procedure executing in rings 39 through 63.

4.2.7.4 Call Brackets–Details

A *call bracket* may be added to the *access bracket* in characterizing any procedure segment (but not a data segment). If the pair (k, l) is the access bracket, then the additional call bracket is, for economy of coding, characterized by a third number m, such that $l < m \leqslant 63$. The call bracket is then the band of one or more rings from $l + 1$ to m, inclusive. Ring-crossing faults occur whenever the ring of the executing procedure is within the call bracket of the target, and segment faults occur when the ring of the executing procedure r, exceeds m, that is, lies outside the call bracket.

The intended access discipline here is as follows: As before, target data or procedure segments are accessible (without induced ring-crossing faults) to any procedures or data segments whose ring number lies within the access bracket. Target *data* segments are entirely inaccessible to procedures whose ring numbers are greater than the access bracket. Access to target *procedure* segments *may* be permitted if the referencing procedure's ring number lies in the target's call bracket, that is, if $l < r \leq m$. Permission is granted in such cases only if the entry point has been established as a gate for inward calls. Gates are specially declared. When the segment's author declares a given entry point to be a gate, the compiler or assembler would then provide an entry in the linkage section having a nonstandard but recognizable format. The Gatekeeper that handles the wall-crossing fault for this case determines whether the faulting procedure has, in fact, been aimed at a gate of the target procedure by examining the format of the entry point. The storage structure of gates is detailed in Section 4.3.6.

4.2.7.5 Ring Brackets—Examples

A ring bracket[16] is recorded in the branch for each segment. It consists of a 3-tuple of numbers. The form of the 3-tuple depends on the ring characterization for the segment, as shown in the following list.

Ring Characterization	Form of the 3-tuple
a. Single ring of access, r.	(r, r, r)
b. An access bracket (k, l), but no call bracket.	(k, l, l)
c. An access bracket (k, l) and a call bracket $(l + 1, m)$.	(k, l, m)
d. A single ring of access r and a call bracket $(r + 1, m)$	(r, r, m)

Some typical uses of ring brackets for system routines and possible data segments are illustrated in Table 4.3. The examples should help you see how ring brackets would be used in characterizing user-created segments.

Figure 4.5 gives pictorial interpretation for two additional ring brackets (1, 1, 1) and (0, 1, 1). What is the ring-bracket characterization for (the rather exotic case of) <a> in Figure 4.4? Answer: (32, 33, 35).

16. The ring bracket is copied from the ACL entry in the file branch at the time the segment is first acquired by the process and subsequently kept in a more accessible per-process table called the KST (Known Segment Table).

Table 4.3 Examples of Ring Brackets Used in the System

Item	Ring Bracket	Effective Mode	Interpretation
1	0,63,63	RE	Every procedure has access to this segment without invoking a ring-crossing fault (target executes in ring of its caller).
2	0,1,63	RE	Procedures in rings 0 and 1 can call without intervention. Procedures in rings 2 through 63 can call via inward ring-crossing fault, but desired entry point must be a gate.
3	1,1,63	RE	A ring-1[a] procedure that may be called as in item 2 from rings 2 through 63.
4	0,0,1	RE	A ring-0 routine. Inward calls are permitted from ring 1 via ring-crossing fault, etc. Calls from rings 2 through 63 are rejected.
5	48,48,48	RW	Data that is RW in rings 0 through 48.
6	5,48,48	RW	Data that is RW in rings 0 through 5 but R only in rings 6 through 48 inclusive.

[a] A point of possible interest is that ring-0 routines may not execute outward calls. Hence if the target has a ring bracket (1,1,63), a ring-0 routine cannot call it directly.

By convention, system-supplied routines, for example, library routines and commands, are given ring brackets of the form $(k, l, 48)$, that is, they are made inaccessible from rings greater than 48. Subsystem designers can take advantage of this convention. They can, for instance, design portions of the subsystem to execute in rings with $r \leqslant 48$. These portions are therefore privileged to use the system routines. whereas restricted users of the same subsystem, whose procedures execute in rings with $r > 48$, would not be able to use these routines. Thus, in a student/teacher subsystem, a student's program executing in ring 49 would, for instance, be "walled off" from, or prevented from using, a system-supplied subroutine, say <cosine>, but might be permitted to use one specially supplied by the teacher.

4.3 Monitoring and Controlling Ring Crossings for Normal Calls and Returns

We are now ready to see how ring access control has been implemented in Multics. First, three important implementation concepts are amplified. (1) A process can have, if necessary, up to 64 rings; user rings are numbered 32 through 63. (2) For each ring in which a process executes there is actually a

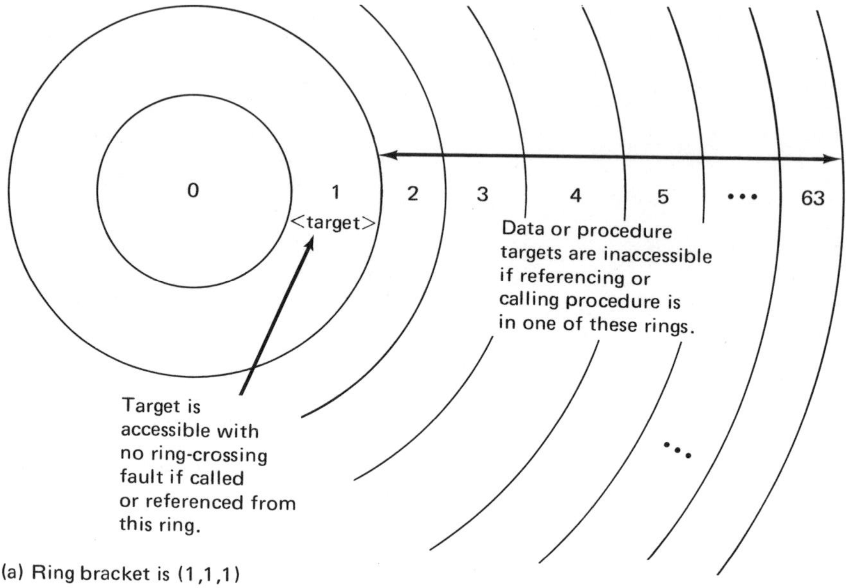

(a) Ring bracket is (1,1,1)

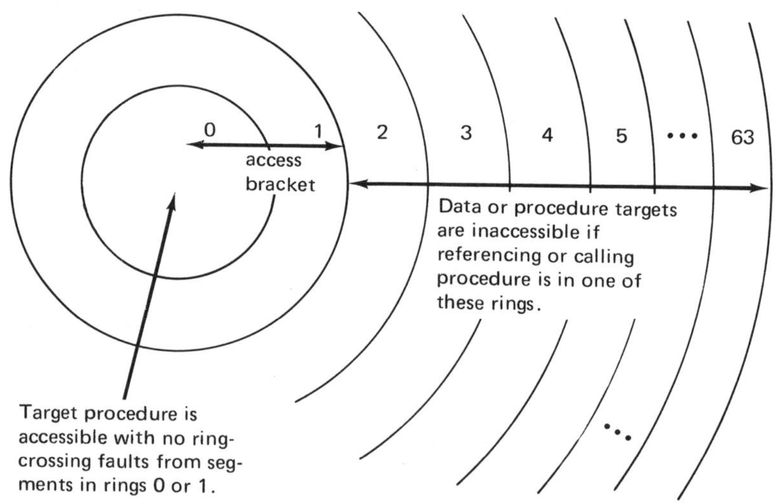

(b) Ring bracket is (0,1,1)

Figure 4.5. Access to a target procedure or data segment

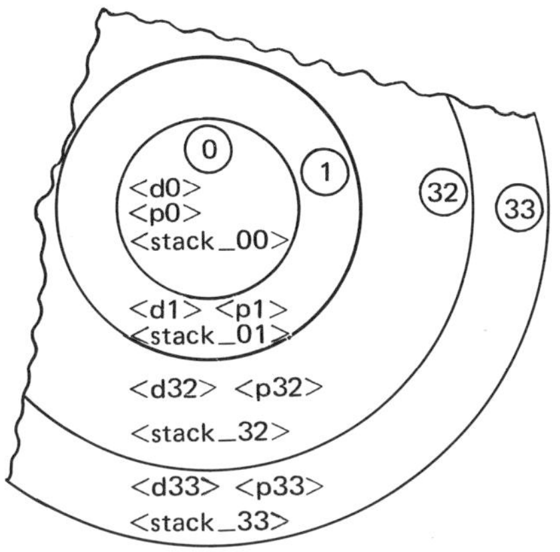

Figure 4.6. A process in miniature (in four rings)

separate descriptor segment. Ring-0 supervisory routines create and maintain these segments as needed.[17] The per-ring descriptor segments differ only in the way fault-inducing bit patterns are placed in the descriptors. The bit patterns are set so as to trap during address formation on all inward data references and on all inward or outward procedure references. (3) There is also a separate stack segment, called <stack_*n*>, created for each ring in which the process executes. Here, *n* is one of the integers 0 through 63 (or, strictly speaking, 00, 01, . . . , 63). Supervisory routines are responsible for creating these stack segments,[18] but once created they are to be treated as ordinary data segments.

4.3.1 Function of the Individual Descriptor Segment

To show how the individual descriptor segments serve in the role of ring-crossing detectors a (hypothetical) process in miniature suggested by Figure 4.6 will be discussed. There are four ordinary data segments <d0>, <d1>, <d32>, and <d33> and four procedure segments <p0>, <p1>, <p32>, and <p33>, one of each in each of the four utilized rings 0, 1, 32, and 33. Also shown are the four stack segments, which, in matters of protection, are to be considered as ordinary data segments. The four descriptor segments are not shown because these are not directly accessible to the user. The use of two

17. Chapter 6 gives an elaboration adequate for initial needs of the subsystem writer. Of course, subsystem and user procedures for ring $i > 0$ will be allowed no direct access to any descriptor segment.

18. Details of stack-segment creation may be found in appropriate sections of the MSPM.

user rings is purely for illustrative purposes and is not to be construed as typical.

Figure 4.7 is a detailed view of access-control bits 30–35 for one of the descriptor segments (ring 32), showing how they could be coded in each SDW so as to detect ring crossings.[19] Dashed lines emanating from the SDWs indicate ring crossings that are detected, causing traps to the Fault Interceptor module. Inward crossings, for example, line ① to an inner-ring procedure, <p0>, or line ② to an inner-ring data segment, <d1>, cause directed faults.[20] Outward crossings to procedures, for example, line number ③ to an outer-ring procedure <p33>, are detected by attempt-to-execute-data faults. To achieve this type of fault, bits 33–35 for <p33> are preset to suggest data. Subsequent attempts to execute an instruction fetch will then cause a fault that forces control to the Fault Interceptor. Outward references to data segments are deliberately not detected, for example, lines ④ and ⑤ to the outer-ring data segment <d33> and to <stack_33>, respectively.

Figure 4.8 shows all four descriptor segments of the process ordered by ring number. Bit details of the descriptor fields in the SDWs are now replaced by schematic markings. Note that the order in which the segments are listed in each descriptor segment of the process must be the same, in order that each segment retains the same segment number from ring to ring. The particular ordering of the segments within the descriptor segment is, however, of little concern to us. Postpone until Chapter 6 any curiosity you may develop as to how and when these access-control bit-fields are preset in the various descriptor segments; such knowledge is not needed now.

This is a good time to observe why, for simplicity, it was chosen not to display SDWs for the procedures' linkage segments in the above example. Recall that entry points to procedures are kept in the corresponding linkage segment. If there is to be a change of rings in a procedure call, the ring crossing must be accomplished while executing the transfer instruction used to reach the target's linkage segment (entry point). For this reason, the ring bracket for a linkage segment is always identical with its corresponding "text" segment. Subsequent transfer from the linkage segment to the target pure procedure would never cause a ring crossing. We see, therefore, that Figure 4.8 could have been made to appear more realistic, but not too much more illuminating, if SDWs had been included for the linkage segments. They

19. For a refresher on the hardware characteristics, first review pertinent parts of Chapter 1 of this guide, especially Table 1.1.

20. Strictly speaking, two types of directed faults are used. More about the distinction between these is given later in this section.

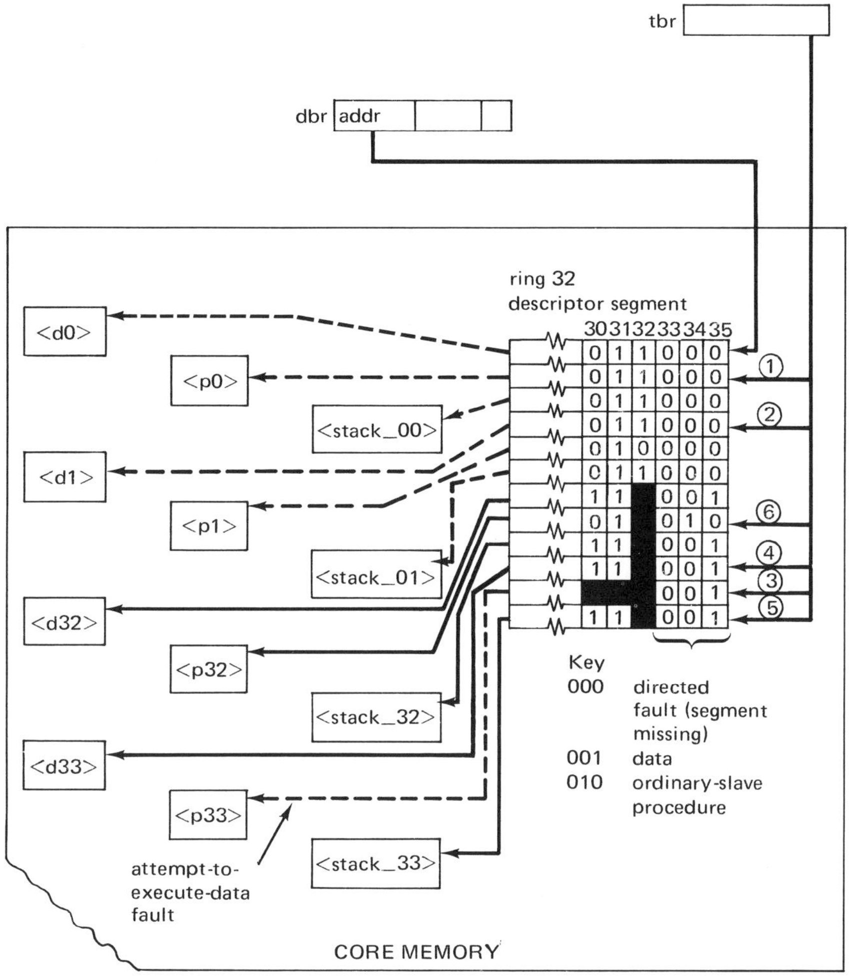

Figure 4.7. Using the descriptor segment as a ring-crossing detector
Consult Table 1.1 for a refresher on the significance of descriptor bits 30–35.

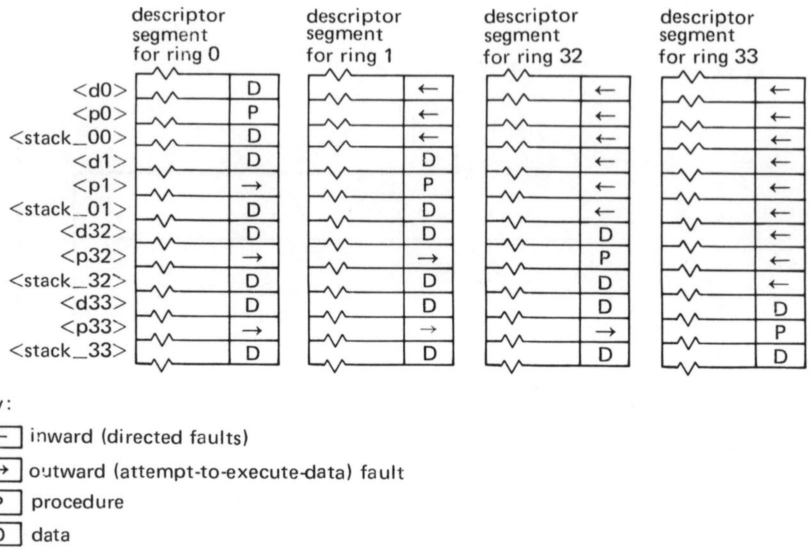

Figure 4.8. All four descriptor segments

would be given schematic markings identical with those of their corresponding procedure segments.

An actual crossing over from one ring to another will take place only if a master-mode supervisory routine (in ring 0) is called to execute the privileged instructions necessary to "switch" descriptor segments, that is, alter the contents of the descriptor base register (dbr) to point it at the descriptor segment of the target ring. Responsibility for calling this dbr-switching routine rests with the Gatekeeper. This is the module described in Section 4.3.2 that takes charge as a result of all attempted ring crossings.

There is no possibility that a user can either write his own master-mode routine to switch dbr values or manage somehow to gain direct access to the routine that does the dbr switching and thereby circumvent the Gatekeeper. The following paragraph explains why.

Recall that master mode is characterized by a bit that is set in the SDW for that procedure. Master-mode routines must be ring 0 because the Basic File System module (Segment Control) that is responsible for setting SDW words will set the master-mode bit *on* for ring-0 procedures only. Moreover, no user is able to create files that have ring brackets that include ring 0. This is because the request to set an ACL entry, which is aimed at the access-control module of the Basic File System, is screened. The lowest ring-bracket value that can be posted by a user is the ring number from which his request to set an ACL entry is issued. This value is always greater than zero.

4.3.1.1 Ring Complexity of Subsystems

It is hard to say how often a subsystem will be designed to execute in more than one user ring. Two prime examples (or types) have been recognized. The teacher/student subsystem, already mentioned, is one of these. The other type arises in subsystems in which there is service to be rendered that involves access to a data base that must be operated on in a protected-ring environment. Subsystem users would gain access to the data base whose ring brackets might be (r, r, r), only by calling inward to a ring r "caretaker" procedure whose call bracket includes r. Even for such systems, it is a safe bet that most segments written for the user rings will be characterized by single-ring ring brackets. Rarely will access and call brackets be employed and even more rarely will complicated patterns of access and call brackets be used. Since this facility is available, however, there will always be some subsystem designers that, if only to satisfy their curiosity, will want to understand how more-exotically protected segments might function in a Multics subsystem. The next two subsections are dedicated to these avid readers. Others may wish to skip directly to the Gatekeeper (Section 4.3.2).

4.3.1.2[21] Determining the Ring of Execution for a Segment Whose Ring Bracket Contains an Access Bracket

A good question to ask is, In which of the rings within a segment's access bracket will a particular segment execute when it is called? There are three cases to be considered. Assume that <a> is the calling procedure now executing in ring r, and that <b> is to be the called or target procedure whose ring bracket is (k, l, m) such that $0 \leqslant k < l < m \leqslant 63$.

Case 1. $k \leqslant r \leqslant l$. (The ring of the calling procedure lies within the access bracket of the target procedure.) *Procedure <b> will execute in ring r.* No ring-crossing fault will be triggered.

Case 2. $r < k$. (Outward fault. The ring of the faulting procedure is less than k.) *Procedure <b> will execute in ring k*, the innermost ring of the target's access bracket. The design rationale for this choice is necessarily arbitrary: Pick the ring "nearest to the caller."

Case 3. $l < r \leqslant m$. (Inward fault. The ring of the faulting procedure lies within the call bracket of <b>.) *Procedure <b> will execute in ring l*, the outermost ring of the target's access bracket. (Of course, the desired entry point must

21. This section may be skipped during a first reading without loss of continuity.

also be found to have the format of a gate.) The design rationale for this choice is again, Pick the ring nearest the caller, because it is also the ring that will involve the least risk.

If used properly, access brackets may increase the flexibility and efficiency of an otherwise complicated multiring subsystem by avoiding the overhead of ring-crossing faults where protection measures are no longer needed. However, there are some pitfalls. If access brackets are not chosen to be functionally meaningful, *superfluous* ring-crossing faults can occur. Thus, the unwise subsystem designer could, in practice, select a set of *straddling* rather than *coinciding* access brackets for procedures that must communicate with one another. The superfluous fault that can occur in such instances is an inward fault, and, if unexpected, the supervisor would have no choice but to abort the process.

The following case will illustrate what happens when the access-bracket facility is improperly (nonsensically) applied. The case is for an elaborate subsystem having segments with ring brackets as shown below.

Segment	*Ring Bracket*	
<super>	(32, 32, 32)	
<a>	(33, 34, 36)	Note: Access brackets for
<b>	(34, 35, 36)	<a> and <b> straddle one another.
<slave>	(36, 36, 36)	

Figure 4.9 schematically illustrates the SDWs for each of these four segments in the descriptor segments for rings 32 through 36. (The descriptor key for this figure is an expansion of the one given in Figure 4.8. The significance of the new symbol (⇐) is explained in a subsequent paragraph.)

Now, consider the four "case histories" shown in Figure 4.10 referring to Figure 4.9 and the given ring brackets. Each case is a possible chain of two calls among the segments.

In case histories (1) and (3) we see calls from <a> to <b>. An outward fault occurs in the first history because <a> happens to be executing in ring 33 rather than 34. A similar situation arises in comparing case histories (2) and (4) where calls from <b> to <a> occur. In the latter history an inward fault occurs because <b> happens to be executing in ring 35 and not 34. If the subsystem designer has failed to anticipate this event by declaring the proper entry point in <a> as a gate, the resulting fault can actually be fatal to the process.

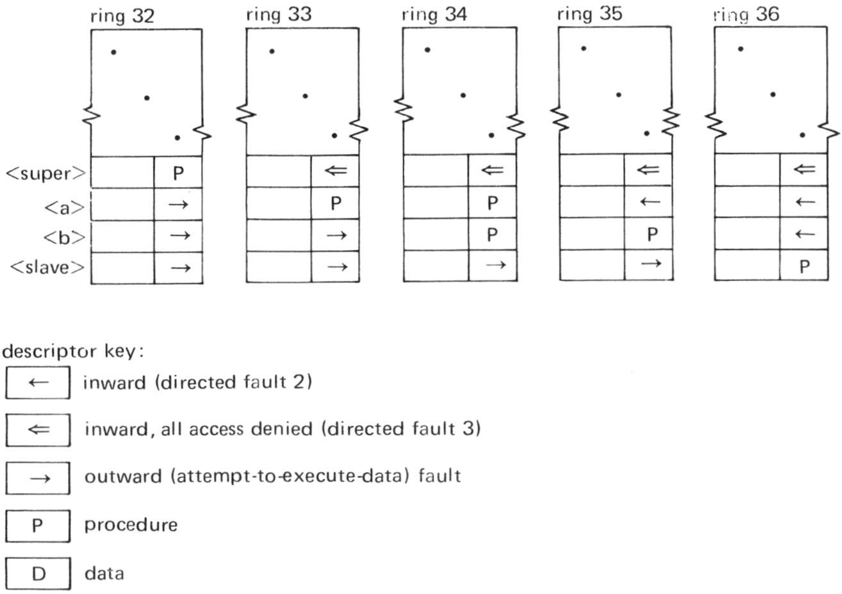

Figure 4.9. Illustration of segment descriptor words for segments having access brackets
Access bracket for <a> is (33, 34), and for <b> it is (34, 35).

4.3.1.3[22] More Details in the Interpretation of the (All Access Denied) Directed Fault

There are, in fact, two types of directed-fault codes used to represent attempted inward crossings, *directed fault 2* and *directed fault 3*. The former, when detected, corresponds to a possibly valid inward call or inward return, as from a procedure whose ring number is within the target's call bracket. The latter, when detected, is interpreted by the Fault Interceptor to mean *all access denied*. This type of inward crossing, by being handled via a separate fault, can be rejected out of hand. The overhead of incurring the Gatekeeper's services to interpret this illegality is thereby avoided. In Figure 4.9 the special symbol ⇐ was introduced to mean directed fault 3 (i.e., all access denied); henceforth the symbol ← will mean, specifically, directed fault 2.

The Basic File System will set all-access-denied faults in data-segment SDWs of higher ring-numbered descriptor segments only when actual references to such targets are attempted for the first time. (Prior to that, the

22. This section may be skipped during a first reading without loss of continuity.

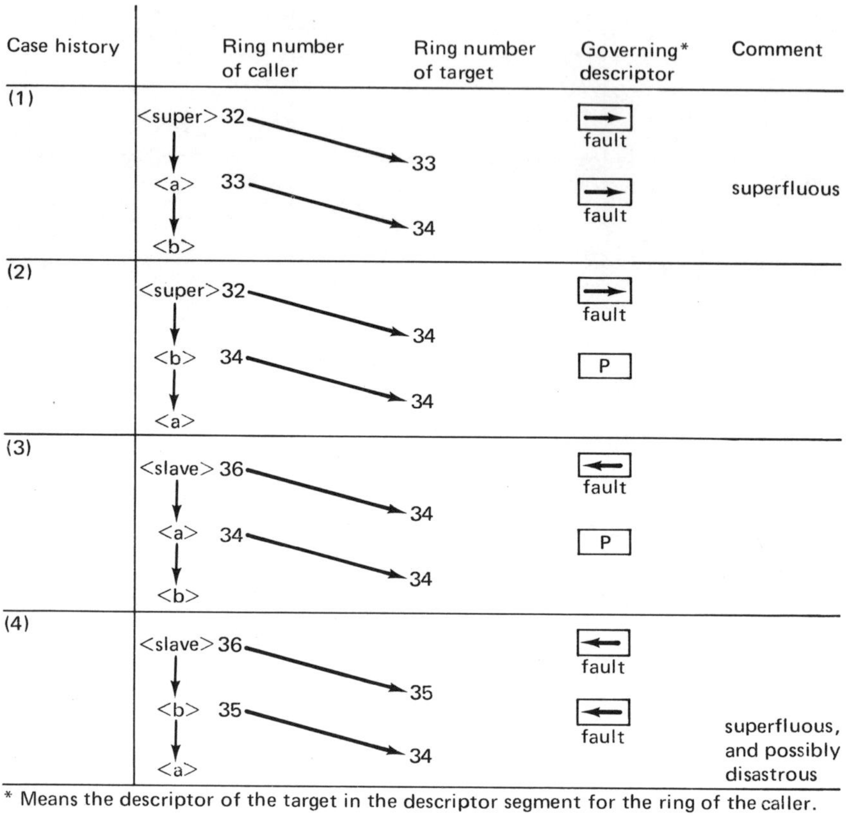

Figure 4.10. Cases of superfluous ring-crossing faults
Cases (1) and (4) show calls between segments whose access brackets straddle one another.

SDWs will have been preset to zero and interpreted as missing segments.) For illustrative purposes (only) the bit coding employed in Figure 4.7 to represent the SDWs for <d0>, <stack_00>, <d1>, and <stack_01> assumes that references to these segments from ring 32 have already been attempted. The same (rather unlikely) assumption was made in displaying the SDW for <p0>, while for <p1>, the SDW was displayed as directed fault 2 on the assumption that <p1>'s call bracket included ring 32.

4.3.2 Management Control over Inter-Ring Crossing (The Gatekeeper)

The Fault Interceptor calls a special ring-0 module, called the *Gatekeeper*, to exercise positive control over all inter-ring calls and returns. An understanding of the Gatekeeper's role and of some of the detailed steps that it carries out or oversees can be very useful to the sophisticated subsystem writer who may want to consider designing a multiring subsystem. I shall attempt to describe most of the important points about the Gatekeeper's tasks but will not always explain them in the order they are carried out. I am more concerned with motivating and explaining the issues of "gatekeeping." Succeeding subsections are divided arbitrarily into a discussion of problems faced by the Gatekeeper and how they are solved.

To make its tasks easier the Gatekeeper first determines which of five types of inter-ring accesses ("wall crossings") is being attempted. The five categories are

a. inward calls,
b. outward returns,
c. outward calls,
d. inward returns,
e. other access attempts (illegal).

The five-way resolution is relatively simple to achieve. The details are the following:

1. Inward versus outward ring-crossing attempts are actually distinguished by the Fault Interceptor. Depending upon the type of fault (directed fault 2 or attempt-to-execute-data fault), the control is directed to one of two appropriate entries into the Gatekeeper, one for inward attempts, one for outward attempts.
2. Calls versus returns are distinguished by examining the faulting instruction to see if it was a tra (call) or an rtcd (return). If neither, it is an illegal request and the Gatekeeper returns an error code to its caller, the Fault Interceptor. If the faulting instruction (on an inward crossing) is a tra, but if after check-

ing the target's linkage section, the Gatekeeper sees that the entry is not a gate, another error code is returned to the Fault Interceptor.[23]

4.3.2.1 Outward versus Inward Calls—Motivation

Compared with inward calls, outward calls, so experience has thus far shown, have limited but important application. Outward calls are used chiefly (as a practical means) for getting a computation started in some desired outer ring so that, for purposes of protection, subsequent execution may appear to originate from that ring. For this objective, outward calls require no arguments (and indeed the current implementation of Multics does not support the passing of arguments in outward calls). This type of application is elaborated at the close of this subsection.

It should be borne in mind that a procedure in ring *r* which makes calls outward to a procedure in ring *s* in some sense compromises the security of the data and procedures of ring *r* to the extent that the results achieved (and returned) by the outer ring callees are "believed," that is, used by ring *r* procedures as a basis for deciding future action. For this reason, outward calls do not extend or support the ring protection structure. If anything, they can compromise it.

Outward calls should be and can be avoided except as a technique for starting up a computation in a specified ring. Indeed, the implementation of outward calls in a general sense, that is, supervisor to user, is not in evidence in other operating systems. There were none in CTSS, for example.

As we shall see later, outward calls with arguments would, if implemented, carry added overhead, because calling arguments that belong to inner rings must be copied into the target ring to become accessible to the callee. Of course, it would be illegal to copy such data for use by the callee unless it was accessible to the caller in the first place. When and if Multics is modified to support the passing of arguments in outward calls, such support will amount merely to a courtesy, since procedures that institute outward calls can always copy the data needed by the callee into segments accessible to him—prior to issuing the outward call. For example, the teacher may copy the initial data to the student ring prior to calling the student program—in the example given earlier. For those especially interested, Section 4.3.5 describes the added details that would be involved in monitoring outward calls with argument lists.

23. Remember, the Gatekeeper is spared from having to examine inward calls from a procedure that is executing "outside" the target's call bracket or, if the target procedure has no call bracket, from outside the access (or single-ring) bracket.

The outward call (with no arguments) has proven to be very useful in allowing users (restricted) access to protected subsystems. For example, picture that there is a subsystem "X" whose key modules are ring-32 segments that are to be reached via a special outer-ring procedure, say in ring 33, known as <X_listener>. Picture that this segment is to be used as the responder and command interpreter by restricted users of X.

Once control passes to <X_listener>, the user can gain the services of subsystem X by issuing commands in the "language of X." Procedure <X_listener> will then interpret these commands by issuing inward calls to the functional modules of X that reside in ring 32. If the user cannot reach command level in ring 32, it will not be possible for him to directly examine, use, or tamper with these ring-32 modules or their corresponding access-control lists.

What is wanted, therefore, is a mechanism to allow a user to state at log-in time that he wishes to use subsystem X, so that his just-created process, which comes to life in ring 32, will then immediately call <X_listener> in ring 33 (before the user ever has a chance to gain command level in ring 32). This mechanism is, in fact, incorporated into the log-in logic of the system's *User Control* module that has responsibility for initiating user processes at login.

Since a user spells out both a project number and his own personal identification at login, User Control is able to consult user-profile information tabulated by the administrator of the specified project. The administrator is privileged to specify through such tables the name and/or ring number of the log-in responder that the just-created process is to call—via an argumentless (possibly outward) call—to put the particular user at command level. (Of course the default responder is the system-supplied standard listener—and its default ring of execution is 32.) In short, a project administrator can, for instance, say to his constituents, "You may log in under my project number but only in (outer) ring y," from which ring the user is then able to gain only restricted access to the services that may be offered under this project number.

Another possible use of outward calls arises in cases like the teacher-student subsystem that was suggested earlier in Section 4.2.3. In this type of system the teacher in his grading process acquires and executes a student-written procedure, making sure before executing the student's procedure to "give it" a higher ring number than the teacher's segments. The call to the student's procedure then becomes an *outward call*.

4.3.2.2 Gatekeeper–After Determining Type of Valid Wall Crossing

The Gatekeeper performs several tasks in handling outward calls, inward returns, and so on, which guarantee the safe handling of information passed to or from inner-ring procedures from or to those in outer rings. For example, in handling an inward return for a faulting procedure <p>, it is necessary to be sure that the return location specified by <p>'s rtcd instruction is in fact, the one supplied by the inner-ring procedure that called <p>. Without this check, the outer ring could, in the disguise of a return, force an entry at any point in any inner-ring procedure, thereby defeating the protection mechanism. The technique used by the Gatekeeper to forestall such disasters is to save a copy of the return location at the time of the outward call to <p>, in a special ring-0 data base which is inaccessible to <p>. Later, the Gatekeeper will insist on a match between the safe-stored return location and the one used by <p> in its faulting rtcd instruction. If no match, the inward return will be declared invalid by returning a suitable error code to the Fault Interceptor, which in turn signals the user of the error.

One final example to show the kind of business the Gatekeeper is involved in is given before proceeding to the details at the bookkeeping level: During an outward call, the argument list and the individual arguments may very well be found in data segments accessible to the caller but not to the target procedure.

In keeping with the Multics protection philosophy, any procedure of an inner ring, say 32, is free, at its own risk, to copy data that are accessible to it into a data segment of any outer ring. Therefore, in an outward call, if argument lists and/or arguments are used that belong to an inner ring, but accessible to the faulting procedure, it should be perfectly OK to allow the copying of these into an outer-ring segment, putting the arguments "within reach" of the target segment.

As suggested in the preceding subsection, a future version of Multics may well support (provide) this copying activity as a service to the user. It is anticipated that the Gatekeeper would be the module to take care of this chore, relieving the programmer of this responsibility for argument management.

The Gatekeeper, in order to do its job properly, would need an argument list especially embellished with pointers to data descriptions. That is, it could not properly copy data without knowing its format. Further details on the required format of these argument lists will be given in Section 4.3.5.

The Gatekeeper would also perform the important function of validating arguments for inward and outward calls. It would see to it that every argument-list element and every argument involved in such calls *is indeed accessible to the faulting procedure*. The basic principle that would be followed is: If a procedure, by virtue of its executing ring number, is not privileged to access a piece of data directly, that procedure should not be permitted to circumvent this restriction by getting help from another procedure that would behave either (a) as an unwitting accomplice (target of an inward call) or (b) as a deliberate accomplice (target of an outward call). Remember, the faulting procedure is ordinarily free to designate anything at all (any virtual address) as an argument pointer.

4.3.2.3 Argument Validation on Inward Calls

A calling procedure could in theory specify argument pointers to data objects for which the caller does not have ring access but to which the target procedure *does* have ring access. We see that an effort must be made to check all argument pointers passed "inwardly" to *validate* that the caller actually had ring access to each of the arguments that has been passed, lest the target procedure act as an unwitting accomplice.

4.3.2.4 Argument Validation on Outward Calls

Assuming it were permissible to pass arguments on outward calls, a calling procedure could in theory *also* specify argument pointers to data objects for which the caller does not have ring access. Something would be done to prevent the Gatekeeper from unwittingly copying these data objects over into the outer-ring segment that would be accessible to the less-privileged target procedure acting as a deliberate accomplice. An effort would be made to validate all argument pointers.[24] In this case, the validation would be done before the copying is performed.

4.3.3 Stack Management in the Multiring Environment

In this section, we consider what must be involved when creating the stack frame as a result of a call to an abritrary segment in the multiring environment. Let us imagine a call to <gamma> has been executed. Further assume

24. The validating technique in the case of either inward or outward calls is essentially the same. For each argument pointer in the argument list the following steps are taken:
1. Determine the ring brackets for the segment defined by the argument pointer. Ring brackets are kept in a ring-0 data base called the Known Segment Table. From the ring brackets, determine s, the highest ring number in the access bracket.
2. Compare s with the ring number t in which the faulting procedure was executing. If $t \leqslant s$, the argument pointer is valid, and it is invalid otherwise.

The ring number t is *remembered* for use in the above test as a special parameter known as the *validation level*. Further explanation of validation levels is given in Section 4.3.4.

that <gamma> is to execute in ring *k*. Ordinarily, as we recall from Chapter 3, <gamma>'s first duty is to execute a *save sequence* so as to add a new frame to its stack segment, which in this case would be <stack_*k*>. In addition to "creating" the frame, we are reminded that there is also the matter of storing in this frame the argument-list pointer passed to <gamma> by the calling procedure (name it <beta>). Also, there is the linking of the frame to its predecessor frame and the resetting of the stack pointer (sp). All is well and relatively simple when <beta> itself belongs to ring *k*.

Are any new clerical problems introduced in creating the stack frame for <gamma> when the calling procedure <beta> is in ring $j \neq k$? Plenty! Fortunately they are all handled for us by the Gatekeeper. We now look at some of these problems and how they are solved by the Gatekeeper.

4.3.3.1 The Housekeeping Problem in Getting Ready to Produce the Frame for <gamma>

The stack frame that <gamma> is to create must be placed in <stack_*k*>. The problem is—How is the segment number for <stack_*k*> determined, and what is the proper offset for the <gamma> frame? Getting stack_*k*# is complicated by the fact that <stack_*k*> may not yet be *known* (i.e., there is no entry for it in the KST). In Multics, after all, stack segments are no different from any others. They are acquired and/or created only as needed. If no procedure in ring *k* has ever been called, <stack_*k*> will be unknown. A special pointer scheme is employed by the Gatekeeper to keep track of segment numbers for stack segments and offsets into them for "next" frames.[25]

25. For those interested in getting an idea how this pointer scheme would work, the following discussion augmented by Figure 4.11 is given. Picture a one-per-process ring-0 data base called the process definitions segment <pdf> that contains a block for 64 its-pair pointers to the stack segments. The Gatekeeper will find stack_*k*# at location

<pdf>|[stacks] + 2*k,

unless, of course, <stack_*k*> is unknown, which is indicated in the block by a null pointer. The Gatekeeper then creates the desired stack segment and initiates the pointer. The address for the last used frame in <stack_*k*> is then seen to be

<pdf>|[stacks] + 2*k,*

The forward pointer at + 18 in this frame then gives the desired location for the next frame (e.g., lines ①, ②, and ③ in Figure 4.11.)

The actual implementation details differ from those suggested above in the following regard. Both <pdf> and <stack_00> are not really separate segments. They are, for the sake of efficiency, actually part of a single (somewhat more inclusive) one-per-process segment that can be called the "process data segment." It is named <pds> (and also contains other vital data for the process such as the "return stack" about which more is said in Section 4.3.3).

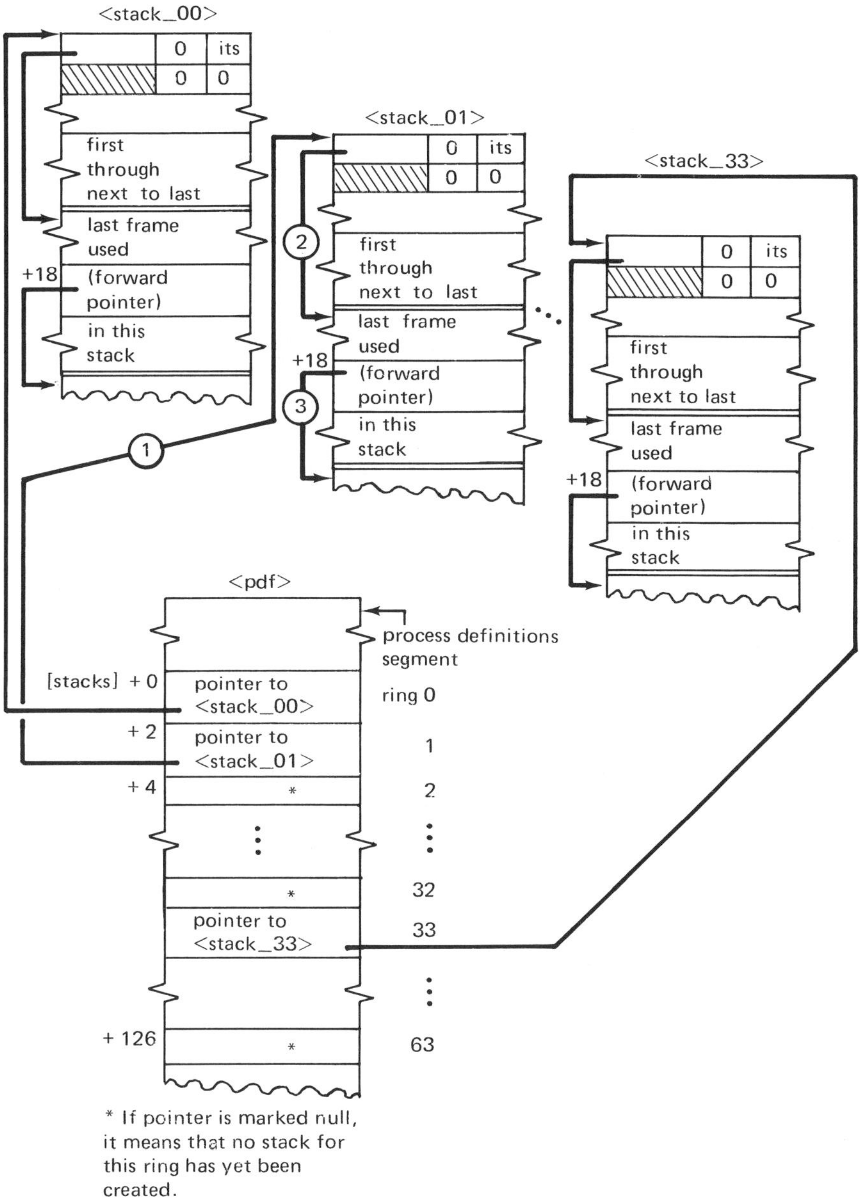

Figure 4.11. Schematic of the pointer scheme for keeping track of the separate stacks of a process (see footnote 25 for discussion of this figure)
The Gatekeeper creates stack segments as needed and places pointers to the head of each one beginning at <pdf>|[stacks].

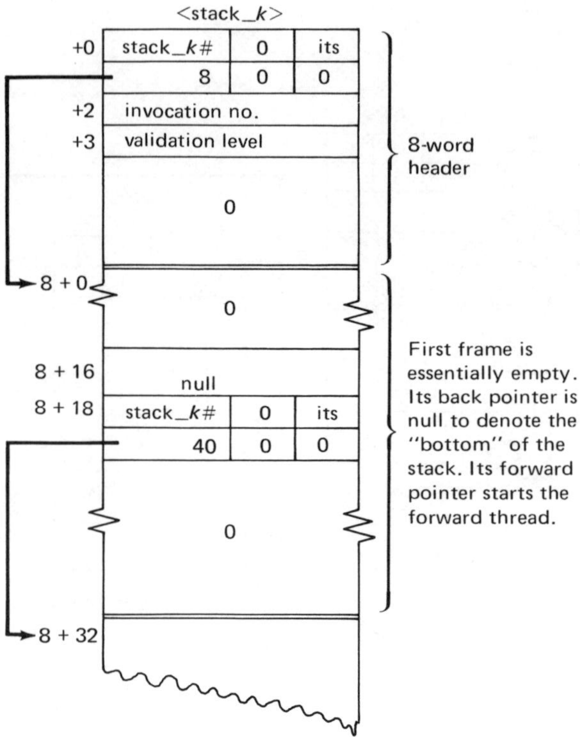

Figure 4.12. Format of a newly created stack segment

The format of a new-born stack segment is shown in Figure 4.12. It is endowed with an 8-word header followed by an essentially empty 32-word frame. This frame's back pointer (at <stack_*k*>|8 + 16) is null to denote the bottom of the stack. Its forward pointer (at <stack_*k*>|8 + 18) is set initially to stack_*k*#|8 + 32 for starting the forward thread.

Upon creation, the first word pair in the stack is set to point to the empty frame, which in this case acts as a *pseudo last-used frame*. The Gatekeeper updates the first pair as one of its housekeeping duties each time it supervises departure from ring *k* to some other ring.

The third and fourth words in <stack_*k*> hold the *invocation number* and the *validation level* about which more will be said shortly.

4.3.3.2 The Stack-Switching Problem

The Gatekeeper has now located the place in the new stack where the about-to-be-called procedure <gamma> is to create its stack frame. But, more bookkeeping problems remain. The normal return sequence in <gamma>,

```
ldb     sp|16,*     reload 8 base registers
lreg    sp|8        reload 8 index registers, etc.
rtcd    sp|20       return
```

should function properly, independent of cross-ring considerations.[26]

The first instruction

```
ldb     sp|16,*
```

is supposed to reload the base registers (all but sb) *from the stack frame of <gamma>'s caller*. Assuming we are using the standard save sequence dictates that the predecessor frame must be found in the same stack segment. (This predecessor is pointed to from

```
sp|16
```

which is the back pointer of the current <gamma> frame.) But, if <gamma> has been called by <beta> from another ring *j*, the stack frame in question actually resides in <stack_*j*>, an entirely different segment. To resolve this apparent conflict, the Multics solution is to place a special copy of <beta>'s header in <stack_*k*> immediately ahead of the frame for <gamma>. The copy of the <beta> frame header is ordinarily referred to as the "dummy" frame.

The Gatekeeper has the responsibility for producing this dummy frame, which serves a number of useful purposes. Figures 4.13 and 4.14 picture this activity. In Figure 4.13 the copying of the <beta> frame header from <stack_*j*> to <stack_*k*> is shown. We also see that the Gatekeeper resets the its pair at <stack_*j*>|0. (Dashed line ① to point to the <beta> frame is replaced by line ②.) The new value in <stack_*j*>|0 will be needed by the Gatekeeper whenever, at some future instant in time, an inter-ring procedure call is made *into ring j*.

In Figures 4.14 and 4.15 we see what the Gatekeeper must do to the dummy frame before it is "usable."

Shaded portions of the dummy frame indicate the following necessary modifications:

a. At $newsp_\beta$ + 28 store an its pair pointing to the original stack frame for <beta>, located at stack_*j*#|sp_β. This pointer is called the *cross-ring pointer*.

26. Segment <gamma>'s compiler will not know <gamma>'s ring number as this could be different for each process sharing <gamma>. Moreover, the compiler will not know the ring of <gamma>'s caller.

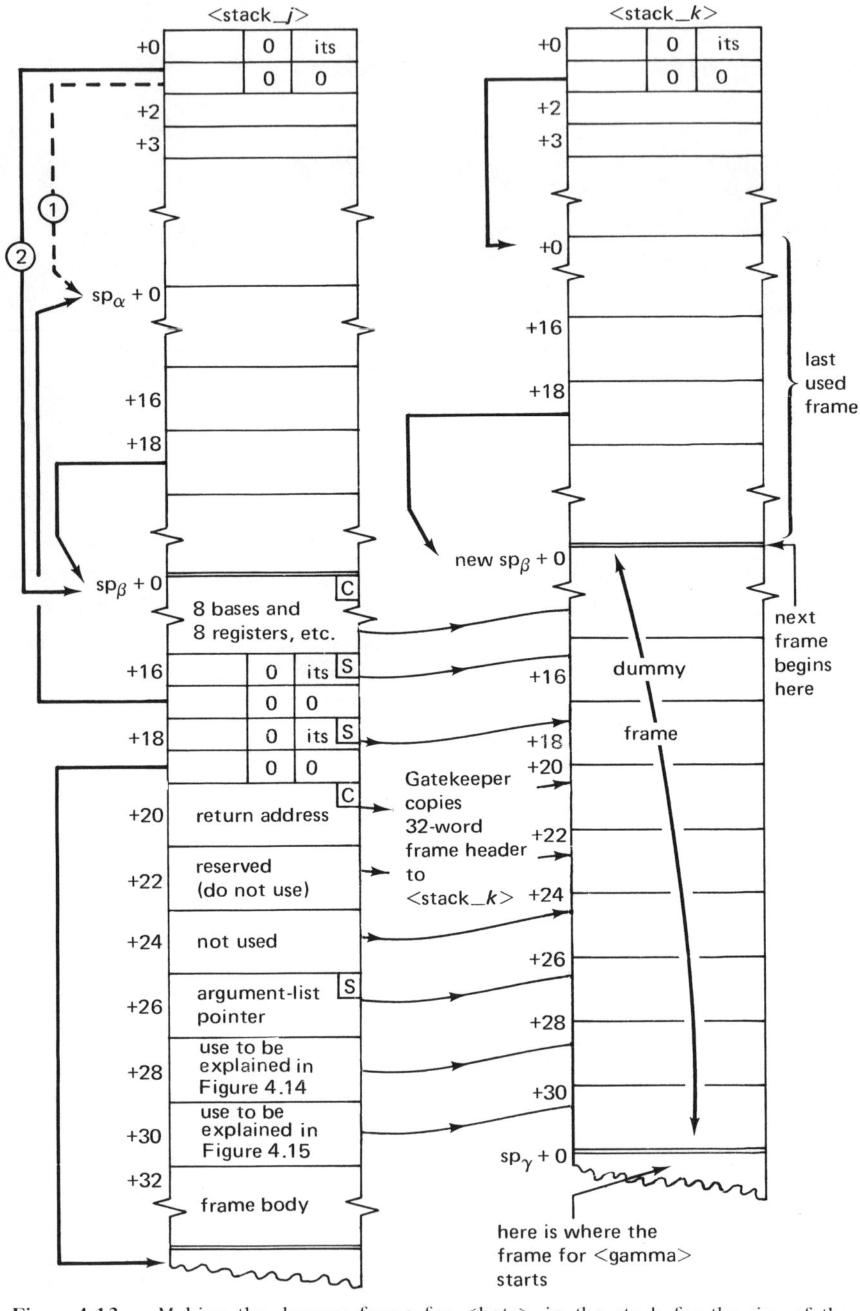

Figure 4.13. Making the dummy frame for <beta> in the stack for the ring of the called procedure

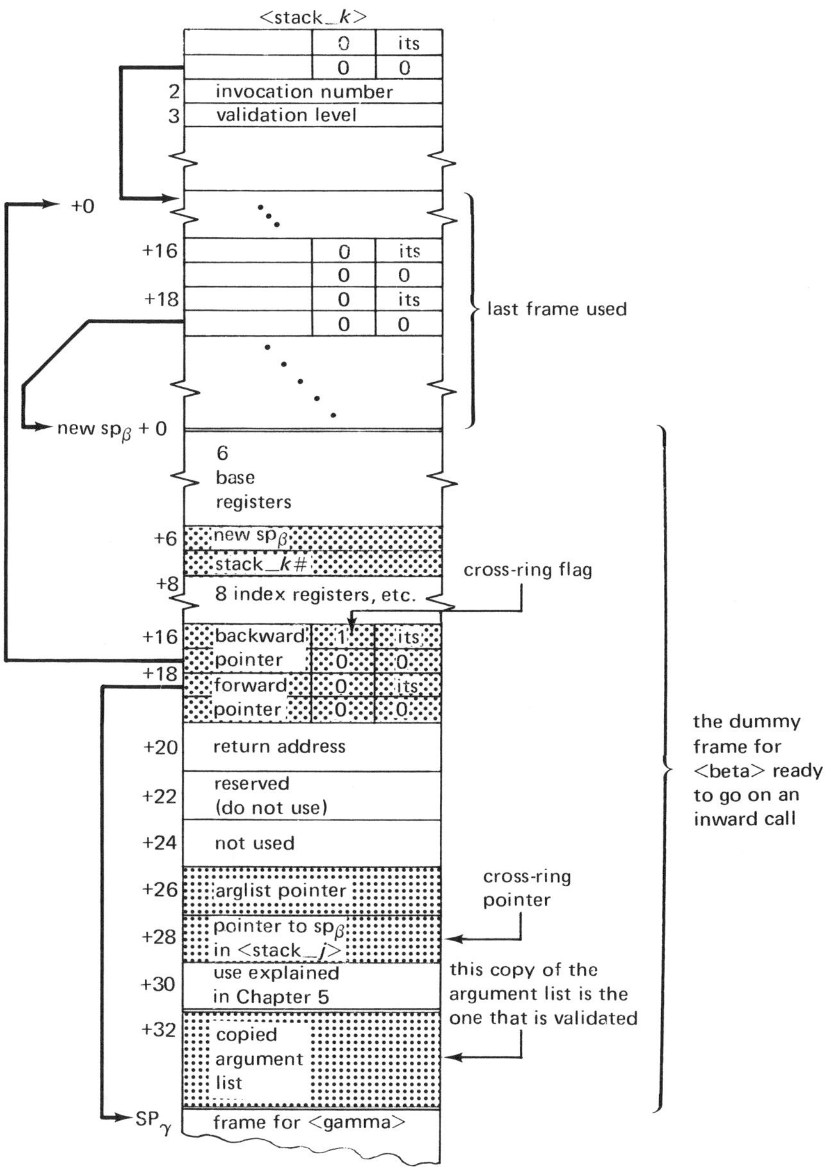

Figure 4.14. Dummy frame for <beta> in <stack_*k*> after being modified for an inward call
Note the last portion where the copied argument list has been safe stored for purposes of validation.

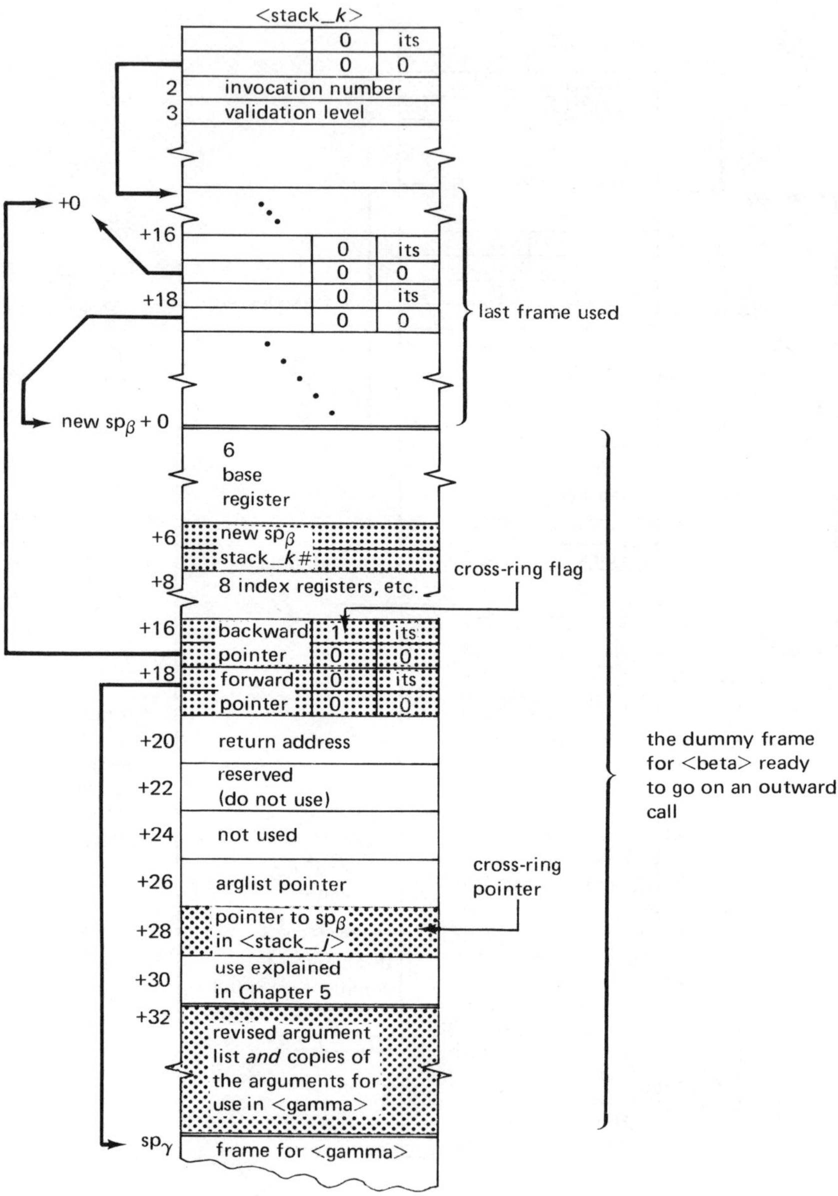

Figure 4.15. Dummy frame for <beta> in <stack_*k*> after being modified for an outward call
(Same as Figure 4.14 except for showing how and where copies of arguments in the call on <gamma> might be placed in the dummy frame.)

b. At $newsp_{\beta}$ + 16 place a *cross-ring flag* (i.e., a 1 in the op code position) to mark this frame as a dummy.

The cross-ring flag and the cross-ring pointer are vital to the success of the condition-handling and unwinding mechanisms to be described in Chapter 5.

Other details of a housekeeping nature are the following:

c. The dummy frame is chained to the preceding frame in <stack_*k*> by adjusting the backward pointer.

d. The forward pointer is reset so it points to the beginning of the next frame, which is to be used by <gamma>.

e. The stack bases saved in $newsp_{\beta}$ + 6 and $newsp_{\beta}$ + 7, which refer to the old stack frame in <stack_*j*>, are reset to point at $newsp_{\beta}$ in <stack_*k*>. This is done in order that the instruction pair

```
ldb   sp|16,*
lreg  sp|8
```

be executable in some meaningful and consistent sense, especially for outward returns. We must bear in mind that an ldb instruction cannot reset the locked sb base register.[27]

On inward returns the effect of the two restore instructions is overridden by similar instructions performed by the Gatekeeper.

Multics cannot (and the Gatekeeper does not) trust an inward-returning procedure to properly carry out the restoration of bases and registers for its inner-ring caller. When the

```
rtcd  sp|20
```

is executed, it faults, of course, to the Gatekeeper—which takes no chances. The Gatekeeper repeats the restoration of the bases and registers, this time using the stack pointer for the original <beta> frame in <stack_*j*> where the integrity of the saved information cannot be questioned. The pointer to the frame in <stack_*j*> is itself safe stored in a special table (the so-called return stack), about which more will be said later.

f. On *inward calls* there is a special (and subtle) type of protection violation that must be prevented. It concerns the possibility of deliberate or accidental changes to argument pointers *after* they have been validated by the Gatekeeper mechanism, but *before* they have been used by the target procedure. For instance, such violations can arise if and when two cooperating processes have agreed to read-write share the outer-ring stack segment that holds the

27. See Chapter 1, Section 1.4, for a review of the ldb instruction.

calling procedure's argument list. To prevent such postvalidation tampering, the Gatekeeper first duplicates the calling argument list in the dummy frame at $sp_\beta|32$ (in the inner-ring stack segment) and then validates from the copied argument list. Of course, $sp_\beta|18$ will have been appropriately set to point to sp_γ, taking into account the length of the copied argument list. The base pair ab $\leftarrow$ ap will be adjusted in the saved copy of the machine conditions for the faulting procedure, so that when the call is completed the arglist pointer in the new frame for <gamma>, placed at $sp_\gamma|26$, will point back to $sp_\beta|32$. The dummy frame is now ready for use in inward calls (Figure 4.14).

g. On *outward calls* these are the activities that the Gatekeeper may be asked to perform—when argument lists are permitted: The Gatekeeper, after validating the original argument list found in the caller's stack frame, then prepares a revised argument list that contains pointers to *copies* of the arguments. Of course, sp_β will have been appropriately set to point at sp_γ, taking into account the extension of the dummy frame for <beta> to include the new arglist and the argument copies. These items are placed in the dummy frame at $sp_\beta|32$. The ab $\leftarrow$ ap base pair will be adjusted in the saved copy of the machine conditions for the faulting procedure, so that when the call is completed the arglist pointer in the new frame for <gamma> (placed at $sp_\beta|26$) will point back to $sp_\beta|32$. The dummy frame is now ready for use in outward calls (Figure 4.15).[28]

In reviewing all these dummy-frame details, notice that the dummy is tied to other frames in two ways:

a. to the preceding and succeeding frames in its stack (sp|16 and sp|18). [The back pointer is primarily for use by system-supplied debugging tools (and for use by the Unwinder mechanism discussed in Chapter 5)] and

b. to the original copy of the frame in <stack_*j*> via the cross-ring pointer at sp|28.

4.3.3.3 Saving Vital Cross-Ring Data on the Return Stack

The Gatekeeper keeps a protected record of each inter-ring call in a special, one-per-process data segment in ring 0. To simplify our discussions we shall call this segment <rtn_stk> (though in actuality the return stack is kept in a multipurpose data segment called <pds>).

The following four items are stored in <rtn_stk> as a consequence of each inter-ring call:

a. the ring number of the faulting procedure. This value is taken from an embellished copy of the faulting procedure's machine conditions.

28. Additional details are shown in Figure 4.20.

b. The validation level of the faulting procedure (explained in Section 4.3.4).
c. A relative pointer to the faulting procedure's stack frame, that is, a protected duplicate of the offset part of the cross-ring pointer.
d. A pointer to the normal return location in the faulting procedure, that is, a protected copy of the value given in the faulting procedure's stack frame at sp|20.

Figure 4.16 shows the overall and detailed structure of <rtn_stk>. A relative pointer to the top entry of <rtn_stk>, called the *invocation number* is updated after each new entry is stacked or removed (popped). Each entry consists of four words.

After completing this entry in <rtn_stk>, a copy of the new invocation number is stored in the *target* ring's stack segment at <stack_*t*>|2, and a copy of the saved validation level is stored in <stack_*t*>|3.

By reading the invocation number in a given stack segment, <stack_*s*>, ring-0 system routines (not user routines) are able to locate the corresponding

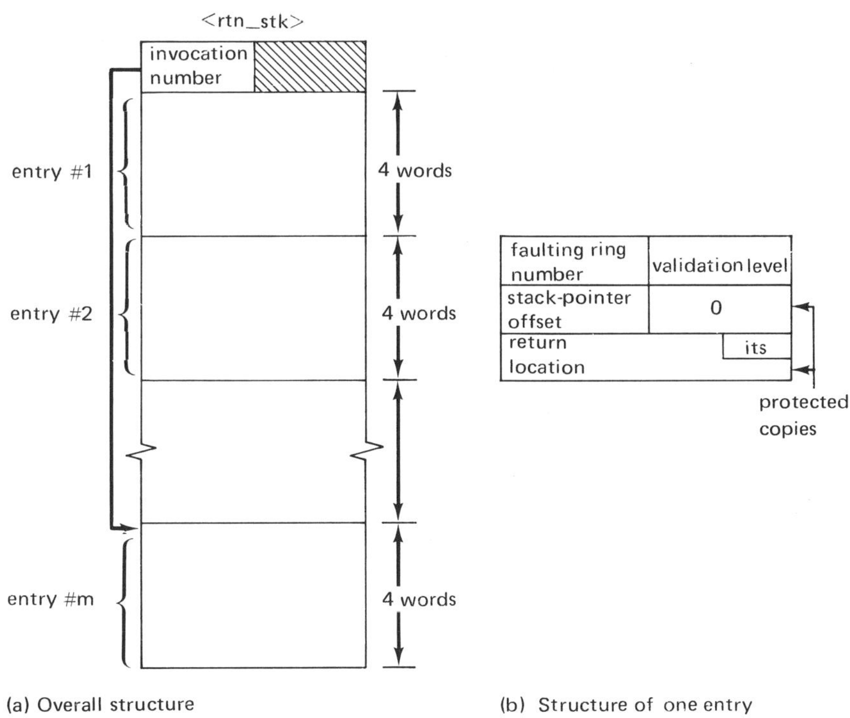

Figure 4.16. Overall and detail format of the return stack (<rtn_stk>)

entry in <rtn_stk>. The entry provides a "trail" back to the procedure (its ring number, and its stack frame) that caused the crossing into ring *s*. The Unwinder mechanism (for abnormal returns) depends on the invocation number for tracing portions of the past history of a process.

The invocation number is also potentially useful to ordinary users as a means of recording when things happen (i.e., with respect to ring-crossing history). Thus a user executing in ring *t* could associate with a certain stored block of data a copy of the current invocation number (call it curinv) found at <stack_*t*>|2. At any later time, the block of data can be identified by the associated value of curinv as to when it was stored.

4.3.4 Validation Levels and How They Are Used

The validation level is the ring number for the segment on whose behalf the call on the ring-*t* segment is being made. It often arises that a user procedure will make an inward call to a "supervisory" module, which, in turn, will call another procedure (either in the same ring or in an even-lower ring) to perform some vital function on behalf of the user. The target supervisory procedure at the end of this "chain" may need to know the ring number (importance level) of the *original caller* in order to perform its task properly. In this way, a routine in ring 0 (Directory Control, for example) will know the importance of the party it is serving and will not be outwitted into "thinking" it is serving another ring-0 procedure that is its immediate caller, when in reality it is a user in ring 32 or greater that is being served. It is seen, therefore, that proper use of validation levels is a means of increasing protection where needed.

When crossing to a target ring *t*, the validation level is always stored in <stack_*t*>|3. The value assigned to this location is a copy of the one in the stack of the faulting procedure. (The Gatekeeper does this copying.) In this way, if there has been a chain of two or more inward calls in reaching ring *t*, the validation level that is set in <stack_*t*>|3 will normally reflect the ring number of the procedure that initiates this chain of ring crossings. The called procedure in ring *t* is then free to interrogate <stack_*t*>|3 as required.[29]

It should be kept in mind, that once execution passes to a target ring *t*, any procedure executing in that ring is privileged to read or write the contents of <stack_*t*>|3. The Gatekeeper will not, however, indiscriminately copy validation-level values. If the current value in <stack_*t*>|3 is lower than the ring number, say *r*, for a faulting procedure, the value passed to the target

29. A system library routine called cu_$level_get is provided for this purpose. See the MPM for more details.

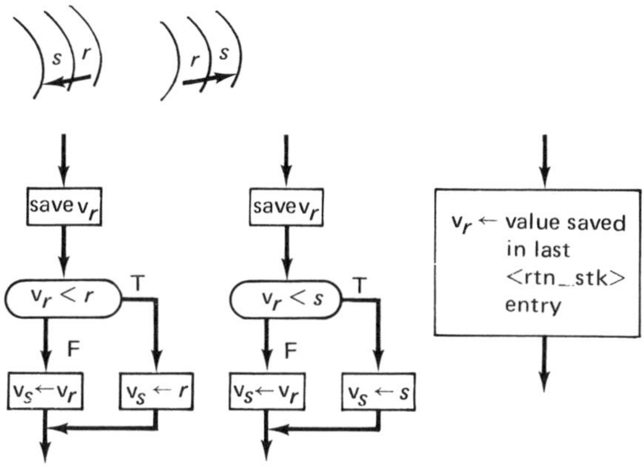

(a) Inward call (b) Outward call

Saving and passing a validation level v_i from ring r to ring s

(c) Restoring a validation level on a normal return to ring r

Figure 4.17. Gatekeeper's algorithm for saving and passing, and for restoring validation levels during ring crossings
Key:

v_i, $i = 0(1)63$, means the variable whose value is the validation level for ring i. v_i is located at <stack_*i*> | 3. *Saving* means storing in the <rtn_stk> entry.

ring will be r. In this way, it will not be possible to trick the inner-ring target into believing that its caller has a validation level that is less than its ring number.

The algorithm used by the Gatekeeper for setting these values is displayed in Figure 4.17. On *calls*, outward or inward, the validation level associated with the faulting ring is saved in the return stack,[30] and a copy of this saved value, possibly altered in a way described below, replaces the current value of the validation level in the stack of the target ring. On inward calls if v_r, the validation level for the calling ring r is for any reason lower than r, then r, rather than v_r, is the value passed to <stack_*s*>. On *outward calls* if v_r is less than s, the target ring number, the value s is passed to <stack_*s*>. On *returns*, inward or outward, the most recently saved value simply replaces the current value in the target ring's stack segment.

In the remainder of this section an example is given aimed at motivating subsystem applications of validation levels.

30. Recall, we are picturing this stack as if it is the separate segment named <rtn_stk>.

Example

Here, a case where it is expedient to check the ring of the caller to determine the nature of the service to be rendered is illustrated.

We imagine a school-records subsystem that operates in four rings (35, 34, 33, and 32), as shown in Figure 4.18.

All personnel and student records are kept in data segments of ring 32. The ring-32 procedure <get_rec>, called from outer rings, retrieves desired information from any of these data files according to the arguments it is furnished and according to the validation level at <stack_32>|3.

4.3.5 Outward Calls with Argument Lists

It was stated earlier that in the initial implementation of Multics the Gatekeeper does not transmit arguments for outward calls, and why the motivation has not been strong to provide this type of system support was explained. A good deal of thought has been given, however, to how such a service would be implemented if ever really warranted. This subsection provides these details for those (probably few) readers that may have become interested in a deeper study of the subject.

Two types of systems that might utilize outward calls with argument lists might be of interest.

a. The subsystem itself is to be coded using outward calls, but the subsystem user is to be so controlled, for example, by limiting his procedures and data to the outermost ring, so that he cannot execute outward calls.

b. The subsystem procedures as well as the user procedures, with the latter no longer restricted to the outermost ring, can execute outward calls.

Some important implications follow in each case.

Case a. The subsystem must be coded in a source language whose compiler can anticipate or recognize outward calls. This is necessary so that the compiler can generate argument lists that are properly embellished with pointers to descriptors of the corresponding arguments.

The Multics PL/I compiler anticipates outward calls in the sense that the argument lists it generates for call statements will contain the information that would be needed by the Gatekeeper to validate and copy arguments on an outward call (if certain simple precautions [31] are taken by the programmer). A compiler that does not automatically construct such an argument list

31. See R. A. Freiburghouse, J. D. Mills, and B. L. Wolman, *A User's Guide to the Multics PL/I Implementation* (Cambridge, Mass.: Cambridge Information Systems Laboratory, General Electric Company, 1970), Section 3.2, "Argument Descriptors." Note: This document will be published by Honeywell in later printings.

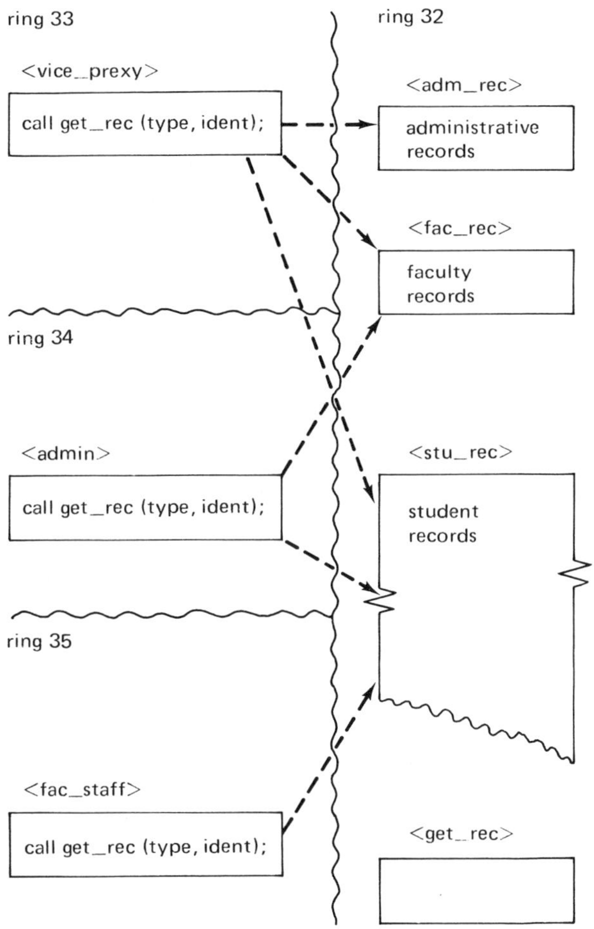

Figure 4.18. School records retrieval subsystem

would have to somehow be furnished the necessary (declarative) information to recognize those call statements for which the special argument lists should be constructed.

If you write your subsystem in any language(s) other than PL/I, you would want to be sure the processor(s) are equipped with this facility. Assuming you don't have to be involved in building this type of software facility, there is no more you need to know. However, if it is your problem to do this job, then read "Case b."

Case b. The coding language of the user need not be the same as the language(s) used for coding the subsystem. If this is the case, and if the user-coded procedures may be written with outward calls, then you must make sure that the processor which handles user codes also has the same capability for recognizing outward calls and for generating suitable argument lists.

Figure 4.19 shows the format of the argument list that would be required for an *n*-argument outward call. The figure shows that for each argument a pointer to its descriptor must also be supplied. Figure 4.20 shows the Multics

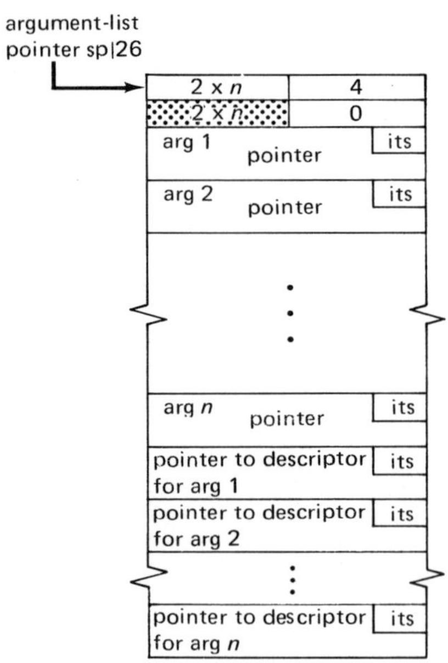

Figure 4.19. Format for an argument list to be used in an outward call

0-----15	16 17	18----------35
data type	I/O	size

Figure 4.20. Multics standard format for an argument descriptor

Key:

data type is an integer code for the type of argument. Some of the different system standard types and their codes were given in Table 3.1. (A full list is provided in the MPM, Reference Data section on standard data type formats.)

I/O is a two-bit code giving the input/output nature of the argument.

I/O Code	Systemwide Interpretation
0 0	I/O nature unknown
0 1	input only
1 0	input and output

size is defined only for aggregates. It represents the declared size of the datum (in bits, characters, or words).

(and PL/I) standard format for an argument descriptor. By consulting the argument descriptors, the Gatekeeper would be able to decide how to copy each argument into the target procedure's stack segment.

What the Gatekeeper would do in a specific instance is now illustrated, Imagine in Figure 4.21 that the procedure <beta> makes an outward call to <proc_hi_ring> with two arguments: X, an integer, and name, an aligned nonvarying character string. The copied block of information is placed at the tail end of the dummy frame made for <beta> in the stack segment for the ring (t) of <proc_hi_ring>. (See also Figure 4.15.)

Note, in the example of Figure 4.21, that each argument pointer in the copied list is now modified to point forward in <stack_t> to its respective argument datum. The descriptor pointers, however, are copied without change. This makes it possible for the target procedure to construct new argument lists for passing the same (copied) arguments to procedures with even higher ring numbers, if desired.

On an outward call to procedure <p>, there may be (copied) arguments whose values are to be altered during execution of <p>. During the inward return the Gatekeeper must see to it that there is permission granted to allow new values for these return or "output" arguments to replace the original values pointed to in the original copy of the argument list. Output arguments (i.e., with write permission) can be recognized by examination of the I/O code (bits 16 and 17) of the argument description, as indicated in Figure 4.20. To deal with these arguments, if any, on an outward return, the Gate-

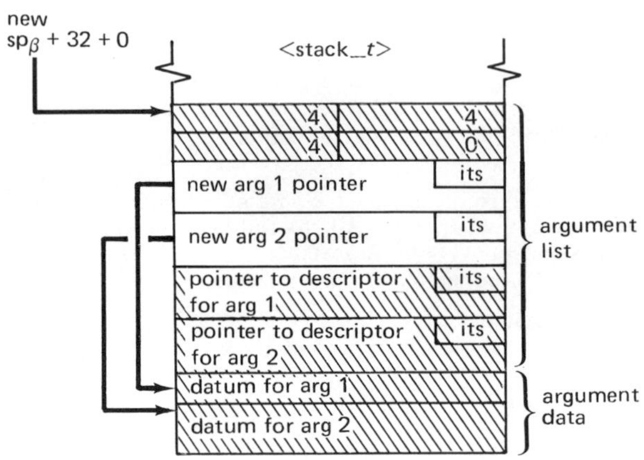

Figure 4.21. Appearance of the copied argument list and copied arguments generated by the Gatekeeper
This information is deposited at the end of the dummy frame created for the faulting procedure. Crosshatched areas represent exact copies placed there by the Gatekeeper.

keeper would search the data descriptors that go with the original argument list[32] for arguments indicated to be of the output type (binary code 10). For each of these, the datum is copied from its position in the outer-ring stack to its original position, wherever that may be.

A review of the foregoing considerations for the copying and recopying of arguments has revealed one reason why a subsystem should provide argument descriptors in standard form; namely, it is a necessity if the subsystem is to interface with the Gatekeeper for processing outward calls and inward returns with arguments. Other Multics service modules, including certain useful debugging facilities,[33] will also require access to argument descriptors in the same standard form.

Normally, the compiler or assembler used to generate code in the subsystem will have the responsibility for generating descriptors for all arguments to be employed in an outward call. Data descriptors for declared variables or for declared parameters (dummy variables) are usually placed in the segment's symbol table produced by the compiler or assembler.

32. It is not the one in the stack of the now-faulting procedure that is executing the return, but the one pointed to in the stack for the inner-ring target procedure. It is not safe to use the argument list in the outer-ring stack because this may have been altered by <p> or by any of its "dynamic descendants" that had access to this stack.
33. See the MPM section on debugging aids, for more details.

4.3.6 Gates

In the description of the linkage section given in Chapter 2 of this guide, no mention was made of *gates* because there was then no way of properly motivating them. This omission is corrected here. As mentioned in Section 4.2.3, a gate has the form of a special *entry* sequence in the linkage section. By way of review, an entry sequence to be found in the linkage section of a target procedure might have the form

```
eaplp    -*,ic
aos      2,ic
tra      linq-*,ic*
arg      0
```

where linq is the offset to the link (pointer) to the program point in the target.

A gate is functionally similar to an entry sequence but is preceded by a no-op instruction whose address field is an offset, at which additional information describing the gate is provided. The form of the no-op instruction is

```
nop    gate_info,du
```

When the Gatekeeper is processing an inward call, the address of the faulting instruction should point to this no-op. Figure 4.22 shows the kind of additional information (at the offset equal to gate_info) that the Gatekeeper would then have available for handling this attempted inward call. Inspection of the gate information will lead the reader to some interesting inferences.

Normally, one would want the Gatekeeper to validate all arguments being passed on an inward call. Whoever writes a translator that generates gates in a linkage section can provide users of this translator with an option to ignore this Gatekeeper's service on inward calls. A user that takes the option to ignore argument validation will eliminate some minor amount of overhead but will risk damage in the target's domain of access.

Whether or not the n arguments are to be validated, the next $[(n+1)/2]$ words provide special 18-bit descriptions. A one in the leading bit position of a descriptor indicates a return argument, that is, write permission for that argument. The arguments may be used *in situ* by the target procedure, because they are (presumed to be) located in the domain of access of the caller.

4.3.6.1 Gate Segments

The six-bit field in gate_info that is marked "cb" (highest *effective* ring number in the *c*all *b*racket) refers to an important design feature. The cb field is always examined by the Gatekeeper when handling inward calls. The

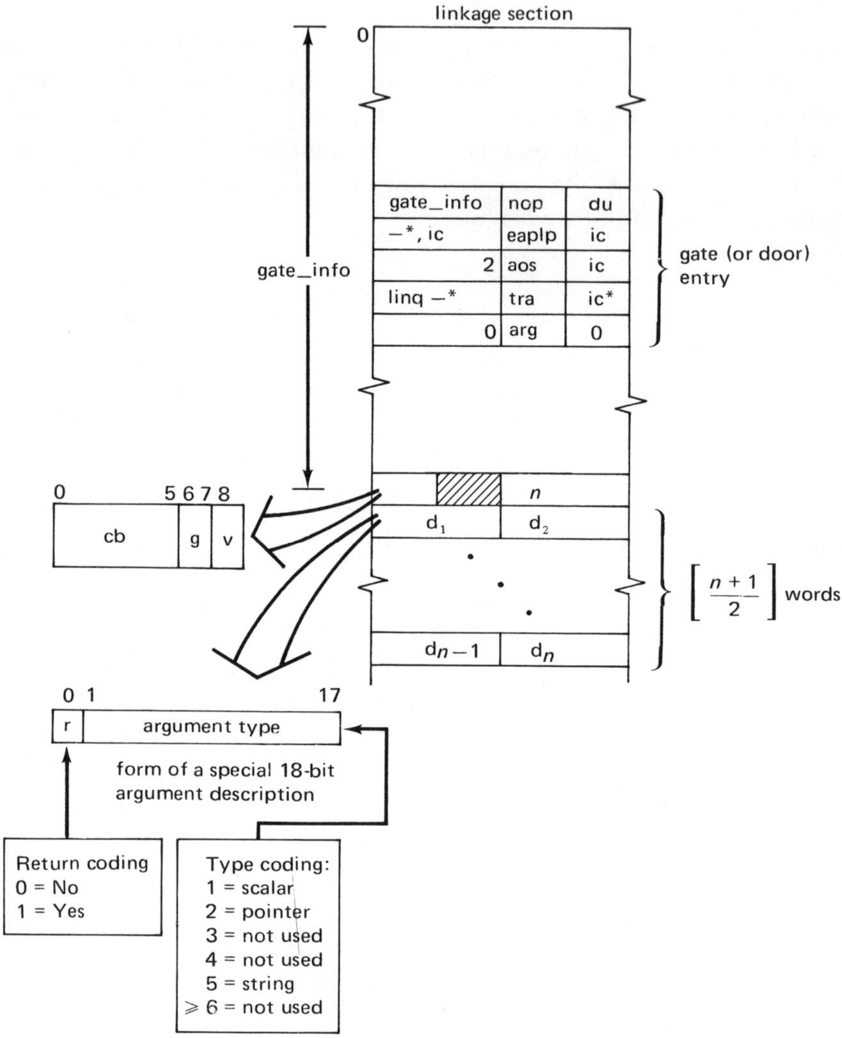

Figure 4.22. Format of gate (and door) information

Key:

cb = outermost ring of the call bracket (used when g = 1).
g = 1 if this entry is a *gate*. 2 if this entry is a door. (See Chapter 5 for explanation of doors).
n = number of arguments for this entry.
v = 0 if arguments *are not* to be validated by the Gatekeeper.
1 if arguments *are* to be validated.
r = 1 if this argument is a return value (ok to use *in situ*).
0 if no value is allowed to be returned for this argument (call by value).

number cb is interpreted as the effective upper bound for the target's call bracket in the event the value of cb is less than the value given in the ring brackets of the segment served by the gate. The cb field may be set arbitrarily ($0 \leqslant cb \leqslant 63$) by explicit coding.[34] A small value of cb (smaller than the outer ring of the call bracket of the target) serves as additional screening of inward calls per entry point.

Most subsystem designers will find few occasions to exploit this extra screening capability for inward calls. When used, it will probably be for the purpose of reducing the linkage segments that are needed in a multiring subsystem. The idea would be to concentrate into one linkage segment a collection of gates for different procedures in the same ring. Such a collection, will hereafter be called a "gate segment."[35]

A gate segment, when properly constructed, would serve as a funnel for access into an arbitrary collection of privileged procedures, for example, in the hardcore ring. The gate segment itself has fixed ring brackets in the executing process, that is, (r_1, r_2, r_3) whose values are given in the file branch for this segment. However, any of the cb values found in the gate segment may be less than r_3.

In the Multics supervisor, for example, the ring-0 segment named <hcs_> serves as a gate segment to minimize the number of linkage segments needed for ring-0 procedures. The ring brackets for <hcs_> are (0, 0, 32). This segment contains gates to all other procedures in ring 0 that are callable from outside ring 0. The gates for some hard-core procedures have cb = 1, while for others, cb = 32. The Gatekeeper will reject any user call from ring 32 to a user procedure whose gate has cb = 1 (even though the faulting segment's ring is not outside the call bracket for <hcs_> itself and even though the desired entry point is a gate).

4.3.6.2 Doors

The last remark I wish to make is for the benefit of readers who may occasionally refer to this subsection from Chapter 5. If the data at gate_info is

34. Eventually source languages like ALM and PL/I will be expanded so a programmer may *declare* an entry point to be a gate. Such a declaration would be expected to result in the generation of gate information in the format shown in Figure 4.22. When declaring a gate, one would specify the value of cb or accept a default value that would probably be 63, a value which would produce no screening effect at all.

35. This segment would function something like the familiar "transfer vector" used in programs that are loaded in conventional batch operating systems. A special command called translate_gate is available for helping subsystem designers to assemble gate segments. See the "System Programmers' Supplement" to the "Multics Programmers' Manual" for details. This document is described in the bibliography.

for a *door* instead of a gate, there will be no arguments involved, because this entry is being used for control of an *abnormal return*, not for a call. Hence, $n = 0$ and the gate information consists of only one word. The gate information in this case serves primarily to identify the entry as a door (thus, making gates and doors mutually exclusive).

5 Condition Handling and Abnormal Returns

5.1 Introduction

Besides ordinary calls and returns, there are two other types of interprocedure (and possibly inter-ring) transfers that the user may wish to make and for which Multics lends system support. These are

1. to execute a "signaled condition,"
2. to execute an abnormal return.

In this section the problems and issues involved in the implementation of each of these will be introduced. With the motivation hopefully provided here, the reader may wish to read either or both of the remaining two sections of this chapter to see the details. As implemented in Multics, abnormal returns, often referred to as "nonlocal GO TO's," are executed in conjunction with the condition-handling mechanisms, so Section 5.3 cannot be effectively read independently of Section 5.2. "Condition handling" is a technical term in programming that is now well recognized as a result of the widely published specifications for PL/I.[1] The term refers to an activity in which the user names in his program a hardware or a software condition and either explicitly or implicitly identifies (or supplies) code to be executed when the stated condition is detected at some later instant in time (i.e., during execution of subsequent program steps). The Multics condition-handling mechanism is adapted from the corresponding PL/I concepts but is extended to serve programmers coding in all languages that utilize the common call-save-return discipline of the system (i.e., the Chapter 3 concepts and details). By way of introduction, in the remainder of this section the pertinent PL/I concepts (and language specifications) that deal with condition handling are reviewed first. Then the approach taken by Multics, which amounts to a generalization of these ideas, is introduced.

In every programming-system environment there exists a priori a class of system-defined conditions, which can arise during execution, that will fault the process. Some of these conditions are recognized (detected) by the hardware, while others are recognized during execution of system-supplied software. Some conditions may relate more strongly to the user's algorithm than to the environment in which it executes. For these conditions, key-word names may be recognized by the compiler that is used. This is the case in PL/I. Examples of such conditions, which we shall henceforth call "PL/I-

1. For a complete list of these see *IBM System 360 Operating System, PL/I Language Specification*, IBM Reference Manual, Form C28–6571 (Armonk, N.Y.: International Business Machines Corp., n.d.), Appendix.

defined"[2] are accumulator overflow, zero divide, and exceeding subscript range. Conditions like these are of the sort that are hardly ever completely avoided and hence are in the category of always-possible-though-always-unexpected. Certain syntactical constructions are included in PL/I to handle occurrences of these conditions, and their use provides the programmer with a measure of choice of action and hence control over his program's fate.

A set of a dozen or so "built-in," PL/I-defined conditions is enumerated in the PL/I specifications. With each of these conditions there is associated a standard action. This "standard" action is executed only in the default case, that is, in the event the PL/I programmer fails to supply any other code for execution when a particular condition has been detected.

Subsystem designers are expected to recognize conditions that are not on the "built-in" list. Hence, additional machinery of similar structure is provided so that the PL/I programmer can name other conditions and, of course, specify the actions that are to be taken when these conditions occur. Unlike the first category of PL/I-defined or built-in conditions, this new category of programmer-defined conditions will not be automatically detected. Consequently, PL/I provides the subsystem programmer with the linguistic constructs that allow his subsystem to behave as a condition detector as well.

More specifically, the following three types of statements have been provided in PL/I:

	Purpose
ON statements	To designate a condition and the associated code that is to be executed when that condition is detected.
REVERT statements	To undo the effect of a previously executed ON statement that refers to the same condition named in the REVERT statement.
SIGNAL statements	To indicate occurrence of a built-in or programmer-defined condition.

A more complete explanation of these statements follows (but as a hint of what is to follow, the reader should be aware that in Multics more direct and

2. (Unfortunately) the PL/I language specifications refer to these as "system-defined" conditions. We shall, however, reserve this term for a broader class of conditions that includes the PL/I group. Thus, in Multics, for example, we have such additional system-defined conditions as access violation, out-of-bounds violation, and linkage error.

somewhat more powerful system calls to accomplish similar effects are also available for use by the programmer—regardless of the coding language used).

ON *statements* identify a PL/I- or programmer-defined condition and designate the corresponding code that is to be executed whenever that condition is detected. The general syntactical form of this statement is

ON <designation of the condition[3]> <action specification>

where <action specification> may be null, a simple PL/I statement, or a block of code.

For example:

```
ON   OVERFLOW   BEGIN;
                      DECLARE SUM STATIC INITIAL (0);
                      SUM = SUM + 1;
                      IF SUM > 100 THEN
                      CALL OVERR;
                END
```

designation of the condition (ON OVERFLOW)

action specification (BEGIN; … END)

The action specification may be thought of as a "handler" for the specified condition. This is because execution of an ON statement has the effect of setting up its action specification as a body of code to be invoked later, as if it were invoked as a procedure. The execution of an ON statement can be said to *establish* a handler for the named condition. Execution of a subsequent statement that results in the detection of the named condition will cause an interruption of the main program sequence and the invocation of the established handler.

A natural question to ask is, What is the program scope in which a given established handler is said to be active, that is, how long does an established handler remain in effect? The answer is—up to but not beyond the point in time where the thread of control exits normally from a procedure block B in which the handler was established. This rule means that after executing an

3. If the condition is PL/I-defined, it is designated in the ON statement simply by its name, e.g., OVERFLOW. If, however, the condition is programmer-defined, it is indicated as such syntactically by placing the name in parentheses and prefixing it with the word CONDITION. Thus,

```
ON CONDITION (UNEXPECTED_DELAY)   CALL PROCA
```

designation of condition (CONDITION (UNEXPECTED_DELAY)); action spec. (CALL PROCA)

ON statement establishing a handler (which we will refer to as) Y for a condition named "X", the thread of control may pass through numerous other procedures (as a result of CALL or GO TO statements) before exiting from block B. All this time the handler Y would remain in effect. A handler is said to remain in effect or *govern* while executing in all the "dynamic descendents" of the procedure block in which it (the handler) was established. However, during execution of any dynamic descendant, one is free to establish a new handler for "X", "pushing down" the original handler by executing another ON statement that designates another handler. Handlers for the same condition that are thus stacked are automatically popped during exits (returns) from the blocks (procedures) in which they were established.

There are two ways, however, to overrule the effect of a handler Y in the replacement or deletion sense. One may either replace Y with alternative code, or one may explicitly nullify Y. A handler Y may be replaced if another ON statement for the same condition is executed in the same procedure block. If the second ON statement designates some other code (which we shall call) YY as the handler for "X", then YY is established and will remain in effect until control passes beyond YY's scope. (This occurs, of course, when a normal exit is taken from the block in which the handler YY was established.) To simply nullify the "rule" of a currently effective handler Y, one uses the REVERT statement.

The REVERT statement names a condition (PL/I- or programmer-defined) whose currently governing handler is to be nullified (i.e., popped from the current stack of handlers for "X").

```
REVERT X;
```

exemplifies the simple syntax of the REVERT statement. If there is a subsequent signaling of condition "X" after executing a REVERT statement, the previously established handler (or a system-defined default handler in case there are no more left on the stack) will be invoked.

The SIGNAL statement allows a programmer to indicate the occurrence of a condition that is named in this statement and thereby to cause its governing handler to be invoked. After execution of the indirectly designated handler, control will (normally) return to the statement immediately following the SIGNAL statement, when and if the invoked handler executes a return.[4] It

4. Experience with Multics shows that invoked handlers frequently *do not* return. This fact relates strongly to the nature of signaled faults in a time-sharing system. In interactive mode, invoked handlers may type out messages explaining the fault, after which the user may well cause an (abnormal) return to command level, aborting execution of the current command.

should be noted that the ON statement that established the currently effective handler for a condition "X" need not, and normally would not, appear in the same procedure(s) that contains the invoking SIGNAL statement.

Although any PL/I-defined condition may be "signaled" with this type of statement, it should be emphasized that executing a SIGNAL statement is the only way a programmer-defined condition handler can ever be invoked.[5] Of course, executing a SIGNAL statement does not alter the scope of the invoked handler. That is, there is no restriction on the number of times a statement like

```
SIGNAL X;
```

may be executed to invoke the current handler for "X".

Signaling via the SIGNAL statement offers the programmer an attractive way to invoke a subroutine without actually having to specify its name, letting its designation be determined dynamically, as determined by the ON statement most recently executed for the same condition. Whether this technique is practical depends on the particular machinery that is developed for the implementation of the ON, REVERT, and SIGNAL statements.

You may be wondering if signaling is merely a fancy programmer's convenience for avoiding the need to set and return proper status arguments. Isn't it the case that a condition can **always** be reflected backward via possibly a chain of such status returns until it reaches the procedure that knows what to do about it (i.e., what handler to invoke)? Certainly, but even this approach has its shortcomings, especially if the chain of returns is long and antecedents on this chain are unable to add any new contextual information (i.e., intelligence) that will clarify or qualify the (recovery) action that should be taken.

As a rule of thumb, therefore, recognized errors and other conditions should be signaled rather than relayed as status arguments whenever the immediate callers are not expected to be "smart" enough to improve the quality of the "recovery" from the given condition.

Fortunately, (overhead) cost need not be a factor in selecting between signaling versus status returns. Careful design of the currently implemented PL/I compiler has made the use of the ON and REVERT statements very cheap. The cost of using the SIGNAL statement is also relatively inexpensive but, of course, depends on the amount of searching through stacked condi-

5. Strictly speaking, the programmer-defined handler could also be signaled by executing an appropriate call to the corresponding system routine called "signal_", which is to be discussed in the next section.

tions that is necessary to locate the governing handler. The same statement about costs can be made about the corresponding system routines discussed in Section 5.1.1.

Observe, therefore, that the Multics signaling system is designed so it is inexpensive to *prepare* for the occurrence of an error condition, though recovery from it may well prove expensive (depending on the nature of the error). Since it is only the recovery action that may be expensive, one is well advised to treat the rarely occurring (bona fide) error via signaling and to treat conditions that occur more frequently via return of status information. The Multics supervisory code itself observes this discipline. It is a heavy user of the system routines supplied for condition handling. All hardware and software faults are converted into (software) signals, whereas commonly occurring conditions such as file_not_found are treated as status information.

5.1.1 The Multics System-Defined Conditions and Condition-Handling Routines

So far we have been content to discuss condition handling and signaling in terms of PL/I-defined conditions and user-defined conditions. The reader should be clearly aware that a third significant class of conditions consists of the Multics- (system-) defined conditions. Typical among these are

linkage_error

and

access_violation

There are some fifty other such conditions, many of which the user will quickly become aware of as he uses the system. A current list of these conditions can be found in the MPM.

With special system-provided procedures, Multics makes it easy to provide *condition handling* in any process, regardless of the coding language that is used. These system procedures are

<condition_>
<reversion_>
<signal_>

They can be used by anyone (including programmers that code in PL/I) to accomplish what can be achieved in PL/I with ON, REVERT, and SIGNAL statements.

The Multics system procedures are in fact a little more general than the corresponding functions compiled for ON, REVERT, and SIGNAL. For example, a call to <condition_> allows one to establish an arbitrary external or internal procedure as a handler that can receive arguments passed to it at the time the condition is "raised" (i.e., recognized). These arguments are passed via the call to <signal_>. This added feature makes it possible to obtain articulate error messages. When linkage_error is raised, for instance, a message like the following can be printed at the console:

"procedure <a> at location 432 died referencing <b>|[y] because it couldn't find the external definition for y."

Note that a signaled condition for which there has been no corresponding handler established will always cause a system-defined (default) handler to be invoked. This safety feature is achieved simply by having <signal_> recursively call itself to signal the condition named "unclaimed_signal" for which the system has a default handler. Thus, in our example, a message like the following would be typed at the console:

"no handler for condition X."

Then, the default handler will call the listener, thereby bringing the user back to command level.

5.1.2 Signaling in a Multiring Environment

If we are going to gain a more sophisticated view of the condition-handling machinery in Multics (present and future), it will be necessary to consider how it couples or might couple with the ring structure. To elaborate this thought, we will do well first to walk through some of the steps of condition handling in the context of the Multics ring structure. (For this purpose we need no longer assume that PL/I is the programming language being used).

Let us suppose a procedure <P> is executing in ring *e*. This procedure may enable[6] (i.e., establish) a condition named "x" simply by calling <condition_> and designating as its arguments the name of the condition, "x", and a procedure entry for a handler. The handler itself, call it <procl>, is a block of code in the form of an internal or an external procedure. Also, let the ring number of <procl> be *h* (for handler).

Procedure <P>, or any of its dynamic descendants is, of course, free to

6. Henceforth we shall be using the phrase *enabling a condition* to mean what in PL/I terminology is expressed as *establishing a condition*. In PL/I there exist additional mechanisms to enable or to disable a previously established condition. We shall not be concerned with this extra level of control in condition handling. Hopefully, therefore, confusion may be avoided.

signal condition x (whether or not <P> has enabled x). The need to issue the signal may be recognized in two basically different ways. Hardware faults may induce this recognition. In this case, a Fault Interceptor module can issue the signal for condition x.[7] Alternatively, simple tests of state variables may be programmed (normally by the user) such that affirmative results are tantamount to event recognition. In this case, the procedure then executing, which shall be called the *signaler*, can execute the call to <signal_>, naming "x" as an argument, and possibly supplying a pointer to other arguments intended for the handler.

Signaler may be written either by the subsystem designer as a utility routine or it may be written by an ordinary user. (It makes little difference.) We shall assume that <signaler> executes in ring *s*.

From the foregoing "exercise" we see that up to three different rings may be involved. These are *e* (for enabler), *h* (for the handler), and *s* (for the signaler). A basic question to be answered is, Should a condition enabled in ring *e* be "signalable" from *s* if $s \neq e$? A *no* answer would be tantamount to making calls to <signal_> and to <condition_> within one ring independent of those in all other rings. A *yes* answer amounts to saying that a condition enabled in one ring may be signaled from any other ring. This in turn implies existence of a mechanism for remembering in what ring the corresponding condition was enabled. It also implies that the same handler <p> can behave differently, depending on the ring from which <p> has been invoked.[8]

Arguments may be offered for both approaches. The first approach ($s = e$ only) has the advantage of conceptual and implementational simplicity. It implies a minimum of execution overhead in invoking the intended handler.

7. System calls to <signal_> will normally transmit, as an optional argument, a pointer to the saved machine conditions, so that the handler may be able to do a more effective job in analyzing the "difficulty."

8. To see why this is so, let the ring brackets of the handler <p> for condition "x" be (u, v, w). Now, any signaler from ring *s* that has ring access to <p> will be able to invoke it. From our study of Chapter 4 we know that <p> would then execute in a ring *r* that lies somewhere in closed interval (u, v), depending on *s*. Suppose the enabled condition "x" is signaled more than once, and from *k* different rings, say, $s_1, \ldots, s_k (k > 1)$. The corresponding rings r_k in which <p> will then execute, may not all be identical. (That is, a handler invoked from different rings, and having an access bracket (u, v) such that $u < v$, may execute in different rings.) Although I may not have mentioned this previously, it is true that for reasons of protection, a procedure <p> is supplied with a separate copy of its linkage section for every ring in which <p> executes and hence may behave differently when executed. This somewhat surprising fact and its interesting implications are dealt with in Chapter 6. There it will be shown that a link (i.e., an its pair), generated by the Linker for the same symbolic reference, may depend on the ring of the link-faulting procedure.

The second approach (s possibly $\neq e$) has the advantage that several useful subsystem applications would be possible if some (perhaps limited) form of signaling across rings were provided in the system. Two of these applications are already well understood.

a. Assume a procedure in an outer ring s has executed an inward call to a ring r where a system-defined condition is recognized. It should be possible for such conditions to somehow be reflected back to the outer ring s, from which handlers established for the reflected condition can be invoked. In "passing the baton" back to the antecedent (outer) ring, it would be desirable to wipe out stack information and any other temporary data that were built up during the most recent period of residence in the inner ring.[9] This activity of restoring the computation to some earlier state (jumping backward a "distance" of perhaps several stack frames) is called "unwinding." The notion of unwinding is discussed in some detail in Section 5.3.

To use a specific example, picture that some ring-49 procedure calls into ring 32, where an overflow fault is then encountered. It would be desirable to offer system support that lets the person that codes the ring-32 procedure signal overflow so as to

1. suitably unwind the computation to the state where the computation was just about to enter ring 32 from ring 49, and
2. then invoke the handler previously established in ring 49.

b. An even more important reason for providing some form of cross-ring signaling would be to make it possible for an inner-ring procedure to intercept conditions raised in an outer-ring procedure (e.g., "send all subscript errors to me"). Thus, in user-designed subsystems, even though signaling may be done from an outer ring where certain restricted users are forced to execute, the designer could see to it that handlers he has established in the inner ring of the subsystem would be those actually invoked.

It should probably be possible to apply a generalization of this interception concept for systems and subsystems of more than two rings. Consider, for example, a three-ring system where the rings are i, j, and k. Suppose procedures in both ring i and ring j are able to ask for interception privileges for condition "x" when raised in outer rings. Then, if procedures in both i and j exercise this same privilege, some discipline for stacking these requests in ring-priority order would probably be desired. (This point has now been

9. At the present time, ring-0 modules do in fact manage to reflect conditions roughly in this same manner to user rings. However, the method used exploits the privilege of ring 0 and hence is not available to user programmers for achieving similar objectives in multi-ring subsystems that they may wish to design.

pursued far enough to ensure that the reader can conjecture further on such cases, if so inclined.)

Finally, note that while we have discovered at least two forms of useful cross-ring signaling, there is at least one form (the *converse* of application b above) that is *undesirable* and should somehow be prevented.

It must never be permissible for an outer-ring procedure to force interception of conditions raised in an inner ring. Allowing such a possibility is tantamount to giving outer-ring procedures control over the destiny of inner-ring procedures, which would be a direct breach of the security objectives of the Multics ring mechanism.

For both of the above approaches, the following interesting problems arise:

a. What ring relationships between *h* (handler) and *s* (signaler) should govern whether or not the signaling procedure should be given access to the designated handler <proc1>? The answer is that the controls which permit the signaler to call the handler apply here. For example, *s* must be less than or equal to the outer ring of the call bracket for <procl>, and, if within <procl>'s call bracket, the desired entry point must also be a *gate*.

b. In any process the condition x may be enabled more than once before it is signaled. Each enabling of condition x, even if from the same ring, may designate a different handler. Moreover, the handler may possibly be located in different rings. In addition to the question raised in problem a, we must now add the question, Which of the handlers is the one that should be asked to *respond* to the signaler (i.e., to which handler do we want control transferred)? The one we want shall be referred to as the *currently active handler.* Ordinarily, the answer is, The one designated when x was last enabled. But, whichever is the active one, how does the supervisory system go about locating it? Obviously, some kind of a stacking scheme must be used.

If one pictures that signals pertain only to conditions enabled in the same ring, then it is easy to visualize how one might implement all three of the primitives, <condition_>, <reversion_>, and <signal_>. A call of the form

call condition_("x", proc);

when executed in ring *e*, might cause a pointer (i.e., entry datum) to <proc> to be pushed onto the top of a stack named "x" for ring *e*. A call of the form

call reversion_("x");

in the same ring *e* would then be expected to cause the topmost element to be popped from the same stack. Finally, a call of the form

call signal_("x");

also executed in ring *e* would cause the issuance of a call to the procedure whose entry datum is the topmost element on stack "x" (of ring *e*).

But what of the more general case if it were implemented in Multics? Here, signaling would not be restricted to the ring in which the matching condition handler was enabled. What selection or searching process would be used to locate the desired handler? Would the programmer, to the extent he is authorized, also have the option to restrict (or guide) the search for an enabled handler? How about reversion? Will the popping that is performed remain limited to the stack for "x" in the ring of <reversion_>'s caller?

c. What practice is followed for the case where a procedure signals a condition that has never been enabled or, if enabled, that has since been fully disabled (reverted)? In this regard it is important to recall the two kinds of conditions recognized in Multics. These are (1) system-defined conditions and (2) programmer-defined conditions. It must be arranged somehow that the system behaves as if every system-defined condition is always enabled, each with a system-defined "default handler," that is, one that will be invoked in case the user fails to impose one or more handlers of his own. A somewhat different mechanism might be devised for guaranteeing default handling of programmer-defined conditions, in such a way that the user still has an opportunity to interact effectively with his process, a prime objective of interactive processing.

Section 5.2 explains the current Multics solutions to the problems just raised.

5.1.3 Abnormal Returns

If, instead of returning to the point of call in the calling procedure, one attempts to execute a transfer to any other point in that procedure or to a point in any other previously called procedure, this is referred to as an *abnormal return.* A satisfactory synonym, which has become widely accepted as a result of PL/I's advent, is "nonlocal GO TO." Imagine, for instance, that <a> calls <b> calls <c> . . . calls <t>. In principle, it is possible to pass a label argument, say *lab*, from <a>, via <b>, via <c>, . . . , to <t>. While executing, <t> can then return to *lab* in <a>. The fact that this is a commonplace facility in such long-used languages as MAD and FORTRAN IV may give you the impression that no problems are presented here. Nothing could be farther from the truth. Severe problems can conceivably be encountered in the proper handling of abnormal returns for programs that execute in a recursive reentrant environment and/or in a multiring environment. The following introductory discussion hopes to reveal these problems. (Imagine for illustrative purposes that PL/I-like programming languages are being used.)

In the course of returning abnormally to <a>, there is a matter of resetting the stack pointer to the target procedure's stack frame and recovering all the saved register values (and the indicators). This can be done relatively easily if all procedures <a> through <t> in the chain are in the same ring.[10] Returning to the earlier stack frame of <a>, which implies resetting the stack pointer, has the effect of recovering the storage allocated in the stack for variables of type "automatic" used in <b>, <c>, and so forth.

There may, however, still be several remaining recovery problems related to resetting the state of the computation to what is was before making its "round trip" from and to the abnormal return point. Some of these problems are enumerated in the following list.

1. Perhaps most obvious is a storage-management problem that arises whenever a procedure allocates temporary (e.g., automatic) storage space in segments *other than a stack segment.* Usually, a procedure that allocates such space should also free it before executing a normal return. However, if such a procedure is bypassed during an abnormal return, there may be no opportunity to execute code in the bypassed procedure that recovers this allocated space. Even if the user makes no explicit effort to allocate temporary variables in this way, the supervisor, or the compiler he is using, may do so. For example, there was the EPL compiler's way of handling varying strings. Space selected for such data was taken from a free storage segment called <free_>.[11] Resetting the stack pointer for the abnormal return would not of itself accomplish the recovery of space that was allocated for such variables.

2. There may be other state-recovery actions whose explicit code might otherwise go unexecuted in bypassed procedures. For example, there may be changes made in various shared data bases, and so forth, that would normally be reversed (reset) if normal returns were taken. If a procedure that effected such changes were bypassed during a normal return, how would reset action be performed?

10. A "standard" abnormal-return sequence can be devised and in fact was once proposed for use in these situations–but was later discarded.

11. The details were given in the MSPM. (Since the EPL compiler has now been made obsolete by the new PL/I compiler, these descriptions are subject to deletion from cited references when all code originally compiled in EPL will have been recompiled in PL/I).

3. During execution of the intermediate procedures (<b>, <c>, . . . , <t>) various conditions may have been enabled. As has already been suggested, each enabling of a condition amounts to the stacking of a pointer to a desired procedure or "handler." These pointers would be popped off such stacks prior to executing a normal return. When an abnormal return to <a> is executed, unwanted pointers should also be popped from whatever stacks they have been put on. If these pointers are held in the stack frames (as they are in the current Multics implementation), reversion of these handlers is automatic. If, however, the pointers are kept in a special segment or segments, as they might be in a more general solution to the condition-handling problem, extra effort would be required in popping these entries from their respective stacks during abnormal returns.

4. The foregoing problems are made more complicated when the procedures and the stacks that are involved in the chain we intend to bypass *reside in different rings*. To perform an abnormal return under these circumstances, it becomes necessary to unwind (i.e., "march backward" through the chain of about-to-be-bypassed procedures, one by one, to locate and revert their respective stack frames).

The system's condition-handling machinery may be effectively employed to help solve the "cleanup" problems already described under items 1 through 3. If, for example, a programmer anticipates an abnormal return that will bypass a procedure <p>, then he might code in <p> a call to establish a handler for a "cleanup" condition. He would define the handler to execute recovery of storage and the resetting of state variables, and so forth, as required. All that is required is to find a "friend" (i.e., some special mechanism) that will be sure to invoke such a cleanup handler when (and only when) <p> is being skipped during an abnormal return. A special system procedure called the Unwinder serves as the "friend" that, not only is trusted to signal cleanup conditions during the execution of abnormal returns, but in fact supervises *all* aspects of the abnormal return, including unwinding across rings.

The Unwinder interfaces with the Gatekeeper as well as the condition-handling procedures for carrying out the unwinding task. For this reason, it is legislated that whenever a user wishes to perform an abnormal return he does so by a call to the Unwinder. In some situations, a user will invoke the Unwinder mechanism without being conscious of it. For example, compilers like the PL/I compiler generate calls to the Unwinder when translating non-local GO TO statements.

5.2 Condition Handling–Details

This section reviews the plan for condition handling, roughly as it is now implemented in Multics. This scheme limits signaling to the ring in which the intended handler has been enabled. Pointers to enabled handlers are always saved in, and reverted from, the current ring's stack segment.[12]

5.2.1 Implementation of <condition_>

Each call to <condition_> has the effect of stacking a pointer to a handler in the current stack frame. If a procedure <p>, executing in ring *s*, calls <condition_>, for example,

call condition_("condname", proc);

the effect is to stack a pointer to the handler (proc) for a condition named "condname", in the current stack frame for <p>. More specifically, what is actually stacked is an information block consisting of the name of the condition ("condname" in our example), and a (six-word) entry datum to the procedure that has been designated as the handler.

Note that proc in the above call may be the name of either an external or an internal procedure, though, for consistency, it will always be referred to here as though it were an external procedure. (Note also that the call to <condition_> can be regarded as being more general and more modular than the PL/I ON statement. The handler itself, rather than a name for it, must be spelled out in the ON statement's action specification, so no arguments can be passed to it as part of the signaling operation.)

When called by a procedure <p>, <condition_> causes the length of the current stack frame for <p> to be extended so that the required information block may be added and, by suitable threading, effectively "pushed" on to the top of a stack of such information blocks in this stack frame. Thus, for each distinctly named condition (designated in calls to <condition_> during this invocation of <p>), <condition_> will have constructed an information block and will have threaded it onto a list of such blocks. The head of this list (i.e., the most recently added block) is pointed to from a specially reserved word of the stack frame's header. (At stack frame-creation time, this relative pointer [at sp|30] is null). Figure 5.1 suggests the appearance of a stack frame for <p> after conditions "Acond," "Bcond," and "Ccond" have been enabled.

12. Though extensions of this scheme to permit some forms of signaling across rings are anticipated, it is very likely that the stack segment will continue to be the choice of storage for the stacking of "conditions" (i.e., pointers to condition handlers).

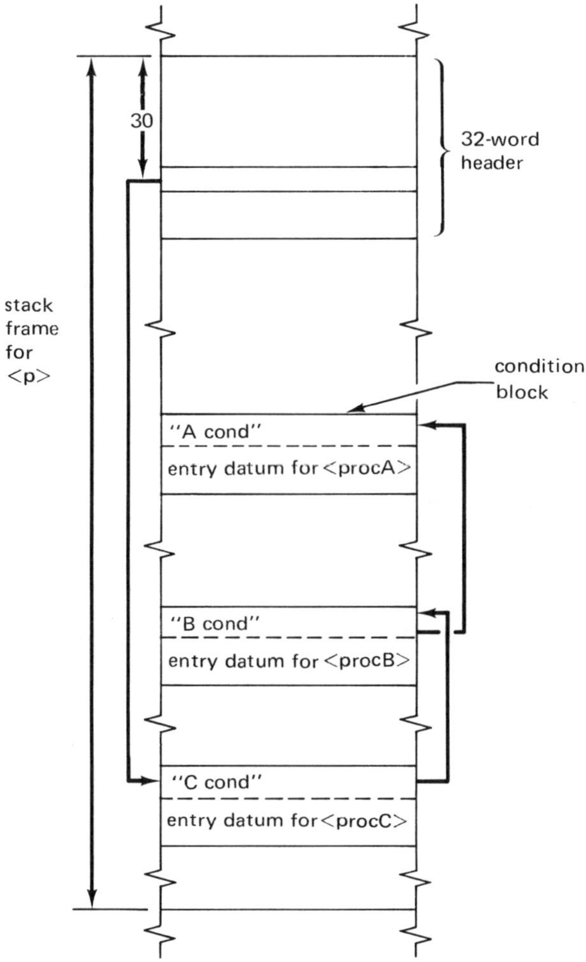

Figure 5.1. Schematic of a stack frame showing the threading of "condition blocks" after three calls to <condition_>

If the call to <condition_> designates a condition name that is already represented in this stack–and a quick search by <condition_> would reveal such a match–then no new information block is stacked. Instead, the current information block is "reused." The new entry datum replaces the one designated in the prior call to <condition_>. In this way, there can be but one handler designated for a given condition in a single procedure block, that is, in its stack frame. For instance, when the stack frame for <p> is as suggested in Figure 5.1, then the net effect of a call of the form

call condition_("Bcond", procB1);

would cause the entry datum for <procB1> to replace the one for <procB> in the condition block for "Bcond". (To "resurrect" <procB>, as the handler for "Bcond" during this invocation of <p>, would simply require execution of another call to <condition_> that pairs "Bcond" with <procB>.)

Thus far, we have viewed the condition blocks of but a single stack frame. If we now consider the set of frames that may "pile up" in a given stack segment, we have the larger context in which blocks for the same condition are to be considered. Suppose "Acond" is designated in calls to <condition_>, executed from procedures <p>, <q>, and <r>, which are related to one another in the dynamic-descendant sense. Then, in effect, the stack segment can contain a *stack of condition blocks* for "Acond" or for any other condition that is enabled from dynamically descendant procedures. Such a structure is suggested in Figure 5.2, which postulates the continuation of the stack that was pictured in Figure 5.1.

5.2.2 Implementation of <reversion_>

Normal returns to calling procedures force the "popping" or reversion of entire stack frames and, hence, automatically revert or pop any and all condition blocks that may "reside" in the affected stack frames. It is, however, possible to explicitly revert a designated condition block from the current stack frame by a call to <reversion_>. One can best see how this is done in the current Multics implementation by first noting the small squares that are shown in the lower right-hand corners of the condition blocks of Figure 5.2. These are intended to represent (schematically)

$$\text{I-}\left\{\begin{matrix}\text{am}\\ \text{am not}\end{matrix}\right\}\text{-reverted flags.}$$

Thus, a call of the form

call reversion_("Acond");

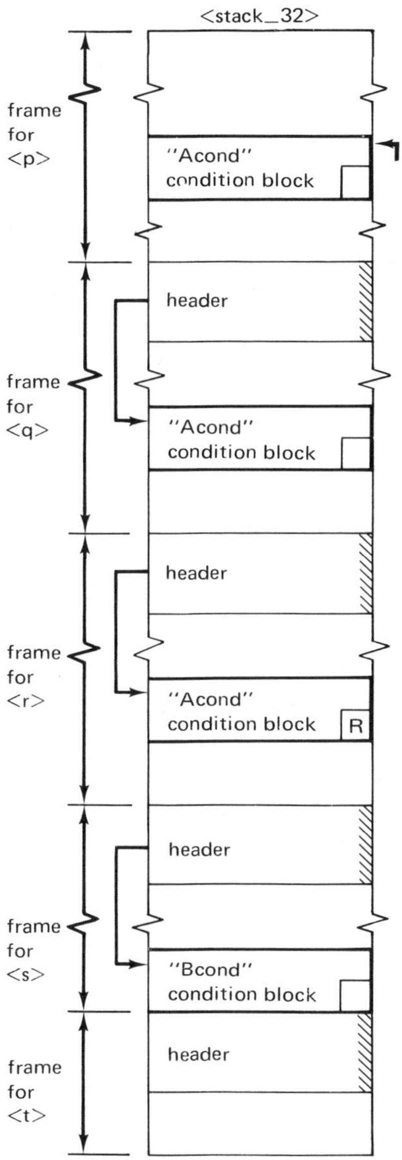

Figure 5.2. Schematic of part of a stack segment showing condition blocks for the same condition stacked in separate frames for <p>, <q>, and <r> in <stack_32>. The condition handler for "Acond" in <r> has been reverted (R).

executed in <r> (at any time following the call to <condition_> during the same invocation of <r> will cause the {I- am / am not} reverted flag to be marked R. The R mark effectively nullifies the containing condition block. (Any subsequent call to <condition_> for "Acond" while <r> is still executing will cause this condition block to be reused and the R mark removed.)

In summary to this point, we see how a stack of condition blocks for a given condition may well develop in a given stack segment. Moreover, calls to <reversion_> may nullify some or all of these condition blocks and hence "disable" their corresponding handlers. There remains to be seen only how such stacks of condition blocks are employed, that is, how the desired handlers are invoked upon calls to <signal_>.

5.2.3 Implementation of <signal_>

The chief purpose of establishing a condition handler is to invoke it when and if proper notice is later given to do so. A call to <signal_> is the act of serving this notice. Consider a call of the form

call signal_("Acond");

To see the effect of such a call, let us suppose that call is executed from <t> in ring 32 with <stack_32> in the state shown in Figure 5.2. The segment <signal_> will invoke the handler whose entry datum has been saved in the "Acond" condition block of the <q> stack frame. This is the topmost (nonreverted) handler in the stack of condition blocks for "Acond". [To find the "active" handler, <signal_> will have searched <stack_32> backward frame by frame to find the first nonreverted condition block with a condition name that matches "Acond". Since the condition blocks of each stack frame are link-listed from the stack header, and since the stack frames themselves are link-listed (also through their headers—as described in Chapter 3), <signal_> has no trouble in making this search.]

Note that in executing the call to the handler via the entry datum (let us say the call is to <procq> in this case), a ring-crossing fault may well occur. If so, the Gatekeeper will respond in an appropriate manner.[13]

Subsystem designers will be interested in one more significant detail regarding signaling. An optional form of the call to **signal_** is

13. Following the rules given in Chapter 4, we see that if <t> is the signaler executing from ring *s*, and if <procq> is the handler, then the ring brackets of <procq> will determine if a procedure in ring *s* may call it. Of course, if *s* is within the call bracket of <procq>, then the Gatekeeper will make the additional check to see if the entry point that is represented by the fault-inducing entry datum is coded as a *gate*.

call signal_("condname", mcptr, opt_ptr);

where mcptr is a pointer (its pair) to a set of machine conditions,[14] and opt_ptr is an optional pointer to data (possibly an argument list) for use by the target handler. Now, <signal_> will always transmit both of these arguments to the handler, when found, by generating and executing a call of the form

```
call handler (mcptr, "condname", hcs_mcptr, opt_ptr);
                          ↑            ↑
                    may also be     null for user-defined
                    a character-    conditions (see the MPM
                    string          write-up of <signal_> for
                    identifier      more details, if needed)
```

For instance, a user-defined condition named "load_limit_reached", whose active handler is <next_try> would be called by <signal_> with

call next_try (null, "load_limit_reached", null, arg_ptr);

if the call to signal_ was

call signal_("load_limit_reached", null, arg_ptr);

The user-written code for <next_try> may or may not utilize the argument information supplied by <signal_>, but it is there if needed.[15] Of course, <signal_>'s caller will have to be put in a position to supply a nonnull value for opt_ptr if full advantage is to be taken of this argument.

5.2.4 Default Handlers

In the event that a search of the stack segment finds no (nonreverted) condition block with a matching condition name, <signal_> will call a special system routine called <default_error_handler_>. The call is of the form

call default_error_handler_(mcptr, "condname");

If "condname" is a (reserved) *system-defined* condition, then <signal_> will normally have been called by a system-provided Fault Interceptor module, in which case that module will have supplied a nonnull value for mcptr. For this

14. This is a data structure that captures values for the address base registers, index registers, scu data, ring number, etc. (The abbreviation "scu" means "store control unit." Data stored in core as a result of executing the scu instruction are called "scu data.") See the MPM write-up on <signal_> for more details, if this information appears to be needed.

15. Handlers established by ON statements, rather than by <condition_>, cannot use opt_ptr even when invoked via a call to <signal_>.

reason, <signal_>'s call on <default_error_handler_> is able to provide the latter with adequate information for determining what to do.

The design is open-ended and modular in the sense that <default_error_handler_> can, in effect, act as a "transfer agent" by transmitting calls to separately coded default handlers for selected system-defined conditions. These individual default handlers are intended to be per-ring in nature. That is, default handling for a given system-defined condition, sys_cond, that is signaled in ring *s* need not be the same as the default handling for the same sys_cond that is signaled from another ring *r*.

If "condname" is a *user-defined* condition, a standard error message will be typed out, giving the user the name of the condition that has occurred. However, the user must be careful to observe that <default_error_handler> may attempt to interpret the machine conditions that it is "handed" if mcptr happens to be nonnull. Since the user cannot normally expect to anticipate such an interpretation (especially if the pointed-to machine conditions are garbage), the response of <default_error_handler_> can easily be unpredictable from the user's point of view.

5.2.5 Condition Handling for PL/I-Compiled Procedures

The current PL/I compiler handles conditions with a few shortcuts so that while the execution of PL/I ON, REVERT, and SIGNAL statements have effects similar to calls on <condition_>, <reversion_>, and <signal_>, the former are somewhat more restrictive but more efficient. Some indication of the implementation differences is provided here. More complete documentation is given elsewhere.[16]

By their nature, PL/I-compiled handlers are always blocks of code that are internal to the procedure in which the ON statement occurs, as exemplified in our introduction to this chapter. Hence, stacked condition blocks contain pointers (rather than instances of the "entry" type of datum) to the body of code that is the handler—and the body itself is compiled as part of the object code.

For each compiled ON statement in a PL/I block, there is reserved (in advance) space in the stack frame for the needed condition block. That is, the stack frame does not need to be lengthened at "run time" since the compiler generates a save sequence that sets the frame to the needed length, providing

16. R. A. Freiburghouse, J. D. Mills, and B. L. Wolman, *A User's Guide to the Multics PL/I Implementation* (Cambridge, Mass.: Cambridge Information Systems laboratory, General Electric Company, 1970), Section 9.8, "Conditions." This is now (1971) to be published by Honeywell.

space for all needed condition blocks. Moreover, the compiler knows the offsets in the stack frame where each condition block will be constructed. For this reason, the compiler is able to generate code for an ON statement, which, when executed, copies into the reserved stack space of the condition block data from a template of that block that has (also) been compiled into the (pure) procedure segment. The template information includes the I-$\left\{\begin{matrix}\text{am}\\ \text{am not}\end{matrix}\right\}$-reverted flag set initially to *am not*, and a pointer to the "body" of the handler that is also compiled into the procedure segment.

Execution of SIGNAL and REVERT statements, like execution of ON statements, employ short-call calling sequences (similar to the one described in Section 3.12) to what are called "PL/I operators." These are in effect built-in functions (and are, moreover, wired down to accommodate ring-0 supervisory code that has also been compiled from PL/I source language). The net effect is that code produced by PL/I ON and REVERT statements is even more efficient than the corresponding code produced via calls to condition_ and reversion_, while code produced from the SIGNAL statement has efficiency comparable to that for a call to signal_.

Programmers in PL/I have a choice of using either the built-in or the system's condition-handling facilities, or both, in any combination for the same condition in the same program. Naturally, the explicit facilities will be needed when PL/I-produced code must interface with code generated from other compilers. It is also true that conditions established by ON statements in PL/I programs may be signaled via calls to signal_ in non-PL/I procedures.

5.3 Abnormal Returns–Additional Discussion

5.3.1 General Concepts

This section is intended to provide background concepts that will lead to a fuller appreciation of the Unwinder mechanism. A procedure may have one or more entry points and *none*, one or more abnormal return points. Here we review the distinction between an *entry point* and an *abnormal* return point. Figure 5.3 will help develop both the differences and similarities.

Even though, from a user's point of view, entry and abnormal return points appear syntactically similar and, in fact, may even have identical storage representations, there is a distinct *functional* difference. The difference has to do with the availability of needed information when control passes to one of these points of a procedure. When *entered* via a call, a procedure should at that instant require no information other than what it is capable of

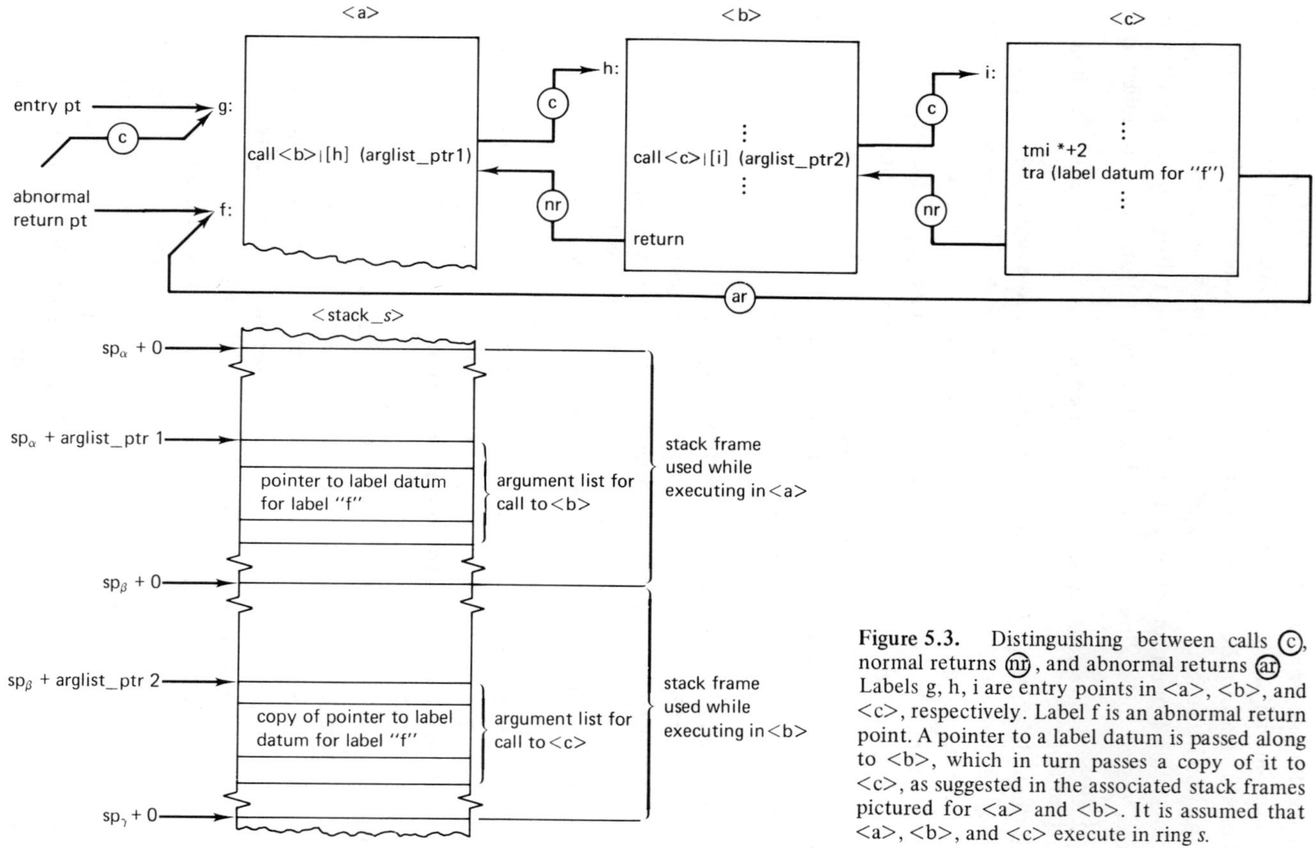

Figure 5.3. Distinguishing between calls (c), normal returns (nr), and abnormal returns (ar). Labels g, h, i are entry points in <a>, <b>, and <c>, respectively. Label f is an abnormal return point. A pointer to a label datum is passed along to <b>, which in turn passes a copy of it to <c>, as suggested in the associated stack frames pictured for <a> and <b>. It is assumed that <a>, <b>, and <c> execute in ring *s*.

developing and what is passed to it in the form of an argument list. Under these circumstances a procedure can and always does begin functioning with a new stack frame. On the other hand, when control passes to a procedure via an abnormal return point, execution *resumes*. This implies that certain information necessary to this resumption of effort may have been previously accumulated, probably in its then-current stack frame. Therefore, resumption at an abnormal return point in the general case clearly forces the need to recover this stack frame, that is, to reset the stack pointer to this frame. The clerical details involved in resetting stack conditions and in recovery of space for all allocated temporary data in the intervening procedures are numerous.

Even if all procedures in the chain of calls being bypassed (including the two procedures at the end points of the chain) have executed in only one ring, the complexity is sufficient to justify a system-provided Unwinder service. If we consider the more general case where procedures in the call chain may have executed in different rings, the clerical complexity is not only compounded, but protection issues dictate that a ring-0 helper for the Unwinder is required.

In the current implementation of the Unwinder,[17] the more limited "single-ring service" is all that is provided. The discussion in this section, however, attempts to anticipate a design for a more general multiring service. A general service is justified on the grounds that the user of a fully evolved Multics should not be forced to be conscious of ring crossings in planning an abnormal return. In many instances, a user may not even know about ring crossings in the path of the abnormal return. The next paragraphs will indicate more specifically some of the complexities that are involved.

Let *s* be the ring of some procedure <a> and let us assume that the pointer to the desired frame in <stack_*s*> is part of the label datum used for generating the abnormal return in an instruction of the form

tra label_datum

(We can normally assume that the value of label_datum has been passed along the call chain as an argument.) One might then imagine that the abnormal return to <a> can be achieved by executing some kind of return sequence that includes the appropriate adjustment of the stack pointer at <stack_*s*>|2 and the address base registers. Adjustment of <stack_*s*>|2 would have the virtue of recovering space in <stack_*s*> for frames of ring-*s* procedures that are bypassed in this return.

17. Listed in the MPM under subroutine calls of the Standard Service System.

The label datum that defines the abnormal return is not necessarily "authentic," however. Suppose, for instance, the stack pointer in the label datum has been inadvertently altered by the user and no longer corresponds to the beginning of *any* stack frame in <stack_*s*> (let alone to the frame that was intended). Clearly, chaos would result if an attempted abnormal return were allowed to proceed using an incorrect stack pointer. To check the given stack pointer for validity will involve, at the very least: (1) a search through the back pointers in the stack frames (at sp|16) for one that matches the given stack pointer, and (2) provisions for error returns in case the search fails to turn up a "good" match.

Even if all goes well, however, two very undesirable side effects must be considered. These would occur if any rings were crossed in the chain of calls from <a> to the point where the abnormal return was invoked. Specifically, suppose the chain is <a> calls <b> calls <c>, and suppose each call involves a ring crossing. At <c> imagine that the abnormal return is invoked by executing an instruction like

tra (label_datum for "f")

as suggested in Figure 5.3.

Side Effect No. 1. Suppose we fail to pop the top two frames in <rtn_stk> while executing this return. What will be the consequence the next time a normal return is executed that involves leaving ring *s* to reach an antecedent of <a>? For example, suppose <a> was originally reached at <a>|[g], via a call from ring *r*. In attempting to oversee the normal return from <a>, the Gatekeeper expects to find a validating return address in the top frame of <rtn_stk>. This address will not be found, because the frame in question is now buried below the top of <rtn_stk>. This failure causes the Gatekeeper to signal an unrecoverable error. The difficulty could be avoided only in very special situations where one can guarantee that all of <a>'s antecedents are in ring *s*.

Side Effect No. 2. What about the other stack segments that hold frames for bypassed procedures? If we fail to pop these frames while executing the abnormal return, then the space involved becomes unreclaimable.

Figure 5.4 suggests why the frame for <b>, pictured in <stack_*t*>, and any other frames that may have been stacked during the most recent "visit" to ring *t* (crosshatched), can never be reclaimed. The pointer at <stack_*t*>|[2] will not have been altered. Thus, after the abnormal return to <a>, any future visit to ring *t* will force the *adding on* of additional stack

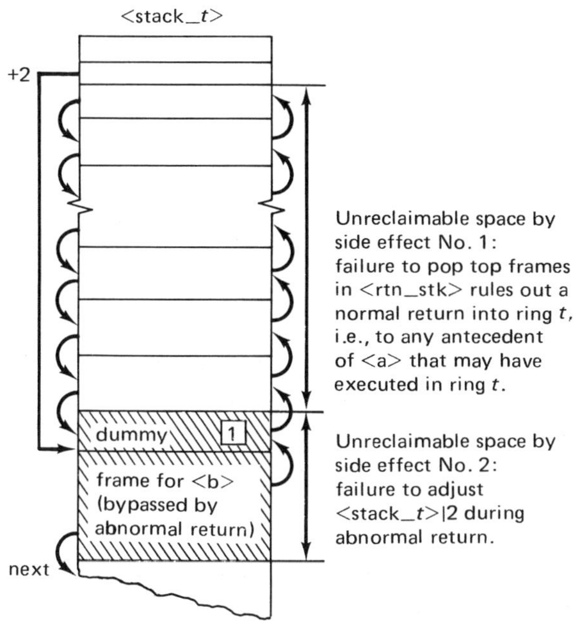

Figure 5.4. A picture of the unreclaimable space in <stack_*t*>

frames beginning at the place marked "next." As a matter of fact, since we have also failed to pop the appropriate frames in <rtn_stk>, preventing a normal return to any antecedent of <a> that may happen to execute in ring *t*, all space thus far used in <stack_*t*> would be unreclaimable.

5.3.2 The Unwinder Details

When the Unwinder mechanism is fully implemented to handle abnormal returns across protection rings, it will perform two principal classes of service. It will

1. validate or screen an attempted abnormal return and, if valid,
2. do various clerical tasks, including those motivated in the preceding subsection, which might otherwise be left undone when normal returns are bypassed.

In subsequent subsections these points are elaborated.

5.3.2.1 Validation of the Abnormal Return

For this discussion the case where <a> calls <b> calls <c>, with <c> attempting to execute an abnormal return to <a>|[f] is again employed as an example. There are two crucial reasons for validating this abnormal return.

1. The ring-access rules that were developed for entry points also apply to abnormal return points. Thus if *s, t,* and *u* are the ring numbers of <a>, <b>, and <c>, respectively, and if *u* lies outside the call bracket of <a>, an abnormal return from <c> to <a> should be illegal. The Unwinder should be (and is) held responsible for making these ring-access determinations.
2. Having determined that <c> has ring access to <a>, and in the event <c>'s ring lies within the call bracket of <a>, it is also necessary to verify that [f] is, in fact, an anticipated reentry point.

If <a> has been coded in a higher-level language like PL/I or ALM, then every such reentry point will be so declared. These declared reentry points are referred to as *doors*. In declaring that [f] is a permitted abnormal return point, that is, a door, it is assumed that the author of <a> is anticipating inward returns at [f] and has presumably programmed accordingly. If [f] is not named a door, the Unwinder should presume that an inward return to this point is not anticipated and cannot be risked, that is, is likely to result in undesirable, even chaotic, behavior.

Such a design philosophy is essential for the protection of supervisor routines that expect abnormal returns. Extending this concept to user-constructed subsystems implies that every abnormal return point designed to take control from an outer-ring procedure must be marked or declared by its author in the source code.

From such declarations the translators can generate doors in the linkage section in the form of specially formatted entry points. The anticipated format for a door is similar to that of a gate. Refer to Figure 4.22 for the details.[18]

Some of the language processors within the Multics system may eventually provide for establishing doors at the user's request.

At the present stage of development, although no doors are recognized and no abnormal returns can yet be handled across rings by the Unwinder mechanism, the PL/I compiler regards all GO TO statements that involve nonlocal label variables as potential abnormal returns. The generated code in each such

18. Although the format for a door has been selected, no doors will be recognized by the Gatekeeper until the fully general unwinder mechanism described here is implemented.

The Unwinder will treat the door pointed to in the no-op instruction of the entry sequence as *door* information, rather than as gate information. Only the first bits of this word are of interest to the Unwinder, i.e., bits 6 and 7, called the "g" field. A value of g = 2 identifies this entry as a door.

instance is a call to the Unwinder, that is, to <unwinder_>. Thus, the PL/I statement

```
go to label_var;
```

in a procedure <p> will result in generated code equivalent to

```
call unwinder_(label_var);
```

unless label_var is known to take on only label-constant values during execution in <p>.

Since nonlocal GO TO statements always refer to the labels within the same PL/I procedure, compliance with the no-ring-crossing constraint is guaranteed.

A subsystem writer who codes in a programming language that does not have this feature must, of course, "manually" call <unwinder_> when attempting to execute an intraring abnormal return.

It is worthwhile to explain briefly the protection provided in Multics in case a programmer *fails* to employ <unwinder_> when attempting to execute an abnormal return, whether intra- or inter-ring. The design concept here is this: Only if the abnormal return is to an inner-ring procedure is system intervention mandatory. This intervention will prevent a user from damaging either more-sensitive procedures within a subsystem or the supervisor itself. Each user should be given the freedom to do what he wants to (or thinks he can do correctly at his own risk, to avoid unnecessary system overhead) with procedures in rings he has full control over. If an inward crossing is attempted, the Gatekeeper should and would in fact intervene. Of course, the Gatekeeper would then properly interpret this transfer as an inward call. We are reminded that every inward call must be verified by determining that it is a gate (g = 1 in gate_info). If a valid abnormal return point is properly declared as a door (g = 2), the Gatekeeper, which is in search of a gate, will necessarily recognize the discrepancy and sound the alarm. It should now be clear why, in the Multics design, gates and doors are necessarily mutually exclusive.

5.3.2.2 Handling Unfinished Business

In its current implementation, <unwinder_> reverts the frames of bypassed procedures. The reversion is achieved by tracing backward through the chain of stack frames that correspond to the pending returns. The backward search (and reversion) ends when a stack frame is reached whose offset is less than or equal to that given in the return label that has been passed to <unwinder_> as the argument.[19]

Cleanup Concepts

Are there other types of temporary data storage besides stack frames that also should be reverted when normal returns are bypassed? Indeed there may be—in some subsystems, as we shall see later in this subsection. Multics must be prepared to serve such subsystems. The segment <unwinder_> is endowed with a built-in capacity of supervising the recovery of such other temporary storage as may have been allocated to segments other than the stack when and if the subsystem programmer wishes this service to be performed. This type of activity is referred to as "cleanup," because in principle, the activity need not be limited only to the recovery of storage. (A cleanup activity might also involve resetting of values for static variables, etc., to correspond with the state of the computation at an earlier point in time.)

Temporary data that a subsystem designer may want kept outside the stack are, for example, complex data structures whose size and shape are made to vary as a result of executing the one or more procedures that are being bypassed in the abnormal return. Thus, one can conceive of certain tree structures that are regarded as alterable, but tempory data, by a group of related procedures, say <a> that calls <b> that calls <c>, and so on. A programmer may then wish to consider any abnormal return to the antecedent of <a> as a signal to deallocate space now occupied by these temporary structures. Other types of recoverable data (external to the stack) may arise and be recognized in the particular subsystem you design. What follows in the next paragraphs is a brief outline of the general cleanup mechanism that has been embedded within <unwinder_>.

Cleanup activity is regarded as a special task to be invoked, when needed, in connection with any (or with each) pending return that is being bypassed in the course of the unwinding process.

Each cleanup task is invoked *as if it were a signaled condition*.

The Unwinder has, in other words, been designed to behave as if it has been instructed to call signal_("cleanup") on behalf of each bypassed procedure (or PL/I block). To implement this signaling analogy, a handler for

19. Eventually, of course, <unwinder_> may be implemented to revert frames in <rtn_stk> as well. Because it has a helper in ring 0, <unwinder_> would be able to consult the top frame of <rtn_stk> when a dummy frame, indicating a ring crossing, is encountered. Each stack frame or <rtn_stk> frame would then be reverted as it is passed over in this scan for the matching stack address.

each cleanup activity is stacked in the format of a bona fide condition handler under the condition name "cleanup".

As each stack frame is about to be reverted, search of that frame is made for a condition block for "cleanup". If found, <unwinder_> generates and executes a call to the designated cleanup-handler procedure before reverting the stack frame. The job that a properly written cleanup procedure must then accomplish is normally one of freeing all space occupied by temporary data that was previously allocated to segments outside the stack segment and of resetting the values for various static variables, and so forth, to the values they held prior to activation of the procedure being bypassed. If no such cleanup handler is found, the stack frame now being considered is reverted and the unwinding process continues.

Who Writes the Cleanup Procedures?

From the above discussion we can see that writing and using cleanup procedures is simple or complex, depending on the job to be done. A main function of a cleanup procedure may well be to prevent undue growth of "dead" storage in a process. A user may write his own cleanup routines and establish them as condition handlers—as many as he wishes. On the other hand, writing cleanup procedures and seeing to it that they become condition handlers (say by calls to <condition_>), and then later reverting them in the event the abnormal return never gets executed, is the sort of mechanical programming we may want compilers or assemblers to generate for us wherever possible. Fortunately, PL/I is one of these compilers whose data types are so represented in memory that all data of class automatic can be and are allocated to the stack. Hence, no explicit use of a cleanup procedure is needed. On the other hand, one can conceive of user programs for which there is need to code other types of cleanup activity such as closing files, terminating I/O stream names that have been previously attached to certain devices,[20] undoing certain changes made to directories or to directory pointers, undoing changes made to I/O modes, and so on.

Such compilers might well generate the needed code for the cleanup procedures and enable the cleanup condition when needed. (It is of historical interest that EPL, the precursor of PL/I in the Multics system, did just that.) The <unwinder_> procedure has been designed to anticipate this need.

To sum up, a call to <unwinder_> (present implementation) is automatically invoked when executing PL/I nonlocal GO TO statements but may

20. This subject will be discussed in Chapter 8.

be invoked explicitly by any user. Prior to reverting each stack frame, <unwinder_> checks that frame for the presence of a condition block for "cleanup". If found, the designated handler is invoked. As mentioned earlier, the frame reversion/cleanup process stops when a frame is reached whose offset is less than or equal to that given in the label-datum argument to <unwinder_>.

You should now be well convinced that a subsystem may be designed within Multics using or permitting others to employ abnormal returns, but the overhead for their oft-repeated use should, of course, be considered. Depending on the nature of the cleanup procedures needed (if any), such overhead might be very high, but the approach may still be practical if the alternatives are sufficiently unattractive. Generally speaking, use of abnormal returns is being avoided wherever possible in the implementation of Multics itself. (Code-value parameters are being used in place of statement-label parameters.) Old MAD or FORTRAN lovers that are accustomed to using statement-label parameters for abnormal returns should please take note.

6 The File System

6.1 Introduction

Chapters 1 and 2 spoke about the file system as a collection of supervisory modules (software extensions of hardware) that provided the virtual-memory environment in which the user's process executes. Chapter 4 touched briefly on the hierarchical (tree) structure of directory and nondirectory segments that has been chosen for implementing the "idealized" memory of the system. This chapter focuses more sharply on the directory structure and on a number of services of the Basic File System that a user is apt to invoke through use of the so-called file-system commands and the many system library routines that are at his disposal, for example, for the creation, manipulation, deletion, and so on, of segments and their attributes.

By way of review I comment on why Multics has retained, for the sake of historical continuity, the somewhat outdated term "file system." Why not now call it a "segment (management) system"? Indeed, readers would be justified in doing so. Recall, though, that the concept of *segment* is in some sense merely an extension of the concept of *file*. In most modern file systems,[1] files (as do segments) carry unique names, have attributes, are created, destroyed, allowed to grow and shrink, have access controls applied to them (i.e., may be shared), and are structured in a directory hierarchy. A file system maintains this structure and offers retrieval services, backup services, and so forth. Only the difference (albeit very significant) that segments are "instantaneously" shareable by virtue of being directly addressable in Multics programs distinguishes the segment from the file. Hence, readers are asked to accept, graciously I hope, the use of terms like "file system" and "Basic File System" in this book, as if "file" and "segment" were entirely synonymous.

The file system plays a central role in the execution of every process. Multics is designed so that, except for the matter of directory maintenance, an unsophisticated user can remain oblivious to the interaction between file-system modules and the remainder of his process. This is true because services of the file system will be invoked indirectly on behalf of the user by other modules, such as by the Linker, as a result of link faults. The Linker may be regarded as a major "customer" of the file system. By contrast, advanced users will typically seek more direct contact with the file system by issuing file-system commands that result in calls to the Basic File System. They may sometimes even forget they are exploiting the Linker to full advantage. The file-system commands permit the user, for example, to obtain listings of his files, create or delete files including directories, modify branches by renaming

1. Following CTSS.

them or altering access-control entries, and so on. They also allow the user to make a segment known so that he can directly address a segment, for example, an ascii file, via a PL/I pointer. As the user constructs subsystems having increased complexity, he is likely to need an increased understanding of the Multics file structure (hierarchy). In particular, he will need to see how modules of the file system maintain and control a dynamic interface between the file structure and his executing process.

In this chapter I hope to explain a number of the functions of the Basic File System with which the subsystem designer will be most concerned and over which he can exercise a degree of control. We shall be concerned primarily with two modules of the Basic File System (BFS), *Segment Control* and *Directory Control.*

Each of these modules[2] offers a significant interface with the user so that each may, upon explicit call or command, perform important service functions for the user. (Naturally, many of the services rendered by these modules are accomplished implicitly; the user is not immediately aware of these.) Segment Control's user interface lets the user deal with (i.e., partially manage) matters concerning the address space of his own process. Directory Control's user interface allows the user to examine and/or alter that portion of the directory hierarchy over which he has appropriate authorization. Hence, in this sense Directory Control offers the user an opportunity to interact with (and affect) the *system's* virtual memory (and not just the address space of his own process).

6.1.1 Segment Control Module (SCM)

This module is responsible for properly interpreting the intent of the user's symbolic references to segments. Thus, it is the SCM that determines to which, if any, of the segments already known to the process a given symbolic name does refer. If to none, the SCM must then determine if any existing segment in the hierarchy[3] is to be associated with the user's symbolic name. If to none, the SCM must then determine if a new segment is to be created and placed in the hierarchy (on a temporary or permanent basis). Questions like the following must be answered: Where in the directory structure should a newly created segment be placed? Is the new segment to be empty, or should it be a copy of an existing one? Finally, the SCM must see to it that,

2. Primary MSPM references for the material in this chapter are the sections that deal with segment management, Segment Control, Known Segment Table, directory data base, Directory Control, and access control.

3. Henceforth, we shall use the word "hierarchy" to mean "file-system hierarchy."

however the segment is identified, it is made known in the executing process (with appropriate access-control rights). Another way of saying this is that the target segment is put into the state where it may be properly written, read, or transferred to by the segment that referred to it.

One of the data bases that will come under careful scrutiny now is the KST (Known Segment Table) to which frequent, but glancing, reference has been made in preceding chapters. In simplest terms, the KST is a dynamically maintained "registry" of the segments that are currently part of the process. Symbolic reference names and other identification are kept in the per-segment entries of the KST. These data also provide context information with which the SCM can determine the intended target when one segment makes symbolic reference to another segment that has previously been similarly referenced, that is, from a point in the process having a matching context.

Depending on the context, for instance, the ring in which a referencing procedure executes, or the parent directory of the referencing procedure, the same symbolic reference name may be intended to refer to the same or to different segments (i.e., to different points) in the file-system hierarchy. Moreover, there may be several different reference names in use that are intended to refer to the same point in the hierarchy. These cases of multiplicity are sure to arise in subsystems involving groups of users, with several directories available as repositories for common routines. The SCM maintains control over these reference-name–segment-number pairings in a given process. Its job is to develop and reuse each name-number pair in its proper context.

6.1.2 Directory Control Module (DCM)

All user requests that deal with creation, deletion, or alteration of files and/or their file descriptions ultimately result in invoking Directory Control to make the appropriate modification to the directory structure. All inquiries about the status or location of segments and/or their descriptions also must ultimately invoke Directory Control, because only this module is permitted to read and alter the contents of the directory segments.

6.2 Directory Structure

In Chapter 4 we began our discussion of the directory structure. Here, we shall review it and amplify it with the introduction to the as-yet-untreated subject of *directory links.* There are actually two types of entries that may be added to a directory–*branches* and *links.*

6.2.1 Branches

A *branch*, you recall, is a detailed description of a segment. Among other things, a branch contains the physical locations in secondary storage of the records that comprise the segment.[4] The segment described in the branch may be another directory, or, if it is not a directory, it can be thought of as a data or procedure segment. Any process that has access to a segment's branch is able to make the segment known in that process. In rarer cases, impure procedures, for example, it is a *copy* of the file, rather than the original, which is made known in the process. Of course, when a copy is made, that copy is a new segment that must be uniquely identified as part of the file system. A branch that points to the copy must be made and placed in an appropriate directory.[5]

At the time it is created, each branch has associated with it a unique identifier (in reality a generated 36-bit serial number). In addition, each branch holds a list of one of more "entry names." These are the official nicknames or aliases by which we as users will normally refer to the segment in our source code. The Multics search rules, described later in this section, are so designed that any entry name in the branch is a permissible *reference name* in our source code.

The alias feature is a necessity in Multics, because it is important, for efficiency and other reasons, to support the binding of two or more individually named segments (not necessarily interrelated logically or functionally). If, for instance, segments <u>, <v>, and <w> are bound into a single segment, that new segment should be known by all three names (<u>, <v>, and <w>), or else existing programs that refer to <u>, <v>, and <w> would have to be recoded (a horrible consequence) to be capable of again linking to the same targets.

4. In point of fact, since the file (segment) normally extends over several records (1024 words each), the *physical location* takes the form of a *file map*, which is an ordered list of the addresses for the individual file records. A zero length file has an appropriately marked file map. As the file's size is adjusted upward to range over one or more records, entries are made in the file map that point to these records. So as not to take up unnecessary storage, a record of a file which has not yet been "written into," is regarded to have all its words in the zero state. Such zero records are not actually allocated secondary storage at the outset. Instead, the file map entry for this record is marked appropriately. Whenever a process makes reference to such a record (as a page of the corresponding segment), a block of core consisting of zeros would be assigned in core memory.

5. If the copy is made for temporary use, i.e., only for the duration of the process that refers to it, the branch is placed in a directory that is associated with this process. It is appropriately called the *process directory*. Every process, while it exists in Multics, will have its own process directory.

An appreciation of the alias concept is enhanced by explaining the following Multics convention. A call reference to an external segment of the form

"<procname>" in ALM (or "procname" in PL/I)

will be interpreted as the entrypoint whose address is

"<procname>|[procname]" (or "procname$procname" in PL/I).

The value of this convention becomes clear when we now consider a single procedure that has two or more aliases. Suppose we picture a library segment whose branch has two aliases, "insert" and "delete". Then assuming insert and delete are declared external, a PL/I call of the form

call insert (A, B);

will be interpreted by the compiler as syntactically identical with

call insert$insert (A, B);

while a call of the form

call delete (C, D);

would be interpreted the same as

call delete$delete (C, D);

and the respective targets will be

s#|insert

and

s#|delete

Here, the symbol "s#" is used to refer to the common segment number that would be returned by the Segment Control Module at the Linker's request. The offsets insert and delete are values that the Linker would obtain by inspecting the insymbol table in the segment.

The converse situation should also be appreciated. Namely, if a segment has only one entry name, say "delete," but the procedure it represents has two entry points, one named "delete" and the other named "insert," then to reach the second entry point the user has no choice but to refer to it as delete$insert, that is,

call delete$insert (A, B);

Another purpose of the alias feature is to permit different programmers on the same project to refer to the same segment with different names, for example, delete and remove. Rather than reassemble or recompile the code written by these programmers to force conformity among several programmers on the same project in the referencing of a given segment, it may sometimes be simpler to guarantee the appearance of both names in the branch of such a segment (and to let both names have the same offset value).[6]

Any programmer that has write access to the directory holding the particular branch may add to it as many distinct entry names as he cares to. Of course, no two branches in any one directory are allowed to have a common entry name.[7] But two or more (different) directories may each have a branch with the same entry name. Figure 6.1a is an attempt to summarize the ideas concerning directory structure given in the foregoing discussions. To conserve space, circles represent directories and rectangles represent nondirectories in this figure (just the reverse of the technique used in Figure 4.1).

6.2.2 Links

A *link* is a special kind of named entry whose purpose is to point to another entry normally in some (any) other directory. Links permit a useful form of cross-referencing capability that can be superimposed over the basic tree structure formed by the branch-type entries. Ordinarily, since segments and their corresponding branches must be one-to-one, no two directories can directly share the same segment. But, for example, with the use of link-type entries that point to branches, a subsystem designer can effectively develop a directory so it *appears to have* segments in it that, in fact, belong to other directories. Thus, in Figure 6.1b, directory q, which "points" directly to only two segments, named v and w, indirectly points to two others, h in n and c in s. Likewise, directory s indirectly points via a link to file m in the superior directory x. This capability for grouping under one directory a selected set of files that, via links, are actually located in other directories is a powerful "packaging" device in the design of subsystems. This packaging is especially effective when the subsystem is later embedded within other subsystems. We will return to this topic later on in this chapter.

Note, also, that if q is a directory belonging to user1 and n is a directory

6. This would probably mean revising the source code for this segment to make delete and remove synonyms (in ALM) or dual labels (of the same PL/I statement) and then recompiling.

7. This restriction is guaranteed by the Basic File System.

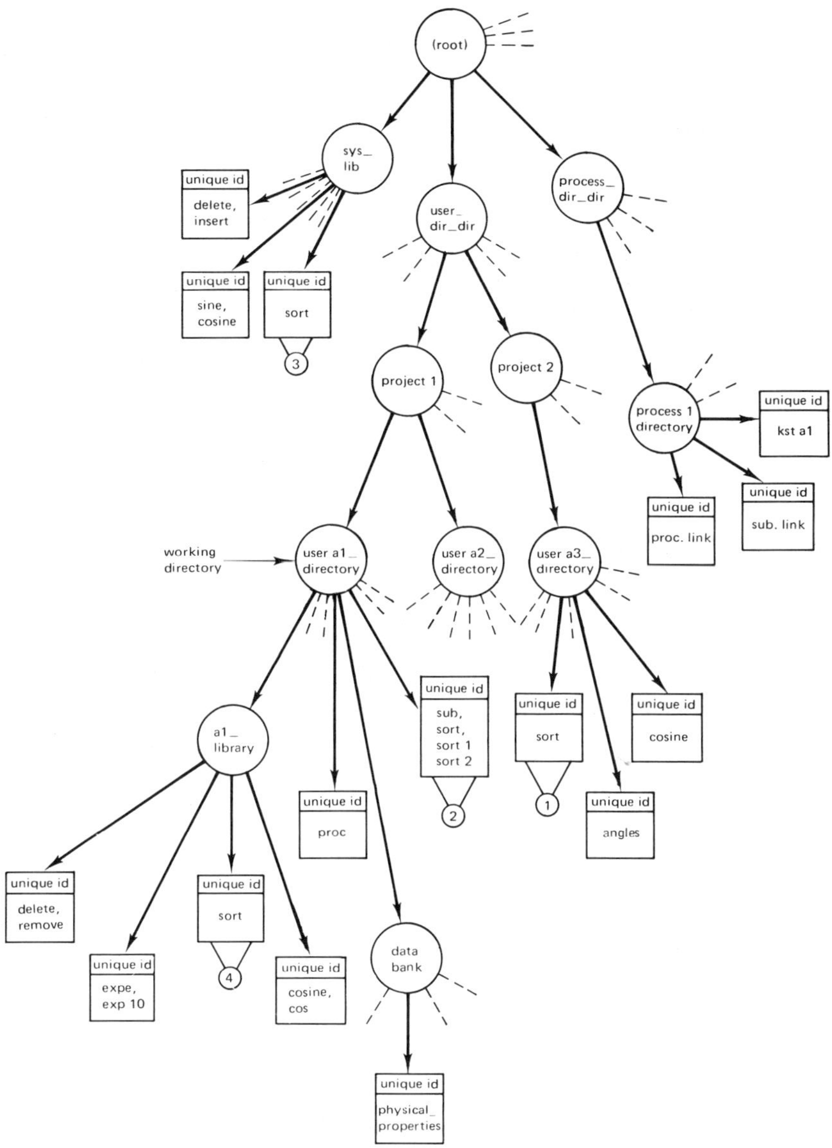

Figure 6.1a. Conceptual model of the file-system tree structure
Circles represent directory segments and squares represent nondirectory segments. In reality, the names shown in the directory segments (circles) and in the nondirectory segments (squares) are, in fact, stored in the branches to these segments, i.e., in the immediately superior directory.

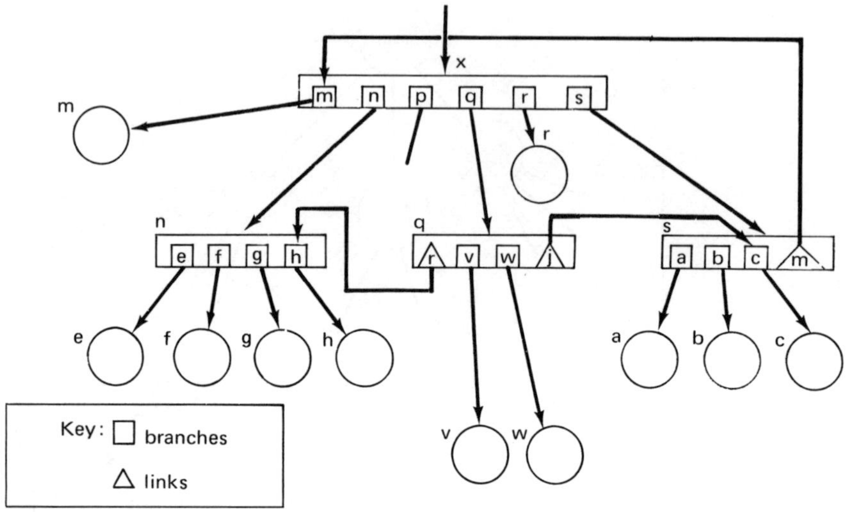

Figure 6.1b. Conceptual model of the file-system tree structure
This shows the cross-referencing that can be achieved with the use of links. Links may be independently named. Thus, in q, the link named j points to the branch whose name is c.

belonging to user2, then user1 may use the symbolic reference "r" while user2 may use the symbolic reference "h," each intending to access the same segment (<h>). Actual access to <h>, however, is another matter. User1's access to <h> is governed by the ACL information in the branch named "h" in <n>. The existence of a link to <h> in user1's directory has no bearing on user1's access privileges to <h>. Only users that have write access to <n> can accord user1 access privileges to <h>.

6.2.3 Path Names

There are several ways by which the system can refer unambiguously to a particular branch (or link) in the hierarchy. As for the subsystem writer, the primary way is by giving the path name for the entry.[8]

A *path name*, in the simplest sense, is a list of the node names from the root to the branch (or link) inclusive. Elements of the list are separated, not by commas as you might expect, but by the ">" character. Thus, the path

8. Another way, mentioned here only for the sake of completeness, is by *unique id.* Uniqueness is assured because the 36 bits include the date and time of day that the branch was created as well as the identification of the hardware system that created it. The ordinary user will not normally know the unique id for a segment he wants to reference.
The MSPM provides more details.

name for the branch in Figure 6.1a named sub would be

“(root)>user_dir_dir>project 1>useral_directory>sub”

This part is never written

Since this same branch has the alternate entry name sort, an equally unique path name would be

“(root)>user_dir_dir>project 1>useral_directory>sort”

directory path name — entry name

path name for the branch (or link)

Note that a path name for a branch can be thought of as having two main parts,[9] the path name for the directory, which points to the branch (*directory path name*), followed by the *entry name* for the branch.

Certain shorthand conventions are expected by the Basic File System procedures. When you write a path name that emanates from the root node, you never (in fact, may not) write the letters “root” as the leftmost part of the path name. Simply begin the path name with “>” as a shorthand for “root>”. Thus, any path name, for example “>a>b>c”, which begins with “>” is recognized as an *absolute path name.*

6.2.3.1 Relative Path Name

An executing process has at all times associated with it a directory that is designated as the *working directory.*[10] This is a directory that the process happens to be currently “using.” It is merely a reference marker to a point in the hierarchy from which it becomes convenient to describe paths to other segments. Thus, tree paths to a particular node may be described relative to the working directory of a process. If a path name begins with some character *other than* “>”, the given path is interpreted *relative to the working direc-*

9. A user can call for services of the Basic File System directly via certain of its “primitives” in Segment and Directory Control, indirectly via such gates as the entry points in the SCM, or indirectly by using one of the many file-system commands described in the MPM. In these calls (or commands), the target procedure in Segment or Directory Control either expects to have a path name passed to it as an argument or expects to return a path name as an (output) argument. Typically, the caller is required to furnish the path name as a *pair* of arguments, i.e., *directory path name* and *entry name*. I will be speaking about some of these primitives in Section 6.4.

10. The user is free to alter the designation of the working directory. The MPM describes a series of commands that allows the user to exercise direct control over the designation of the working directory.

tory. Use of this convention greatly shortens the length of most path names. This is illustrated by referring again to Figure 6.1a. Assume that usera1_ directory is the working directory at some instant in time.

Example 1

The path name for proc is simply "proc"; for sub it is simply "sub". Thus, for branches (or links) in the working directory, the entry name and the path name are identical.

Example 2

The path name for physical_properties (relative to the working directory) is "data_bank>physical_properties".

Example 3

It is also possible to use the relative path-name convention when referring to a branch that is not a descendant of the working directory. This is done with the aid of the character "<". It is interpreted to mean *parent of* the working directory. Moreover, "<<" would mean *parent of parent* of the working directory, and so on.

Thus, a suitable (relative) path name for <usera3_directory> is "<<project2>usera3_directory". This is a somewhat more attractive alternate to the (absolute) path name,

">user_dir_dir>project2>usera3_directory",

especially since users will not normally know the names of all the parent directories.

Example 4

As another example of the same type, the (relative) path name for the segment named "angles" would be "<<project2>usera3_directory> angles".

6.2.3.2 Retrieving File-Branch Information

When Directory Control is handed a path name for the purpose of retrieving corresponding file-branch information, the desired directory entry is retrieved and its type (link or branch) determined. If it is a branch, the target has been reached; if it is a link, the path name found in the link is then employed for a repetition of the retrieval process. A *chain* of links eventually leading to a branch is also a possibility. Directory Control is coded to prevent the repeated retrieval process from getting out of hand, as could occur in the event the links loop back on themselves. Figure 6.2 shows a chain of two links leading to a file branch. The chain depicted in Figure 6.2 can conceivably arise in the following way. User4 grants permission to user3 to use the routine

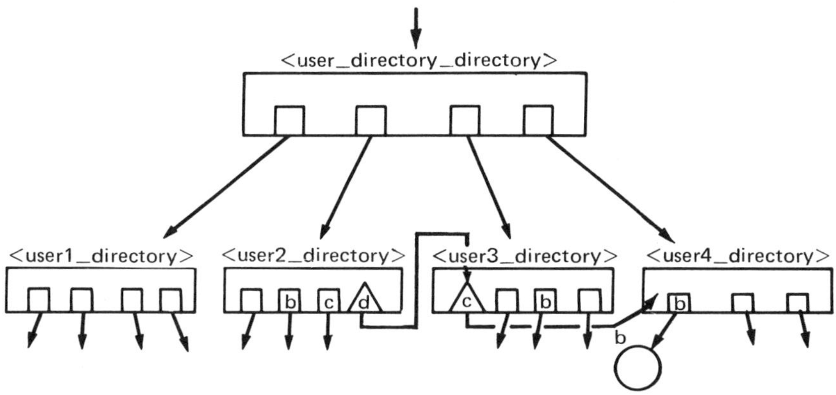

Figure 6.2. Chain of links
If user2 and user3 appear in the access-control list for <b> in user4's user directory, then user2 may use "d" as a symbolic reference and user3 may use "c" as a symbolic reference to the segment whose branch entry is named "b".

called "b". But, it is inconvenient for user3 to refer to the same procedure as "b" because he already has a routine in his directory called "b", so he chooses to refer to the user4 procedure as "c". At some other time user3 persuades user2 to use the same routine, only user2 chooses to call it by still another name, "d", for similar reasons. When and if user2 makes a reference to "d", he may find he has no access to it, if user4 has made no provision to include user2 in the permission list for "b".

6.2.4 Programming with Reference Names Instead of Path Names

If every programmer were forced to unambiguously designate every segment by its path name (absolute or relative), the job of the administrative modules would be made a great deal easier, but they would have few, if any, customers! A major design objective of Multics is to shift the burden of unambiguous segment designation, or as much of the burden as possible, from the user to the system. Certainly, for example, the ordinary PL/I or FORTRAN programmer should be entirely freed of this burden.

The purpose here is to show in a general way how this is done and to provide further details in later sections.

In ordinary usage, the reference name given for a segment is the name given to the segment's directory entry (normally a branch). This reference name can be thought of as the path name for the file *stripped of its front end* (i.e., stripped of its directory path name). It is the omission of this front end that, while making it easier for the users, complicates the problem for the SCM when it is asked to obtain a segment pointer for the symbolically referenced segment.

If the target of this reference is already known, and moreover known by the same reference name, a search of the KST for a match on the name as the search key will be successful (and relatively fast) so the SCM can return the wanted segment pointer (containing the index of the indicated KST entry) forthwith. However, if the target is either not known or known by some alias reference names–and these are permitted in Multics[11]–then the SCM has a more complicated task to perform.

As a preface to the explanation of this task, I observe that when a segment is made known to a process, the full path name (together with its unique identifier), and not merely the reference name, is recorded in the KST.[12] The SCM's first step, therefore, is to expand the given reference name into a full path name (by applying certain search rules explained shortly) and to use the path name to fetch the wanted segment's unique identifier, which is found in that segment's branch. Armed with the unique identifier of the target as a search key, a search is made to see if there is a KST entry with a matching unique identifier. If yes, then the target is already known by another reference name. If no, then the target is unknown and must now be made known.

match was found is used to construct the wanted pointer; but, before returning to its caller, the Linker, the SCM appends the new reference name to the KST entry so that from now on the segment will also be known by the new name. Any new link faults to the new name will then be handled expeditiously.

The interesting question that remains is, How does the SCM go about expanding a reference name to a full path name when this proves necessary? Indeed, is there any guarantee that the SCM can *always* decide on a path name? To set the stage for answering these questions, a hypothetical case for study is created, again relying on Figure 6.1a for a frame of reference.

Suppose the procedure named proc is executing in a process which shall be called process1. Now, let <proc>, in particular, be the segment whose branch is in <usera1_directory>. Further, let us suppose <proc> now incurs a link

11. These are discussed further in Section 6.3.1.
12. To be more precise, the KST entries for directory segments contain full path names. The KST entries for nondirectory segments contain reference names.

fault to someplace in <sort>. The Fault Interceptor passes the baton to the Linker, which, after extracting the string "sort" from <proc>'s outsymbol table, now calls the SCM, asking it to return a segment pointer to <sort>, that is, an its pair of the form

sort #	0	its
0	0	0

Assume that the SCM's attempt to find a match on the reference name "sort" in the KST has failed. The SCM now has the problem of deciding which of the many possible segments named "sort" is the one desired by the faulting procedure. Looking over Figure 6.1a, we see four branches, each having an entry name "sort". Some are more "likely" than others, but, in principle, any one of these may be the *intended* segment.

Most likely, however, the one marked ① is *not* intended. But, any one of the other three, that is, ②, ③, and ④, might very well be the one the user had in mind.

Clearly, the use of a reference name for <sort> rather than its full path name results in an apparent ambiguity that must somehow be resolved. In Multics a set of system conventions is provided by which this ambiguity is removed. These conventions are called *search rules.* They are stated in the next subsection. The important point here is that a programmer that employs reference names in his program must understand these rules if his programs are to reference their intended objects.

The idea is to search an ordered set of directories for an entry that matches the given reference name. The directory that is most relevant, from the point of view of the context in which the external reference is being made, is searched first; then, the next most relevant directory is searched, if necessary, and so on. If a match is found in a given directory, the path name of the matched entry is immediately known and is presumed to be the one that is wanted.

Failure to find any match among the directories in the search set results in a failure to construct the path name, even though some other directories in the hierarchy, not in the search set, may have entries whose names match the given reference name. News of a failure propagates back to the user, as described in Section 6.2.7.

Note that from the point of view of a tree search, use of the search rules constitutes a heuristic rather than an algorithm. This is not to say that a user does not have full control "over his own destiny" since he is using known and advertised search rules. He presumably arranges his work in accordance with these rules. Hence, the results are always predetermined.

6.2.5 Standard Search Rules

As pointed out in the MPM,[13] every programming system employs a set of search rules in one way or another. Consider, for example, the early batch processing system. One furnished a job deck of cards consisting of a main program followed by a set of subprograms. During the loading process, external references encountered in the program or subprograms of the job were assumed to refer to subprograms in the same deck, or else in the system library (on tape or disk). The ambiguity that could occur (if one of the subprograms in the deck had a name identical with a program in the library) was resolved by virtue of the prescribed *order of search*—the deck of cards (first in the order of search) being regarded as contextually more relevant than the system's library.

In a like manner, the Multics search rules amount to a sequence of trial assumptions and tests for their validity. The first trial assumption is that the intended target is a segment having a branch in the same directory as the one holding the branch for the faulting procedure segment. That is, the first directory to be considered is the so-called *caller directory* abbreviated as "cdir". In our example of the preceding subsection, the cdir for <proc>, the faulting segment, is "usera1_directory". Hence, the branch marked ② in Figure 6.1a would be selected because a search among the branches of usera1_directory would result in a match with "sort". In general, however, if no entry can be found in cdir having a name that matches "sort", the SCM falls back on a *secondary* search strategy. This is to search a (system prescribed) ordered set of other directories. First in this set is the user's current working directory dubbed "wdir". (Frequently, cdir and wdir will be the same, in which case only one is searched.) Following this is a set of system library directories, and finally the *process directory*. The first match found is then considered to identify the intended target.

To summarize, the Standard Search Set is given in Table 6.1.

6.2.6 Alternate Search Rules

A design objective of Multics is eventually to provide users the option to specify their own search rules, even perhaps in a purely dynamic sense, that

13. See Chapter I of the MPM for a well-developed and concise discussion of the search rules in current use and the reasons for selecting them.

Table 6.1 Standard Search Set

	Directory	Name (or metaname)
Primary Strategy	1. The directory holding the branch to the faulting procedure	(cdir)
Secondary Strategy	2. The user's working directory	(wdir)
	3. The Multics command and systems library	system_library_standard
	4. Several additional special libraries. The list is given in the MPM	
	5. The user's process directory	(pdir)

is, on a search-to-search basis. Also intended is a provision such that the search of individual directories may be qualified using various logical relations, possibly even letting the user specify complete algorithms that would be used to examine the directories.

As an interim measure and a step toward this objective, readers should note that use of the library routine,

set_search_dir

(described in the MPM) will permit a user to cause any specified directory to be inserted between cdir and wdir in the Standard Search Set.

6.2.7 Permission to Search

The scan of each directory in SCM's search set is performed by Directory Control. Each search of a directory is done on behalf of the faulting segment. Consequently, Directory Control, a ring-0 module, first ascertains the faulting segment's right-of-search, determined by its ring number. In essence, the rules are as follows. Suppose the faulting segment is <a> and it needs to know if "b" is an entry name in <directory1>. Although Directory Control does the "looking," it first checks that the user has search privileges in <directory1>. This check amounts to determining if the user_id (for the process that is calling Directory Control) appears in the access-control list for the branch describing <directory1> and, moreover, that the E (execute) attribute is *on* in the effective mode of this branch. For a refresher on what the user_id is, review Section 4.2.2 of this book.

If any directory on the search list fails to meet these criteria, it is skipped, and the next directory in the set is searched.

As another example, if <proc> took a link fault using the reference cosine, a path name to the branch named "cosine", found in sys_lib, would be returned. If prior to taking this link fault the user had executed the "change_wdir" command,[14] designating the path name "<usera1_directory>a1_library" as the working directory, then his own library cosine routine would be selected instead of the Multics-library cosine routine.

Finally, note that in the hypothetical situation given in Figure 6.1a, if useral's <proc> takes a link fault to sort while the working directory is set at usera1_directory, it would appear impossible for the SCM to return a pointer to the sort procedure in a1_library, that is, to ④, unless the user makes some deliberate effort to achieve this objective. This is because usera1 already has a branch named *sort* (one of four aliases) in the same directory that holds <proc>, the caller.

In order to give <proc> the opportunity to reference the a1_library routine called sort, one of two approaches must be taken.

a. Prior to the call to sort, make an explicit request of the SCM to "initiate" the desired file as a segment and therafter refer to it not by name but by direct addressing [e.g., by a pointer-qualified (based storage) reference, if coded in PL/I]. A segment pointer will have been returned to the user in the call to initiate the wanted segment. To initiate a segment in this way, a programmer must be able to furnish the SCM with the path name of the desired file. Note that the same problem can recur again during execution in another similar process. The explicit call to the SCM for initiating the desired sort file does not alter the basic directory structure or search strategy, so it only provides a per-process "remedy." Additional discussion of this type of expedient will be deferred until Section 6.4.

b. Make some change to the directory structure itself at any time prior to the implicit invocation of the SCM. One possible change that might be made is as follows: First, delete the alias sort from the list of four names given to the branch marked ②. (The "deletename" command can be used for this purpose.) Second, add a link to usera1_directory that points to the branch named sort in al_library, as sketched in Figure 6.3. (The "link" command can be used for this purpose.)

The foregoing actions exemplify the type of control a user can exercise on the directory structure whose root node is his user directory. In later sections, especially Section 6.3.3, the case where the same reference name may

14. See the MPM for a description of this command and others mentioned in this chapter.

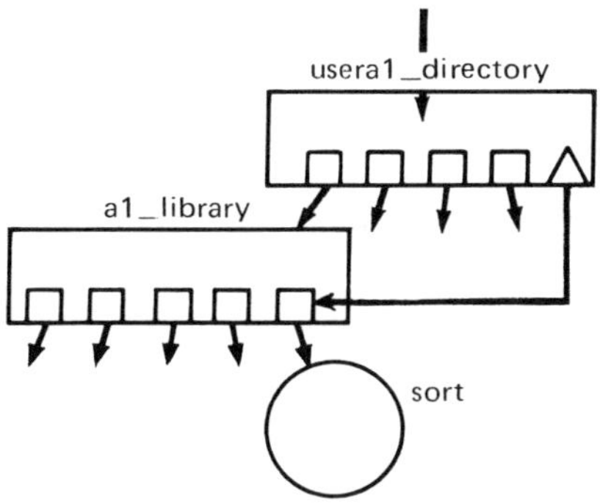

Figure 6.3. Linking to a branch named sort

be used (in the same process) to mean different segments in the hierarchy will be considered. This conflict-of-names problem and ways to solve it or avoid it is one with which subsystem designers will frequently be confronted.

6.2.8 The Case of a Search Failure

If, after considering every directory on the search list, no entry is found, this failure will be considered to be an error, and the error code is returned by the SCM to the Linker and thence to the Fault Interceptor, which signals a linkage_error condition in the ring of the faulting segment. If the user has not provided his own handler, a system-supplied default handler will be invoked. It will print an articulate message, telling precisely what could not be found and wait for a (hopefully remedial) response from the user at his console. In this way the nature of the error is reflected back to the user.

6.2.9 Access Failures

If the target of the search is found by Segment Control, the access rights to the user whose procedure has link faulted to this target (or whose procedure has called explicitly for the initiation of that target) may well be nil.[15] This

15. For convenience I mention here some of the access-failure logic (much of which was described in Chapter 4) that would result in nil access rights for the target. First a check is made to see if the user's user__id appears on an ACL (access-control list) entry in the branch. Failure to find the user__id (or a class name that includes user__id as a member) in any ACL entry of the branch is, in fact, only a partial indication that the creator of the target wishes access to be denied to this user. Each directory is actually provided with another access-control list. It is called the common access-control list (CACL). The access-control logic also includes a check of the CACL after failing to find the user__id in the ACL of the target branch. If the user__id is found in the CACL, then the associated (REWA) access rights listed therein are applied. Failure to find a listing on the CACL seals the verdict. (In Chapter 4, I deliberately omitted a discussion of the CACL when I described the structure of a directory. The reader can see these details in appropriate sections of the MSPM.)

fact does not "perturb" either Segment Control (or the Linker). The target will still be made known and the (REWA) access rights, whatever they may be, duly recorded in the KST entry. Only when an actual (first) reference is made to the target, that is, after Segment Control is reinvoked to create the needed segment descriptor word, would an access violation (if any) be detected by the user. These steps are elaborated in Section 6.5.

In short, two types of access failure have been discussed in this and the preceding subsections. An access failure to a directory in the search causes rejection of the make-known request ("The operation was a success, but the patient died" immediately.). An access failure to the target itself will not be detected at make-known time but rather at the time actual use of the target is made (The patient may die later.).

6.3 Making a Segment Known–Fine Points

Assuming the search activity has been successful, that is, the SCM now has a complete path name for the desired segment, and, assuming a search of the Known Segment Table, using the unique identifier as the key, fails to find an entry with a match on this key, the next job is to create a new KST entry for this segment. In this section we focus on the details of the KST entry and the way it is embedded in the KST. We also look at some of the fine points, that is, ways the user can take advantage of this closer look at the KST and its structure.

The act of creating a KST entry is often referred to as *initiating* a segment. Here, we are still thinking about this step as part of a chain of events that began with a link fault. However, other implications of interest to subsystem writers will be considered in Section 6.4. How the user is able to explicitly cause the initiation of any desired segment (provided he can designate its path name) is explained there.

In making a segment known, any directories that must be searched to locate the given segment, must themselves be made known to the executing process. As a result, KST entries for all "superior" directory segments, of a given segment <s>, that is, all those along the tree path from <s> to the root node, will already have been constructed when the entry for <s> itself is created and placed in the KST.

Each entry is threaded back to the entry that corresponds to the immediately superior directory in the hierarchy. In this way, KST entries form a tree structure.[16] In essence, the KST tree is a subtree of the entire file-

16. A complete description of the KST and its storage structure is given in the MSPM.

system hierarchy and characterizes the current state of the executing process.

Table 6.2 lists the items in each KST entry.[17] Item 3 serves as the backward thread referred to in the preceding paragraph. The very first item is a dynamically maintained list of reference names by which each segment is *known* in the process. More will be said about this item momentarily. Items 6, 7, 8, 9, and 10 represent information copied from the corresponding branch at the time the segment is initiated. The effective mode and ring brackets (items 7 and 8) are used by Segment Control to construct (and possibly later to revise) SDWs (segment descriptor words). Items 2, 4, and 5 will be disregarded in the present discussion.

Only the Basic File System is privileged to use or modify KST data. This is because the data kept here are the basis for policing the process's use of each segment, and for this reason must remain compatible with the latest access-control information given in the branch for this segment.

6.3.1 Listing Reference Names in the KST

In a single process the same target segment may be referred to by one of several different reference names. The first of these names that is actually used as a reference will trigger the initiation of the segment (i.e., the construction of a KST entry). The segment will then initially be known by this first reference name. Later, if a second reference name is used and if the SCM determines that this, too, is a valid alias for the same segment, this alias is also entered into the KST (as an appendage to the list in Item 1 of the same entry).

Any of the following are valid reference-name aliases for a segment:

1. Entry names in the branch for this segment.
2. Entry names in a link to the branch for this segment.
3. Any name that the user may wish to declare (by an explicit call to the SCM) to be an alias for the segment. Unlike entry names embedded in the branches of the hierarchy, however, aliases that are declared in calls to the SCM are temporary, that is, for the life of the process. This is because the KST vanishes when the process is destroyed and so does the temporary alias. Section 6.4 mentions how these alias declarations are made.

6.3.1.1 Ring-Context Prefixes as Additional Qualifiers

There is more detail that has thus far been withheld from the reader—in an effort to build up the full picture in stages—some of which must now be revealed and the rest discussed in Section 6.3.3.

17. Items 7, 8, and 10 are updated from time to time as a result of subsequent changes made in the corresponding branch.

Table 6.2 List of Items in a KST Entry

Item No.	Importance Level of Item for Discussion in This Chapter (1 is most important)	Item Description	Applicability Check on the Type of Segment: Directory Segment	Applicability Check on the Type of Segment: Nondirectory Segment
1	1	*List of reference names*[a]	√	√
2	nil	Number of currently known segments in this process for which this directory is the parent directory	√	ignore
3	1	*Pointer to the branch* for this segment (Includes segment number for this segment's parent directory)	√	√
4 & 5	nil	Transparent usage and transparent modification switches	√	√
6	4	*Directory segment switch* (*on* if a directory)	√	√
7	1	*Effective mode* (R, E, W, A)	√	√
8	1	*Ring brackets* (r1, r2, r3)	√	√
9	3	*Unique identifier* (36 bits)	√	√
10	2	*Date* and *time* the *branch* for this segment was *last modified*	√	√

[a] If this entry is for a directory, the list consists of the (one or more) full path names for the directory.

Each reference name that is stored in the KST entry has prefixed to it an important bit of context information, namely, the validation level.[18] This number is the ring in which the referencing procedure is executing when it makes the symbolic reference. The KST form is

"*nn*_refname"

where *nn* is the validation level. If the SCM is subsequently asked for a segment pointer to the same "reference," mere discovery of this name in a KST entry will not be sufficient; the prefixed validation level must also be matched against the current validation level. Only then will the SCM easily deduce that the index of the KST entry where the match was found is the appropriate segment number for use in constructing the requested segment pointer.[19]

By associating the validation level *nn* with each recorded reference name in the KST, the SCM is able to offer the user an extra degree of control over the mapping of names to their intended target segments. A user may, if he chooses, use the same reference name to mean two or more different segments, each target being determined in the context of the ring in which the reference to it has been made.

6.3.1.2 Examples

A somewhat elaborate and admittedly contrived series of examples is given here to illustrate the points that have just been made. Assume that the file-system hierarchy includes the files and file branches as shown in Figure 6.4. Suppose further that in usera5's process a sequence of symbolic references are made in the order shown in Table 6.3.

Each line in the table gives values for the pertinent state variable (columns 2, 3, and 4) that were extant at the time the symbolic reference was made. It also shows the identified target segment (column 6) and the name, if any, that has been added to the corresponding KST entry (column 7). The response of the SCM (columns 5–7) for a given line in the table is clearly dependent on the process's history. For our purposes, the history begins at Line 1.

The table must be read one row at a time. As you read a row you are expected to be consulting Figure 6.4. The first 11 lines show the process executing a chain of calls

p ⟶ q ⟶ r ⟶ s ⟶ t

18. For a refresher on validation levels, see Section 4.3.4.

19. Failure to find this match will trigger the task of expanding the given reference name to a full path name, getting the unique identifier, and instituting a search with it.

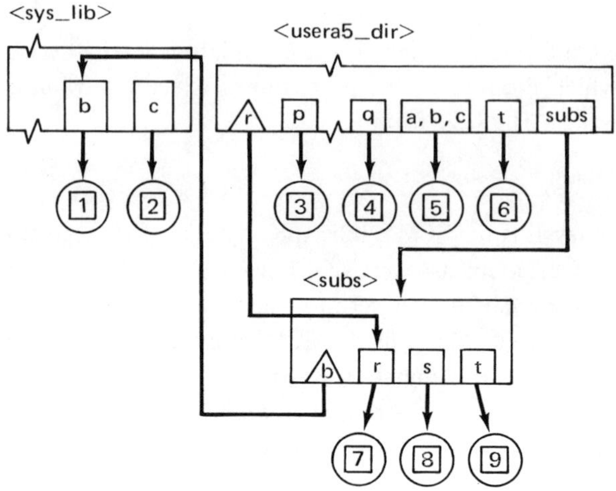

Figure 6.4. A portion of the file-system hierarchy

The next paragraphs amount to a walk through the first few lines of the table. Depending on your interest, you are invited to finish the walk through the first 11 lines as one exercise and, if the spirit really moves you, to complete the remaining lines as an additional exercise.

Walk through Lines 1–6 of Table 6.3

Line 1

Procedure <p> executing in ring 32, using <usera5_dir> as its working directory, makes a reference to a segment using the name a. Since this is presumably the first time the reference name a has been used in this process, there will be no KST entry having a reference name of the desired form (32_a), so a search of the hierarchy is begun, beginning with the caller's directory. The caller directory is <usera5_dir>, and a search of this directory finds a branch (to file 5) with an entry name a. The KST is re-searched to see if there already exists an entry whose unique id is 5.[20] This could be the case if the file had previously been initiated under a different alias. We assume here that this possibility in fact did not occur. Hence, a new KST entry is created and the entry name 32_a is added to its (empty) list of reference names.

20. It should be clear that our use of a number inside a square to represent a unique identifier (actually 36 bits), is merely a graphical convenience.

Table 6.3 Buildup of Entry Names in the KST

			State Variables			Response by the SCM					
	Line No.	1 Name of Referencing Procedure	2 Ring of Execution	3 Current Working Directory	4 Symbolic Reference Name	5a Directory Search Required (yes or no)	5b Name of Directory in which Matching Entry Is Found	6a Unique Designation (schematic) of the Target File and Its Corr. Segment	6b New KST Entry (yes or no)	7a New KST Entry Name	7b Form of New KST Entry Name
<p>	1	<p>	32	<usera5_dir>	a	yes	<usera5_dir>	$\boxed{5}$	yes	yes	32_a
↓	2	<p>	32	<usera5_dir>	q	yes	<usera5_dir>	$\boxed{4}$	yes	yes	32_q
<q>	3	<q>	32	<usera5_dir>	b	yes	<usera5_dir>	$\boxed{5}$	no	yes	32_b
↓	4	<q>	32	<usera5_dir>	r	yes	<subs>	$\boxed{7}$	yes	yes	32_r
<r>	5	<r>	33	<usera5_dir>	b	yes	<sys_lib>	$\boxed{1}$	no	yes	33_b
	6	<r>	33	<usera5_dir>	c	yes	<usera5_dir>	$\boxed{5}$	no	yes	33_c
↓	7	<r>	33	<usera5_dir>	s	yes	<subs>	$\boxed{8}$	yes	yes	33_s
<s>	8	<s>	33	<usera5_dir>	b	no	–	$\boxed{1}$	no	no	–
	9	<s>	33	<usera5_dir>	c	no	–	$\boxed{5}$	no	no	–
↓	10	<s>	33	<usera5_dir>	t	yes	<subs>	$\boxed{9}$	yes	yes	33_t
<t>	11	<t>	33	<usera5_dir>	c	yes	<usera5_dir>	$\boxed{5}$	no	yes	32_c
	12[a]	<q>	32	<usera5_dir>	a						
	13	<q>	32		t						
	14	<t>	32		b						
	15	<t>	32		r						

[a] It is presumed that prior to reaching the occasion of Line 12 normal return has been executed from <t> to <s> to <r> to <q>.

Line 2
Procedure <p> (still executing in ring 32) calls <q>, thereby making the symbolic reference q. Since (we assume that) no entry in the KST has the reference name 32_q, a search of the hierarchy yields the fact that file [4] in <usera5_dir> fulfills our search requirements. Assuming a second search of the KST shows that no entry now has the unique id equal to [4], the appropriate KST entry is then formed and the name 32_q is added to its list of reference names.

Line 3
Procedure <q> executing in ring 32 makes a reference to a segment using the name *b*. Assuming the search of the KST fails to find an entry name that matches 32_b, a search of the hierarchy will result in again finding file [5]. A re-search of the KST now shows there already is an entry for a segment whose unique id is [5]. So, no new KST entry is needed. It is merely necessary to add 32_b to the list of reference names in the existing entry.

Line 4
Procedure <q> calls <r> with the symbolic reference r. A search of the hierarchy is again assumed necessary. This time Directory Control will discover that a *link* in <usera5_dir> (not a branch) has the matching entry name. The path name found in this link points to a branch in <subs>, thus identifying file [7] as the target. Again, we assume a new KST entry for this segment must be made on grounds that there is no existing KST entry having [7] as its unique id.

Line 5
Since <r> executes in ring 33, when <r> makes symbolic reference to b, a match must be found with 33_b in a KST entry. No such match will be found in this case, so again the hierarchy is searched. But now, the caller directory is <subs>. This is the first directory in the search list now. The link named b is found in <subs> leading Directory Control to come up with file [1] in <sys_lib>[21] as the intended target. A new KST entry is formed, initiating file [1] as a segment, and making it known by the name 33_b.

Line 6
Procedure <r> refers to c. There is no branch nor link named c in the caller directory <subs>. The standard search rules next dictate a search in the working directory <usera5_dir>. The search succeeds in locating the branch

21. This is our "private" shorthand for <system_library_standard> that is mentioned in Table 6.1.

for file [5], one of whose aliases is c. The reference name 33_c is now added to the list of names by which the segment for file [5] is now known.

In case the subsystem actually intended that the target be file [2] in <sys_lib>, it would be necessary to have previously established a link named c in <subs> pointing to the branch named c in <sys_lib>.

6.3.2 More on Ring-Context Implication

If a procedure <p> has an access bracket of two or more rings, it is possible (and perhaps occasionally desirable) for the meaning of <p>'s symbolic references to depend on the particular ring within the access bracket in which <p> happens to be executing. To be more specific, Figure 6.5 shows a sequence of symbolic references that will help to explain the point just made. In this situation the service procedure named p can execute in ring 32 or in ring 33. Rules for determining in which ring of its access bracket a procedure will execute were developed in Section 4.2.2.1. Applying these rules we see that if called from procedure <x> whose ring brackets are (33, 33, 33), then <p> will execute in ring 33. If called, say, from a procedure <y> whose ring brackets are (32, 32, 32), then <p> will execute in ring 32.

Figure 6.5 suggests that while <p> executes in ring 33 and references sort, the intended target segment could very well be one routine, say, a radix sorting procedure; whereas an entirely different target is intended, say a binary sorting routine, when <p> executes in ring 32. Moreover, if the thread of control shifts back and forth between ring 32 and ring 33, the meaning of sort, as used in repeated calls from <p> could alternate!

One way this alternation of meaning for a symbolic reference could be explained is by picturing that there is a physically different copy of the link

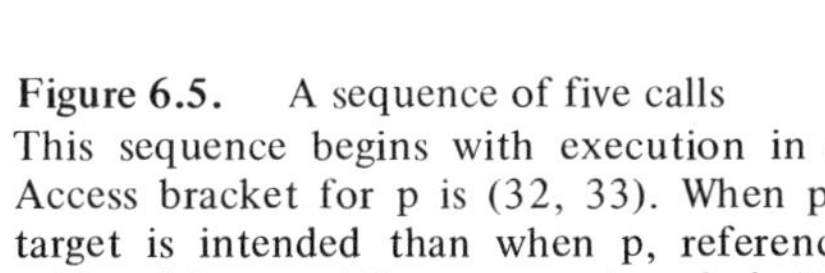

Figure 6.5. A sequence of five calls
This sequence begins with execution in a segment known by the reference name x. Access bracket for p is (32, 33). When p, referenced by x, refers to sort, a different target is intended than when p, referenced by y, refers to sort. This dual intent is achieved by providing two copies of p's linkage section, one for use when executing in ring 32 and one for use when executing in ring 33.

pointer used to address the target. Each of the two link pointers would be formed by the Linker, but to distinct targets. As a matter of fact, this is precisely how this dual intent occurs in Multics. The two different link pointers reside in different copies of linkage sections for <p>. One linkage section (part of the combined linkage segment for ring 33) is used when <p> executes in ring 33 and the other (part of the combined linkage segment for ring 32) is used when <p> executes in ring 32.

We shall now take a more complete look at the idea of multiple copies of linkage sections. Having done this, we will consider how the situation described in Figure 6.5 is appropriately reflected in the KST.

Ring protection considerations dictate that, for each ring in which <p> executes, a separate copy of the linkage section must be used. Here is why: While <p> is executing in ring 32, the corresponding linkage data must be protected from procedures executing in higher-numbered rings. Hence, the ring brackets for <p>'s linkage section for ring j must be of the form (i, j, j), where $i \leqslant j = 32$. Now, we can employ a similar argument when <p> is executing in ring 33. Granted that <p> must have access to its linkage data, but how can it have access to the particular linkage section made earlier? Clearly, a new copy of the linkage section must be formed whose ring brackets are of the form (i, k, k) where $i \leqslant k = 33$. Extending this argument to the general case, we see that a procedure <p> whose access brackets are (l, m) may require (as necessary) a separate copy of its linkage section for each of the rings $l, l + 1, \ldots, m - 1, m$ in which <p> actually executes.[22]

We are now ready to view the action taken by the SCM in handling the five

22. Certainly these copies need not be made in advance. The Linker, in fact, orders these copies to be made as it handles link faults to <p> from each new ring in the range l through m.

As first suggested in Chapter 2, it would be very costly if the system let each new linkage copy stand as a separate segment. Some of the consequent costs are longer descriptor segments, longer KST's (and other such ring-0 segments whose entries are on a per-segment basis), wasted space in individual linkage segments and more segments that can be missing from memory when they are needed. To avoid these expenses, the Linker whenever possible will place each created copy of a linkage block onto special, one-per-ring segments called *combined linkage segments.* This type of segment contains linkage blocks or *sections* for other segments that have also been referenced in this ring; call it r. The combined linkage segment for this ring has the ring bracket (r, r, r). It is actually of no great importance to the subsystem writer whether a linkage section "stands alone" or is combined with those of other segments. The important net effect relative to this discussion is the same; namely, multiple copies of linkage sections are made for a segment when it is referenced in different rings. It is, however, far simpler for our discussion to picture each of these linkage copies standing as separate segments. So in all subsequent discussions the terminology of linkage *segments* rather than linkage *sections* will be reverted to occasionally.

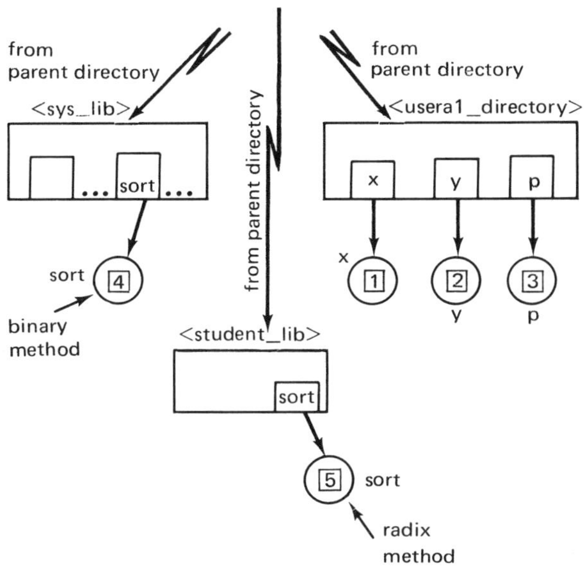

Figure 6.6 A possible directory structure
This structure is consistent with the call sequence in Figure 6.5.

symbolic references depicted in Figure 6.5. This is done with the aid of Figure 6.6 and Table 6.4. The former shows the kind of directory structure that would be needed to support the "ambivalence" of sort in the Figure 6.5 example. What appears to be required is that branches for neither of the two targets called sort may appear in the same directory as the branch for <p>, the calling procedure. Line numbers in Table 6.4 correspond to the five numbered symbolic references of Figure 6.5. Note that for the references documented on Lines 1, 3, and 4 of Table 6.4, the target is found in the caller directory, but for the references on Lines 2 and 5 the target is found, by design, in the working directory. It is necessary that the working directory be adjusted at least once during the sequence of references. Two changes are assumed in the trace depicted in the table. It is assumed that wdir is set to <student_lib> prior to the ring-33 call on <p> and that wdir is set to <sys_lib> prior to the ring-32 call on <p>.

6.3.3 The Duplicate-Names Problem—and How It Is Resolved

Wherever the same reference name, used in different parts of the same process, represents two (or more) different segments, there arises a potential confusion (conflict of names). This is illustrated with the following example.

Table 6.4 Buildup of KST Entries for the Case Shown in Figures 6.5 and 6.6.

		State Variables			Response by the SCM				Remarks
Line No.	Referencing Procedure	Ring of Execution	Current Working Directory	Symbolic Reference Name	Unique id of Target	New KST Entry Required	New KST Entry Name	Form of New KST Entry Name	
1	<x>	33	<student_lib>	p	$\boxed{3}$	yes	yes	33_p	First copy of <p.link> is made.
2	<p>	33	<student_lib>	sort	$\boxed{5}$	yes	yes	33_sort	Radix sort is selected
3	<x>	33	<student_lib>	y	$\boxed{2}$	yes	yes	32_y	Wall-crossing fault (inward).
4	<y>	32	<sys_lib>	p	$\boxed{3}$	no	yes	32_p	<y> sets working directory to <sys_lib> before making call on <p>. Second copy of <p.link> is made.
5	<p>	32	<sys_lib>	sort	$\boxed{4}$	yes	yes	32_sort	Binary sort is selected.

Suppose a subsystem writer, say a civil engineer, wishes to package a set of related segments as a subsystem called "truss" for computing forces in arbitrary structures. For simplicity let us assume this subsystem consists of the principal procedure <truss>, a data segment called <formulas>, and the special routines <cosine> and <arctangent>.

Ideally, the user of a "package" developed by another (i.e., a *borrower*) should not need to know the internal structure of the borrowed package in order to obtain effective use of it. This theme, to encourage "system users to build upon the work of others," has been emphasized in long-range design goals of information utilities.[23] In terms of this example, therefore, we should hope that borrowers of the truss package would not be expected to know what procedures or data segments <truss> refers to during each of its invocations nor where in the hierarchy they are located. Now the difficulty is that some of these procedures may be referenced in <truss> using the same reference names as other (probably different) procedures used by the borrower, who may be a customer that has arranged for the use of truss.

We see that the user's process now not only needs to make reference to different segments having the same reference names, for example, cosine or arctangent, but worse, the user will not be aware of this apparent ambiguity. If, prior to calling <truss>, the user's process has already initiated one version of, say cosine, how can we be sure that, when called, <truss> will link to the cosine it needs? Or, if, after a return from <truss>, the user wants to compute cosine(x), won't the cosine routine that is called necessarily be the one initiated by his process while executing in the <truss> package? In short, how can the user be sure that each portion of his process will get the cosine of its choice without making an elaborate advance study of <truss>'s "inner works." Clearly, the person that packages the truss subsystem and "sells" others on using it must guarantee that all subsidiary procedures and data targets of the truss subsystem will be properly selected (names paired with the right segment numbers and no interference with name-number pairs needed when executing "outside" the truss package).

This conflict-of-names problem was anticipated in the original Multics design and a general solution for it was not only proposed, but implemented. An SMM (Segment Management Module) was designed that enabled a pack-

23. See these papers by Project MAC's first director, R. M. Fano, "The MAC System: The Computer Utility Approach," *IEEE* [Institute of Electrical and Electronics Engineers] *Spectrum* 2 (January 1965): 56–64; and R. M. Fano, "The Computer Utility and the Community," *IEEE International Convention Record*, pt. 12 (1967): 30–37.

ager of a subsystem to *relate* one or more uniquely identified segments to a uniquely identified caller or "parent" segment. Thus if <x> is regarded as the parent, it would be, for example, possible to declare segments <u>, <v>, and <w> as being related to <x> in such a way that when reference names, u, v, and/or w are used within <x> (and only within <x>), links are formed to the intended segments, say, <u>, <v>, and <w>, notwithstanding the possibility that the same reference names u, v, and w had already been used (or would in the future be used) to refer to other segments in the hierarchy. Establishing the required relationships among the segments could be achieved via explicit calls to the SMM. Unfortunately, the initial implementation of the SMM proved too costly to use because it required that for every segment <x> there be listed in the SMM's data base the name of every other segment, <u>, and so forth, that <x> referenced. For every possible referencing couple of the form (<x>, <u>), a separate name block had to be built in the SMM's dynamic data base. This cross-reference table could not only grow very large and become expensive to maintain because of its complex structure, but there was no adaptive procedure applicable to make construction and insertion of new table entries (or search for existing entries) progressively easier.

The current SCM does not provide the very general "relate" facility previously mentioned. It does provide a simpler, less general mechanism, however, which in the long run may well prove equally effective. This present mechanism has the virtue of being automatic in the sense that no explicit calls are normally necessary to prevent name conflicts. Before describing it, in order that the reader better appreciate its elegance and simplicity, I digress here for a moment to consider what, if any, user-initiated practices or conventions are available for "manually" avoiding name conflicts. Three such approaches are listed. The third one has real merit but is far from being fully satisfactory.

First Approach (poor)—Change the reference names used within a subsystem (package) to increase the likelihood of their uniqueness (or change the ring of the procedure that executes these symbolic references, or both). Clearly, by qualifying the names used (or changing the context rings), for example, truss_cosine in place of cosine, there will be substantial reduction in the possibility for name conflict.[24]

Second Approach (poorer)—Terminate names (and/or segments) that may have been previously initiated before making new symbolic references with the same names. This approach appears to have little or no merit, especially in

24. Up to 32 characters are permitted in a reference name, which leaves a good deal of room for qualifiers.

cases where extensive looping and/or logical complexity occurs within which the name conflict resides.

Third Approach (good)–Bind the subsystem package into one segment. A subsystem designer, after debugging his package, can execute a system command[25] to *bind* the segments of his package into a limited number of segments (normally, one for the procedures and one for the (static) data segments, if any). When, for example, procedure segments <a>, <b>, and <c> are bound into one segment, their corresponding linkage sections are also bound into one linkage segment. I use the term *bind* rather than *combine* to emphasize that in binding, the links for all the former intersegment references among the segments of the set being bound, for example, a call from <a> to <b>, are resolved (i.e., eliminated) in the binding process. The bound package can, therefore, be executed without further fear of conflict between reference names used within the package and those employed by the user of the package. There is some disadvantage of binding for the subsystem designer that may wish to maintain his package by periodic updates. The cost of updating may be higher, since even minor changes will necessitate rebinding the entire package.

We are now fully ready to discuss the mechanism currently implemented within the SCM for resolution of the problem under discussion. In essence, the recorded reference name (in the KST entry) is further qualified, not just by the validation level (of the referencing procedure), as revealed in Section 6.3.1.1, but also by the identification of the directory in which the referencing procedure resides.

In short, the recorded reference name is in actuality a 3-tuple. On a link fault to a reference name y, the SCM will search for a KST-entry reference name that must match not only y and the faulting segment's validation level, but also the id of the faulting segment's parent, that is, the caller directory (cdir). In the next paragraph we focus on the remarkable effect that the directory id qualifier can have in preventing name conflicts, provided the subsystem writer will "package" his subsystems within individual directories.

This is illustrated with Figure 6.7 on behalf of our "friend," the truss_system designer. This figure suggests the kind of directory structure that usera3 (the designer) should create for the truss subsystem.

Let "idt" represent the (36-bit) unique identifier of <truss_system_dir>. Further, let <truss> be the first procedure to execute in the subsystem, say in ring 32, let <truss> be the "entrance" of the truss subsystem. Then, recalling

25. The bind command is described in the MPM.

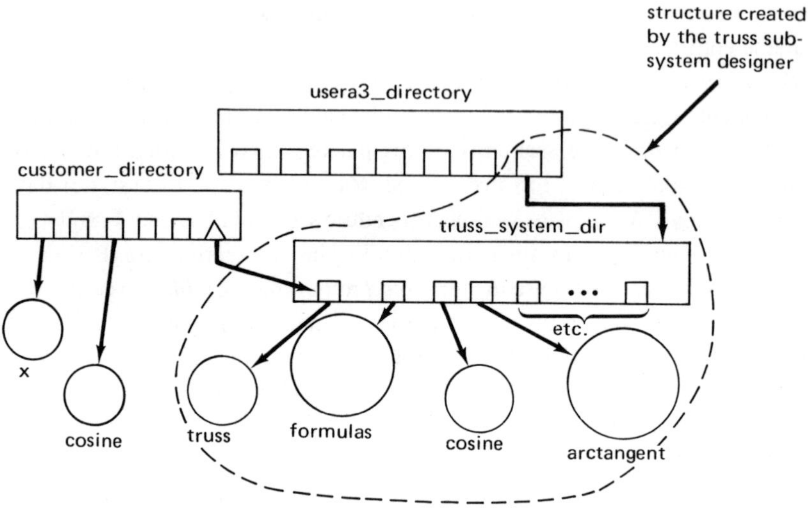

Figure 6.7. Separate directory structure created by usera3 for a subsystem whose primary name is "truss"

the nature of the cdir search rule, a first reference from <truss> to cosine, unknown to the process thus far, will result in the initiation of the desired target with a recorded reference name of the form

32_idt_cosine

Now—and here is the clincher—any other procedure segment in the directory truss_system_dir that subsequently executes (within the same subsystem) and that references cosine, will, of necessity, link fault to this same segment named cosine. No other target is possible. Moreover, no component of the subsystem (other than <truss>, of course) can be mistakenly referenced from outside the subsystem. Thus, if procedure x in the customer's directory references cosine, either before or after a first use of the truss subsystem, the nature of the search rules will dictate that either the customer's <cosine> will be made known and linked to (if such a segment appears in his directory) or a library cosine will be chosen.

Figure 6.8 illustrates one additional important observation: It is possible for one subsystem to link to another subsystem via its primary name (and to another, and another, and so on) without inducing any new danger of name conflicts. The obvious reasoning is left to the reader.

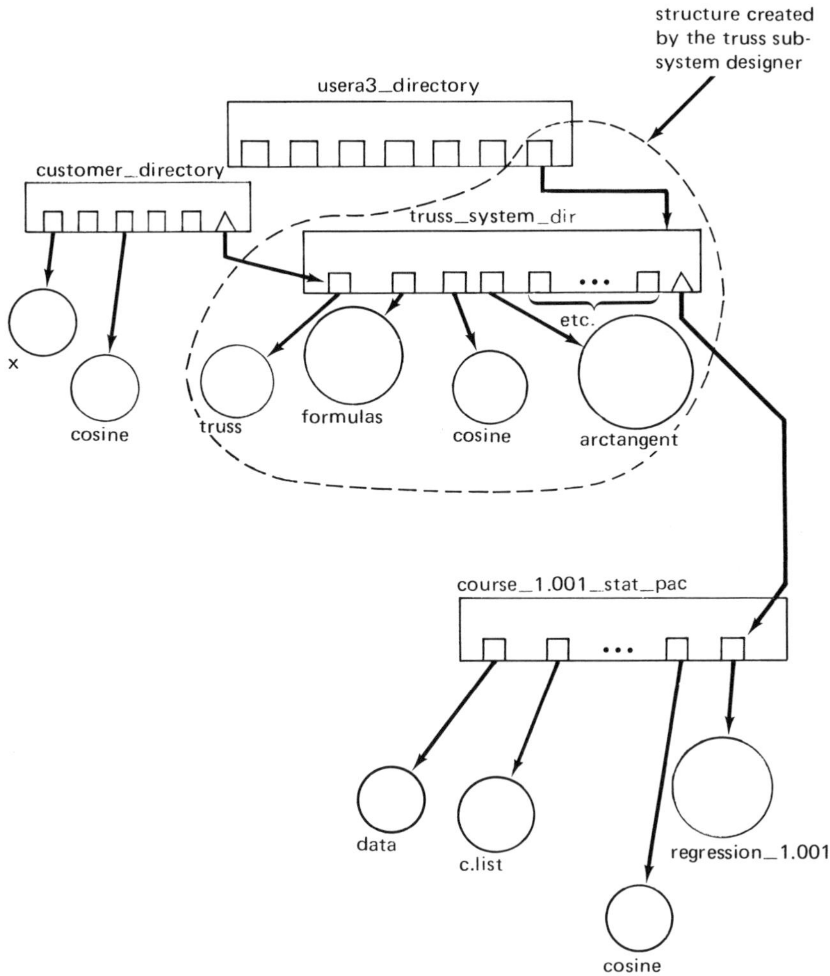

Figure 6.8. The truss subsystem executing in another subsystem
The truss subsystem can execute in any other subsystem, through its primary name, e.g., in course_1.001_stat_pac through regression_1.001, without risking a conflict of name (over cosine).

6.4 Explicit Calls to the Segment Control Module

Thus far we have been viewing the SCM as a module that is normally called by the Linker in search of a segment pointer for use in forming a link to a target segment. Now that we understand the task involved in making a segment known, we can consider reasons why a user may wish to cause the initiating or terminating of a segment (or reference names for segments) in a more explicit manner, that is, by calling the SCM directly. For example, by explicit call to the SCM, or by a corresponding command, a user process may declare that an arbitrary alias is to be meaningful as a reference name for a particular segment of the process. The declared pairing of reference name and segment, which is defined by giving its full path name, can then remain in effect throughout the life of the process. Temporary aliases are not made part of the directory structure, since they are stored only in the KST entry for the stated segment. Subsequent to the declaration that "initiates" the alias (in actuality a call to the SCM entry point, hcs_$initiate), link-fault references can be made to the declared alias just as if it were a valid entry name in the directory hierarchy.

It is frequently useful to ask for the initiation of a segment in order to learn information *about that segment*, possibly in anticipation of referencing the segment itself at a later time. Because a successful call to initiate a segment returns its segment pointer as a return argument, subsequent use of this pointer enables the caller to address *directly* into the now-made-known segment (without link faulting or recourse to other indirect means). Such direct addressing is especially convenient to achieve if coded in PL/I using based storage referencing, as will be illustrated at the end of this section. Use of this facility—and here is a crucial point—essentially gives the user potentially direct access to every segment in the Multics virtual memory!

Table 6.5 contains a selected list of tasks that a user's process may need to have completed. These tasks can in each instance be accomplished by the appropriate call or sequence of calls to SCM entry points, or by issuing the equivalent commands.

Most of the listed calls to the SCM are relatively safe for a subsystem writer to make. [The calls and their calling sequences (as well as equivalent commands) are described more fully in corresponding SSS section (Standard Service System) of the MPM.] There is one exception, namely, a call to the entry point hcs_$terminate_seg, the associated risk for which will be explained momentarily. It is worth noting that all calls to the SCM return a value for an error code argument that indicates the success or failure of its

Table 6.5 A Partial Set of User Calls to the Segment Control Module

Task	Appropriate Entry Points in the SCM
1. Given a valid path name for an existing file, initiate a segment and obtain a pointer for it. Optionally, supply a reference name as well, so that it will thereafter be associated with the segment being initiated. Optionally, supply a reference name that is to be regarded as a copy of the one identified by the given path name.	hcs_$initiate
2. A variant of hcs_$initiate that returns an integer argument that gives the bit count (length in bits) of the initiated segment. The bit count is an attribute that is kept in the branch.	hcs_$initiate_count
3. This routine sets the bit-count attribute according to the integer value supplied as an input argument.	hcs_$set_bc
4. Find the segment number for a segment, given its reference name.	hcs_$fs_get_seg_ptr
5. Find out the path name of a segment, given its segment number.	hcs_$fs_get_path_name (If not previously initiated a returned error code tells you so.)
6. Create and make known an empty segment by a given name and in a designated directory having certain designated attributes, e.g., size, effective mode.	hcs_$make_seg
7. Terminate a segment identified by a particular segment number. (Terminating a segment is the inverse of initiating it.)	hcs_$terminate_seg
8. This routine deletes a given nonnull reference name from the list of reference names by which the corresponding segment is currently known. (A call that deletes the last nonnull name triggers termination of the segment itself.)	hcs_$terminate_name
9. A variant of hcs_$terminate_name explained in the text.	hcs_$terminate_noname

Note: Each call is to the gate segment <hcs_>. The full set of calls is given in the MPM.

mission. Thus, an attempt to initiate a segment from ring 32 with the reference name zilch will fail if there already exists a KST entry with the name "32_idt_zilch" and the returned error code will so indicate.

To initiate a segment, a user must supply the SCM with a path name. To terminate a previously initiated segment, a user must supply a segment number (pointer) that is supplied as a return argument in the call to initiate the segment. Herein lies a real danger. This segment number is normally freed for a reassignment (by analogy to a reuse of a telephone number) the next time the process initiates another segment. When a segment number *n* is terminated, KST entry numbered *n* is deleted and the SDW numbered *n* is set to zero to induce a segment fault the next time access is attempted through it. As long as this number remains "deactivated" in this way, links that have been previously set to segment *n* will induce segment faults and the user will be alerted via error messages if such unintended events occur. However, if prior to executing via these links, that is, addressing through them, the user's process initiates another segment that is assigned segment number *n*, chaos can surely occur. Any unintended address formation which reemploys links that are set to the former segments will go undetected. Errors and possibly faults of unpredictable nature (and of hard-to-recognize origin) are likely to occur shortly thereafter.

There is a simple rule (or philosophy) one can follow to completely prevent confusion like that just described. If a segment is made known via the Linker, and a set of access paths (links) are made to that segment, it is dangerous to terminate that segment without first reversing the linkage process, thereby removing these access paths. The library subroutine

term_

can be called to unlink or remove all such access paths (in the process) to any known segment of that process (in the preparation for terminating the segment). If a segment is made known by bypassing the Linker (e.g., by one of the calls to initiate a segment), then it should be terminated in a corresponding manner (bypassing the Linker). Any "cross products," for example, initiating through the Linker and terminating via an explicit call to terminate the segment, can cause problems and is to be done at the risk of the user.

In a similar philosophical vein, whenever a user calls hcs_$initiate (see Table 6.5) to supply a nonnull reference name for a segment, he is in effect deliberately communicating with the Linker—trying to "tell it" something that the Linker would ordinarily never learn about on its own. When a user takes this type of initiative it also is his responsibility to recognize the consequences and possibly to prevent some of these by interacting further with the file system (taking even more initiative). For the sake of completeness (only) the accompanying footnote[26] suggests still another type of initiative (opportunities to interact with Segment Control) that can be taken to deal with the access-path problem.

The examples given in the next subsections involve the initiating and terminating of segments, but all of the risks or complexities described in the foregoing discussions are avoided. This is because references to the initiated segments are accomplished by direct addressing (i.e., using based storage referencing), thus bypassing the Linker's mechanisms entirely.

The other SCM entry points listed in Table 6.5 may also be of occasional use to the subsystem designer and are representative of a still larger set of available entry points—all of which are described fully in the "Multics Programmers' Manual."[27] Commands are available that correspond with some of these SCM entry points, and these are also described in the MPM. Generally speaking, however, the commands offer fewer options than do the calling sequences for the corresponding subroutines.

6.4.1 Illustrative Example 1—Copying a Segment

This example, couched in the form of a PL/I procedure called copy, shows how a segment may be copied from one directory to another. The procedure's parameters are

from_dir	the path name of the directory that currently contains the segment.
to_dir	the destination directory's path name.
file_name	the name of the segment being copied.

26. In terminating a segment (via a call to hcs_$terminate_seg), the user may optionally specify that its segment number be held in reserve, i.e., not returned to the "pool" of available segment numbers. Exercising the option eliminates the risks just described and also offers other interesting possibilities that may be of positive use to the subsystem writer. To appreciate the latter possibilities, one must also be aware of a companion option that may be exercised in the call to hcs_$initiate. This option permits the user to specify a segment number to be assigned (if available) for the segment being initiated. Employing both options, a user may terminate a segment named x and later initiate another segment with the same number that also has the same name. In principle, then, a user has the power to let a given name take on two (or even more) different meanings, albeit one meaning at a time. He can even cause a reversion to an original meaning (by terminating the second segment named x and reinitiating the original one that was named x). If done carefully, then at no time need there be a risk that a completed link would be used to address a spurious target.

27. Further insight can be gained in some cases by examination of appropriate sections of the MSPM.

To appreciate the program about to be given, a word or two of general explanation is needed concerning the use of the entry point hcs_$terminate_noname. It is possible to ask the SCM to render unknown any currently known *nonnull* reference name for a segment using calls to hcs_$terminate_name.

Among the acceptable reference names for a segment, however, is a *null name* (""), which by convention is not usable by the Linker (and thus one can add a null name and remove it with impunity).

A null reference name would normally be supplied as the reference name when initiating a segment if only direct addressing to it is intended. A subsequent call to the special entry point hcs_$terminate_noname will terminate that segment if and only if the only reference name listed for it in its KST entry is the null name. If in the interim other reference names have been added (for instance as a result of link-fault action), hcs_$terminate_noname will only delete the null name but will not terminate the segment itself. We are now ready to view the PL/I coding of our copy procedure

```
copy:      procedure (from_dir, to_dir, file_name);
declare    (from_dir, to_dir, file_name) char (*);
declare    bit_count fixed bin;
declare    (fp, tp) pointer;
declare    segment bit (bit_count) based;
call hcs_$initiate_count (from_dir, file_name,"", bit_count, fp);
call hcs_$make_seg (to_dir, file_name,"", 1011b, tp);
tp -> segment = fp -> segment;
call hcs_$set_bc(to_dir, file_name, bit_count);
call hcs_$terminate_noname (fp);
call hcs_$terminate_noname (tp);
return;
end;
```

Here are some points to be noted about this procedure.

1. Direct addressing of the two initiated segments, using based storage referencing, takes place in the PL/I assignment statement

```
tp -> segment = fp -> segment;
```

Explanation of this remarkably powerful statement is provided in this paragraph for those that may be a bit slow in reading PL/I code. In the above statement, fp and tp are pointer variables that have been assigned segment pointer values as a result of the calls to hcs_$initiate_count and hcs_$make_seg, respectively. The based variable "segment" defines a string of bits whose dimension, bit_count, has been given its value during execution of hcs_$initiate_count.

The expression

tp -> segment

is a reference to the new segment (a bit string) while

fp -> segment

is a reference to the original segment, also a bit string. Pointer-qualified variables are compiled into direct addressing of their targets, that is, completely avoiding the linkage mechanism. This results in compiled code that takes less space and executes faster than ordinary symbolic referencing.

2. The third argument in the calls to initiate_count and make_seg are the null reference names. The fourth argument to make_seg is the use mode (R₵WA) of the new file, expressed as a binary constant. The calls shown in the above example are abbreviated versions (poetic license) of those documented in the MPM. They lack the copy switch and error code arguments, which are slightly irrelevant to the current discussion.

3. If by chance this procedure, copy, is called to copy itself, for example,

call copy (from_dir, to_dir, copy);

this copy will copy itself without terminating itself, albeit it initiates both segments (itself and its copy) using null reference names. This property has been found useful in Multics for generating copies of the Multics system itself. Subsystem writers may find this useful!

6.4.2 Illustrative Example 2—Editing a Segment

This example, also couched in the form of a PL/I procedure (called remove_semi), shows how a segment may be edited using direct addressing only. Input to the editing procedure consists of the path name (dir_name and file_name) for the subject segment. The same SCM calls used in the preceding example are used here. The reader should have no trouble following the logic of this program.

```
remove_semi:    proc(dir_name, file_name);
declare         (dir_name, file_name) char(*);
declare         (bit_count, i,j) fixed bin;
```

```
declare              p ptr;
declare 1 segment based aligned,
          2 ch(262144) char (1) unaligned;
call hcs_$initiate_count(dir_name, file_name, "", bit_count, p);
j = 0;
do i = 1 to (bit_count/9);
   if p -> segment.ch(i) ^= ";" then do;
        j = j + 1;
        p -> segment.ch(j) = p -> segment.ch(i);
        end;
   end;
bit_count = j * 9;
call hcs_$set_bc(dir_name, file_name, bit_count);
call hcs_$terminate_noname(p);
return;
end;
```

The lines in the above program where direct addressing of the segment undergoing editing takes place are

```
if p -> segment.ch(i) ^= ";" then do;
```

and

```
p -> segment.ch(j) = p -> segment.ch(i);
```

6.5 Segment Descriptor Management

Initiating a segment, that is, giving it a KST entry, is only one of the steps necessary for a user's process to gain access to the segment. At the point of initiation, no segment descriptor word will yet have been constructed for the segment in this process.[28] Moreover, the segment itself (or, more precisely, the page table and the referenced page of the segment) is quite likely not to be in core at the time the segment is initiated.[29] Building the SDW and placing in core the page table for the segment and the required page that is implicit in the user's symbolic reference are functions relegated to Segment and Page Control.

28. Of course, if this segment was once initiated but later terminated, the SDW is actually being constructed for a second time.
29. The segment might be in core in the event that some other process had recently referenced that same segment, i.e., a segment having the same unique identifier.

A segment is said to be *active* (a per-system concept) when its page table is in core and is said to be *connected* (a per-process concept) when its SDW holds a pointer to the page table such that the hardware can now address through the SDW to the page table (no missing-segment faults).[30] Activating a segment or connecting it are normally tasks to be completed, whenever necessary, only after the segment has been made known to a process.

Once a segment is made known, a reference to it may be made through its SDW. (For instance, if the segment was made known as a result of a linkage fault, then the faulting procedure can now resume its attempt to form the target address–now held in the completed link.) No matter how the target address may be formed for subsequent reference, it will now point to a (preset) zero-valued SDW. The hardware then interprets this zero as a directed fault that the software then interprets as a missing-segment fault. It is this induced fault that will invoke the service of Segment Control to complete the accessing path to the target.

In summary, numerous symbolic references to the same segment may result in an equal number of link faults, each leading to a call on the SCM for a segment pointer. But, only the first of the link faults to the same segment will require that the SCM initiate the segment. Likewise, it is approximately correct to say that use of only the first of the formed links to a segment will result in a segment fault to trigger activation and connection. So long as the segment remains active and connected, additional references to the same segment can, of course, pass successfully through the SDW, but they may incur page faults in the event the desired page is not in core. A page fault induces the transfer into core of the referenced page.

In the foregoing and in the remainder of this chapter the segment fault is pictured occurring as if always to achieve three objectives at once, namely, activating the segment, connecting it, and computing its access rights (the descriptor field of the SDW) for the faulting process. Actually, segment faults will also occur on occasions for which two or only one of these objectives must be attained. The three cases are the following:

1. The segment is inactive. It must be activated, connected, and have the access rights to it computed. (This is the case assumed in earlier discussions.)
2. The segment is already active (because some other process is currently

30. Page Control has responsibility for maintaining the page tables of active segments and for transferring pages to (from) core memory. Segment Control has the responsibility for activating and connecting segments.

sharing it), but it must be connected and have its access rights computed for the first time for this process.

3. The segment is active, but has been disconnected because another process, authorized to do so, has forced a change in some of the segment's attributes. When this occurs, segment control disconnects the segment in all processes that are now sharing it, forcing each of these to attempt a reconnection and a recomputation of their respective access rights before making the additional references to that segment.

The remainder of this chapter attempts to show how Segment Control constructs the SDWs, as needed, from the information stored in the KST entries. This discussion is provided not so much because of its immediate utility in the design of subsystems, but because it may help some avid reader tie together a number of "loose ends" regarding segment addressing, access control, and protection in the Multics operating environment. It would be perfectly reasonable to skip this material, especially during a first reading.

6.5.1 Constructing Segment Descriptor Words after a Segment Is Made Known

We start by picturing the various descriptor segments of a process, that is, one for each ring in which the process has thus far executed code. At the time segment number i is initiated, the contents of each descriptor segment at the offset = i are (preset) to zero.

We now consider what happens after some segment has been made known and some procedure then references it for the first time (perhaps via an its pair constructed by the Linker). As mentioned in an earlier paragraph, a directed fault will occur immediately upon attempting to construct the desired memory reference. (The fault occurs, of course, because the address-formation mechanism of the GE 645 will attempt to employ the word at offset = i in the currently employed descriptor segment. A zero SDW is interpreted in Multics as a missing-segment fault.)

The Fault Interceptor is again involved via the segment fault, but this time it calls Segment Control to remove the fault (to construct the proper segment descriptor word). Figure 6.9 summarizes the sources of information used by Segment Control in constructing an SDW.

Figure 6.10 shows the logic exercised by Segment Control in determining the six-bit descriptor field. First, there is a four-way resolution (boxes 1, 2, and 3) of the relationships between the ring number of the referencing procedure and ring brackets of the target. The logic for inward and outward types of inter-ring references is seen by following the heavy lines in Figure 6.10.

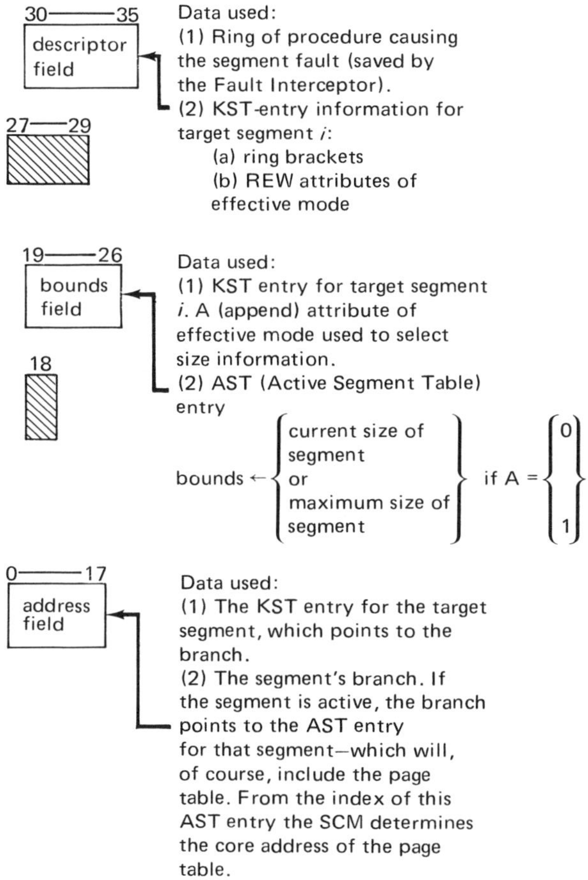

Figure 6.9. Sources of data used by Segment Control in constructing the descriptor, bounds, and address fields of an SDW for a target segment *i*

Note: The AST is another ring-0 data base. This per-system table is discussed in Chapter 7. Among other things, the AST contains all page tables.

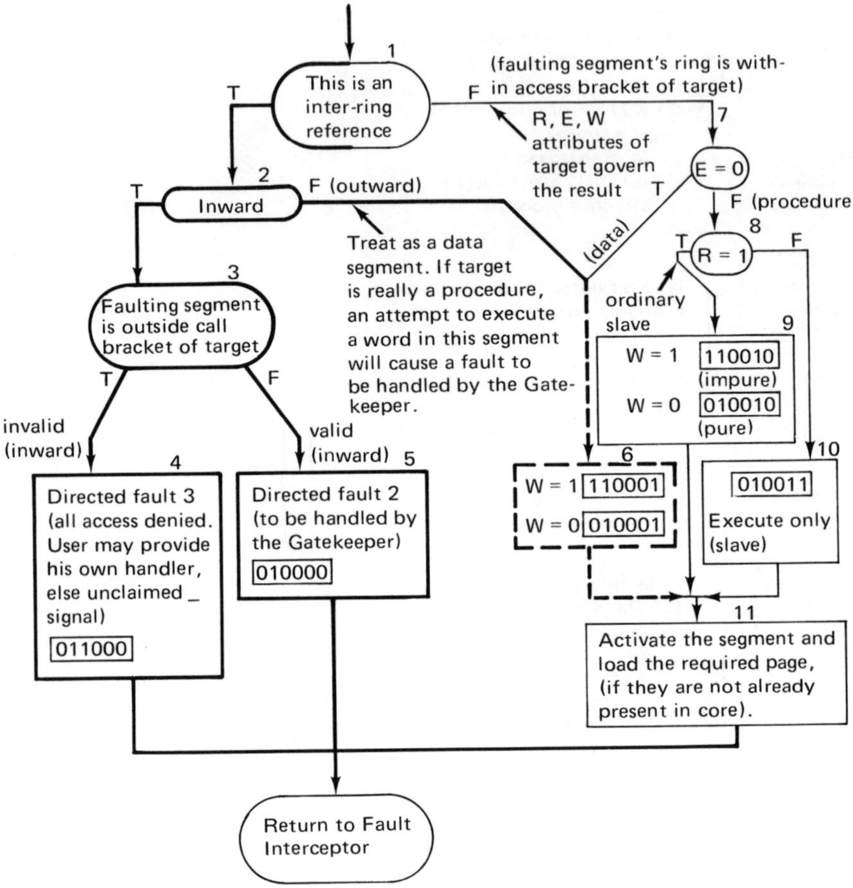

Figure 6.10. Logic used by Segment Control in constructing the six-bit descriptor field of the SDW
Key:
R means read attribute
E means execute attribute
W means write attribute
A means append attribute

For these cases, the protection rules described in Chapter 4 govern the determination of the descriptor bits (boxes 2, 3, 4, 5, and 6 of the logic). For data and procedure references that are neither inward nor outward (in the ring sense), the R, E, W mode attributes of the target (found in its KST entry) govern the determination of the descriptor field (boxes 7, 8, 9, and 10). Also, as indicated in box 11, a page table is created for this segment; if necessary, a pointer to it is placed in the SDW, and, if needed, the transferring to core of the wanted page is initiated.

Upon completing the SDW, Segment Control returns via the Fault Interceptor to the faulting procedure, which can now again attempt to complete execution of the instruction that faulted. Although the SDW is not now zero, it may nevertheless have been coded as one of the faults or potential faults indicated in Figure 6.10.

If the coding corresponds to an inward or outward procedure reference (flow chart boxes 5 or 6), then the *executing procedure will fault again*. This time the fault handler will be the Gatekeeper. During the course of its work, the Gatekeeper effects a ring change by causing the descriptor base register (dbr) to be reset so it now points to the target ring's descriptor segment. Eventually, the Gatekeeper will return control via the Fault Interceptor to the faulting procedure. If the target has never before been referenced in the target ring, then the SDW found at the same offset (= i) in the target ring's descriptor segment will again be zero and cause another segment fault.

This fault is again handled by Segment Control. The Fault Interceptor will have recorded, as part of the saved machine conditions, the segment number and core location of the SDW causing the fault, and the (new) ring number of this target segment. Consequently, Segment Control is fully able to proceed with the task of forming the new SDW using, of course, the same set of rules (Figure 6.10) as before. (This time, however, the logic in boxes 7, 8, 9, 10, and 11 will be followed.) When control is returned to the faulting procedure, address formation will be allowed to proceed through the newly formed SDW to the now-active target.

We are now in a position to picture the evolution of multiple descriptor segments in the multiring environment. The SDWs are set dynamically, that is, one at a time[31] in the rings where they are used, on an as-needed basis.

To illustrate how this activity would proceed, I deliberately choose the

31. For efficiency reasons, the file system may opt to produce some SDWs that the user is unaware of. Thus, if a segment fault is taken in ring r, the SCM will construct (or adjust) an SDW in the ring-0 as well as in the ring-r descriptor segments.

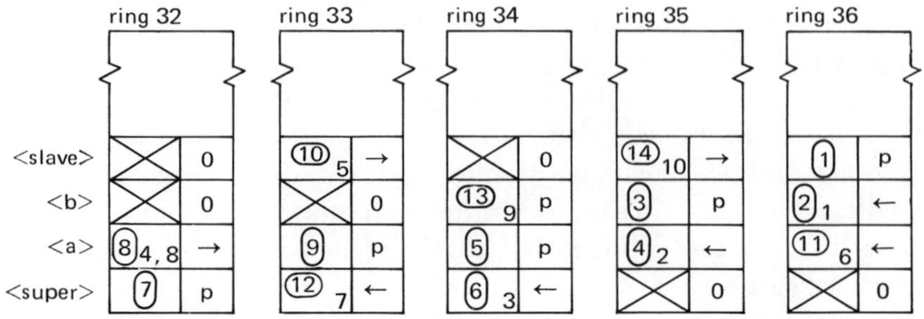

Figure 6.11. The sequence in which segment descriptor words are created
This shows the sequence in which segment descriptor words are created (circled numbers) via segment faults. Noncircled numbers refer to the sequence of calls and returns as follows:

<slave> ⇄ (1, 10) <b> ⇄ (2, 9) <a> ⇄ (3, 8) <super> ⇄ (4, 7) <a> ⇄ (5, 6) <slave>

(36) (35) (34) (32) (33) (36) ← executing rings

Assumptions: No prior references have been made to <a>, <b>, or <super>. Moreover, <slave> has been referenced for the first time by a call from within ring 36. Ring brackets for the segments in this figure are

(36, 36, 36) for <slave>
(34, 35, 35) for <b>
(33, 34, 34) for <a>
(32, 32, 32) for <super>.

rather exotic (in fact, unlikely) case first displayed in Figure 4.9. This case involved four procedures, <slave>, <a>, <b>, and <super>, each with different ring brackets.[32] If <slave> has just been initiated in the process, and if a chain of calls emanates from <slave> to <b> to <a> to <super>, these additional procedures will become initiated in the course of executing this chain.

Figure 6.11 gives a particular hypothetical chain of calls and shows the sequence in which the SDWs would be created via segment faults. Note that the positions of the SDWs in their respective descriptor segments reflect the order in which the corresponding segments are initiated in the process. Each descriptor segment will typically have some SDWs that have not been set. The

32. The straddling access brackets of <a> and <b> cannot be justified in a typical application. They are used here to illustrate the coordination between Segment Control and the Multics protection rules and mechanism, which were described in Chapter 4.

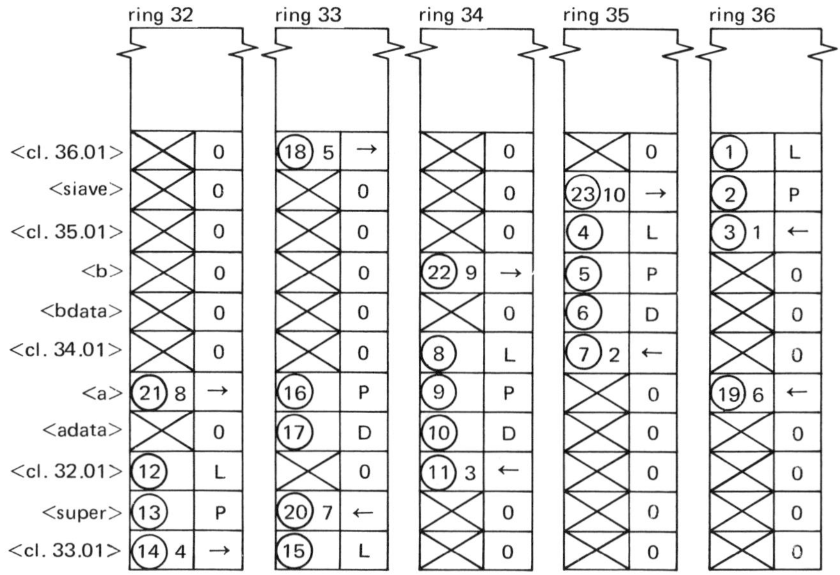

Figure 6.12. Further details for developing segment descriptor words
Further details in the steps followed for developing segment descriptor words in the sequence of calls and returns:

$$
\langle\text{slave}\rangle \underset{10}{\overset{1}{\rightleftarrows}} \langle\text{b}\rangle \underset{9}{\overset{2}{\rightleftarrows}} \langle\text{a}\rangle \underset{8}{\overset{3}{\rightleftarrows}} \langle\text{super}\rangle \underset{7}{\overset{4}{\rightleftarrows}} \langle\text{a}\rangle \underset{6}{\overset{5}{\rightleftarrows}} \langle\text{slave}\rangle
$$

(36) (35) (34) (32) (33) (36) ← executing rings

Key to descriptor symbols:

L – means a segment whose effective mode is REWA (used for linkage segments)
D – data
P – procedure
← – inward call or return
→ – outward call or return

setting of the SDWs is strictly a dynamic affair, depending upon the particular thread of control that has been followed in the process.

Figure 6.11 is still oversimplified in some respects, for instance, the following:

1. The possibility that the various procedures shown in Figure 6.11 may also make intersegment *data* references was disregarded. Naturally, linkage faults resulting therefrom would eventually cause segment faults to the referenced data segments as well.

2. When executing in a ring *r* for the first time, segment faults would first be taken when addressing through the linkage section corresponding to the target procedure in ring *r*. This linkage section normally resides, you will recall, in the combined linkage segment for ring *r*. In Multics notation, a combined linkage segment for ring *nn* that may extend beyond 64k words by growing into another 64k "instance" *mm* has a name of the form <cl_*nn.mm*>.

Figure 6.12 is a more realistic version of Figure 6.11, taking the aforementioned omissions into account. In this figure it is suggested that <a> and <b> reference data segments <adata> and <bdata>, respectively. It is also assumed for this example that the access brackets for these data segments are, respectively, identical to those for <a> and <b>.

7 Resource Sharing and Intercommunication among Coexisting Processes

7.1 Introduction

The earlier chapters gave us an increasingly larger view of an executing process. We began in Chapter 1 with a microscopic view that focused on the minute, but nontrivial, details of fetching and executing the individual GE 645 instructions of an executing process. Upon completing Chapter 6, we have managed to enlarge our view of a process in execution about as far as possible from the "*in vacuo*" point of view taken thus far. That is, for the most part, we have been considering the process in isolation, as if it were the only one employing the computer system's resources. We know that each executing process *coexists* in some sense with other processes: some may be executing simultaneously on other processors (if there is more than one in service); some may be waiting a "turn" to execute on a processor; and still others may be waiting for some event whose occurrence will enable the process to proceed with execution. The collection of these coexisting processes clearly implies (a competition for and) a sharing of hardware resources, a sharing of system software and data bases, and a *control* over this sharing. Most of the control functions described previously were of a *per-process* nature, and the data bases considered were of a one-per-process type, for example, stacks, descriptor segments, KSTs, and so forth. In this chapter we will be examining controls of a *per-system* nature. Of course, the data bases that associate with these functions are central to the operation of the entire system. It is hoped that when a subsystem designer understands how a process functions (cooperates and/or competes) in a milieu of other processes, he can better anticipate the performance of the processes in which his subsystem(s) resides.

7.1.1 Types of Coexisting Processes

In this overview section I shall anticipate what follows by summarizing the types of processes that coexist in Multics and provide a rough indication as to the nature of their interaction. Three kinds of coexistence can be identified.

1. Sets of seemingly unrelated user processes (multiprogramming)

Experience with Multics, as with earlier operating systems, including CTSS, has shown that only certain types of console users, for example, workers in artificial intelligence, have processes that may at times fully utilize a fast processor. Characteristically, a user process makes frequent requests for relatively slow-to-commence block transfers of information from drum, disk, or other I/O devices. Even with devices that have high transfer rates, there is, to begin with, an associated latency of several milliseconds or more, that is, a *delay* before the to- or from-core transfer may begin. During the delay and subsequent transfer time, it may not be possible for the requesting process to do any useful work. (This is certainly the case in Multics when a page fault has led to the initiating of the request for a drum or disk transfer to core of the desired segment or page thereof.) In principle, either the CPU must remain effectively idle while the process waits for completion of the block transfer or the process must somehow relinquish the processor to another process that *is* in a position to execute on a processor at this time. Systems for "passing the processor around" among several processes, so as to prevent the idling of a CPU during I/O waits or other delays, are known as *multiprogramming* systems. Multics is, among other things, a multiprogramming system.

The set of processes that share a processor in the fashion just crudely described need not be related to one another in any explicit way. They may, for instance, be a set of arbitrary user processes. Nevertheless, interaction among these processes is clearly implied. First, they share the same supervisory procedures and certain system data bases (tables) as segments in their respective address spaces. Second, each process is compelled, while executing in its (shared) supervisory procedures, to occasionally assist an idled process that is waiting for a particular event to "arrive." Although in each case the executing process *must* cooperate, the user should be, and is, completely oblivious to the fact that his process is performing as a *Good Samaritan*. This is because all such activities will occur while his process is trapped in certain ring-0 supervisory routines. Since these routines are common to all user processes, all processes are likely to serve as Good Samaritans.

There are several ways an executing process may know about the arrival of an event that is of interest to another (nonexecuting) process. However this knowledge is acquired, the waiting process is alerted so that it may again compete for time on an available processor, or possibly even preempt the processor.

An executing process may, for example, be interrupted (by an identifiable signal from another active unit) and in this way "told" about an event of interest to another process. Should this occur, the interrupted process is forced to (in some sense) *wake up* the process or processes for whom the interrupt signal is of primary interest. Alternatively, the executing process may of its own discover the apparent arrival of such events while it executes in supervisory mode. This type of discovery happens with great frequency in Multics. When a process incurs a page fault and must wait for the arrival of a requested page from the drum, it must put itself into a *wait* state. Just before doing so, it always checks a certain systemwide I/O request list in which it can discover which, if any, paging requests (of other processes) have been completed. The executing process then "notifies" the appropriate waiting processes before putting itself into a wait state.

2. A user process and a system process

Multics provides a set of "ever-present" *system* processes that offer specialized services to user processes. Among these, for instance, is the *I/O daemon,*[1] a system process that drives line printers and other output devices to produce copies of user-designated segments. A user will usually communicate implicitly with such a process by executing a system library subroutine call. This routine in turn executes the explicit steps needed to communicate an unambiguous work request to the system process so the user is, in fact, insulated from the details of interprocess communication.

Because the system process is a separate and fully independent process, its functions may be achieved as a parallel operation. The system process is free to fulfill the requests it receives at its convenience. With the current implementation, the user process proceeds to other chores without waiting for an acknowledgment from the output driver that the requested output task is done. For illustrative purposes, however, we can also imagine that, when requested, such a system process could send a meaningful completion signal to any user process. The latter might either wait for and be awakened by the completion signal or periodically inspect a special "mailbox" for the presence of a message sent by the former to indicate completion of the task.

3. Sets of deliberately cooperating processes

The computation structures of many algorithms exhibit parallelism that can never be taken advantage of when using only one processor. There is an increasing interest in the computer community in providing the operating system machinery that would permit parallel computation. The Multics design provides a simple capability of this type.

The ordinary programmer notices parallelism at various levels, from the PL/I-statement level on up to the subroutine. Thus, in the right-hand side of the statement

Y = (A*B + C)/(D*F + E);

computation of the numerator can, in principle, be carried out in parallel

1. A (Clerk Maxwell) daemon is a beneficent being that performs tasks in an autonomous fashion.

with that of the denominator. Likewise, but at a more *macro*scopic structural level, it is conceivable that in the statement

T = det(A)* cos(x);

the function for computing the *det*erminant of the matrix A could be executed in parallel with the computation for the *cos*ine of x, if each subroutine could be invoked to execute in parallel on separate processors.

If one could invoke separate and parallel computations, a mechanism for *synchronizing* the two parallel functions would also be needed. Thus, the multiplication of det(A) and cos(x) clearly must be delayed until it is known that both subroutines have returned values. Suppose, for instance, we consider a flow structure as depicted in Figure 7.1. Boxes 1, 4, and 5 are representative of the logic required to invoke and to synchronize the parallel action. Boxes 1, 4, and 5 can be carried out only if some common data cells are shared between the two computations for use, so that one computation can communicate with the other.

Clearly, there is some trade-off between the savings in time that can be achieved in the parallel computation and the extra costs associated with use of the machinery for achieving these gains. In Multics, opportunity for such computation is provided. Parallel computation can be achieved by executing

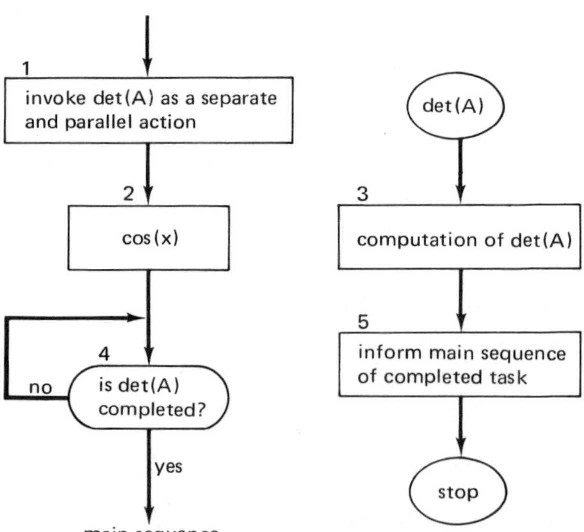

Figure 7.1. Invoking and synchronizing a parallel action

two or more processes concurrently. However, in a Multics system with several CPUs, the user is never given an opportunity to force their simultaneous allocation to his separate processes. Hence, "parallel computation" is just a possibility, never something that can be guaranteed. Although it is more realistic to regard the execution of such separate computations as *asynchronous* rather than *parallel*, I shall generally use the latter term, and it should be understood in its properly qualified sense.

Even in the absence of a second processor there can often be time savings realized by programming a computation to split or "fork" into logically independent (conceptually parallel) and intercommunicating sections. For example, let a computation reach a fork at which either leg *a* or leg *b* may now be followed. Suppose that if progress down leg *a* must be halted, say to await the occurrence of some event, then leg *b* might be pursued (or resumed, if its waited-for event had arrived), and vice versa. If the events needed to proceed down each leg are assumed to occur in random order, the ability to switch, if need be, from leg *a* to or from leg *b* at each wait point could make for greater progress for the computation as a whole, than if it were programmed to execute one leg to completion before beginning on the second leg. As we shall see in Section 7.5.3, Multics provides users the machinery to permit such multiple (serial) processing within a single process.[2]

Machinery for interprocess communication is provided in Multics by which to create and/or invoke other processes and also to synchronize with other processes using shared data bases known as "event channels." With this machinery, meaningful cooperation (e.g., parallel computation) can be conducted. (The scope of the parallel tasks may be large or small, as the user or users desire.) Explicit user programming, of a type to be described in this chapter, is required to achieve this objective. Moreover, the programming for each such "subsystem," for we can indeed regard such planned cooperation as a subsystem design, is specific to the objective at hand.

In review of the above three types of coexisting processes, we see that the following hold in all cases:

1. "Cooperation," whether voluntary or involuntary, preplanned by the system or explicitly planned by the programmer, implies communication between processes through the use of shared data bases.

2. An example of such a process might be one that forks to drive a common output device on behalf of two or more user processes that are its customers. We can picture that driving the output device on behalf of each customer requires execution of code peculiar to that customer and that this code can be executed (or can resume execution) whenever a customer "sends it work."

2. Of necessity, all coexisting processes, whether they cooperate or not, also *compete* for processor time and core space.[3]
3. By design, *all* processes share common supervisor modules and certain system tables.

For gaining additional perspective, it is well to consider how Multics differs in its design approach for achieving and controlling parallelism from the approach taken in more traditional operating systems.

In earlier operating systems, parallel operations were limited to I/O activities, hence the mechanisms for controlling parallelism (interrupt handling and dispatching) became embedded in supervisory packages called I/O control systems. Of course, in the context of the more "modern" multiaccess, multiprocessor systems, the same or equivalent mechanisms together with some new ones are also inherent in (a) achieving the multiprogramming of unrelated coexisting processes (type 1), and (b) in the invoking and synchronizing of parallel computations in coexisting processes (type 3). The additional mechanisms include appropriate locking controls on shared data bases and the means of communicating (e.g., sending signals) between the independently operating hardware processors. For this reason, Multics has split out the traditional aspects of I/O control systems having to do with parallelism (interrupt handling and dispatching) and has combined these with the other aspects of parallel processing.

The combination resulting from this unified viewpoint has led to the development of a single, general-purpose supervisor subsystem for control of all parallel operations. This subsystem is known as the Traffic Controller.[4]

7.2 Multiplexing Processors

Our immediate goal is to see how Multics achieves the orderly and effective multiplexing of its processor(s) among the coexisting processes. The reader

3. We make the implicit assumption that nearly always there are more processes able to execute than there are available processors. A similar assumption is made with respect to core space; i.e., there is not enough to "go around."
4. The Traffic Controller was first formulated by J. H. Saltzer in a lucid Sc.D. thesis, "Traffic Control in a Multiplexed Computer System," Department of Electrical Engineering, M.I.T., 1966. This thesis has been distributed as a project MAC Technical Report (MAC-TR-30). A modification of Professor Saltzer's original design, developed in the M.S. thesis by Robert Rappaport ("Implementing Multi-Process Primitives in a Multiplexed Computer System," Department of Electrical Engineering, M.I.T., 1968), has been incorporated in Multics. This thesis has also been distributed as a Project MAC Technical Report (MAC-TR-55). The more recent work of other members of the Project MAC staff, including the work of S. L. Webber, is reflected in the current implementation.

The principal references for this chapter are the appropriate sections of the MSPM.

will learn about the functions of the Traffic Controller (or TC) in an incremental fashion. First, those functions needed to support multiprogramming are viewed. These are the mechanisms to give away and get back a processor when predictable time delays, such as those due to paging, are forced on a process. Next, the TC will be viewed as a general mechanism for time sharing, for interprocess communication, and for achieving still other control functions.

7.2.1 A Simple Mechanism for Multiprogramming

Consider a set of n seemingly unrelated user processes in a system of k processors ($k < n$). Each process coexists in one of three "execution states": running, ready, or waiting.

A *running* process is one that is currently executing on a processor. (At most, k of the processes are in the running state.)

A *ready* process is one that would be running if a processor were available for it to run on. (There are at most $n - k$ ready processes.)

Since we picture that processes will frequently incur page faults, some of the $n - k$ nonexecuting processes will be waiting for the completion of previously invoked paging requests (normally from the highest-speed auxiliary memory device). So, a *waiting* process is defined as one that cannot make immediate use of a processor (even if one were available), because it is waiting for a so-called *system event* to happen. Arrival of a page in core is an example of a system event, which can be defined as an event that (a) is of interest to at least one coexisting process[5] and (b) the waiting time for the occurrence of which has a predictable upper bound. Waiting processes compete for processors in the sense that once the waited-for event has occurred, the processes should then be regarded as being *ready*.

The Traffic Controller's tasks for multiplexing processors among this class of processes are conceptually simple. Its activities center around the maintenance of a list of the coexisting processes. This list is called the Active Process Table (APT). For each process on the list the Traffic Controller associates the current execution state and other vital data. Thus, for a process that is marked as *running* there is also recorded a code that identifies the particular processor on which the listed process is now executing. Entries for some processes that are not running are marked *ready*. Still others are marked as

5. Two processes could conceivably take page faults for the identical page of the same shared segment. The page fault in the second process could occur after the page fault taken by the first process but before the page request initiated by the first process has been completed. The net result is that when the system event (completing the page request) finally occurs, it will be of interest to *two* waiting processes.

waiting. For these there is also recorded an identifier for the event being waited for.

An interrupt is caused to go off upon completion of a page request. The interrupted process is forced into ring 0, where it notes that a waited-for system event has arrived. It then calls the Traffic Controller to "notify" the appropriate process(es) that has (have) been waiting. The TC then uses an event identifier that is associated with the interrupt to *notify* the appropriate processes in the following manner. For each given event identifier the TC locates on its list of processes those that are waiting for the identical event. For each such process, the TC then alters the code for its execution state from *waiting* to *ready*, and any now-readied process with sufficiently high priority can now preempt the processor. There is further discussion of the preemption mechanism in Section 7.4.

All processes that are running, ready (can run), or waiting (should run) are maintained in a priority sublist of the APT. In due course, every ready process will get its turn, that is, will be selected from this priority list, to run on a processor (at which time the identification code for the processor given to that process is recorded in the APT entry).

In summary, we see that notifying a process of a system event does not immediately place it in the execution state. A process must first pass through the *ready* state en route from *waiting* to *running.*

It may have occurred to you to ask the following question: Once put back into the running state, is there any iron-clad guarantee that the page for which a process had been waiting will, in fact, be there? There is some possibility that in the interim, between the time the process was first "notified" that its requested page was in core and the time it finally reacquired a processor to reference that page, the page has again been removed from core. This situation could arise in the following way. Let "x" be the page in question. Then, during the said interim, which could be a long one, other running processes may have page demands that are satisfied by "pushing out" page x. If in fact this situation were actually to occur, the victimized process, when it regained the running state, would reexecute the original faulting instruction and again cause a page fault. The running process would reinitiate the same page request and again call the TC to "put itself" into the wait state and give up the processor to one of the ready processes.

The hypothetical situation just described pictures a process cycling through the running-wait-ready states without ever accomplishing anything but page faults. This situation is one of several types of "system thrashing" that the system designer is always bent on preventing. Thrashing is prevented in Multics in the following way. The number of processes eligible for CPU attention is controlled so that (estimates of) their combined core requirements are approximately equal to the core available. The number of processes in this *eligible* group[6] may vary as the core requirements of the respective processes vary but is never allowed to increase simply to find work for the CPU. That is, under this form of control, the CPU may become idle occasionally. Moreover, a process that is forced into the wait state never loses its priority relative to the other eligible processes. So, when the process has been notified that it may resume execution, there can be at most a limited number of processes queued ahead of it. (There is even a built-in preemption mechanism to allow a just-notified process to preempt a processor if that process has a relative priority higher than any of the now-running processes.) The possibility that the desired page would be pushed out before it can be used by each process that has faulted on it is thus made negligible. A full elaboration of how this fine control is achieved is deferred to Section 7.4.

7.2.2 The TC Used for Time Sharing

If a running process is executing in a computation loop (deliberate or accidental) such that it takes no page faults over an extended period, what prevents this process from "monopolizing" the processor? The scheme for multiprogramming that was described in the preceding subsection does not indicate any way that other processes (ready or waiting) can get their "turn." Clearly, an additional mechanism is needed to force a sharing of the processor on the basis of elapsed time in execution. This mechanism is provided in the TC by assigning to each coexisting process an appropriate execution time allotment q, such that when a process has executed for a total of q time units, it is forced to give up the processor. The time allotment is a value that is under control of the system administrator. The control is achieved with the help of hardware as elaborated slightly in the following discussion.

First, it should be noted that the time allotment q for each process is assigned by a module of the TC called the "scheduler." The value for q is stored in the Active Process Table entry for the process. Also kept in the same entry is the amount of time r that has already been used in execution against the allotment q. When a process enters the running state, one can picture that the TC sets a timer register with the value $q - r$. The CPU's timer register

6. The system estimates core requirements for each process and periodically updates these estimates. They are treated as core *commitments* to the eligible processes. Typically, the number of eligibles fluctuates in the range from one to ten.

then counts down to zero. When it reaches zero, a combination of hardware and software causes the generation of a *process interrupt*. The interrupted process then calls an appropriate entry point in the Traffic Controller that causes the process to lose its eligibility and give away the processor to the "next" ready and eligible process. In addition, the process may be rescheduled. The term "rescheduling" refers to the tasks of –

a. giving the interrupted process a new time allotment q' (not necessarily equal to its last value of q) for use the next time it is allowed to enter the running state;

b. putting the process into the ready state by marking the execution state as ready, resetting the value of the time used (r) to zero, and making other updates to its APT entry;

c. placing the entry for the process in a possibly new (priority) position in the queue of ineligible processes;

d. running the highest-priority process available. Note that for want of a "better" one, the selected process could well be the one in item b that was just taken out of the running state.

When a running process moves to the wait state because it has incurred a page fault (or is forced to wait for some other system event, e.g., the unlocking of a system table), the value of r is kept in its APT entry and is incremented by an amount inferred from the reading of the timer register. There is no loss of eligibility incurred when a process moves to the wait state. Typically, the process's current time allotment is, in fact, used up over a sequence of short executions, each punctuated by a page fault or other system delay that causes the process to pass through the wait and ready states. Eventually, the time allotment is used up, at which time the process will lose its eligibility and (probably) be "rescheduled." It is current policy to give that process a larger time allotment but also a lower priority, which in effect means that its "insertion point" in the queue is made correspondingly less favorable.

In addition to giving a more detailed look at rescheduling, Section 7.4 also describes an *eligibility restriction* and a *preemption mechanism*. *Eligibility* refers to the depth or "degree" of multiprogramming. It is the number of processes that are permitted to compete for core memory at any one time. The number of eligible processes is necessarily restricted in order to prevent severe thrashing, that is, destructive competition for the limited core resources. Eligibility is first conferred on a ready process when that process attains highest relative priority among noneligible ready processes and when its core requirements, when added to those of the eligible processes, do not exceed the total available core.[7] Eligibility is withdrawn when a process uses up its time allotment, completes an interaction, or otherwise enters a dormant period to await a process event (blocked state).

Preemption amounts to one eligible process taking the CPU away from another eligible process of lower relative priority. Typically, this occurs when a high-priority (eligible) process in the wait state becomes ready.

7.2.3 Block, Wakeup Functions for Use in I/O Control and in General Interprocess Communication

Two more mechanisms are provided in the TC that are designed mainly to facilitate the synchronizing of deliberately cooperating processes. These are called the *block* and *wakeup* functions. They are functionally different from the previously described wait and notify functions. The wait, notify mechanisms, which can be called only from ring 0, allow a process to wait on (and later be notified of) system events; block, wakeup mechanisms allow a process to wait on (and later be notified of) so-called process events.

By a *process event* I mean an occurrence that can be of interest to only a specific process (or set of specific processes). The waiting period for such an occurrence will not, however, be either predictable by the supervisor or bounded. To retain the distinction between the two types of waiting, it is said that a process enters the *blocked* state when a process begins waiting for a process event.[8] It is said that the process receives a *wakeup* when it is notified of the occurrence of that event.

Before going further into detail of these TC mechanisms, it will help to consider an illustrative example (somewhat contrived) of a user process synchronizing its activities with a hypothetical system process that manages teletyped I/O (tty manager).[9] An I/O operation involving the typing out of a string of several thousand characters will be pictured.

Suppose the tty manager shares a segment with the user process that can

7. Should the process require all available core to run, it will acquire eligibility and will run by itself after all eligible processes ("ahead of it") have lost their eligibility.

8. Having defined what we mean by the blocked state, one is justified in viewing the wait state as an important special case–a state reached when the process becomes blocked while executing in ring zero–such that much is known about the nature of the waiting period to follow and how notification of its termination will come about. Multics designers have chosen to split out the wait state (from the blocked state) principally for reasons of efficiency.

9. Readers should realize that in the present implementation of I/O control in Multics, I/O supervisory procedures that control teletypes are part of each user process. No manager process is needed as a "middle man" or broker to execute these I/O functions. The hypothetical example of the manager process, once thought to be useful for systemwide service, is instructive and may prove applicable in the design of special subsystems.

be regarded as an output buffer. For simplicity, let it be 270 characters in length. Picture that the tty manager copies characters out of the buffer in amounts that range up to 270 characters at a time (enough to type up to three full lines on a certain brand of teletype). The user process attempts to move up to 270 characters of the long output string into the smaller buffer area on each transit through its write loop. With the aid of pointers into the buffer, each process is able to interpret the information in the buffer in an appropriate way. Thus, the pointers identify and delimit the next group of (up to 270) characters in the buffer that may be moved out (in groups of up to 90 characters) by the tty manager. The same or other pointers tell the user process which set of spaces within the buffer are "open," that is, which may be filled with the next group of characters from the output string. Two situations are apt to arise.

a. The user process may find at this instant that there is not enough room in the buffer for the next group of $i \leqslant 270$ characters to be copied into it. We will presume that under these circumstances, *the user process would want to place itself into the blocked state* until the tty manager has had an opportunity to "empty out" enough of the buffer to provide the room needed by the user process.

b. The tty manager may find it has emptied out the buffer, that is, there is no information in the buffer to be moved out. In the event there is nothing else that the tty manager can do, it would then have to wait for the arrival of more data into the buffer. *The tty manager would then want to put itself into the blocked state to await the desired event.*

Note (according to our earlier definition) that the events for which both the user and manager process might wait are *process events*. Thus, no other process but the manager will be interested in being notified that there are now characters in the buffer that are to be copied out onto the teletype. Moreover, there is no general way to predict how long the manager might have to wait for this notification, because the user process may incur various delays (including delays due to paging, due to computations of arbitrary length, or due to entering the blocked state) in the course of cycling through its write loop. Thus, the user process might be preempted or timed out during any one transit of its write loop.

There is, in fact, a symmetry here in the synchronizing of these two processes that can easily be seen. If one process, say the user, blocks itself, the other process (in this case the manager process) wakes up the first process and vice versa. Also, note the important implication that when each process blocks itself it is *counting on* the other process to "wake it up." It is usually unimportant for the blocked process to know when it will be awakened, but it is always crucial for that process to know it *will be* awakened.

We are now ready to see how the mechanisms *block* and *wakeup* that are provided in the TC would be applied. Our initial view will of necessity be greatly simplified. A more complete description is given in Section 7.5. Figure 7.2 will be helpful for the present purpose. It sketches some of the details in the write loop of the user process and in the synchronized read loop of the tty manager, which, taken together, characterize the buffered write operation. The synchronizing steps (loops) being described correspond to the set of actual interactions with the tty manager that from a source-language level is but a single logical interaction (I/O call). In this chapter it is not my purpose to show how the I/O control system might convert user-written calls such as

call ioa_(a,string);

into the steps being described in Figure 7.2, that is, boxes 1 through 5. Chapter 8, however, will shed some light on this translation process. Here the reader should accept the fact that such conversion is needed.

It is advisable to begin the discussion of Figure 7.2 at box 1. If the user process fails the test in that box (i.e., no place open in the buffer), it calls the "block" entry of the TC. The three dots on the line between boxes 1 and 2 are provided to suggest that the call to block is really handled indirectly, that is, through a chain of intermediate (supervisory) routines to be described in Section 7.5. In actual fact, a user will not be aware that his process is calling block. The argument in the call is a returned pointer to a location where A can expect to find a "message" signifying the event(s) being waited for has (or have) arrived. Basically, what the TC does when called at box 2 is the following:

The APT entry for process A will be marked *blocked* and the processor will be switched to the ready and eligible process of highest priority.

Process A has now been taken out of the running state and hence cannot return from its call to block (box 2) until after the event it waits for has arrived. This is why the line from box 2 to box 3 is shown with a break. A can return to the running state and thereby "jump the line break" in the flow diagram (so to speak) only after process B has executed a call to the wakeup entry of the TC (in box 6). In this call, process B names as arguments A's

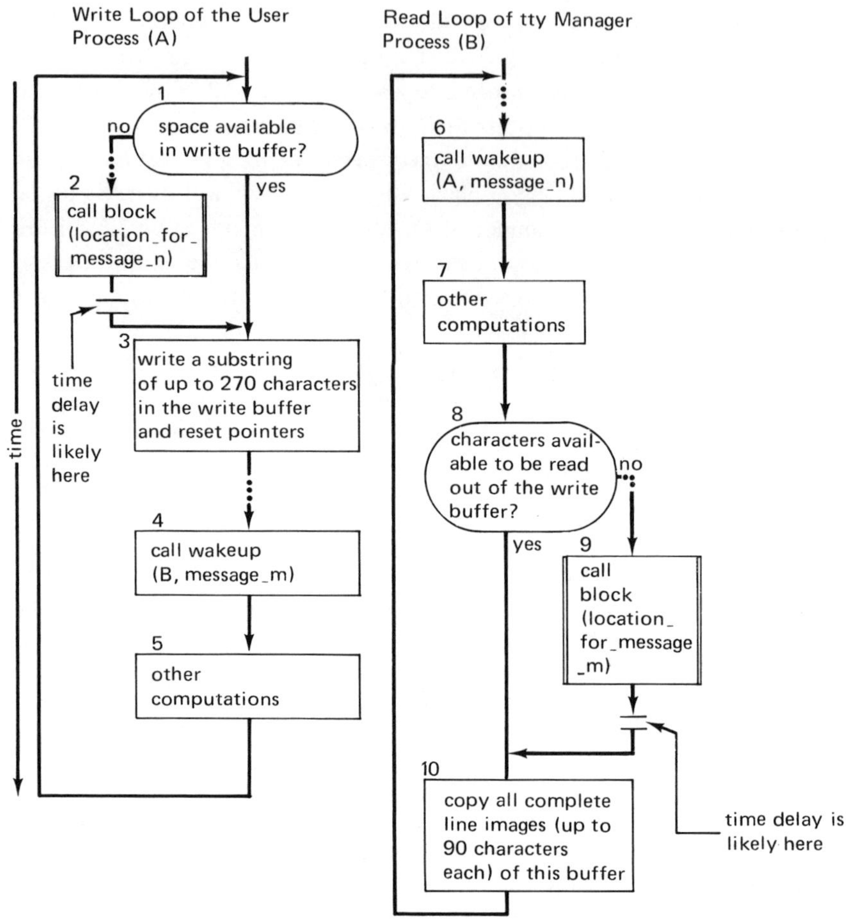

Figure 7.2. Schematic showing the synchronizing of a user process with the hypothetical tty manager process for a write operation (simplified view)

unique process identifier and a message, message_n, that represents the event A is expecting.[10] The message must later be recognized by process A before A can reenter the running state.

The TC upon being called at box 6 will place the given message_n in a systemwide shared data base that is, of course, accessible to process A while it executes in the supervisor (only). The TC also places a pointer to the message in the APT entry for process A. Here, bear in mind that only TC is allowed access to the APT (which is also a systemwide shared data base). Next, the TC places process A in the ready state. The wakeup procedure now returns to its caller, and execution in process B proceeds through box 7.

Now that A is in the ready state, it can compete again for a processor. When A subsequently gets a processor, it will resume execution within the TC module in which it (A) was last executing and then return from block at the exit of box 2. Block returns the pointer to the message sent by B as a return argument.

There is an intermediate step between box 2 and box 3 that was omitted from Figure 7.2 to keep its structure as simple as possible during a first view. Before proceeding to box 3, an intermediate system routine makes a check to be sure that it is the *expected* event message and not a spurious or irrelevant one that has been received.[11] If spurious, then box 2 is repeated. The schematic in Figure 7.3 replaces box 2 and the delay that follows. A similar loop structure is appropriate to replace box 9.

7.2.3.1 Conversion of I/O System Interrupts into Wakeups

Here the detail of box 10 of the model given in Figure 7.2 will be expanded. We now picture that having initiated teletype output, the manager process can do nothing else until this relatively slow output operation is completed. Suppose that under these circumstances it is appropriate for the tty manager to give up its processor by calling block. In this case it would be more realistic to consider detail shown in Figure 7.4 to replace box 10.

How, then, will the tty manager receive word of the completion of the I/O operation? That is, who (what process) wakes up the manager so that execution may proceed to box 12? The user process A may itself be in one of the

10. It will be seen in Section 7.5 that there is in fact one more important argument in this call, the event channel name, which, for the sake of simplicity here, has been deliberately left out of the discussion.

11. For example, a process P may be in communication with more than one other process, say B and C. At any one point, however, process P may enter the blocked state to await a wakeup signal from B. Suppose that shortly thereafter C sends P a wakeup signal, for whatever reason. Chaos would then result if P were awakened and permitted to proceed on the assumption that its expected signal from B had been received.

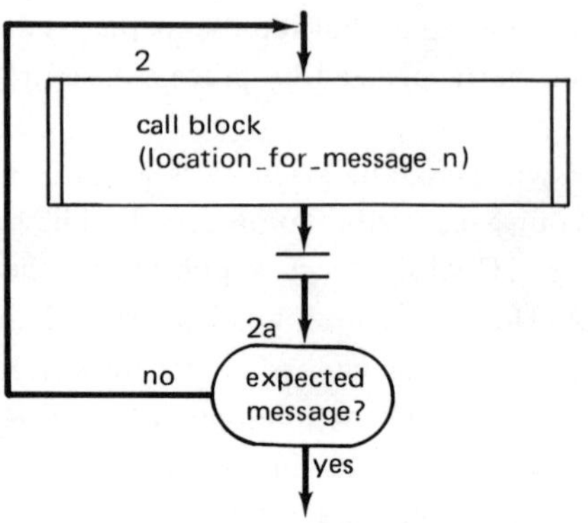

Figure 7.3. More detail for box 2

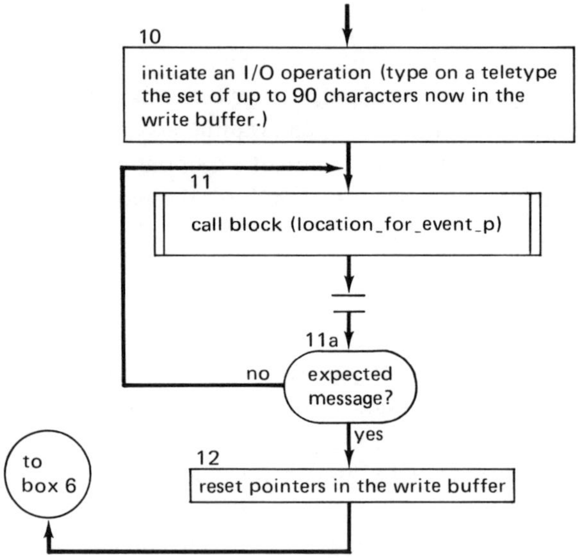

Figure 7.4. More detail of the initiation of an I/O operation

nonrunning (blocked, waiting, or ready) states while the tty manager is blocked. Thus, process A cannot be counted on for any help. Clearly, some "third" process must be involved. In the Multics I/O system design, the third process is any process that happens to be executing on the processor when it receives a hardware interrupt signal that is intended to indicate completion of the invoked I/O operation. The executing process is forced to play a Good Samaritan role because all system interrupt signals (I/O completion signals are examples of such interrupts) are handled by the Traffic Controller. By design, an I/O completion signal comes into the GE 645 memory and triggers the interruption (trapping) of whatever process happens to be executing on the affected processor. An invoked interrupt-handler program then converts this signal into a wakeup call to the TC, identifying the process that should be waked up and providing it a message that signifies the device on which the I/O task has been completed. Just as soon as the call to wakeup is completed, control returns from wakeup, and routine execution of the interrupted Good Samaritan continues. The foregoing concepts are suggested in Figure 7.5.

7.2.3.2 General Interprocess Communication

The test in box 2a of Figure 7.3 (and in box 9a, if it were drawn in a similar fashion) suggests an essential characteristic of meaningful communication among coexisting (and cooperating) processes. A process may receive more than one message or signal (from one or more processes.) Each legitimate signal could have different significance to a receiving process. In most instances it is essential that the reawakened process be able to identify the sender and the nature of the message, if proper interpretation of the "reawakening" is to be made.

For example, consider our hypothetical tty manager as the receiver of messages. Such a process could serve, not just one user, but all users that are using teletype consoles for output or input. In that event, the loop (boxes 6 through 10) of Figure 7.2 would clearly be an oversimplification. When awakened, the tty manager must identify which user process is sending a message and moreover which type of message it has received, so that it can act accordingly, that is, so it can resume a write loop to initiate more output on the teletype, or so it can resume a read loop to initiate more input—to read a buffer from the teletype—for some process. While the manager is not running, it must somehow be in a position to receive such messages in an orderly way, so that when again in the running state the message(s) received in the interim can be properly interpreted.

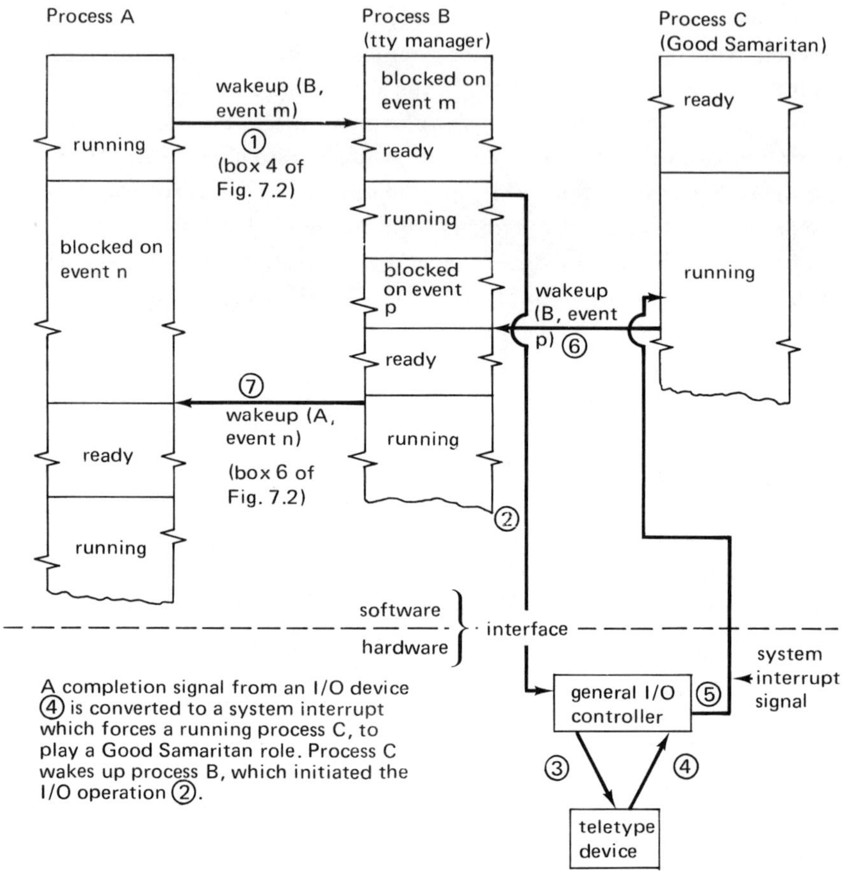

Figure 7.5. An illustration of the conversion of system interrupts to process wakeups

Multics provides a general mechanism known as the IPC (interprocess communication facility) to achieve the transfer of messages (signals) between processes. "Receipt" of messages can occur while the process is in any execution state, because the sender, using the IPC facility, can place a message in a shared data base that the receiver will examine and interpret at a later time, also with the aid of the same IPC facility. Subsystem designers will have little interest in the details for transmitting messages between user processes and system processes like the I/O driver, since these are entirely controlled by built-in functions of the I/O control supervisory procedures. On the other hand, the same techniques for interprocess communication also apply to subsystems in which two or more user processes must communicate with one another for effective operation. Here, the designer must provide the explicit calls on the IPC facility. For such subsystems, the designer must become more fully acquainted with the IPC. Section 7.5 provides the basics.

A final observation is in order in this introduction concerning interprocess communication. This has to do with the distinction between *data* communication and *control* communication. In the example of Figure 7.2, the data passing into and out of the write buffer may be regarded as *data* communicated between the two processes. The messages transmitted by the wakeup function and examined by the block function, though also data in one sense, nevertheless serve as *control communications* in that their net effect, like stop and go signals, permit the starting-up of a blocked process.

7.2.4 Other Control Functions of the Traffic Controller

The Traffic Controller contains modules needed for the purpose of creating processes, for destroying them, and for halting processes in anticipation of destroying them. Additionally, the TC is able to cause the *loading* of a process. Loading a process amounts to placing in memory a limited number of selected segments, page tables, and other information whose guaranteed presence in memory is essential if the process is put into the running state. This set of process information will be referred to as the minimum core image (MCI). Among the components of MCI are the APT entry for the process, a ring-0 descriptor segment, a descriptor segment for the current user ring, and a special ring-0 process-state segment named <pds> (process data segment).

Generally speaking, the subsystem designer need pay little attention to these essential supervisory functions, since they must be carried out as a matter of course in normal operations. Thus, during login a process is automatically created for the user, and during the logout that process is destroyed.

Moreover, it is also the responsibility of the Traffic Controller to see to it that a process acquiring eligibility has a minimum core image. In other words, loading of the MCI is supervised on behalf of the process whenever necessary.

With all this machinery for "managing processes" already necessary (and available) as supervisory functions, it is not surprising that the Multics design is aimed at giving a sophisticated user the opportunity to exploit some of these functions for his own purposes.

Two types of user applications are envisioned. The first is almost fundamental because of its relationship to console debugging. The second relates to the user's management of a subsystem in which one process spawns others.

1. Stopping a Process to Debug It

During a console session the user will often find cause to stop a process in execution (running, ready, or blocked). He may notice, for instance, that his process is in an endless (or undesirably long) output loop, suspect an endless computation loop is in progress, or for other reasons wish to halt the process and take stock of the situation, that is, enter into certain on-line debugging activities. The Multics design makes it feasible to carry out such console debugging by providing the user with a simple-to-use facility to accomplish the following:

a. Cause his current process to be "stopped." In the stopped state a process may not be awakened, that is, made ready. A process that is to be terminated (i.e. destroyed), say, by another process created by the same user, should be in the stopped state. This prevents the chaos that would result if, for instance, one process were to try to remove the APT entry for another process while the latter is actually running, perhaps due to an unexpected wakeup.

b. Cause a new process to be created and activated on the user's behalf that will now respond to his console commands. (No new login is necessary, mind you.) The new process can now be used to "inspect" segments such as the stacks of the stopped process, using debugging procedures that execute in the newly created process.

When Multics is fully implemented, a user will be able to achieve steps a and b simply by pressing the quit button and then issuing a "save" command on his console. The effect will be to signal an always-coexisting process, called the *answering service*, asking it to do these chores.

c. If, after inspecting the stopped process, the user deems it "resumable," possibly after "doctoring" one or more of its segments in some fashion, then he may destroy the new or current process and *resume* (put back into the ready state) the old process. This step, of course, implies that the console will be reattached to the resumed process. (See Chapter 8 for a discussion of attachment.)

Step c would be accomplished by typing the simple command, resume.

d. Alternate decisions might be either to *save* the old process for future resumption or save certain of the temporary segments of this process. Saving a previous process or any of its temporary parts is simple enough and is achieved by typing the simple command, save. Providing the system support for the practice of resuming a saved process at a *much later time* (say more than two weeks hence), however, is not considered practical. This is because such a practice implies that the "state" of the Multics supervisor and the Multics library will, at the time an old process is resumed, be sufficiently like its original state to make resumption of the process meaningful. But how can we be sure that the option to resume the process at some time, or any later time, can be successfully exercised? (This problem is intrinsic to all information utilities whose supervisory code and system libraries evolve at some finite rate.)

There is, indeed, a need to define a "canonical state" of a process so that the system itself can stop a process (when it reaches that state) for the purpose of performing some system operations. Examples are (a) the automatic logout of a user process so that it can be resumed when he (the user) is permitted to log in again, and (b) stopping a process to convert it from one that runs under control of an absentee monitor to one that runs under control of an interactive user and vice versa.

In addition, a user should be able to stop a process so as to perform certain routine checks on his process before resuming it. He should also have the convenience of stopping his process to "take a break," for instance, leave his console for a few hours to attend class or a committee meeting. The support of all these valid objectives is achieved through certain system practices and conventions. These are the following:

1. A process is never stopped in ring 0. (So, it never resumes in ring 0.)
2. The only user interface with the hard-core supervisor is <hcs_> which has a fixed segment number for all processes. Moreover, the offsets for all current (symbolic) entry points within <hcs_> are fixed. New entry points will be appended and traps will be set at existing entry points, should they ever be removed.

Items 1 and 2 assure that resumption of a process will find a consistent and safe set of system services—even if the system itself has changed somewhat in the interim.

3. Any library procedure that has been obsoleted will remain in the system library for a well-advertised period, say two weeks. During this grace period, a library procedure <X> will be renamed using a standard renaming convention that indicates the date this procedure became an old version, for example, "old_X_7/24/70".

We conclude our discussions concerning the stopped state by reviewing it from the perspective of the Traffic Controller and its design. The TC is not only designed to assist in the stopping of a process but is also able thereafter to recognize such a process, by marking the execution state (in its APT entry) as *stopped*. We see then that there are in actuality a total of *five* execution states that are recognized, namely,

running, ready, waiting, blocked, and *stopped.*

A process is marked "stopped", as explained hereafter, when it has no use for a processor and has no expectation of needing one, that is, is not *expecting* a wakeup. Putting a process in the stopped state prevents later wakeups received from cooperating processes from accidentally restarting a stopped process.

2. Stopping a Process in the General Subsystem Case

A special entry is provided in the TC that can be used by one process (A) to stop another process (B). The form of the call is

```
call stop (id_of_process_B);
```

Of course, the call must be (and is) quite privileged. No user can be permitted to use it in an indiscriminate fashion or the entire system would quickly collapse. On the other hand, with proper safeguards, it would be very useful to grant such permission for user-process A to stop (and possibly even then destroy) user-process B, provided, however, A and B were related to one another in a meaningful way. For example, Multics provides a subsystem with the capability for one process to spawn one or more other processes (much as certain system processes must be capable of doing). Each such spawned user process would then belong to the same "process tree" (as those that have a common ancestor user process). In a fully implemented version of Multics, a supervisory module, such as the TC, would conceivably be able to recognize members of the same process tree [12] so as to screen requests of the form

```
call stop (B);
```

12. The coding scheme that will permit this recognition is not yet finalized as of this writing.

A subsystem designer will, therefore, be able to write code that makes an initial working process A spawn processes B, C, ... Any of these may be coded to spawn others. All belong to the same process tree. Any one process might reach a decision to stop another process inferior in the same tree, on the basis of "cross talk," that is, interprocess communication between or among two or more of those coexisting within the group. I leave to the imagination of the reader the possibilities for subsystem design that are implied by virtue of these capabilities. Further consideration of this topic here would be premature prior to an examination of the Multics interprocess communication facility (IPC) itself, which is introduced in Section 7.5.

7.3 Core Resources Employed and Managed by an Active Process

In this section we shall examine core requirements of an active Multics process during various phases of its existence (from the time the process is created until it is destroyed). The system implications of these core requirements in the multiprocess environment in which all coexisting processes compete or tend to compete for core will also be considered. (When a user logs in, a process is created on his behalf by a preexisting system process that responds to the login command. The newly created process is registered in the Active Process Table (APT), and a small number of key segments for the process are made active by giving them entries in a systemwide data base known as the Active Segment Table (AST). Each AST entry includes a page table that is initialized to no-pages-in-core. The process normally remains active until the user logs out, at which time the process is destroyed.[13]

The execution state of a process not only characterizes the process as a competitor for a processor, but it also implicitly suggests how a process functions as a competitor for core.

A *running* process will attempt to (and in fact may) capture as much core as it needs. It will be restricted from doing so *while it is executing* only by virtue of competing demands of processes that are simultaneously executing on other processors. Of course, processes that "demand" core may execute on the same processor. So, in a single-processor environment, the longer a

13. The initial Multics implementation rigidly couples activation and deactivation of a process with its creation and destruction. A more flexible connection, e.g., *dynamic activation*, is also possible, and in principle, could be added to the system at some later time. Dynamic activation would make it convenient for Multics to support subsystems that exhibit a large number of only-occasionally used processes.

A user's process can spawn other processes, which become "active" in the same way.

process is allowed to execute without interruption, the larger can its "core holdings" become.

A *ready* process competes for a processor mainly with other ready processes. At any given time, a ready process will be queued in some fashion dependent, among other things, on the respective priority levels of the members of the set of ready processes. The specific queuing discipline currently used is discussed in Section 7.4. If it is not eligible, then, as a competitor for core, a ready process is a "loser." Because it is not executing, a ready process is unable to initiate the acquisition of core. Attrition can occur in its core holding due to the demands made by the executing process(es). A new page is brought into core for an executing process normally at the "expense" of some other page. The Multics algorithm for selecting pages to be "thrown out" in favor of new ones is such that least-recently referenced pages tend to be preferentially selected for removal. Thus, in principle, the longer a process remains in the ready and ineligible state (hence, not making references to the core-resident portion of its address space), the more likely it will suffer a loss of pages.

Only a ready process that is *eligible* will retain in core that portion of its address space that it needs to execute effectively. The eligible process gains frequent enough use of a processor to ensure that its most-recently referenced pages will not be purged (during any period of its residence in the ready and eligible state).

A *waiting* process is one that cannot make immediate use of a processor because it is waiting for a so-called system event to happen, for example, the arrival of a page into core, the request for which was initiated while this process was last executing. As a competitor for core, a waiting process would be expected to be a loser in roughly the same sense as a ready process. However, because a process that goes to the wait state for a system event is expected to remain there for only a brief and predictable period of time, it is allowed to retain its eligibility during this period. It also retains its favorable position in the queue. If its position is sufficiently favorable, then, when readied, it may in fact preempt the processor. In general, residence in the wait state will tend to be for short periods; hence there will be short periods *between* execution states and therefore minimal, if any, attrition of the process's core holdings.

A *blocked* process is waiting for a (process) event whose time of "arrival" is not in general predictable. As a competitor for core, the longer the process remains blocked, the more of its (nonshared) core-resident pages will be removed. If a process is blocked long enough, all its unshared pages, including its descriptor segments, will be paged out. Page tables for most of these segments will also be deleted as these segments are deactivated. Care is taken, however, in the system design to retain the page tables for several critically important segments (such as for the KST, the process data segment (pds), and the descriptor segments).[14] By retaining page tables for these important segments, the process remains capable of reactivating other segments—as required. Page tables and pointers to the branches for these segments (and for all other segments that remain active) are retained in the Active Segment Table (AST),[15] which is wired down. Of course, there will always also remain a "core residue" consisting of pages and page tables of the shared supervisory segments and perhaps also some shared library segments (both wired-down and otherwise).

A *stopped* process is the same type of core competitor as is a blocked process. The only difference is that a stopped process may be destroyed at the request of another process. In the course of being destroyed, segments that are categorized as *temporary* (and filed in its "process directory") are deleted along with their branches. These include the KST, the various individual and combined linkage segments of the process, and so forth. The space occupied by these segments, on whatever device they happen to occupy, is returned to the free storage pool of that storage device by the storage-allocating routines of the system. Thus, core space occupied by pages (and page tables) for temporary segments is immediately reclassified as *free*. (Free space is dispensed first in satisfying page requests of executing processes. Only after this pool is exhausted will other pages be removed.) Blocks occupied by the remaining pages and page tables of the destroyed process will be reused as needed by the system's paging algorithm.[16]

From the above discussions we see that, as a process cycles through its execution states, its core holdings ebb and flow cyclically. The system's scheduling and page-removal algorithms are designed to help keep this potential loss of efficiency from becoming significant. As previously mentioned, the Traffic Controller limits the number of users that may compete for a CPU

14. Strictly speaking, even these page tables would be removed if the process were unloaded. A process is typically unloaded or loaded (key core holdings written out or read in from auxiliary store) at the instigation of the Traffic Controller whenever that process loses or gains eligibility.
15. The AST is discussed further in the next subsections.
16. An excellent view of this algorithm can be found in the paper "A Paging Experiment with the Multics System," by F. J. Corbató, in *In Honor of Philip M. Morse*, edited by H. Feshbach and K. U. Ingard (Cambridge, Mass.: M.I.T. Press, 1969), pp. 217–228.

at any one time. The eligibility restriction has the effect of keeping the paging activity in the system at a tolerably low level (as a percent of CPU usage). The by-product of this restriction is that the average number of pages allotted to each competing process can be kept above some desirable minimum value. If the number of eligible processes is made too low, however, eligible processes may compute efficiently (i.e., for very long periods between page faults), but there will be too much idle time when the page faults do occur, and there may be some wasted core, while at the same time the system's response to the noneligibles may become unacceptably poor. (So it may pay to "tune" the system so that it thrashes a little bit.) As experience in the use of Multics grows, the sophistication of the various controls employed by the Traffic Controller can be expected to increase in the resultant direction of an optimal balance among these conflicting needs.

7.3.1 Minimum Core Requirements of an Active Process

I have already alluded to the idea that there exists in Multics a minimum core commitment for each active process. In this section you will begin to gain insight into the core-management aspects of Multics that relate to these memory-resource requirements of an active process.

From an overall view, core can be viewed as composed of three parts:

a. wired-down supervisor code (very roughly, about 25,000 words as of the summer of 1969),

b. systemwide tables and I/O buffers (perhaps 50,000 words),[17] and

c. the remainder, consisting of core blocks of a pool that is managed by a core allocator. These blocks are for the pages of nonwired procedure and data segments (approximately 300,000 words maximum, in the present configuration at Project MAC).

Of the systemwide tables mentioned in item b, the AST (Active Segment Table) is of chief importance in this discussion. This is a table that includes an entry for every active segment in the system and that cross-references each of these segments with the processes that presently share them. For each active segment there is also included in the AST its corresponding page table. Saying that a segment is *active*, therefore, mainly reflects the fact that its page table is currently in core.[18] Segments are limited to 64 pages (1024 words each) so that their page tables may be stored as 64-word blocks.

17. Space allotted in these tables is a function of the total core space available and of the anticipated number of active processes permitted in the system at any one time.

18. The AST provides page-table space for enough page tables (npt) to ensure that there is, in fact, always an excess of page tables over the number of segments (nseg) having a page or more in core. The excess, npt − nseg, is used to retain page tables for vital

In terms of the overall view of core just presented, we now discuss two types of minimum core requirements for an active process.

1. A *static minimum*, which is the core committed to the active process while it is *not running* and not loaded. This is the core needed for an effective transition into the running state. As long as the process remains active (i.e., has an entry in the APT), the static minimum is retained. In the present implementations (fall, 1970) it is a core space of approximately 130 words and, apart from the 32-word entry in the APT, is drawn entirely from the AST.

2. A *dynamic minimum*, which is the core needed when the process is loaded for running. The additional core space implied in this minimum, while partly drawn from the AST, is mainly drawn from the general pool of 1024-word core blocks. Three blocks are currently needed for pages of several "vital" system-provided segments.

It will be useful to enumerate components that make up each of these minimum "sets" even though continuing implementation improvements may make these details rapidly obsolete. Table 7.1 lists the static set and Table 7.2 lists the dynamic set. The following discussion provides some functional explanation of these two sets. It is not intended as a complete discussion, only as the beginning of a plausible explanation for the curious.

First I shall suggest the reason for maintaining, in active status, the three listed segments of Table 7.1. The system is designed so that resumption of the running state will result in references to each of these segments, and hence segment faults to them, which either should or must be avoided, are indeed

---

segments of all active processes (including those not eligible) and also to retain page tables for segments that are the *ancestor* directories of all active segments. Experience shows that keeping page tables for these segments in core drastically depresses the number of segment faults (and by-product page faults) that are normally incurred as a result of process switching and as a result of file-system operations. This amounts to a form of "preventive maintenance" for system efficiency, since each segment fault currently costs around 10 milliseconds and each page fault around 2 to 4 ms. Processing the page fault takes only 0.7 ms of this amount. The rest is consumed in the interrupt handler, and in the Traffic Controller for giving up the processor and selecting another process to run. Clearly, reducing the number of these faults also means reduced delay or latency in the execution of any one task. The system appears to be optimally tuned when sufficient page tables are retained so that a segment remains active for a (grace) period of about one minute beyond the time that its last page has been removed from core. At this balance point, i.e., a grace period of one minute, approximately 1 percent of CPU time is consumed in segment-fault processing (and about 10 percent in page-fault processing). Letting the grace period drop, for example, to 40 seconds to achieve some space saving (in the AST) causes segment-fault processing to creep up to 2 to 3 percent of CPU time (while page-fault processing rises to about 12 percent).

Table 7.1 The Static Set (minimum core requirement for an active process)

Item		Number of words
1. APT entry		32
2. AST entries for segments:[a]		
(a) ring-0 descriptor segment	<desc_0>	12
(b) "process data segment" (combines in one segment the functions of <pds> <pdf> <stack_00> and <rtn_stk>)	<pds>	36
(c) Known Segment Table	<kst>	24
(d) ring-*i* descriptor segment	<desc_i>	12
(e) process directory	<pdir>	12
Total		128

[a] Hardware modifications to the GE 645 address-formation mechanism were recently completed that enable Multics to use arbitrary-sized page tables–i.e., page tables whose size is whatever appears to be suitable to the system designer. A normal AST entry is now 12 words in length. (In the earlier design, page-table lengths were fixed at 64 words.)

avoided. At least two of the listed segments (2a and 2b) will almost immediately be referenced when the process resumes the running state. These are the process data segment, that is, <pds>, and the ring-0 descriptor segment. [In the current implementation, the process data segment includes data areas previously allotted to separate ring-0 segments, e.g., <pdf>, <rtn_stk>, and <stack_00>. In making references to the first two of these, neither segment faults nor page faults to certain pages therein[19] can be tolerated; so actual pages for these segments (<pds> and the ring-0 and ring-*i* descriptor segments) will be read (back) into memory, i.e., preloaded along with pages for several other key segments *before* the process is switched to the running state.]

19. The process executed last while in the Traffic Controller (ring 0). It was using page 1 of the ring-0 descriptor segment and a special stack (called the "process concealed stack") that is kept in the process data segment. This segment also contains vital process-state information, such as the current ring number, which must be accessible to the system while it is processing page faults.

Upon returning from the *block* (or *wait*) entry of the Traffic Controller, the process will still be in ring 0, so the ring-0 stack, also embedded in the process data segment, will also be needed.

Table 7.2 The Dynamic Set (minimum core requirement while an active process is loaded)

Item		Number of words
1. Items listed in Table 7.1 (5 AST entries and 1 APT entry)		128
2. Pages for segments		
(a) ring-0 descriptor segment	(1)[a]	1024
(b) process data segment (see Table 7.1)	(1)[a]	1024
(c) ring-*i* descriptor segment	(1)[a]	1024
Subtotal		3072
Total		3200

[a] These pages are preloaded before the process begins to run. All other pages are brought in as a result of page faults. A page of the process data segment, the first page of the ring-0 descriptor segment, and the first page of the ring-*i* descriptor segment, once loaded, are treated as wired down so long as the process remains loaded and eligible. The system considers pages for other useful segments, such as for the ring-*i* stack and the ring *i* combined linkage segments, as nonessential candidates for this "charmed circle" of preloaded pages. This is because in principle a smart user is free to code impure procedures for ring *i* that would not have to use a combined linkage segment or stack for that ring during extended periods of execution.

Typically, the Traffic Controller was entered either as a result of a process interrupt, while the process was executing in some ring other than 0, or indirectly, as a result of a call from another ring *i*. The Gatekeeper must be able to effect a return to ring *i*, implying need for the presence of the page table to (and a page from) ring *i*'s descriptor segment.

Once a process enters the running state, the pages of its core holdings (beyond those three that are preloaded for it) will rapidly expand in number. Some segment faults may also be incurred in referencing other segments not listed in Table 7.2, item 2.

A segment fault may result in the creation of an AST entry (72 words) and a page request for the referenced page. In a "busy" system new AST entries can be created only at the expense of old ones that are in some sense candidates for removal. Just as new pages replace ("old") pages that have not recently been referenced, new AST entries replace those for segments which have had no pages in core for some time. (Of course, certain types of AST entries, such as the per-process segments listed in Table 7.1, are not candidates for removal while the process is active.)

As shown in Table 7.2, a typical process will tie down a minimum of five AST entries and a minimum of three pages while it performs even the simplest of tasks. Additional core space is needed for its nonsupervisory procedures and data segments. Normally, the pages and AST entries in Table 7.2 will be referenced so frequently that the system removal algorithms will never select them as candidates for removal while the process is *eligible*. Presumably, the same will be true for frequently-referred-to pages of the user-provided segments of a process.

The Working Set

Following Denning[20] I shall refer to the Table 7.2 list plus the other pages and page tables of the user segments that are being referred to very frequently as the *working set* of a process. The page removal and AST-entry removal algorithms of Multics "honor" the working set in the sense that its components tend to remain in core over the period of time the process is executing. During this time, demands by the same or coexisting processes for a large number of *less-frequently needed* pages and their AST entries can also be satisfied without seriously affecting the working set (or working sets of the eligible processes). Section 7.3.3 explains how the working set for an eligible process is maintained.

7.3.2 The Active Segment Table and Shared Segments

This subsection and Section 7.3.3 describe some of the inner workings of the file system's key modules and data bases used in creating and managing the Multics virtual memory. The material is provided mainly for the sake of completeness.[21] It is certainly not essential in the flow of ideas for this chapter. These subsections do, however, help one to appreciate some of the challenges that have faced the Multics system designers and show why the success of a subsystem may well depend on how effectively its designer has minimized the load (segment and page faults) that the subsystem has placed on the file system.

Since space for entries in the AST is limited, it will be the usual case that some segment must be *deactivated* so that another may be activated.

20. Peter J. Denning, "The Working Set Model for Program Behavior," *Communications of the ACM* [Association for Computing Machinery] 11, no. 5 (1968): 323–333. See also Peter J. Denning, "Resource Allocation in Multiprocess Computer Systems," Ph.D dissertation, M.I.T., 1968. This dissertation has been issued, under the same title, as a Project MAC Technical Report (MAC-TR-50).

21. A more complete discussion of this topic may be found in "The Multics Virtual Memory" by A. Bensoussan, C. T. Clingen, and R. C. Daley, *Second Symposium on Operating Systems Principles, Princeton University, October 1969* (New York: Association for Computing Machinery, 1969), pp. 30–42.

Deactivating a segment, therefore, means relinquishing AST table space for its AST entry. Each such entry consists of an 8-word entry and an associated page table. An active segment becomes a candidate for deactivation if it satisfies these conditions:

1. The number of its pages in core is zero.[22]
2. The "entry hold" switch in its AST entry is off.
3. If this is an AST entry for a directory, its *inferior count*, that is, the number of its immediate descendents that are active, must be zero.

An entry that satisfies the above conditions is flagged, and when later selected for removal, it tends to reflect the segment that has had no pages in core for the longest period of time.

When the entry for such a segment is selected for deactivation, the corresponding SDW for the process that lists this segment in its address space must be located and marked appropriately with segment-missing bits. (Recall that in Chapter 6 this task was referred to as *disconnecting a segment*.) In this way one is assured that a subsequent reference to this segment will incur a segment fault and thereby invoke mechanisms to recreate an AST entry and page table. Having put a "stop" in the appropriate SDW, Segment Control is then free to proceed with the construction of the new AST entry and page table, which will allow Page Control subsequently to page-in the referenced page. The faulting SDW word is then altered appropriately and made to point to the newly constructed page table, that is, the segment is *connected*.

If we consider that the deactivated segment may have been *shared*, then removal of its AST entry and page table implies the need to disconnect the segment *from each process that shares it*.

Recall that the AST cross-references every active segment with the processes that share it. Segment Control, by proper use of the AST, is therefore able (and is sufficiently privileged) to identify each process that currently shares any given segment and also to determine its segment number in each of these processes (i.e., determine the SDW in each sharing process). To be more precise, the cross-referencing design of the AST permits Segment Control to get at and alter SDWs in each descriptor segment of every process that shares the segment that is being deactivated.

Suppose we picture that process A is deactivating a segment <s> that is shared by processes B, C, D, and so on. Clearly, the job of marking with

22. If no segment can be deactivated that has zero pages in core, segments having only one page in core are then considered, then two pages in core, etc. Such pages will be forced out in the deactivation process.

segment faults a sizable number of SDWs (i.e., disconnecting a sizable number of segments) cannot be done instantaneously. This means that some care must be (and is) taken to prevent page-faulting references to <s> from being serviced by processes B, or C, or any other, while A, still executing in Segment Control, is attempting to deactivate <s>. To permit the freedom for other processes to request a new page in <s> at this time is to invite chaos.[23] Process A prevents this confusion from happening by setting certain flags and locks at key places in the AST at the start of its deactivation task. The result is that any other process sharing <s> must wait should it fault to a page of <s> while <s> is being disconnected. When fully completed, and all SDWs have been set with segment faults, the flags and locks are reset, permitting the sharing processes once again to reference <s>. The first such reference will incur a segment fault that will then result in a new activation of <s>. More details for those interested are provided in the accompanying footnote.[24]

7.3.3 Handling of Segment and Page Faults

Segment faults and page faults add CPU time, and wherever possible the subsystem designer should be on the lookout for ways to avoid triggering these faults unnecessarily. Before examining ways to avoid these faults (see Section 7.3.4) it is a good idea first to get a feeling for how these faults are handled.

7.3.3.1 Segment Faults

Segment faults currently require on the order of 8 to 15 ms of CPU processing time. In addition, segment faults will usually trigger page faults and possibly other segment faults as a by-product since both the segment fault-handling procedure and the data bases it looks at, that is, the directory and the KST, are not wired down. The steps taken are roughly as follows. For purposes of

23. This is because such references, if permitted, would imply that Page Control would be working at cross purposes for different processes. For one process it might be attempting to add a page for <s> (and remove a page fault in the corresponding page-table word of <s>'s page table), while for another process it would be attempting to reset the page table so it can be used for another segment. Although this situation is rather unlikely, it is nevertheless possible, and hence provision must be made to prevent it.

24. If another process takes a page fault in the segment being deactivated, Page Control will notice the set flags and will properly interpret what is happening. It will then "tinker" with the process so that the process will "believe" it has taken a segment fault instead of a page fault. This is accomplished by altering the SDW of the segment that has incurred the page fault so it will cause a segment fault when next referenced. Following this adjustment, Page Control simply returns, whereupon a repeated execution of the faulting instruction will cause a segment fault. When the process next attempts to solve its segment-fault problem, it will be forced to wait on a lock (of the parent directory) that has been set and will remain set until the process doing the deactivating of the segment has finished its job. Whereupon, the flags and locks are reset, permitting other processes to again activate the deactivated segment if necessary.

illustration we shall picture that the fault is taken for a segment <t> in ring *i*. Here we imagine the branch for <t> is found in a user directory whose path name is >w_dir_dir>John.

1. Consult the KST entry whose index is the same as the segment number of <t>. (This t# is determined from the saved machine conditions.) Since the KST is itself always active, there will be no segment fault incurred in referencing it, but since the KST is a *paged* segment, a page fault may be induced before a reference to the desired KST entry is eventually achieved. Segment Control will obtain from the KST entry the segment number and offset of the directory branch for <t> in the segment <John>. (See Table 6.2.)

2. Appropriate information needed for activating <t> is then copied from its branch if <t> is not already active.[25] In referencing the branch, another segment fault may be induced if <John>, although guaranteed to be active (by the ancestor-is-always-active rule), is not *connected* to its page table.[26] (Admittedly, the possibility that <John> is not connected is extremely unlikely since active segments are normally also connected.) However, the particular page wanted from <John> may be missing, thus inducing a page fault. The data copied from <t>'s branch is used to create a new AST entry and page table. Page-table words (PTWs) are set with missing-page faults and file-map data. That is, the address field of the PTW is either set with pointer information for the page's address in auxiliary storage or is set to null (for page numbers that are either beyond the current length of the segment or that correspond to pages yet to be created).

3. After the page table is constructed and the new AST entry is cross-referenced, that is, connected, to the process requesting it, the SDW words are appropriately set in the ring-0 and ring-*i* descriptor segments, pointing to the new page table.

7.3.3.2 Page Faults

Page faults currently require on the order of 2 to 4 ms. of CPU processing time, including time spent in interrupt handling and "visits" to the Traffic Controller. The type of tasks that are involved in handling page faults has already been suggested in earlier discussions, so not much more detail on the matter will be provided here. Briefly, when Page Control is called to get a page,

25. References to branches can be thought of as being made by Directory Control on behalf of Segment Control.

26. In fact, a recursive sequence of such segment faults can occur in the unlikely event that all parents (except the root) have fault-inducing SDWs (i.e., are disconnected). The recursion ends at the root node because this item is by design always immediately accessible.

it is handed, via the faulting machine conditions, a pointer to the faulting page-table word. Moreover, since the page-table address in which the PTW is found has the same index as the corresponding AST entry, the latter's address in the AST can also be determined. The AST entry would then be consulted to ascertain if it is OK to proceed with the fetching (or creation) of the page. (As you may recall, this entry may have been flagged to indicate that the segment is in the process of being deactivated.) If the PTW address field is nonnull, it contains device address information for the wanted page, but if null, it indicates that a page of zero-valued words is wanted.[27] Page Control invokes a core-allocating routine[28] to obtain the address of a free core block. (Such a request can easily trigger a page-removal request if the number of free core blocks is low.)[29] Page Control zeroes out this acquired block, resets the faulting PTW to point to the new block, adjusts the AST entry to reflect the new condition of the page table, and returns control to the faulting procedure.

If the pointer in the PTW is not null, Page Control also asks for a core-block address, then initiates the drum or disk I/O request, as appropriate, to get the wanted page from secondary storage and calls *wait* in the Traffic Controller. You can see from the foregoing discussion that processing time for a page fault will vary according to several factors.

Page faults that call for the creation of a new page (of zeros) will be least expensive, because although it takes approximately 1 ms to make the zeros vs. 0.7 ms to initiate a page request (of a similar set of zeros) from disk, other costs such as interrupt handling and process switching are avoided—that is, loss of the processor and delay while in the subsequent wait and ready states. Additional time is required in processing page faults, up to 2 milliseconds, if the page-removal algorithm must be invoked and the attendant I/O request(s) initiated.

7.3.3.3 Maintaining the Working Set of an Eligible Process

In this section I shall describe how the system is currently organized to help the user keep the working set of his process in core memory whenever the

27. Space for such "empty" pages is created only when first reference is made to them. It is never created and stored ahead of time. Hence, no page needs to be "transferred" from secondary storage.

28. Additional details on the core-allocating activity associated with Page Control may be found in appropriate sections of the MSPM.

29. To remove a page involves invoking the page-removal algorithm, about which I spoke earlier, which "fingers" pages that are candidates for removal. Also invoked would be the appropriate machinery to copy out the contents of said removal candidates on to auxiliary storage. Copying of a page is performed only if the respective PTW indicates, via its page-has-been-written bit, that the page has been altered while in core.

process is eligible. For each process Page Control maintains a so-called page trace, which is a list of the last (200) page faults taken. Upon unloading a process, this list is processed to decide which pages to postpurge (now) and which to prepage (later), when the process is reloaded. (Those worthy of prepaging are remembered and paged in if not already in core at reload time.) The decision process (to postpurge or prepage) involves these six criteria, which are applied to each page in the page trace.

a. Is the page still in core?

b. Has it been used (referenced bit *on* in the page-table word)?

c. Has it been modified?

d. Is this page part of a per-process segment?

e. Would the page be sent back to—or come from—a paging drum (or not)?[30]

f. Has the page been used during the (current) eligible period?

The 0/1 replies to these six questions yield a six-bit integer argument used as an index to a ring-0 table called the "prepage, postpurge driving table." Each of the 2^6 entries in this table holds a 4-bit action code that tells what to do with and how to regard the subject page [31] as follows:

bit 1:	postpurge this page (now).	These are not necessarily mutually exclusive.
bit 2:	prepage this page (later, if necessary).	
bit 3:	consider this page to be part of the working set.	
bit 4:	move the page in the "core map" list, so that the page becomes the next to be considered for removal when space is needed.	

The count of all pages that "compute" to be part of the working set in this fashion represents the current estimate of working-set size that is then recorded appropriately in the APT entry for that process.[32]

When computations make rather abrupt "changes of direction," their working sets (and sizes) would be expected to change abruptly too. Accordingly, a way has been found to make the working-set estimator more responsive to such changes and indeed to be responsive to advice from the user

30. The paging drum, with its hardware queuing feature, effectively manages 16 request queries, i.e., one per drum sector. Hence, transfer to or from the paging drum, which normally incurs shorter delays than to or from disk storage, is relatively attractive.

31. Multics system programmers are able to adjust this systemwide driving table (using a privileged command) during tuning studies.

32. At process creation time (during the log-in phase) the system supplies an initial estimate of the working set size, knowing just how many pages are needed to begin effective execution of any process.

should he care to give it. More specifically, there is a system routine,

hcs_$reset_working_set

provided for this purpose. The system is a heavy user of this routine. Upon each return to command level, the Listener calls hcs_$reset_working_set, which goes through the page-trace table resetting every *used* bit (to zero) in page-table words of the corresponding pages that are still in core. Upon return from this call, the Listener completes its activity on behalf of the user in the course of putting the process into a blocked state to await another interaction. In so doing, the computation (quite conveniently) touches pages of all the key segments that should remain part of the working set and be preloaded when the process becomes eligible once again, for instance, ring-0 and ring-1 stacks, ring-1 combined linkage segment, the typewriter I/O mechanism and its data bases, the interprocess communication facility and its data bases, and so on (including the Listener itself, naturally).

Subsystem designers may call hcs_$reset_working_set at any time, at a point where there is a known abrupt change in the nature of the computation, as, for instance, between two passes of a compiler, or after having executed some section of a computation that is known to be a low CPU user but has touched numerous pages that will not be referenced again. Proper use of hcs_$reset_working_set causes the unwanted pages to be purged sooner and so frees core for more immediate use during the processing of subsequent page faults. Such practice also lowers the core commitment for this process and may generally work for the mutual benefit of all processes in the system (more throughput through more effective utilization of core).

7.3.4 Ways to Reduce Segment Faults

By now the subsystem designer reading this chapter should be more than mildly receptive to suggestions for reducing the incidence of segment faults (that are under his control to reduce). Two relatively obvious principles serve as a guide.

1. Because other eligible processes compete for page-table space in the AST, a process having a large number of segments will tend to suffer a larger number of segment faults than a process with fewer segments. Hence, a conscious effort to keep the number of segments to a reasonable minimum will tend to reduce segment faults. For example, a computation may have data arrays A and B that are logically independent, so one may be tempted to code each as a separate segment, though the arrays may easily be made part of the same segment.

2. For a given number of segments in a process it should be possible, by conscious programming effort, to organize a "computation" for a minimum of segment faults. Intuitively, this could be achieved if it were possible to sustain a high enough frequency of reference to the segments that were most recently referenced. In other words, if it is possible to design the process so that it maintains a high degree of *locality*[33] with respect to its segment references, the process will incur fewer segment faults due to deactivation.

Here are several approaches the subsystem designer can take to reduce or limit the number of segments of a process:

a. Avoid specifying multiple rings unless necessary, because each ring in which the subsystem executes automatically adds a number of segments to the process, for example, a descriptor segment, a stack segment, and a combined linkage segment.

b. Bind[34] procedure segments that belong to the same ring, and bind, where feasible, data segments of the same ring that are to have the same access controls. Bind procedure (and data) segments that are related more by the typical flow of control through them (or by references to them) rather than by their functional similarity. Thus, if <alpha_sort> and <num_sort> are two separate sort routines, they should not be bound together on the strength of their functional similarity if only one, but not both, is typically called to do a sorting task. On the other hand, certain string-handling procedures employed by <alpha_sort> might well be bound to it rather than to other string-handling routines.

c. Proliferation of procedure segments can be limited by a conscious effort to define internal functions and procedures, that is, those that are defined within the body of external functions. ALGOL, PL/I, and MAD, for example, provide good facilities for defining internal functions. FORTRAN does not.

d. Use internal static and automatic variables (i.e., that will be placed in the ring-*i* stack or (combined) linkage segment) whenever possible, in deference to creating separate (external) segments for variables.

Here are three approaches the subsystem designer can take to increase the degree of locality of his process:

1. If the subsystem is multiringed, try to confine the computation within

33. A thorough discussion of the locality concept is given by P. J. Denning in a paper entitled "Thrashing, Its Causes and Prevention," *AFIPS* [American Federation of Information Processing Societies] *Conference Proceedings, Volume 33, Part 1, 1968 Fall Joint Computer Conference* (Washington, D.C.: Thompson Book Co., 1968), pp. 915–922.

34. Binding was discussed in Chapters 2 and 6.

one user ring (or within as few rings as possible) for *as long* as possible. That is, try to organize the computation so that as few rings as possible (2) are involved in any one console interaction. Wall crossings are relatively cheap compared to segment faults, so going back and forth between the same two rings need not be too costly. However, a less-frequent reference to a third ring may trigger a number of segment faults if the segments for that ring were deactivated since the last execution in that ring.

2. Avoid frequent use of loops in which there are explicit calls to the ring-0 supervisor.

3. Group external variables and data structures that are referenced in the same activity into one segment or into as few different segments as possible.

7.3.5 Ways to Reduce Page Faults

There are no revelational remarks that can be made on this subject. Following the logic in preceding discussion on segments, it is clear enough that a process with fewer pages will, in the long run, generate fewer page faults. What is really wanted is the recipe for minimizing page faults when the number of pages in a process is already at its minimum, and to accomplish this, locality is again the key! A high degree of locality within (the pages of) each segment is wanted, and this is a property that only the individual programmer can, with his conscious effort, attempt to achieve. In some cases this will be easy and in other cases very difficult.

Achieving a high degree of locality at the segment level (see the preceding subsection) will normally reduce page faulting as well and perhaps with an even greater percentage improvement. It is also possible in certain cases for the user by conscious (but not too great) an effort to achieve increases in the locality within (the pages of) a segment. Stronger locality will be achievable in many procedure segments if cognizance is taken of the flow of control within the procedure itself while it is being coded.

Locality may sometimes be even more easily controlled within a data segment. For example, let there be two arrays, A and B, each having 2^{10} entries, 32 characters each. Suppose references to these two tables are always made to pairs (A_i, B_i). Further suppose both arrays are stored within the same segment. Which storage structure would tend to yield stronger locality of reference, an array of pairs (A_i, B_i), or a pair of arrays, A, B? Compare the following alternatives in PL/I:

```
declare 1 table (1024)
            2 a char(32),
            2 b char(32);
```

or

declare (a(1024), b(1024)) char(32):

Clearly the former gives stronger locality of reference.

7.4 Assignment of Processor Resources

The assignment of processors to processes that need them is a central management problem in any information utility. In Multics, two management functions are, in fact, to be simultaneously fulfilled in the second-by-second, minute-by-minute solution to this assignment problem. These are time-sharing decision-making and multiprogramming decision-making. Both functions quite naturally influence the kind of system response that can be expected in the execution of subsystems developed by users. Introductory details, hoped to be adequate for the needs of the subsystem designer, are provided in this section.[35]

The time-sharing function guarantees each user a chance to gain an equitable share of processor time. The term "equitable" is explained in the next subsection. Roughly speaking, sharing is always among those users that have the *same priority*. For reasons we shall see shortly, a user's relative priority may well vary with time. An ideal time-sharing system should therefore anticipate (or correctly guess) each user's current need for processor time and accord him a (higher or lower) level of priority that is consistent with this need, that is, with the load he would place on the system when allowed to run. (It is current Multics policy that the higher this load the lower should be the relative priority.)

Principally because of core-memory limitations, however, a processor cannot be effectively time-shared with an unlimited number of equal-priority processes. The multiprogramming function is therefore restricted so that the processor is assigned in fact to a sufficiently small subset of the "most deserving." The subset, called the eligibles, is chosen small enough so that the work that is done for each member is *effective work*, and is not degraded, for instance, by excessive thrashing. An implication of the "subset-of-eligibles" idea is that the processor may occasionally be forced to *idle* for very brief periods of time until an already eligible process is again ready to run. (Occasional idleness is preferable to the alternative of always adding another process to the list being multiprogrammed. The latter approach would greatly

35. The principal reference material is in the MSPM.

increase thrashing. If this occurred, the cost of recovery would prove greater than the small amount of deliberate idle time.)

7.4.1 Time-Sharing Philosophy

To understand the basis for the scheduling algorithm used in Multics, one begins with a crude model in which every user is an "interactive user"; his process consists of executing a series of normally short spurts of computation, for example, commands. If the execution time for each command were short, invariant, and known in advance, then a sensible scheduler might allot each user the time q_k that is needed to execute command k to completion. Users would be queued on a single list and permitted to execute in FIFO (first in, first out) fashion. No timer run-out interrupts would be required.

A few commands may be fixed in duration, but, for most, their duration are functions of their arguments, such as the FORTRAN command whose argument is the program being compiled. Nevertheless, it is useful to pursue this line of reasoning, that is, temporarily ignoring the fact that command duration is often unknown, because it provides us with a useful conceptual basis from which to understand the more realistic scheduler used by Multics.

A Conceptual Model

Let q be some (albeit fuzzily defined) *average* duration for commands in the system. Suppose current experience indicates that q_0 time units is an appropriate approximation to q. If the scheduler were initially to allot each user an amount of time q_0, then a sizable fraction of users would complete their tasks before their time "ran out." Accept as a premise that the system should, in the default case, be designed to favor users that execute short commands (highly interactive users) by according such users a relatively high priority. Let each command be classified into one of n categories (numbered $1, 2, \ldots, n$) according to its duration. Commands in category 1 would correspond to short durations with priority level 1 (highest priority), while lengthiest commands in category n would be in priority level n (lowest priority).

The next step is to associate a separate queue with each priority level. If a user wishes to execute a command that falls into category j, where $1 \leqslant j \leqslant n$, his process would then be added to the queue numbered j to wait his turn. Following the management principle that higher-priority jobs should be executed before lower-priority jobs, the following default rule is promulgated for the conceptual-model scheduler.

No entry on queue numbered j *shall be considered until all higher-priority queues are empty*. This rule discourages users from executing long-duration commands while the load is high. There is also presumed to be a mechanism for overriding this rule, so that under certain circumstances a user can be "credited" with an interaction and so obtain an increase in priority level for his command. (He might, for instance, be requested to attract the attention of the supervisor by pressing a special button on his console.) This completes our first model.

The Real Model (Multics)

Here we shall realistically presume that a command's duration is in general *not known in advance*. However, we shall take the attitude that the unknown duration must be determined if meaningful scheduling is to be achieved. Some type of adaptive technique suggests itself. In the Multics scheduler, it is assumed that every process arriving on the ready list for the first time deserves a position on a high-priority queue on grounds that the command to be executed will be a short one. Associated with the queue is some fixed time allotment q_0 (say one second). When a process on this queue is picked to compete (in the eligible-for-multiprogramming sense), the command may run to completion. If so, the process will then call block before the allotment q_0 is used up. On the other hand, if the allotted time is exhausted, execution will be halted by a timer run-out mechanism. The command is then assumed to belong to the next category. The containing process can no longer compete on the first queue, so the process is awarded an additional allotment of time, say $2 \times q_0$, and placed at the end of the next lower priority-level queue.

Each time the current time allotment is exceeded, execution is stopped so that the command's category can be "reappraised." That is, the process is given an additional allotment, say twice the preceding allotment (e.g., $2 \times (2 \times q_0)$) and placed at the end of the next lower priority-level queue. In this fashion we see how the system learns adaptively about the "true" duration category l of a command's activation. When command execution is completed at some priority level l (or, speaking more strictly, whenever an interaction is accomplished), the process is rescheduled, anticipating execution of another command. Specifically, the process is dissociated from queue l and reassociated with the top priority-level queue with allotment q_0.

A price has been paid to learn a command's "true" duration category when more than q_0 time units are needed. This price amounts to premature processing of a variable portion of its total execution. During this time the process is allowed to compete briefly with more-favored commands. Thus, if a command's execution is in the range $q_0 \times 2^r \leqslant \text{duration} \leqslant q_0 \times 2^{r+1}$, then at least half of its processing ($q_0 \times 2^r$) will be completed at a perhaps unnecessarily high priority.[36]

7.4.2 Multics Design Details [37]

The Multics solution to the processor assignment problem is made conceptually simple when it is discussed with the APT sublist of ready processes as the focal point. For then, albeit at risk of some oversimplification, one sees that—

1. the decision process that determines where new entries will be *inserted* in the ready list and what time allotments to give them (scheduling) amounts to fulfilling the time-sharing decision function.
2. the decision process that determines which entries on the ready list to run amounts to fulfilling the multiprogramming decision function. (Removing an entry means awarding a processor to the process associated with that entry.)

7.4.2.1 Insertions in the Ready List (Scheduling)

The ready list may be viewed as a set of n queues (each a ready list), one per priority level. At the time it is created, each user process is assigned a range of priority levels (l_1, l_2) with initial execution started at level l_1. The range (l_1, l_2) offers some clue as to the type of time-sharing service the process will be given. At any given time a ready process has a current priority level l such that $1 < l_1 \leqslant l \leqslant l_2 < n$. For interactive and absentee user processes, the ranges (l_1, l_2) fall on the scale 1 to n as follows:

Interactive processes would range from 1 to some value k_1 while absentee processes would range from some value k_2 to n, with k_2 perhaps having a lower priority level than k_1 as suggested by these straddling brackets:

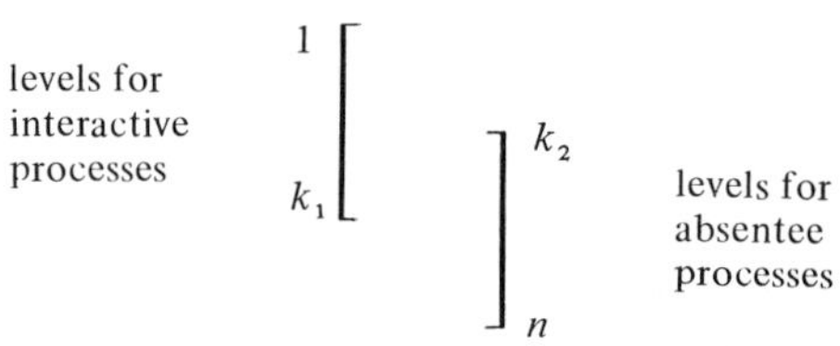

36. If we assume there are cost vectors C and R such that c_i is the charge to execute for q_0 seconds at priority-level i, and r_i is the cost of rescheduling the process from priority-level i to $i + 1$, then the excess cost, EC, to learn the true category s of a command's particular activation is at most

$$EC = \sum_{i=1}^{s-1} [(c_i - c_s) \times 2^i + r_i]$$

Of course, a user would not necessarily be charged in this manner. The quantity EC is mainly of conceptual value in understanding the nature of the Multics scheduler.

37. Modular design of the central supervisor has made it feasible for the Multics system architects to try many variations of the basic traffic control and scheduling algorithm

Consistent with the current policy of giving good response to short interactions, priority level 1 is awarded to processes that are expected to make brief use of a processor. For instance, a process that has initiated a console read call and has given up the processor (is blocked) while waiting for the console typist to type the next input line wants the opportunity to resume (with a short spurt of execution), that is, to *respond*, when the input step, that is, an interaction, has been completed. The Traffic Controller will ready a blocked process with (highest) priority level of 1 (i.e., will credit the process with an "interaction") when it knows that the following two criteria have been satisfied:

a. The process has previously called block (via the privileged console read subroutine) after initiating (but being unable to complete) a request to read data from a terminal.

b. The requested data have actually arrived from the terminal (and an indication of this event has "reached" the Traffic Controller).

Lower priority levels would be reserved for longer-running interactive processes and for absentee processes. Absentee processes are akin to foreground-initiated background jobs in CTSS.[38] (The priority range for absentee processes is expected to be (k_2, n), where $1 < k_2$. Note that if $k_2 \leqslant k_1$, there would be some straddling of the interactive user's priority range, which is $(1, k_1)$. In any case, service for short absentee jobs will be better than for longer absentee jobs.)

7.4.2.2 Eligibility Management–Design Details

Eligibility management superimposes a needed control on the number of processes that are being multiprogrammed so that the combined core requirements of these processes matches the amount of available core memory. A good match prevents wasted core at one extreme (too few processes) and excessive thrashing at the other (too many processes). There should be no substantive alteration of the general multilevel scheduling algorithm's efficacy as a consequence of superimposing eligibility control. This subsection and the next one on *preemption* outline the design details.

---

whose concepts have been sketched earlier. The details presented here are, to the best of the writer's knowledge, consistent with a version of the scheduler used in the summer of 1970 and are useful for illustrative purposes. Details of the actual scheduler may differ from those described here, but, in all likelihood, differences from those described here should be of no significance to the subsystem writer. System designers wishing to learn about the current algorithm should consult the appropriate sections of the MSPM.

38. Absentee processes are being implemented in the current Multics. Sections of the MSPM show the design plans for implementation of absentee processes.

Although the number of eligibles is basically a function of available core memory and the working-set estimates for the most-favored processes, there are certain built-in parameters in the Traffic Controller, which can be varied by the system administrator, that have the effect of altering the number of permitted eligibles (by inflating or deflating the working-set estimates).

The APT entries for the running, ready, and waiting processes can be thought of as linked in a list so as to maintain their relative priority. The first few of these linked entries also represent the eligible processes. When a running (and eligible) process enters a wait state for the occurrence of a system event, the CPU will be given to the ready and eligible process that has the highest relative (or positional) priority. When the event waited for occurs, the now running process notifies the waiting process by marking its APT entry accordingly (changing its state bit to ready). If the process so notified has higher relative priority than one of the running processes, the notifying process (executing in the supervisor, of course) will cause the processor now running for the process having the lowest priority to yield to the notified process. If necessary, the notifying process will send a preempt interrupt to another processor to accomplish this objective. In this way the system favors the higher priority eligible processes.

Available core memory is a system resource that can be allocated among the eligible processes. Processes gain and lose eligibility cyclically. The cycle can be traced as follows:

An ineligible process is made eligible when it appears on the top of the ready list at the time an eligibility vacancy occurs and when the working set of that candidate can fit in core. (If it cannot fit in core, then the candidate's "elevation" is delayed and no other process will be chosen. There will be another attempt to make the candidate eligible after another eligibility vacancy occurs, and so on, until there is finally enough room in core.)

A vacancy will occur when a process *loses* its eligibility. This will occur when

a. an eligible process enters the *blocked* or *stopped* state

b. a process incurs a timer run-out interrupt and is rescheduled.

Since a process specifically retains its eligibility when it enters the *wait* state, it is entirely possible for all the eligible processes to be in the wait state simultaneously. In this event, there being no eligible processes to run, the processor is given to an idle process that can be regarded as always ready and always has the lowest priority.

Each time a process gains or loses eligibility, its APT entry is marked accordingly. When the process loses its eligibility, the Traffic Controller selects the next candidate to be marked eligible. If that candidate is not loaded, the TC calls a "friend" in the file system to load the process. Loading includes the prepaging of all those pages so identified at the time the process was last unloaded.[39]

7.4.2.3 Preemption

The mechanism provided to let one eligible process preempt another assists in the implementation of the policy of giving good response to interactive users that issue commands of short duration. Note that a preempted process reschedules itself immediately. If it belonged at a priority level k, the process is rescheduled by being placed on *top* of the queue at level k with a time allotment equal to whatever time is still unused from its last scheduling allotment.

The net effects are as one would like them to be, namely, that a preempted process is favorably treated, relatively speaking. Thus, suppose B, at priority level 3, preempts C at level 4. Process C is rescheduled at the top of level 4. If shortly afterward, B incurs a timer run-out, it will lose its eligibility and be rescheduled at the *bottom* of the queue at level 4. Now C will be picked to run next, if no other process has been added to the ready list ahead of C while B was running. This, we should note, is precisely the behavior pattern we want. Namely, other things remaining the same, a preempted process should be placed in a favored position to recapture the processor when the preempting process next loses its processor.

7.4.3 Expected System Response

With the benefit of the foregoing discussions on scheduling, eligibility control, and preemption, a user is now ready to anticipate the type of system response that can be expected for his process. These ideas are summarized here.

It is the current policy that system response will be a function of the burden added by the user's request and of the current (overall) load on the system. Response to a request that adds trivially to the current load (e.g. a simple edit command) will be less sensitive to that load. Response to a request that adds significantly to the system's current work load, for instance, compilation of a very large PL/I program, will, on the other hand, be quite sensitive to the system's load. In short, when the system begins to be loaded,

39. Loading, you recall, also involves placing and wiring into core the pages listed in Table 7.2.

the first users to feel it are those whose processes are on the bottom queues (the long jobs) and the last to feel it are those in the top queues (the short jobs). The next paragraph offers some graphical elaboration.

During slack load periods, for example, two o'clock Sunday morning, the ratio R, defined as

$$R = \frac{\text{elapsed time for completion of a command}}{\text{virtual time}},$$

(virtual time: actual CPU processing time for the command)

will approach *one* irrespective of the commands that are executed. During peak load periods, however, users that execute commands of long duration are likely to observe that execution appears to proceed rapidly at first, then slower and slower, as suggested by the solid curve in Figure 7.6. Thus, commands that under light system loads might require three minutes of processor time may require hours to complete in extreme cases. This is because the user's process sinks to lower and lower priority levels as virtual execution proceeds. A point is likely to be reached where the process is rarely or never picked to execute simply because there are many processes that are always queued at higher priority levels. Only after the peak load subsides (fewer users logged in) will the long-duration command again have a good chance to be picked for execution.

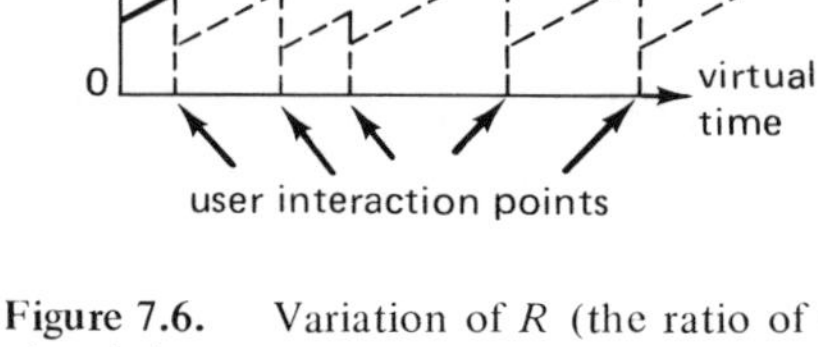

Figure 7.6. Variation of R (the ratio of elapsed time to virtual time) as a function of virtual time
Key:

Solid curve assumes no user interaction. *Dashed curve* shows points of user interaction.

User Recourse to Slow Response

A user that is impatient with this response is encouraged to

1. reexamine what he is doing, by considering alternative attacks on the same problem, for example, converting his process to run in absentee mode, or

2. determine if his requirements are of a special-case or emergency nature. If so, he may wish to push his process through using "quits and starts." More specifically, he can force one or more "interactions," each of which will have the effect of rescheduling his process (back up) to level 1.

The simplest way to force an interaction is, first, to press the "quit" button on the console and, after it responds by typing

ready

then type

start

and then strike the "carriage return" key on the console. The effect of hitting the quit button is to cause the user's (console) process to enter command level and accept the user's next input. The desired effect of typing start and striking carriage return is a consequent rescheduling to priority level 1. The effect of using the quit button is suggested by the dashed line in Figure 7.6. Users will learn that the use of the quit button for purposes of speeding up execution will prove to be an *unpleasant* way to use the system. (It turns out to be not much fun hitting *quit* and typing "start" repeatedly, especially if it must be done a large number of times.) It is basically useful only as a brute force method when there appears to be no other choice.

7.5 Interprocess Communication

7.5.1 The Nature of Processes and the Nature of Their Intercommunication

In the overview of this chapter (Section 7.1), I initiated a discussion of interprocess communication–although without taking a serious look into the nature of intercommunication among processes. Here a more thorough discussion of this topic is provided. I shall also provide, for interested readers, a description of the tools available (and how to use them), that is, for the operation of subsystems that comprise two or more intercommunicating processes.

You already know from previous discussions that processes may properly function to achieve a common goal only if they communicate as senders and as receivers of messages via shared data bases. Hence, an understanding of communication mechanisms, for example, information content of messages, "mailboxes," message switching and routing techniques, validation and protection of messages, and so on, is likely to be essential for detailed subsystem design.

A process A that wishes to alert a process B of an event of interest to the latter must send a wakeup and a message to B. The message must be formatted in a standard fashion, so that its source (process A) and its target (process B) and the specific receiving point within the target's address space (i.e., a mailbox) may be recognized, validated, and accessed. The receiving process must in turn exercise known scanning habits that will find, properly interpret, and dispose of messages that have been received in its mailboxes. Details are discussed in the following section.

7.5.2 Communication Mechanisms

A process may reach any number of *suspension points*, as suggested in Figure 7.7 where, for example, three such points are marked. In a very simple process, these suspension points, however many in number, may occur at *the same program point*, that is, the process loops through this program point. For n transits of the loop, there will be as many as n suspensions. In each case, then, the nature of the event waited for will be the same, and even the sender of the notifying message that permits resumption of the active state may be the same. In a more general case, however, we can expect suspension points at *different program points*, possibly occurring in different procedures and even in different rings. Suspensions at different program points will, in general, be for different reasons. (Such program points will hereafter be referred to as *wait points*.) This means that the nature of the events waited for at different wait points will in general be different. Moreover, the corresponding sending processes need not necessarily be the same either. Basic to all of this discussion is the following observation that can be made about most user processes: *For each distinct wait point of a process it must be assured by prior arrangement that some process (at least one) will send a wakeup message when the looked-for event has occurred.* Suppose, then, a

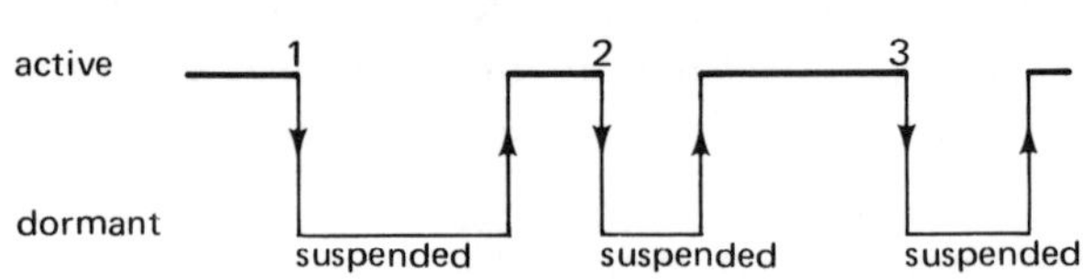

Figure 7.7. Time-line characteristics of sequential processes

process that has several distinct wait points reaches one of them. The process must now be prepared to wait, if necessary, for a particular message to arrive (possibly from a particular sender). Of course, there need not be any waiting at all if the wanted message has already arrived. However, whether or not waiting is required, either upon reaching the wait point or after being awakened following a suspension, the suspended process must be sure that the wanted message has been received before continuing with its active efforts.

What is involved in searching for the wanted message? If one pictures that the receiving process has a single mailbox for all messages, then determining if the wanted message has arrived is simply a matter of scanning the contents of one mailbox—either by an indexed or by an associative search, depending on the data structure of the mailbox. But, wait! Won't protection considerations dictate that there may be at least one mailbox per ring of the process? The answer is yes, but since the reasons are secondary to the main line of thought here, the explanation is left to a footnote.[40]

Are there cases where one mailbox per ring would be insufficient? In principle, perhaps the answer is no, provided each message fully identified the wait point, the sender, and the exact time that the message was sent. In practice, however, the Multics designers have chosen to implement the system in such a way that any number of different mailboxes per ring are available. For example, a process may contain a programmed wait point that asks to wait for receipt of a message in any of a given list of designated mailboxes. These ideas will be discussed in more detail later. I mention them here only to motivate the notion that a process may have what amounts to sets of mailboxes (each mailbox possibly empty), one set per ring.[41] Clearly, each

40. A one-mailbox approach would mean that a ring-32 procedure, for instance, could read mail intended for a ring-1 procedure! Clearly, this is unacceptable. So we must picture a process arranging for the receipt of mail in different, ring-related mailboxes. In this way, a ring-1 procedure can scan mail in a ring-1 mailbox (and even in a ring-32 mailbox if desired), but a ring-32 procedure would be allowed to scan mailboxes only in rings $\geqslant 32$.

41. There is one by-product benefit that comes from the implementation decision to have multiple mailboxes per ring. Let the distinct wait points in some ring r of a process A be designated as wp1, wp2, . . ., etc. Suppose the wait at each of these points is for a message from a correspondingly *different* process, e.g., from processes p1, p2, . . ., etc. Prior arrangements between the process pairs (A, p1), (A, p2), (A, p3), etc., for the sending of messages to A need not be fully coordinated in the sense that A is not forced to give (or to divulge) to p1, p2, p3, etc., the very same mailbox name. One can regard this flexibility as an advantage in that there may be less risk of confusion if separate senders are asked to send messages to different mailboxes, with each mailbox having a different meaning.

mailbox must bear a unique designation within the receiving process so that a sender can transmit messages to their proper destination.

7.5.2.1 Messages, Mailboxes (Event Channels), and Transmission

The technical name used in Multics for a mailbox is *event channel.* An event channel is uniquely designated by a 72-bit identifier.[42] This name is generated by the system as a result of executing a user-written subroutine call for the creation of an event channel.[43]

Origin of the Message

By added convention, every *message* originates as a 72-bit item of arbitrary content (set by the sender). (However, in the course of transmitting the message, system routines expand it with additional information, such as time of day and the sender's process id.)

A message is sent in the form of a call to the hard-core system routine, hcs_$wakeup:

```
call hcs_$wakeup (receiving_process_id,
                  channel_name,
                  message,
                  code);
```

Note that although the actual text of a message is small and fixed in size, it is large enough to be used as a pointer to messages of arbitrary size. I defer momentarily answering the obvious question, namely, How will the sender know both the process_id of the receiver and its receiving point (the event-channel name)? This matter is taken up in the section entitled Setup for Interprocess Communication.

The hcs_$wakeup subroutine makes some simple (routine) checks on the first two arguments so that if they are obviously erroneous,[44] due to programmer error, the caller can be alerted if he chooses to examine the returned

42. The substructure of the event-channel name includes three items: a ring number, a *key* (52 bits), and an ECT address. The key is a unique name representing the wall clock time in microseconds at which the event channel was created for this process. The ring number identifies the ring in which the receiver expects to examine messages placed in this channel. Received messages are saved (until inspected) in a one-per-ring segment called an ECT (Event Channel Table). The ECT address is simply the offset within this segment at which the (possibly queued) messages for this channel may be found. A channel is in effect a FIFO list. Details of the ECT data structures should be of no interest to users. They may be found in the MSPM.

43. Creation of event channels is further discussed in the next subsection.

44. For example, if the process id or certain of the subfields of the 72-bit channel name are zero, this is clearly an error.

error code. After this partial validation, the Traffic Controller's *wakeup* entry is called, at which point steps are taken to forward the message to the intended receiver, as subsequently outlined.

1. If the message indeed *has* a receiver, then it must be possible to match the receiving_process_id with the id of one of the processes that now have entries in the Active Process Table. Failure to find such a match results in an appropriate error code being reflected to hcs_$wakeup's caller. (Note that a post office analogy to this case is "addressee unknown at this address–return to sender.")

2a. A message aimed at a bona fide target process will be copied into a ring-0 system table where it is properly augmented (see below) with "truthful" information about the sender. The system table (central storage) is called the ITT (for Interprocess Transmission Table). The receiving process will later draw the message out of this table.

2b. The last step is to call the Traffic Controller at its entry point *wakeup* to wake up the receiving process, that is, make it ready if it was blocked.

The above steps are summarized in the Figure 7.8 flow chart. Note that hcs_$wakeup serves as the user's only interface with the otherwise inaccessible *wakeup* entry of the Traffic Controller. Protecting this entry from direct user calls simplifies the logic of the Traffic Controller, which, because it is locked to all other processes when entered, must be kept as simple (and fast-executing) as possible.

Receivers must be protected against receipt of false messages, whether accidentally or intentionally sent. Certain information about the sender is therefore added to the copied message that is placed in the ITT. This information, which is of critical importance for the protection of the receiver, consists of the sender's process id and the validation level of the sender's call to hcs_$wakeup (i.e., the ring in whose behalf this call was made). The user cannot be trusted to transmit these items accurately. Figure 7.9 shows the message format as stored in the ITT. The Interprocess Transmission Table is a systemwide table in ring 0 that holds messages for all active processes. The table is organized as a set of message queues, one per process. The head of each queue is pointed to from a fixed position in the APT entry for the corresponding active process, so that when any process reenters the running state in the Traffic Controller as a result of being awakened, it can quickly determine if there have been any messages deposited in the ITT on its behalf since the last time it *ran.*

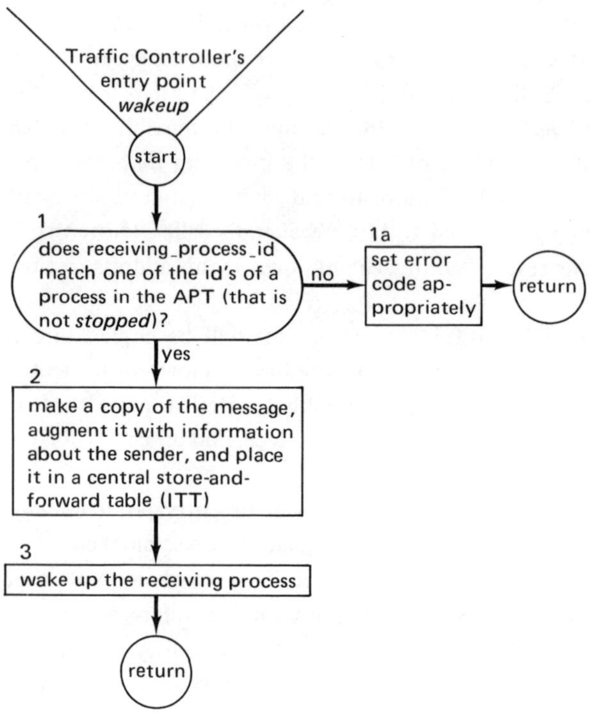

Figure 7.8. Some details of the Traffic Controller's entry point *wakeup*

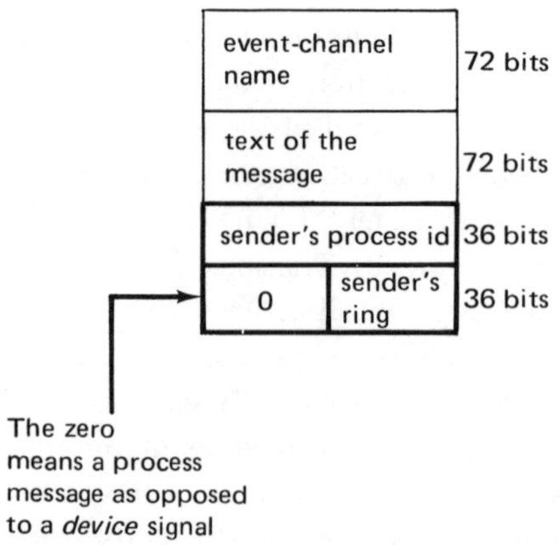

Figure 7.9 Message as placed in the ITT, augmented with (heavy border) information about the sender

Getting the Message from the Central Store-and-Forward Point to the Receiver

So far we have considered mainly the mechanics of sending a message as far as a central forwarding center. In a postal system analogy, such as shown in Figure 7.10, this is the halfway point, for instance, a regional post office. No ordinary citizen is able to walk up to this center and ask for his mail. Nor, by analogy, can the Multics user expect to get his mail by attempting to read messages while they are still in the ITT. He needs help in moving the messages to data areas that are ring-accessible for his purpose. While the postal system automatically pushes the mail through to its receiver from the central post office without any special coaxing, the Multics analogy is somewhat different. Here some initiative is always taken by the receiver to *pull* the message(s) out of central storage and to place them into the individual ring-accessible event channels of the process. Recall that a receiver's process will have a table of one or more event channels (an ECT) in every ring in which there occurs a distinct wait point in that process.

A wait point is always programmed as a call to ipc_$block, which is the entry point in the so-called *Wait Coordinator*, the heart of the interprocess communication facility. A user program should call this entry point whenever it must enter the blocked state while awaiting the receipt of a message.

The form of this call is

```
call ipc_$block (wait_list_ptr, message_ptr, error_code);
                       ↑                ↑
          pointer to a list     pointer supplied as an input
          of one or more        argument that specifies the
          event-channel         location where the caller
          names                 expects to receive a message
                                which he can examine
```

When called, ipc_$block scans the event channels in the list pointed to by the first argument. Scanning of the channels is done in the listed order, and if lucky enough to find a message in one of these channels, ipc_$block transfers the first such message found into the location given by the second argument, and returns to its caller. The message that is actually transferred consists of the six-word message whose format was shown in Figure 7.9, augmented by a seventh word consisting of the wait-list index. Thus, if a message is found in the *third* of eight channels on a wait list, the seventh word of the returned message will have the value 3.

Note that ipc_$block has been executing in the ring of its caller. The

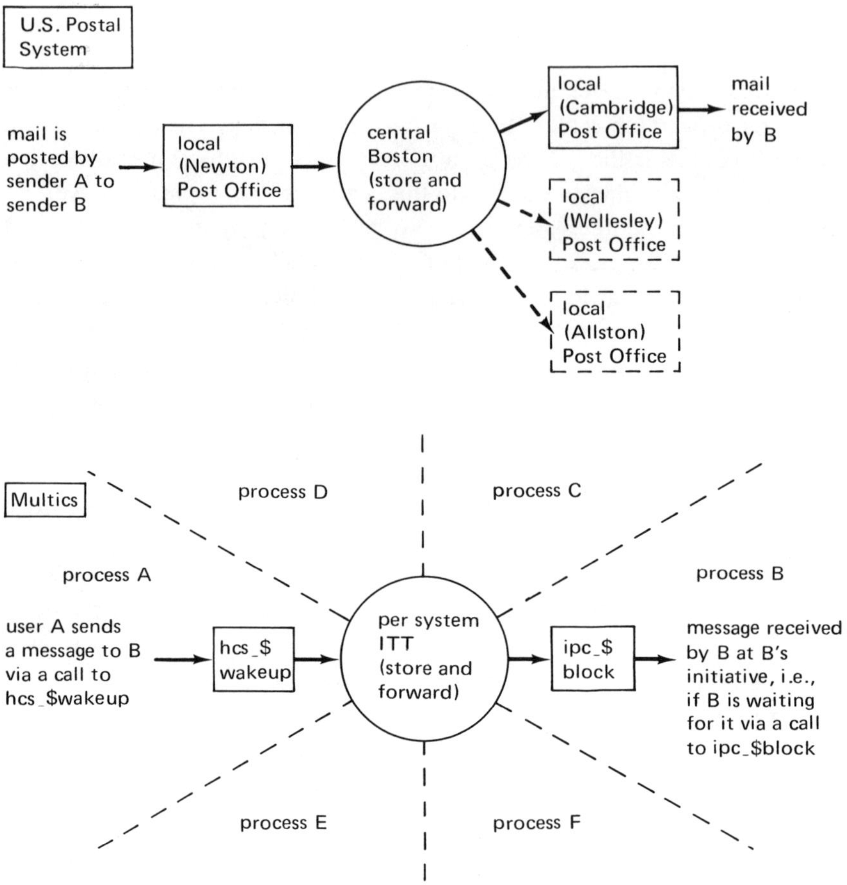

Figure 7.10. Postal system analogy to the Multics interprocess message transmission system

procedure ipc_$block has ring brackets which are (1, 48, 48). Consequently, this procedure does not have ring access for scanning central storage (i.e., the ITT), which may have received one (or more) of the desired messages. Therefore, ipc_$block is forced to call a privileged routine in ring 0 (at an entry point hcs_$block). This routine in effect transfers all valid messages that have accumulated in the ITT event queue for this process. Each message is placed in the event channel that is designated in that message. Invalid messages, such as those whose channel names do not match existing channels in the receiving process's ECTs, are summarily discarded.

If, in the course of making these message transfers, not a single message was transferred into a ring ⩾ the validation ring (i.e., that of the call from ipc_$block), then it is clear that the wanted message cannot yet have been received. Hence hcs_$block, which is fully privileged to do so, calls the corresponding entry in the Traffic Controller to give away the processor.[45] If, on the other hand, at least one such message was moved to a ring that is accessible to ipc_$block, then hcs_$block will return to its caller so that the former can again scan its given list of channels in hopes of finding the wanted message.

The chain of calls just discussed is summarized in Figure 7.11 (but with the details cited in the preceding paragraph omitted). If we follow the return path from the TC backward toward the user's point of call to ipc_$block, it becomes easy to see how a fresh message, received at hcs_$wakeup can be thought of as being forwarded from central storage to the appropriate event channel of the receiver.

It should be recalled that when an awakened process finally recaptures a processor, effective execution will resume as a *return* from the block entry in the TC to its caller, hcs_$block. The latter then "transfers" all newly arrived messages from its ITT event queue into the appropriate event channels. If no messages were transferred into rings ⩾ that of the caller, ipc_$block, then the process cannot have received the message it was waiting for. Hence, hcs $block again calls the TC at entry point *block* to give away the processor. But if at least one potentially suitable message was transferred from the ITT, hcs_$block returns to its caller (ipc_$block). Note that the return

45. To be absolutely precise about things, there is still a possibility for a last minute "reprieve"; if, anytime up to the very last instant before giving the processor away, a wakeup arrives, control will return to the TC's caller. For more details you could review J. H. Saltzer's Sc.D. thesis or appropriate sections of the MSPM to see the function of the so-called *wakeup waiting* switch.

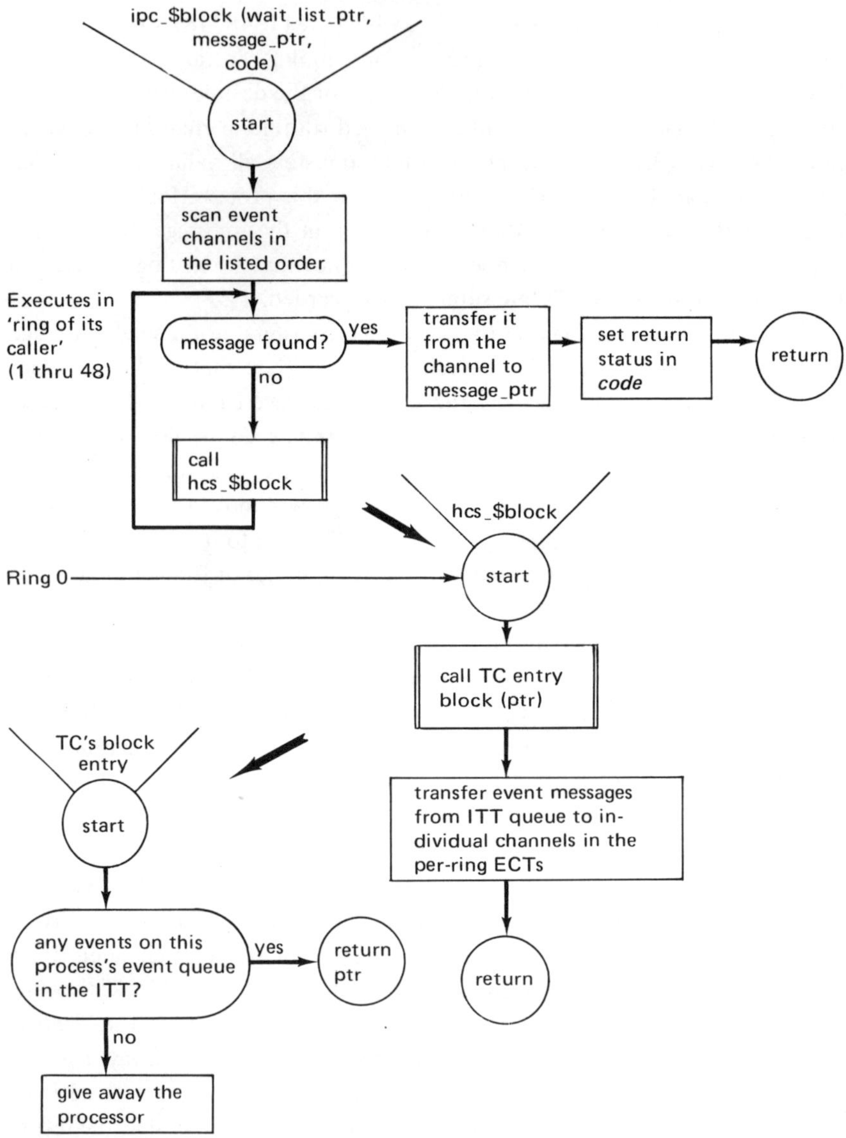

Figure 7.11. The chain of calls: → ipc_$block → hcs_$block → TC block entry Illustrating how event messages are *pulled* out of the ITT queue and distributed to individual event channels in the user rings. (Readers should note that Figure 7.14 is a more complete description of ipc_$block.)

to ipc_$block is no guarantee of a return to its caller. If ipc_$block finds no message in one of the listed event channels, it simply calls hcs_$block once again.

7.5.2.2 Setup for Interprocess Communication[46]

Here we shall discuss how a sender learns the identification of a receiver process and the identification of that receiver's event channel. For convenience let us adopt the following notation.

Let *B-to-A setup info* be that basic information that is required by a sender process B so that it can send a message to a receiver process A. This information consists of A's 36-bit process id and A's 72-bit event-channel name.

Let p(A) and p(B) refer to the *p*eople responsible for programming A and B, respectively. (To be sure, they may be the same individual, wearing "two hats.") Clearly, the system-provided message transmission facility (IPC) cannot be employed to transmit B-to-A setup info, or setup info would not be needed in the first place. Note also that p(A) cannot supply p(B) with the B-to-A setup info by telephone or by other direct personal communication *until after A has been created.* This is because a process id is a clock-dependent unique bit string that is generated by the system at process creation time. Furthermore, A's event-channel name, which is also a clock-dependent unique bit string, will not be known until after A executes the system call that creates the event channel. There appears to be only one sensible, perhaps obvious, plan for passing setup info. The plan is as follows:

1. Persons p(A) and p(B) agree *in advance* on the (unambiguous) name of a segment that is to be shared by A and B. Call this segment <shared>. Also agreed upon is an offset within <shared> (call it [setupBA]) that is to be regarded as a mailbox (3 words in capacity). Moreover, this mailbox should initially be set to zero.
2. After A and B have been created, and after A has created the appropriate event channel, A will be able to (and does) place in shared$setupBA the desired setup info.
3. Process B fetches the three words at shared$setupBA, and if nonzero, assumes, by convention, that the required A-to-B setup information has been obtained.

46. For a more basic discussion of this topic, the reader may wish to examine the paper, "The Multics Interprocess Communication Facility," by M. J. Spier and E. I. Organick, *Second Symposium on Operating Systems Principles, Princeton University, October 1969* (New York: Association for Computing Machinery, 1969), pp. 83–91.

Note that if A is also to become a *sender* to B (not just a receiver), then A-to-B setup info (as opposed to B-to-A) is also needed. This info can be sent by a similar prearrangement, although in fact a form of "boot strapping" can now be achieved if it is desired, to avoid further use of<shared>. That is, the first message B sends to A can, by further convention, contain the A-to-B setup information.

But how does A know its B-to-A setup info so that it can place it at shared$setupBA?

How A Obtains Its Own Process ID

A function reference to the system routine (described in the MPM)

get_process_id_

will retrieve the process id for the process that makes this reference. Thus,

bit_string = get_process_id_;

will assign the wanted identification to bit_string.

How A Obtains an Event-Channel Name

A user creates an event channel simply by calling ipc_$create_ev_chn. The first of two return arguments in the call contains (upon return) the 72-bit name that the IPC has established for this channel. Henceforth, it is the user's responsibility to keep track of this name.

Summary

The steps that would be coded by p(A) and p(B) to establish interprocess communication with B as a sender and A a receiver can now be summarized.

1. Person p(A) codes the following steps in some procedure of A:

a. Call ipc_$create_ev_chn(channelBA, code); this call creates an event channel that can hereafter be referred to by the value assigned to channelBA, because the value of the first return argument is a 72-bit unique id of channelBA.

b. Assign to the three-word mailbox at shared$setupBA values of channelBA and the process id. Illustrative PL/I coding is provided in the accompanying footnote.[47]

2. Person p(B) can code B to pick up the required setup info at any time

47. In PL/I, this might be accomplished with coding that relies on a three-word based structure for a mailbox:

```
dcl   1 mailbox3 based (p),
      2 chname fixed bin (71),/*a channel name*/
      2 pid bit (36)/*a process id*/;
```

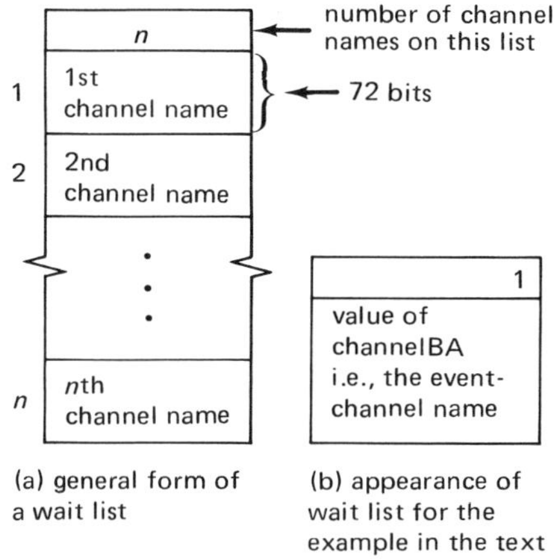

Figure 7.12. Wait lists–general and specific

and use it to send a two-word message to A. Illustrative PL/I coding is provided in the accompanying footnote.[48]

3. Person p(A) is now able to code appropriate calls to ipc_$block at various points in A to wait for messages from B. A call of the form

call ipc_$block (argptr, msgptr, code);

gets the job done on the assumption that the first two arguments are pointers to the base of structures, the first being to a wait list of channel names, and the second to an area of sufficient size for receipt of the message.

The general structure for the wait list is of the form shown in Figure 7.12.

Then, the executable code that would follow creation of the desired event channel might look like:

```
p =     addr(shared$setupBA);
p - > mailbox3.pid = get_process_id;
p - > mailbox3.chname = channelBA;
```

48. We shall assume that B also uses a declaration for a three-word mailbox identical to the one in the preceding footnote. Then coding in B might appear as:

```
p = addr(shared$setupBA);
receiver_pid = p -> mailbox3.pid;
channel_name = p -> mailbox3.chname;
if^(receiver_pid = 0 & channel_name = 0)
    then call hcs_$wakeup (receiver_pid, channel_name. message, code);
    else call print_error;
```

Here message is a 72-bit message and print_error might be a routine to print an appropriate error message before proceeding with whatever steps are then deemed appropriate.

7.5.2.3 Applying the IPC Tools

In the preceding two subsections I gave the details whereby one process might wake up another process, block itself (Section 7.5.2.1), or perform the setup steps to communicate with another process (Section 7.5.2.2). Here we shall apply what we have learned to the early example given in Figures 7.2 and 7.3 in which process A synchronizes with a (hypothetical) tty manager. Below PL/I coding is shown that includes:

(Part A) declarations in the code for process A,

(Part B) setup statements that would precede flow-chart box 1 of Figure 7.2, and

(Part C) the coding of interest to us here for flow-chart boxes 1 through 6.

Readers that follow this PL/I code should, as an exercise, have no trouble in coding the corresponding steps in the tty manager (boxes 6 through 10).

Part A–declarations

```
declare 1 waitlist,
          2 n fixed bin (35) initial (1),
          2 channelBA fixed bin (71);
declare 1 message,
          2 chname fixed bin (71),
          2 message fixed bin (71),
          2 sender bit (36),
          2 dummy bit (72);
declare 1 buffer based (q),
          2 first fixed bin (18),
          2 last fixed bin (18),
          2 body char (270);
declare 1 mailbox3 based,
          2 chname fixed bin (71),
          2 pid bit (36);
declare   (p, r) pointer;
declare   char_string char (3000);
declare   tty_mgr_id bit (36),
declare   (write_buffer, shared$setupBA, shared$setupAB) external;
declare   code fixed bin (35);
declare   (channelBA, tty_mgr_channel) fixed bin (71);
```

Part B–IPC setup steps

```
setup:    p = addr(shared$setupBA);
          q = addr(write_buffer);
```

```
        q->buffer.first = 1;
        q->buffer.last = 251;
        r = addr(shared$setupAB);
        msgptr = addr(message);
        argptr = addr(waitlist);
        call ipc_$create_ev_chn(channelBA, code);
        p->mailbox3.pid = get_process_id_;
        p->mailbox3.chname = channelBA;
        tty_mgr_id = r->mailbox3.pid;
        if tty_mgr_id = "0"b then go to error_return;/* if tty_mgr has
        failed to give us his process_id, set error code
        and return */
        tty_mgr_channel = r->mailbox3.chname;
```

Part C–coding for flow-chart boxes 1 through 5 in Figures 7.2 and 7.3

```
box 1:  if q->buffer.first ^= q->buffer.last then go to box3;

box2:   call ipc_$block(argptr,msgptr,code);
box2a:  if message.sender ^= tty_mgr_id then go to box2;
            .
box3:   /* move characters from char_string to fill the write
        buffer from addrel(q,first) to addrel(q,last)
        with wrap-around implied when last>first */
            .
            .
            .
box4:   call hcs_$wakeup(tty_mgr_id, tty_mgr_channel, channelBA,
        code); /*channelBA is A's message to tty_mgr */

box5:       .
            .
            .
        go to box1;
```

7.5.3 Programming of a Multipurpose Process

A Multics process is basically sequential in nature by virtue of the fact that but a single execution point (or point of control) is free to traverse over its address space at any one time. For this reason, it is natural to think of such a process as having a *single purpose*.

If two or more independent computations are to be performed, albeit related to one another, it is entirely appropriate for the programmer to create a separate process, one per each defined purpose, and have these processes execute in any interrelated fashion that seems appropriate. In fact, this approach is recommended for most initial efforts of this kind.

Subject to processor availability, concurrent computation of the separate but related processes may occur in some fashion, but it is not predictable, of course, since the Traffic Controller and its functions are outside the control of the programmer. In any case, by proper use of IPC, the separate processes (purposes) *may* synchronize with one another.

It is worth noting, however, that the establishing and maintaining of separate address spaces, one per process, incurs some system overhead.[49] Such costs are ultimately passed on to the user directly or indirectly. Hence it may well be worth considering under what circumstances it is feasible to coalesce (and condense) the address spaces of several processes into a single, now *multipurpose process* having one address space (and one execution point).

Certainly, it is necessary that concurrent pursuit of the separate purposes, that is, parallel executing of the separate tasks be no requirement. (But, then, such a requirement, even without coalescing, cannot be guaranteed in Multics anyway.) Beyond this, the order in which these tasks may be initiated and executed should in some sense be of secondary importance and perhaps be independent of the tasks themselves. This set of circumstances may obtain in the case where events external to the process drive the multipurpose process. That is, IPC messages received by the process are the basis for deciding which task to execute next. Examples of multipurpose processes are common among *system software processes*, for instance, answering services, I/O device managers, automatic recorders, data samplers that periodically gather and record statistics, automatic file dumpers, and so on.

A process that must behave in multipurpose manner, can in principle be coded using flow-chart logic described in Figure 7.13. The basic idea suggested in the figure is to create *n* event channels, one for each of the *n* distinct purposes of the process. After furnishing setup information for use of each of the *n* channels to the *n* senders (not necessarily *n* different processes) the process calls ipc_$block to await one of the *n* types of events. Each time an event arrives, ipc_$block *returns* with a message. The message is examined (in box 5 of the flow chart) to determine which channel (type of event) has occurred so as to invoke the associated task. When the task is completed, a call is again issued to ipc_$block.

49. The create process command, for instance, consumes approximately 2 seconds of CPU time (equivalent to the time required for a medium command).

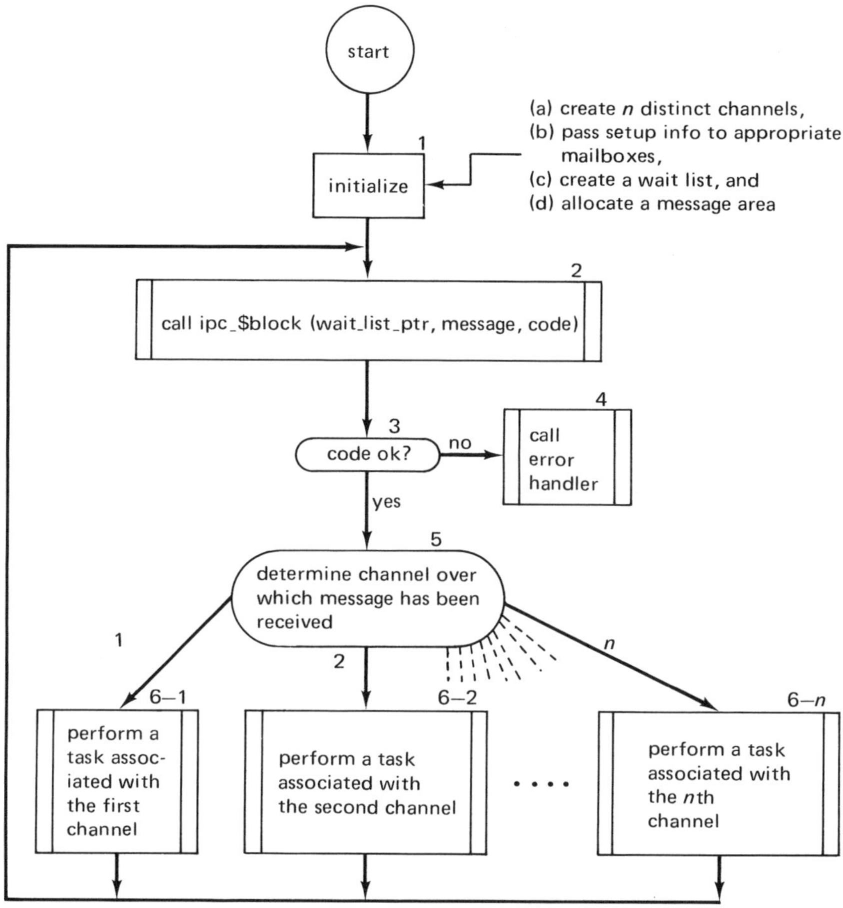

Figure 7.13. A possible structure for a multipurpose process

I have not yet defined what is meant by a *task*. The simplest idea is to suppose it corresponds to a call to a procedure that is associated with the corresponding event channel. We will be interested in understanding what restrictions are imposed, if any, as to what may go on inside the called procedure. For instance, are calls to ipc_$block to be permitted from within the associated procedure and/or from any of its dynamic descendants? This possibility will be considered in the next subsection. For the moment, however, we shall assume that such recursive calls do not happen.

There are also restrictions in an associated procedure's use of data that should not be overlooked. Thus, if the same associated procedure is "shared" by two or more tasks, one should consider how the static data that are task-related should be handled. The linkage section of the associated procedure is an appropriate repository for static data, such as a usage counter, that relates to *any* use of that procedure. But what about task-dependent static data, that is, data that are a function of the repeated use of the associated procedure when it serves a particular task? For a simple example, one can picture a counter j that should be incremented by the associated procedure whenever invoked in task j. Clearly, such shared procedures will need access to separate, task-related, static data blocks. A more realistic example is the system's Answering Service, which is a process whose structure is similar to that of Figure 7.13. Each task can be regarded as a response to a console user to help him log in. As such, the associated procedure is shared by all tasks, all logins being basically similar. The Answering Service must therefore maintain separate data blocks, one per each log-in conversation, and see to it that, whenever called, the associated procedure references the appropriate data block.

7.5.3.1 Event Call Channels

Note that further logical simplification of Figure 7.13 arises (from the user's viewpoint) and some slight increase in efficiency can be gained if the control logic of boxes 3, 4, 5, and 6 are made part of ipc_$block. At the topmost logic level the process would be characterized simply as the execution of boxes 1 and 2. That is, initializing of channels, transmitting of setup information, and so forth, followed by a single call to ipc_$block. There would be no return and, therefore, no repeated calls on ipc_$block. Of course, it would be necessary to furnish IPC with more information so it can perform its more elaborate job. Basically, this amounts to telling IPC what are the procedures that should be called (invoked) upon receipt of respective messages.

The "simplification" we have been discussing is in fact provided for in Multics by allowing the user to designate event channels of his choice for special interpretation. Event channels marked in this fashion are referred to as *event call* channels, as opposed to the ordinary *event wait* channels. Messages found in event call channels are examined *and interpreted* while the process is executing inside the IPC. Interpretation amounts to execution of a call to the associated procedure if the associated event has occurred.

7.5.3.2 Concept of the Wait Coordinator

As can now be seen, the code associated with entry point ipc_$block is in fact more sophisticated than a simple scanner for messages received in event channels, since some action decisions (i.e., interpretation) are in fact delegated to this procedure. The code is referred to in MSPM documentation as the *Wait Coordinator*, and aptly so.

Once an event channel has been created, a programmer is free to declare, by a call to an appropriate IPC entry point, that the said channel is thereafter to be regarded by the Wait Coordinator as event call type. Subsequently, when the process is executing inside the Wait Coordinator, a scan of event channels that turns up a message in an event call channel will trigger a call to the associated procedure. It should be stressed that return from this call is to a return point *within* the Wait Coordinator. The net effect, therefore, is that, in the case of event call channels, the action of boxes 5 and 6 of the Figure 7.13 flow chart is accomplished implicitly, that is, on behalf of the procedure that calls the Wait Coordinator.

When a Multics user wishes to establish an event channel to be of the call type, he takes the following action:

1. Creates the event channel by a call to ipc_$create_ev_chn. (This step sets up the channel, but its default interpretation is of the *event wait* type, i.e., while given this interpretation it may only be used as pictured in Figure 7.13.)
2. Declares said channel to be of the *event call* type by a call to ipc_$decl_ev_call_chn. The form of this call is

```
                         obtained from step 1
                                   ↓
call ipc_$decl_ev_call_chn(channel_name, associated_procedure_entry_
name; data_ptr, priority, code);
```

The second and third arguments in this call are saved in the Event Channel Table (ECT) for later use by the Wait Coordinator so it can construct the desired call to the associated procedure. Since a user is free to declare more than one event channel to be of the call type, it is necessary to provide the Wait Coordinator a scanning order for these channels. The user furnishes an integer argument, priority,[50] to be used by the Wait Coordinator as a scanning index. Thus, if channel_billy and channel_tilly are both declared to be event call channels and priorities 2 and 1 are associated with them, respectively, then if messages have been received on *both* channels, the procedure associated with channel_tilly will be called before the one associated with channel_billy.

The next three subsections (7.5.3.3, 7.5.3.4, and 7.5.3.5) round out the design details of the Wait Coordinator that may be of interest to some readers. They can easily be skipped on a first reading.

7.5.3.3 Call-Wait Polling Order

Although I have just suggested the rule for scanning event call channels, I have yet to explain the dependency relationship that exists between rules for scanning event *call* channels and those for scanning event *wait* channels. Each call to the Wait Coordinator (in reality a call to ipc_$block) is in fact a request to scan, not one, but *two* lists of channels, the *wait list* and the *call list*. The wait list is the list of event wait channels that is pointed to (first argument) in the call to the Wait Coordinator. The call list is the list of event call channels that are currently kept in the ECT for the ring of the Wait Coordinator's caller.

We shall say that a *W-C polling order* is one in which the wait list is scanned first and then the call list, while a *C-W polling order* is the reverse (i.e., call list before wait list). The system's default polling order is W-C, but a user is given the opportunity, by calling a special entry point in the IPC,[51] to reverse the current polling order.

It should be remembered that whenever a message is found in a channel of the wait list, channel scanning ends immediately. The discovered message (augmented by the wait-list index) is copied into the caller's message area, and the Wait Coordinator returns to its caller. This means that when functioning in the default (W-C) polling order, the event *call* list is scanned only if no event wait message is found.

Whenever a call list is scanned, it is scanned in its entirety or until a message is found. If one is found, however, the associated procedure is called

50. Strictly speaking, this argument is a priority *level*, the lower the integer (level), the higher the priority.
51. The full set of IPC calls is given in the MPM.

and, following a return from this call, if any, a rescan of the entire list is begun. The above scanning logic is summarized in the Figure 7.14 flow chart.

7.5.3.4 Invoking an Associated Procedure and Controlling Its Repeated Use

A designer of a subsystem that uses an event call channel will, of course, be required to designate the name (or pointer) of the associated procedure at the time he declares the channel to be of event call type. We will call the associated procedure "AP" for convenience. The Wait Coordinator, when it issues the call to AP, will always use a standard form for this call. The author of AP must therefore code it so that it is compatible with this standard call. The rules are explained in the accompanying footnote.[52]

Several messages can be queued up over the same event call channel. But the Wait Coordinator must see to it (and does) that it treats only one message at a time (the topmost). It should not recognize the next message in the queue until processing of the topmost is completed. This means that an associated procedure must *return* control before the Wait Coordinator can permit itself to again inspect the same event call channel. The following paragraphs show why the controls are needed and how they are achieved.

It is easy to see how the Wait Coordinator could get into this situation. Suppose AP1 is called for the first message of a call channel "1", and suppose that during its execution AP1 must call ipc_$block to await a message on some event wait channel. Further, suppose this message has not arrived at the time of this fresh call to ipc_$block. The Wait Coordinator might then find itself scanning channel 1 once again, and if it finds another message (assuming no controls were set to prevent it), it would call AP1 once again. We would then have a situation that there are *two* invocations of AP1, each permitted to perform operations over the same set of external (and static internal) variables. Since the first activation could be suspended after making incomplete alterations to such variables, chaos could easily result.

To avoid this kind of confusion, the Wait Coordinator associates and maintains an *inhibit flag* for each event call channel. This flag is set immediately prior to the call to—and is reset immediately following the return from—the

52. Conventions used in calling associated procedure (AP) are the following:

1. The AP has one argument, message_ptr, which is a pointer to an eight-word based structure, the first six words of which are as given in Figure 7.9.

2. Before issuing the call, the Wait Coordinator appends to these six words a word pair whose value is that of data_ptr. This item, you recall, is the third argument furnished in the declaration of the event call channel. The data_ptr can, therefore, be thought of as an ordinary arglist pointer of a procedure, except it is available only indirectly in the message argument. In addition, of course, AP has access to the first six words of the message area, which is also useful information.

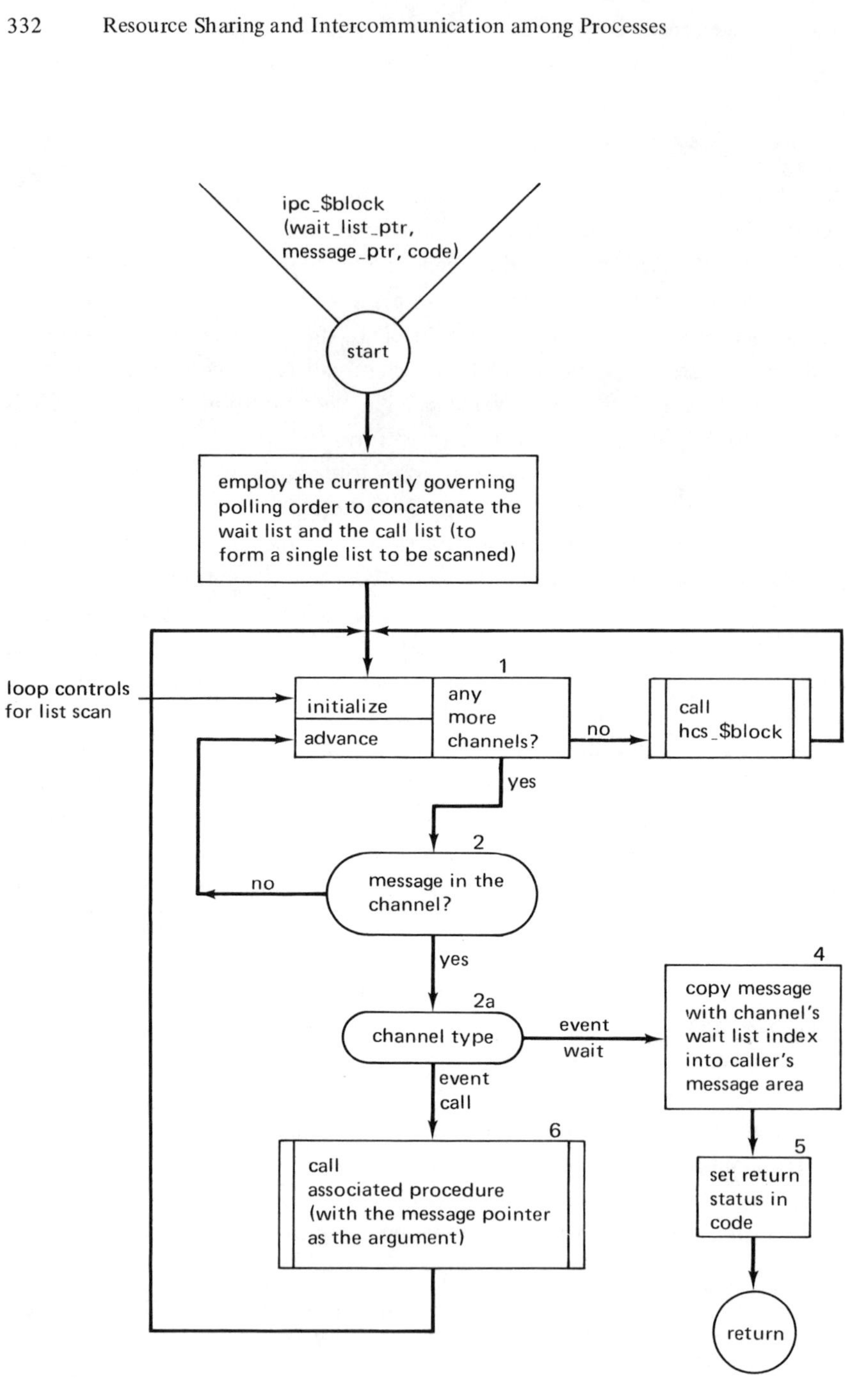

Figure 7.14. How the ipc_$block functions as a Wait Coordinator (Note that this is an expanded version of the flow chart given in Figure 7.11.)

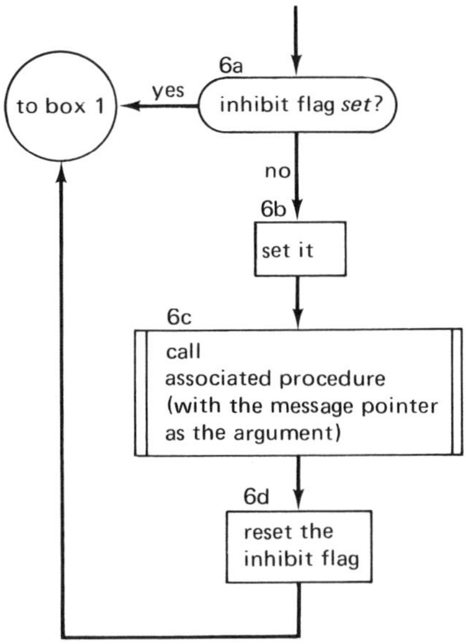

Figure 7.15. Amplification of Figure 7.14

associated procedure. Moreover, event call channels that have inhibit flags *set* are ignored by the Wait Coordinator whenever the list of channels is scanned. This simple set of controls has been omitted from the picture given in Figure 7.14 to keep things simple, but it could be added simply by replacing box 6 with the amplification shown in Figure 7.15.

7.5.3.5 Other Channel-Management Functions

The subsystem designer that has a further need to know about event channels and their management will be pleased to learn that the IPC offers a number of other services. Using these capabilities, a user may, for instance, control the polling order, delete as well as add new event channels, drain or flush out unwanted messages from existing channels, cause a given list of channels to be masked during certain periods, that is, skipped over during normal scanning by the Wait Coordinator, convert event call channels back to the event wait category, associate a given call channel with a new procedure and/or data pointer, and last, but of considerable importance, *read the messages in a given channel (without waiting)*. Details for making the appropriate IPC calls can be found in the MPM.

7.5.4 Limitations of Multipurpose Processes

The study of the Wait Coordinator has provided us with a new frame of reference for discussing multipurpose processes. With additional study we can understand the potential as well as the limitations of such Multics processes.

Because each task of a Multics process would ordinarily share the same stack with its sister tasks, the order in which events arrive and their time spacing clearly determines the order in which tasks are started and completed. A feeling for this event dependency can be gained by studying timing diagrams for specific cases. In Figures 7.16 and 7.17 two cases are presented, each for a multipurpose process having four event call channels whose associated procedures are EC1, EC2, EC3, and EC4. The respective priorities for these channels are assumed to be 1, 2, 3, and 4. It is hoped that the reader who chooses to study Section 7.5.4.1 will conclude that a process structure which would give rise to the case illustrated in Figure 7.16 may be well worth the effort, but that one which would exhibit the characteristics of Figure 7.17 may not.

7.5.4.1 Two Case Studies Using Timing Diagrams[53]

Figure 7.16 covers a period of time that commences while associated procedure EC1 is executing. Events arrive for channels in order 2, 3, 4, 2, 1, spaced as shown in the vertical time line on the left side of the figure. The vertical line segments in columns marked EC1, EC2, . . . , correspond to execution times for the respective tasks, which are carried out in the order 2, 3, 4, 1, and 2. This is somewhat different from the order in which the event messages were received due to priority considerations.

Figure 7.17 is a similar case, but it exhibits one important complication; namely, at some point during its execution each task must make a call to ipc_$block to await a specific message (on an event wait channel). Arrival times for event wait messages are labeled ew_1, ew_2, . . .

We gain valuable insight by "walking" through this timing diagram to see why things happen the way they do.

① When task EC1 has *called* the Wait Coordinator to await arrival of event ew_1, the Wait Coordinator discovers event ec_2, so it triggers task EC2, which proceeds until it reaches a wait point.

② During execution of EC2, the event ew_1 that task EC1 has been waiting for has arrived but *cannot be recognized by the Wait Coordinator* when it is called by EC2 to await event ew_2. Consequently, the process is forced to block itself until the next recognizable event

53. This section may be skipped on a first reading without loss of continuity.

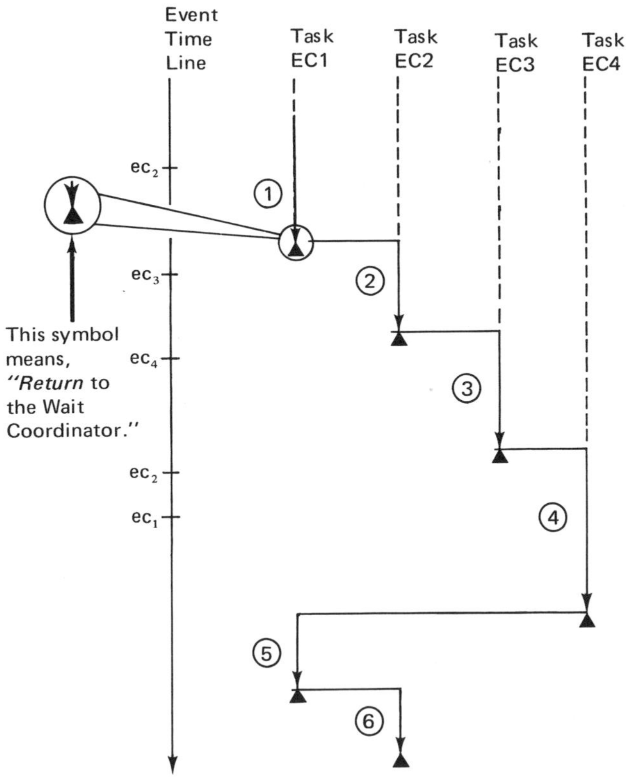

Figure 7.16. Timing diagram showing execution of tasks EC1, EC2, EC3, and EC4 when triggered by events that arrive at points in time labeled ec_1, ec_2, etc, as indicated on the (vertical) event time line. Circled numbers show the sequence in which tasks are executed in virtual time.

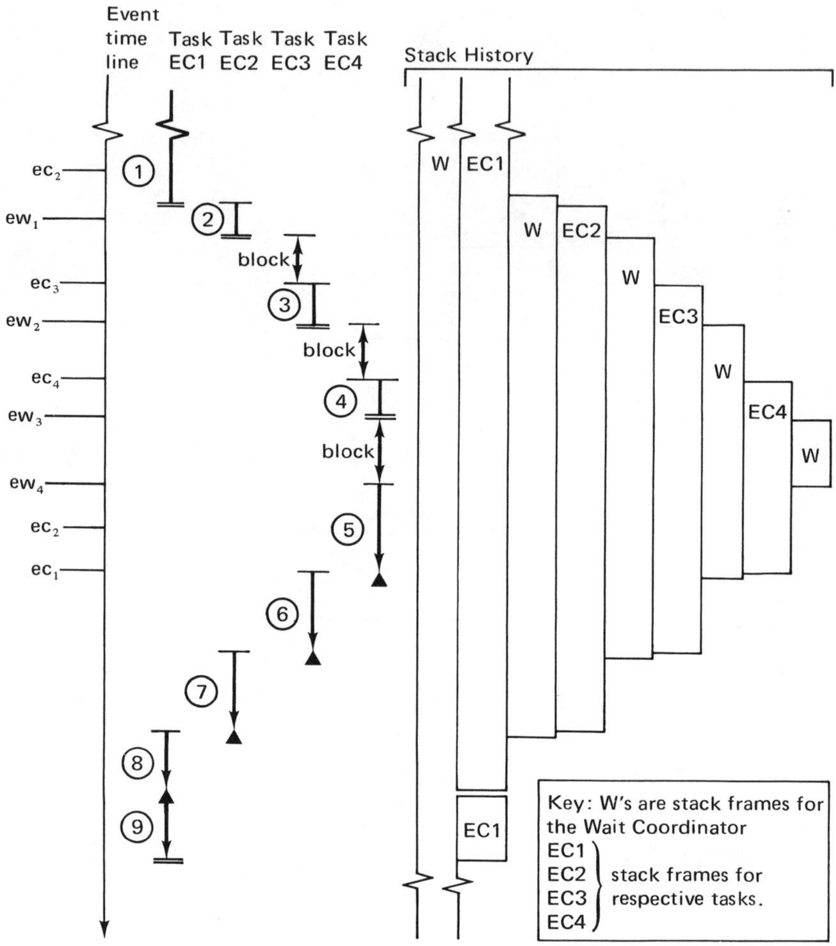

Figure 7.17. Timing diagram showing execution of tasks EC1, EC2, EC3, and EC4. This example assumes each task executes one call to ipc_$block to await distinct events, labeled ew_1, ew_2, ew_3, and ew_4, respectively. Note that a W-C polling order is assumed.

arrives, which, in our particular example, is ec_3. Arrival of this event causes the Wait Coordinator to invoke task EC3.

The reason why the Wait Coordinator fails to recognize ew_1 when it is called by task EC2 is simple: the event ew_1 is not on the wait list of this call! The Wait Coordinator is in fact executing with a new stack frame. Hence, this activation of the Wait Coordinator will not be "looking for" ew_1. When will the Wait Coordinator again look for ew_1? In a moment we will have the answer to this question, but first let us continue our walk through Figure 7.17.

③ As a result of invoking EC3, this task executes until it reaches a wait point and calls the Wait Coordinator with the wait list, ew_3. Since this event has not yet arrived, and since no event call message is initially present, the process is again forced to block itself.

④ The process is revived following arrival of ec_4, at which time task EC4 is invoked.

⑤ After going blocked again for a short period, ew_4 arrives. The Wait Coordinator recognizes ew_4 because it is on its wait list, so task EC4 resumes, executes to completion, and returns to the Wait Coordinator.

⑥ A *return* (as opposed to a *call*) to the Wait Coordinator implies reversion to a preceding stack frame of the Wait Coordinator (i.e., to a prior activation). Execution in the prior activation means that the Wait Coordinator can now recognize the arrival of ew_3. It may be noted that events ec_2 and ec_1 have also arrived. However, we are assuming a W-C polling order in the example. As a result, ew_3 will be the first message discovered in the scan. As a consequence, task EC3 is resumed and completed.

⑦&⑧ The above reasoning may be repeated to see how tasks EC2 and EC1 may be completed in this order.

⑨ Upon completion of task EC1 and the return to the Wait Coordinator, events ec_2 and ec_1 are discoverable, since there are no event wait messages on hand. The message for ec_1 is discovered first because it has higher priority causing EC1 to be invoked (Thus endeth this nine-step walk.)

7.5.4.2 Ways to Prevent Sluggish Event Wait Response of Event Call Tasks

A serious shortcoming of the multipurpose process should now be evident. A difficulty may arise any time an event call task is forced to call ipc_$block for an expected event. Even though that event may arrive with reasonable dispatch, there is no guarantee that the Wait Coordinator will "respond" in a reasonable length of time by giving this task an opportunity to resume. For instance, suppose the following sequence of events occurs.

a. Task EC1 calls ipc_$block to await event ew_1.

b. The Wait Coordinator then invokes task EC2, and shortly thereafter ew_1 arrives.

c. Then task EC2 calls ipc_$block for an event ew_2, which takes an unexpectedly long time to arrive.

Nothing can be done to give control back to EC1, even though its awaited message has long since arrived. (Changing the polling order does not help.) The difficulty stems from the fact that a stack history has been built up of the form:

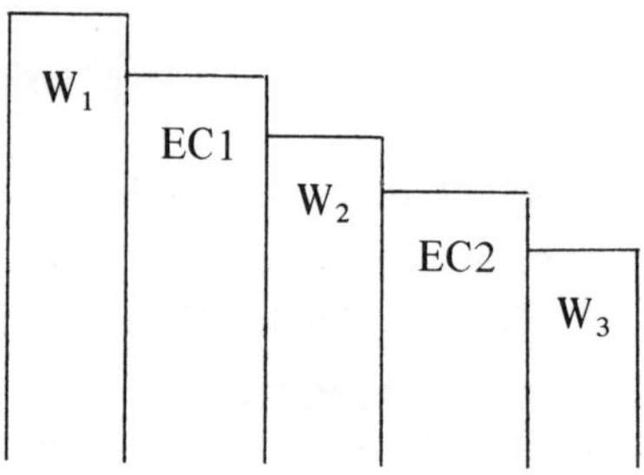

It is impossible to resume EC1 without doing an *abnormal return*, that is, from W_3 to EC1. But this action would have the effect of aborting task EC2, which could cause chaos.

Three approaches are open to the programmer to circumvent this problem.

1. Program all associated procedures so that they and all their dynamic descendants (if any) execute no calls to ipc_$block. This could be difficult because if an associated procedure or any of its descendants calls a system library routine or one written by another individual, there is no easy way to be sure, without reading the code, if said targets do or do not call ipc_$block.

2. Program each associated procedure so that–

a. the first thing it does upon being called is to execute an IPC call that *masks* all event call channels, that is,

call ipc_$mask_ev_calls (code);

b. the last thing it does, prior to returning, is to execute an IPC call that *unmasks* all event call channels, that is, call ipc_$unmask_ev_calls (code);

This approach has the merit that any task that is invoked is treated as having absolute top priority. In a sense, it can be regarded as an extreme approach to solving the problem. Figure 7.18 illustrates what we mean. Here the effects of masking and unmasking event call channels are shown, using the same event timing sequence as in Figure 7.17. Note that task EC4, because of its low priority, is not even begun during the time span being considered.

3. Give up trying the multipurpose approach in the first place! Go back to the principal design approach of Multics, and let each task that is now programmed as an event call task and in need of better response from its Wait Coordinator be made into an independent process to accomplish the same objective. Each such created process would have a single event call channel

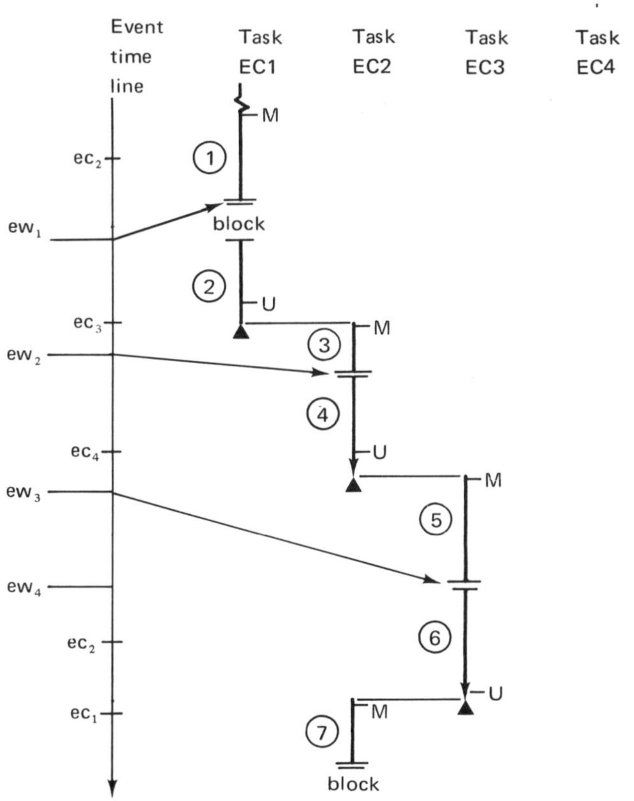

Figure 7.18. Same case as in Figure 7.17 except that calls to ipc_$mask_ev_calls and to ipc_$unmask_ev_calls are made at points marked M and U, respectively.

over which it can be signaled. Hence, competition for good response by its Wait Coordinator will now be eliminated.

Bear in mind, however, that after establishing separate processes for the several tasks, these can now, in principle anyway, be executed in parallel, whenever two or more processors can be awarded to these tasks during a single period of time. The mere fact that execution *can* proceed in parallel as a result of following this approach carries with it the need for greater care in the handling of shared data segments.

We can see that the constraints for the first approach (no calls to ipc_$block) make it less than fully satisfactory for a broad range of applications. However, it is in fact a recommended approach when

a. the special nature of the tasks to be executed lets one "live easily" within the constraints, or

b. the tasks to be executed are so specialized (e.g., in the Answering Service process) that the effort required to "live" within the constraints is justified, or

c. the tasks to be executed are very simple ones, for example, in a data sampling process, where the constraints are not encountered.

The second approach, for reasons of its complexity and biased response to certain event calls, cannot be regarded as fully satisfactory.

The last approach has the merit of being the most widely applicable and in some sense conceptually the simplest, although it, too (along with the first approach), merits the admonition that it should be used with care. Creating an independent process becomes especially attractive when the amount of work to be done by the created process (say, as measured in consumption of CPU time) is easily sufficient to justify the cost of its creation.

Each application must, of course, be judged on its merits. The system's Answering Service, for example, is one application where creation of separate processes was not justified. That is, conceptually, the Answering Service creates a separate task to respond to each dialup (hangup, etc.) at each terminal. But, separate processes per each task are not justified, because the work to be done per terminal is trivial compared with the cost of creating the per-terminal process. For this reason the extra design effort associated with using the first approach, which may be thought of as multiprogramming within a single process, was considered appropriate.

8 The Input/Output System

8.1 Introduction

In many early operating-system designs the software known as the input/output control system (IOCS) played a central conceptual and functional role. In the premultiprogramming, batch operating systems, in fact, many supervisory functions had to do with input/output control—for example, control over queued jobs, control for management and operation of secondary storage, control for operation of display devices and other peripheral equipment, and so on. A system programmer (or subsystem designer) for such operating systems could hardly prove his professional competence without acquiring a reasonable familiarity with the intricacies of the IOCS for his "installation."

By contrast, the role played by the input/output control system in a long-lived Multics system is decidedly secondary, at least from a conceptual point of view, and certainly tends to diminish over time. Even from a functional point of view the relative importance in Multics enjoyed by the software having responsibility for I/O may tend to attenuate in time. In fact it will probably prove true that many or even most subsystem designers may be able to achieve their respective objectives while remaining entirely oblivious to the IOCS details of Multics. In the next few paragraphs of this introduction this viewpoint will be justified and enlarged upon.

One of the objectives of this chapter is to describe the *degrees of involvement* in or *awareness* of I/O system details that are appropriate for the reader, depending on his interest and on the type of subsystem he may be planning to design. Before this objective can be reached, it is believed that a reasonably complete top-down view of the Multics I/O system organization is needed. This is attempted in Section 8.2. Those reading this chapter in its entirety will (it is hoped) gain some insight on the relationship of the I/O system to the central supervisory functions of Multics (especially the file system) that have been described in preceding chapters.

There are two related views of Multics that suggest a secondary role for I/O in Multics:

First, there is the central fact that the file system makes known and dynamically links files that are stored in the hierarchy, that is, within the system, to the processes that legitimately request this service. It does not matter whether these files reside on drums, disks, or tapes. The users (or for that matter other supervisory modules) are unaware of any explicit data movement in accessing these segments even though physical transfer from actual secondary devices to central memory may in fact be involved and some

duly incurred. The required data or procedure object from the hierarchy is made part of the virtual memory of the "requesting" process in a manner such that any data movement that is involved is entirely transparent at the level of ordinary source coding. In other systems, particularly in most earlier ones, a request for an information object on secondary storage always required an explicit request for an I/O transfer in the "source/sink" sense. That is, the source of the object desired had to be identified as a named object and/or location. Correspondingly, if information was to be removed from main memory, it was necessary that the destination (sink) be identified as a named object and/or location, and the transfer (often along with parameters to afford control for a particular type of transfer) had to be explicitly initiated.

The second view stems from the fact that the information storage within the Multics file system is open ended, being basically a *growing* storage. Hence, over time there will be a tendency for an increasing proportion of the information needed by a process to be made known (added to virtual memory) through the service of the file system. The corollary observation is the diminishing frequency of need for data and programs that are "original," that is, that originate *outside* the system during execution of the process and hence must be input via an I/O activity. In the limit, the Multics I/O activity will be related only to the one or more I/O devices that a user's process would have direct control over, normally for conversation with the system. In most cases this is simply his typewriter or TV console. Moreover, in such cases, thoughtfully designed system default mechanisms are supplied, offering the programmer the option to remain oblivious to specific functions of the I/O system and to the fact that his process is actually making use of this facility.

The reader should not jump too quickly to the conclusion, however, that the Multics designers' principal objective has been to erect a barrier that prevents the (system or user) programmer from acquiring and exercising full control over I/O devices, whatever they are, be they tapes, special display devices, special communications channels, or other devices. On the contrary, user processes are able to "negotiate" with the system administrator, who controls distribution of I/O resources, to acquire particular I/O devices (and/or channels). Then, with user code, the user process may program the control of these I/O devices (and channels) and operate them with the full freedom that is normally accorded a hard-core system programmer. One of my purposes in this chapter is to provide at least an initial guide to this programming flexibility for those interested.

In brief, the Multics I/O system has been designed using guidelines that would be followed in the design of any good multipurpose tool.

a. The simplest, most commonplace use of it requires only a minimum of knowledge and skill—and the overhead for such simple (common-mode) use is also minimized.

b. To extract more tailored (special-purpose) services there is added cost—both in the time that must be committed to understand how the tool works and in the actual overhead that will be incurred in execution.

8.2 Input/Output System Organizational Overview

In the introduction I claimed that there are different levels or degrees of potential involvement in I/O system implementation that would be appropriate to each subsystem application. These will be enumerated and exemplified in succeeding sections. But, first, we are in need of an effective frame of reference to guarantee meaning for the delineations that will be made. An organizational overview of the I/O system is what is wanted for this purpose.

Such an overview must begin by recognizing an overriding design objective for any general I/O system; namely, the input/output operations stated in the programs or service procedures that a user writes should specify only those device functions that are required for the application at hand, leaving to the system the responsibility for gauging the degree of device independence implied by the user's request. In this way a user that invokes such service procedures is free to designate substitute devices as may be appropriate, while adhering to the device dependencies that are implied by the stated I/O function requests. (For most ordinary users whose sole I/O device is normally just the console, this objective amounts to an opportunity for the user to state his I/O requests in a manner that implies device independence. Moreover, the identity or special idiosyncrasies of the particular I/O device used in this fashion is of no concern to him either.) For this reason user-coded I/O operations of a process should ordinarily be independent (or as independent as feasible) of the particular device and model, or even of the type of device, for example, typewriter, as opposed to teletype or tape.

There are two clear reasons for this crucially important objective. First, we must presume that at any given time a system will generally accommodate several types of I/O devices and models. Each is likely to require different programmed control. Each may have different character sets, and may be intrinsically different in various respects (e.g., line printers are not backspaceable, tapes are; some tapes can be read backwards as well as forwards, while card readers are never designed to read cards backwards; etc.). Second, we presume that I/O devices become obsolete and, over time, are replaced by new models of the same or different types, for example, keyboard-TV versus typewriter. Clearly, if programs are to be reusable, if processes are to be repeated with minor or no variation in the nature or effect of their I/O operations during reuse of these programs, then recognition of device independence must be a planned part of the programming system for I/O operations.

One approach to design for the needed device independence is to regard the I/O resource needed to complete any given I/O operation, not as a *real* or physical resource, as, for instance, a particular card reader, but as a *virtual* (pseudo) I/O resource that is described in terms of the functions it must be capable of performing, which is mapped by the system to a particular real resource at run time, using whatever I/O device is available and convenient. The analogy here is with virtual memory, regarded as a resource, which is mapped by the system into particular blocks of core memory using the segmentation and paging features of the hardware and in a way that is transparent to the user. Such an approach implies that all available input devices, regardless of type (or location), are in some sense acceptable equivalents and that all output devices are correspondingly equivalent.

Unfortunately, even if we exclude the user's own console, which normally must be fixed during the life of the process, it is still a poor analogy if interpreted too strictly. The user must, when he so chooses, be able to decide what I/O devices he wants used (when there is a choice available to him). If, for instance, he wants to develop a subsystem whose output may optionally drive either a dedicated line printer, 30-column card punch, or 80-column card punch, he must be allowed to specify which one, or which combination of two or three, and in what prescribed order. In short, a completely flexible I/O system must provide for user designation of the specifics of certain I/O operations—and even of user-provided devices (or simulated devices) in certain cases. For example, a user develops a subsystem whose output will drive a newly acquired display device. He may be required to furnish the detailed I/O coding for the control of that device (later referred to as a Device

Interface Module or DIM). [It is hoped that those interested in seeing what is involved for such an application will find this chapter helpful, but they should regard this entire chapter as merely a jump-off point for more extended study.]

Certainly some kind of compromise arrangement is needed whereby some users (most, in fact) may code their processes so that I/O is regarded as employing virtual resources while others may code I/O operations by partially or completely specifying the devices to be used and the programmed control to go with it. The former use the so-called *package I/O* calls, such as ioa_ and ios_$read_ptr, while the latter will come to grips with and effectively utilize the basic functions of the I/O system itself in varying degrees of involvement. Some details of these calls and related techniques are described in Sections 8.3 and 8.4. Readers may already have encountered descriptions of these calls in the MPM.

The particular design approach taken in Multics is based on two practical requirements. One has to do with the discharge of the system's responsibility for dispensing and recovery of all real I/O devices; the other has to do with the run-time mapping of valid user-coded I/O operations, regardless of their degree of specificity, onto specific devices in the manner appropriate to those specific devices and with appropriate controls.

First, it is recognized that at any given time, as a consequence of the I/O-device needs of a process, certain specific I/O devices (or device capabilities) must be allocated to each given (user) process. The system's decision to allocate from available I/O device resources to a process will be made for any of several reasons. For ordinary situations the system is easily able to infer those needs, for example, the console is needed on which a user logs in. In more exotic cases, the user can negotiate these allocations with the system's administrator in advance, or eventually obtain these resources at run time via commands or library subroutine calls.

Second, any programmed I/O operation should, at source level at least, be expressed (coded) in a general way that specifies the I/O source or sink, not by its device designation, but only by a placeholder name for that source or sink. (Moreover, as an added convenience to users, it may be possible to code certain standard I/O operations so that even this name may be inferred from context.)

For example [and here the illustration is only schematic], rather than use a specific device designation, even though that device may in fact already be allocated to a process at the time its use is wanted, such as in the following forms:

```
read from "card_reader_2" into area_23;       ⎫
or                                            ⎪
input ("card_reader_2", area_23);             ⎪
or                                            ⎪
read ("device 35_2", area_23);                ⎬ (1)
or                                            ⎪
input ("console 204", area_23);               ⎪
or                                            ⎪
call io (input,"console 204", area_23);       ⎭
```

we might instead say

```
read from the stream named "Billy" into area 23;  ⎫
or                                                ⎪
read ("Billy", area_23);                          ⎪
or                                                ⎬ (2)
call read ("my_console", area_23);                ⎪
or                                                ⎪
call io (read, "my console", area_23);            ⎭
```

depending on the syntax of the coding language being used.

Here in examples (2), "Billy" and "my_console" are simply identifiers for *sources* of data. For such a read statement to have any meaningful effect, the specific device represented by that identifier must be *bound* to, or "attached" to (i.e. associated in some way with), "Billy" or "my_console" at some time *after* the device is allocated to the process and *before* the read statement is executed. The Multics I/O system is responsible for maintenance and supervision of these device-source name associations. Likewise, for output, names for *sinks* are used in write statements rather than actual output device designations. Thus by analogy to the read examples in (2) above we could conceivably picture something like

write ("his_console", "format 12", area_22); (3)

in which "his_console" is here intended to suggest the name of some sink (output device). The attachment at any given time may be to one of a set of several (different) devices. Thus, if a single process had several consoles allocated, the process could simulate a "party-line" conversation on the several consoles where the name "his_console" could be attached and reattached, possibly cyclically, among the several different allocated devices.

A generic name for elements of the set {source, sink} that has now found favor is *stream*. We shall use this term frequently hereafter. Thus the term "stream name" refers to either a name of a source or a name of a sink. [It is clear why the word stream is selected, since an input or output operation suggests a stream of information (words, characters, bytes, or bits) flowing from a source (input device) or to a sink (output device).] Conceptually, the attaching of a stream name to a particular device is a form of parameter binding. The device designation plays the role of the actual argument and the stream name that of the formal parameter. In order to apply more than one "argument" to the same "parameter," Multics provides for the detaching of a device (designation) from a stream name, so that subsequently another device can be attached to the same stream name.

To carry out a read or write operation (call) of the type suggested in (2) and (3) above, the following steps can now be visualized. The system module that receives and is responsible for "interpreting" this call must first perform a table lookup (in a per-process, per-ring data base) to determine the device designation (and type of device, constraint rules, if any, for use, etc.) that is currently associated with the named I/O stream parameter. (Because attachments are maintained on a per-ring basis, a subsystem that executes in a special ring can have a distinct set of stream-name "meanings.")

In principle, assuming the I/O call parameters are consistent with the data kept in this so-called *attach table*, this same I/O control module can then convert this request into an I/O action—that is, by initiating the desired I/O operations after generating the required channel commands,[1] and so forth. Because the system must be capable of supporting an open-ended number of

1. IBM set a trend by calling the I/O channel instructions on its model-709 computer *commands* to distinguish them from the instructions of the CPU. This distinction became a rather conventional notation that has remained popular for over ten years. In the GE 645, however, these channel instructions are called "data control words" or DCWs.

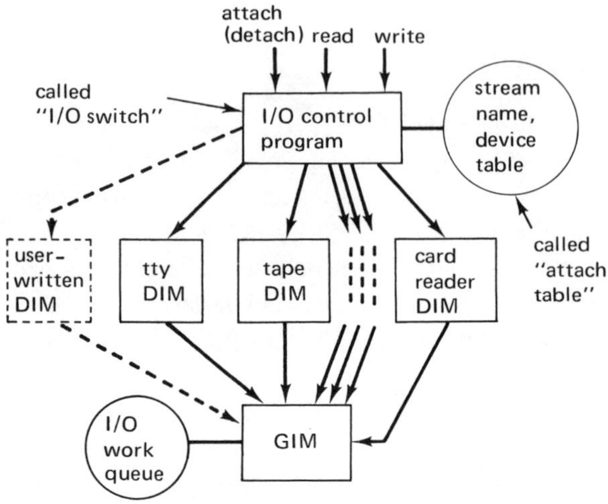

Figure 8.1. First simplified view of I/O system organization

devices, device types, and controllers, considerably more modularity is called for. So, in actual fact, the I/O control module merely transmits the now more specific I/O request as a call to an appropriate "specialist" module (called a Device Interface Module, or DIM). There is one such specialist module for each type of device. This DIM in turn takes charge of getting the I/O request accomplished as suggested in Figure 8.1.

To get a better grasp of what the specialist module's job is, it is worth while to digress momentarily to consider some of the special characteristics of the GE 645 I/O controller hardware.

The input/output controller hardware of Multics is designed so that each individual I/O device may be (and in fact normally is) in effect connected to a separate I/O channel. By I/O channel I mean (here) conceptually a separate I/O processor capable of accepting commands that carry out I/O operations.[2] Hence, when we speak about allocating a device to a process (group), we shall also take for granted that the system also more or less permanently allocates a channel for this device. The identity of the channel, the identity of the device connected to it, and the identity of the current owner process (group) can be regarded as system-maintained in conveniently organized (ring-0) system data bases available to the modules of the I/O system.

2. Those that later have occasion to study the reference literature on the GE 645 I/O controller hardware will find that the term *channel* is used in a more restricted and technical sense. There, several such channels, taken together, comprise what I speak of in this chapter as an I/O channel.

Communication with the channels, that is, initiating their activity and supplying them with their needed commands, receiving and interpreting the status information that they return, and so on, is achieved in the GE 645 system by providing a peripheral processor called a GIOC (Generalized I/O Controller). This active hardware device acts as a high-speed "broker" to manage (and multiplex) the communication between memory and the many I/O channels (which are themselves packaged in the GIOC). Each GIOC is logically organized to provide half-duplex (one-way) communication service for up to 2000 input devices, output devices, or devices that alternate as input and output devices,[3] or up to 1000 full duplex units, such as typewriter or keyboard-TV consoles.

We can now return to complete our view of the I/O system's handling of read/write calls as suggested in Figure 8.1. Each Device Interface Module (DIM) performs a number of functions: The description that follows is inspired by a recent description by Graham.[4]

The DIM converts a device-independent request into a device-dependent one. In doing this, it must compile a program for the hardware input/output controller GIOC (which it can in turn supply to the target channel). The compiled program reflects the idiosyncracies of the particular device to which the stream is attached. It (the program) may include line controls in the case of remote terminals, select instructions in the case of tapes, and so forth. In addition, the Device Interface Module may need to convert the internal character code used by the system into an appropriate character code for the device. Typewriter terminals, for example, come in many different varieties. Virtually every different variety has different character codes.

The Device Interface Module, after compiling a program for the GIOC, calls a module that serves as an interface for the GIOC to start the I/O using this GIOC program. It is the DIM's responsibility to interact with the GIOC Interface Module (abbreviated as GIM) until this I/O request has been completed. This may require several calls to the GIM depending on the format of the channel programs that the GIOC can provide to the channels for execution.

The GIOC Interface Module (a ring-0 CPU program) is responsible for the overall management of the GIOC. Thus, the GIM is also responsible for overall monitoring of the operation of the GIOC. The GIM answers interrupts

3. Such as the IBM 2741 typewriter console.
4. "File Management and Related Topics," by Robert M. Graham, © 1969, p. 48. Course notes issued at the 1969 Engineering Summer Conference on Computer and Program Organization, University of Michigan.

(i.e., its code acts as an interrupt handler for the GIOC), recognizing completion of tasks and transmitting to the GIM's caller status information deposited by the GIOC.

A final point of explanation for Figure 8.1 regards the four indicated entry points to the I/O control program. The entry point *attach* is always employed (to establish the appropriate stream-name-device association in the attach table) prior to utilizing the entry points *read* or *write* for the same streams. The entry point *detach* is used to nullify a previous attach stream-name-device pairing.

Generalization of the Device Concept to Include Files

If we now add one powerful, in fact crucial, generalization to the I/O system organization picture painted thus far, we can then see the actual Multics design overview in its entirety. That generalization is the one that permits segments to be substituted for I/O devices in the association with stream names. (Let us pause briefly to let the last sentence sink in.) What I mean by this remark is that any named segment of a user's process may be employed as a source or sink for a read or write function, as if it were (or in lieu of) an actual I/O device.

There are a number of important applications that are now possible as a result of this type of generalization. For instance, during a console debugging session, information can be read out of storage onto the user's console for visual verification. Once verified, the results of subsequent but similar computations might be more appropriately output to segments and thus saved as files. To achieve this objective, the programmer might follow these steps:

1. (For debugging.) Call *attach* to associate the stream name, say, "user_output" with his console, for example, tty302.
2. (For production runs, after debugging.) Call *detach* to nullify the previous call to attach. Call attach once again, this time to associate the same stream name "user_output" with, say, <results_file>.

Other applications are those that make it possible to simulate I/O devices for interactive or conversational interplay, for sending mail, that is, output to data bases shared with other users, or for converting console sessions to run absentee by placing on one file the sequence of commands that can be *read* as an input file and by placing (writing) the series of resulting responses on another file. (In the last-mentioned application, the dialogue's results can be examined later at leisure by asking for a printout of the output file.)

This remarkable generalization of the notion of input/output is achieved in a mechanically almost trivial manner in Multics. The trick is simply to create

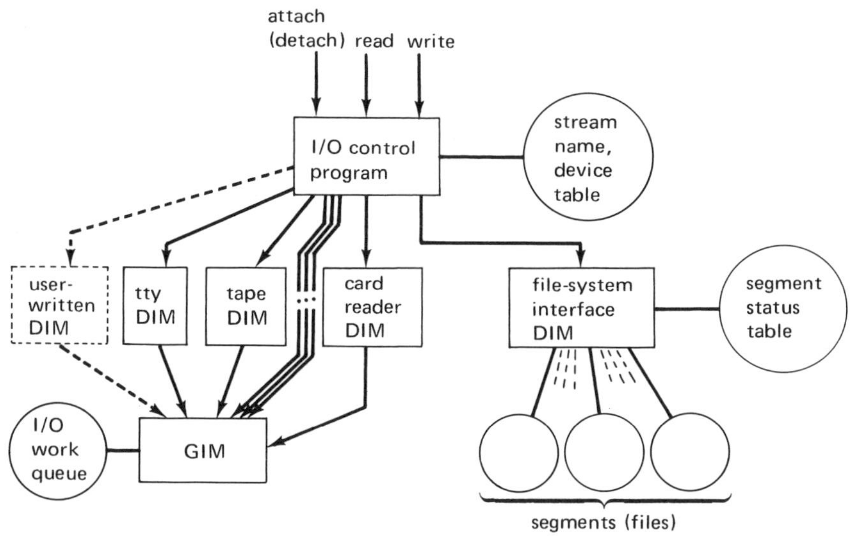

Figure 8.2. Complete simplified view of the Multics I/O system organization

another specialist DIM called the file-system interface DIM, as shown in Figure 8.2, which completes the I/O system organization overview. Again we follow closely Graham's description of this module's function.

The file-system interface DIM functions like any other DIM. However, it does not call the GIOC Interface Module. *The file-system interface DIM is used to make a segment look like an I/O device.* In its (per-process) static storage, the file-system interface DIM maintains a table holding status information for each segment that is being referred to as a device. When an attach call is made to the I/O control program for attaching a stream to a segment (instead of to an actual device), the requested segment is initiated as a known segment (if not already known). (See Chapter 6 as a refresher for the details on making a segment known.) The file-system interface DIM maintains in the table of status information separate read/write indexes of the current positions in the segment where reading or writing is taking place. Subsequent read or write calls are processed by the file-system interface DIM and consist of copying the requested information into or out of the segment at the position of the appropriate read/write index. After the copy is made, the index or "current pointer" is updated to the new position in the segment.

We have just seen how the I/O system may behave as a "customer," of the file system, which supplies needed services. One might wonder if the reverse of these roles is ever true. That is, does the file system through its Page Control Module, when seeking to transfer a page of information from/to core and disk or tape storage, ever find itself to be a customer of the I/O system? Emphasis on objectives of modularity might cause one to guess the affirmative. In actual fact, however, considerations of efficiency have dictated that paging I/O in Multics be treated with special-purpose I/O software that greatly streamlines the processor's task in initiating and controlling such I/O. The details of this special-purpose software should be of no interest to subsystem designers and for this reason will not be covered here.

8.3 Packaged Input/Output for Communication with the Console

Typical of all operating systems that support interactive processing, Multics furnishes several routines (and enables them) to satisfy the typical user's need for an easy-to-express console I/O request, that is, one that requires a minimum of acquaintance with the I/O system organization. These routines have been referred to as "packaged I/O."[5] They serve effectively as interfaces with the I/O system by mapping the received call into the appropriate (and more technical) calls to the I/O system.

One of the simplest of the interface routines currently available is the simplified print routine called ioa_, which can be used to construct and print messages made up of character strings, integers, and pointer values. For instance, a call written in PL/I syntax, might be:

```
call ioa_("date          ^a   ^d,   ^d,      time   ^d: ^d",
                    "June",   20,      1969,   2014,   36);
```

When executed this call would produce a typed line that might appear as

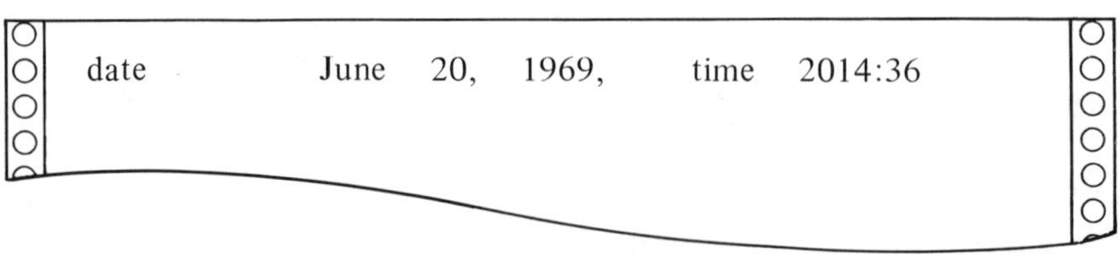

As another example, the statement

```
call ioa_("overflow   at   ^   ^p",   pointer_variable);
```

would produce when executed a typed line that might appear as

5. This is terminology used in the "Multics Programmers' Manual," Chapter II.

```
overflow   at   274|3263
```

The first argument is a control string that is a form of format code somewhat similar to a FORTRAN format (but more limited in purpose). We'll not dwell on the details of this routine or its variants as they are well described, with additional illustrations, in the MPM. We only consider here how functions like ioa_ behave in the context of the operating system organization structure just overviewed in the preceding section.

To understand how ioa_ is able to do its intended job we must appreciate the following system service conventions that are obeyed for each process created at login.

First, the identification of the console device-channel pair on which the login attempt is made is noted by the user control process (i.e., the "Answering Service") that responds to the dialup. When login validations are completed and the process is created on the user's behalf, the console device is allocated to that created process, and the stream name "user_io" is "attached" to this device by calling the I/O control module at the entry point *attach* and supplying as arguments the necessary information to complete a suitable entry in that process's attach table. (Note that the interface routine can be oblivious to the type of device the user is logging in on. The I/O control module has responsibility for directing the I/O request to the appropriate Device Interface Module). In Section 8.4 we shall take a closer look at this bit of business, but for the moment merely note that in fact several calls are made to the attach entry, resulting in a table entry that shows the names "user_output" (as well as "user_input") *as synonyms* for the stream name, "user_io", where "user_io" means the tty he logged in on. Second, we must also appreciate that ioa_ is written to call the write function using "user_output" as the I/O name. In general, packaged I/O interface routines always use the fixed names "user_output" or "user_input" as I/O names for their function calls to the I/O system.

We now see that when the log-in process is completed, and the user is "put in charge," the necessary connections that essentially enable ioa_ to perform properly have all been made. The same connections (i.e., attachments) are also made for other packaged I/O routines. Of particular interest in this category is a pair of routines for reading or writing typewriter I/O. These two routines, whose full names are ios_$read_ptr and ios_$write_ptr, are fully described in the MPM.

For example,

call ios_$read_ptr (stringv_ptr, rdmax, rdcount);

requests that up to rdmax characters be accepted from the console for assignment to the character string variable, pointed to by stringv_ptr. The output argument rdcount reports the number of characters actually read from the typed line.

A subsystem writer will be pleased to observe that the effective sources or sinks for packaged I/O routines are easily changed to any device or file of his choosing. For instance, if the only explicitly called I/O routines in the subsystem are of the packaged variety, then to convert the subsystem to run absentee, the only requirement for the change is to cause execution of an I/O system call to detach the "user_input" and/or "user_output" synonyms from the stream name "user_io", and then cause explicit attach calls to reassociate the names "user_input" and/or "user_output" with the designated files (named segments). These I/O system calls could be executed (preferably at command level) just after login or at any time afterward when absentee mode execution becomes appropriate. This flexibility may motivate some readers to investigate the attach call and the related I/O system calls that are discussed in the next section.

8.4 Input/Output System Calls (ios_)

These direct calls to the I/O system, a total of over twenty by current count, are enumerated and fully described in the MSPM as well as in the "Multics Programmers' Manual." (The details for specifying all the arguments for these calls, however, are somewhat scattered throughout the latter.) Here I shall give brief descriptions of some of these calls and their use but avoid a detailed technical description. Four of the most frequently used entry points are listed in Table 8.1.

8.4.1 ios_$attach

To attach a device to a stream name, the programmer must specify the following (indicated arguments[6] are given to the left):

ioname1 – the stream name.

type – the type of device, to designate the appropriate DIM, for example,

6. The first three arguments (ioname1, type, and ioname2 must be supplied as character strings).

"tdsm" for the tape DIM, or "file" for the file-system interface DIM.

ioname2 – The device designation, for example, "tty138" for a typewriter, or "Harry" for a file (i.e., a relative path name).

mode – a code to designate the kind of restraints to be placed on the use of the device, its method of accessing, and its interpretation of the data representation (and any other type of constraint, or optional use, or function, that is deemed appropriate during this particular attachment).

status – the name of a (72-bit) variable to record the response of this request–that is, in which to receive the reflected error messages, warnings, or other advice from the modules that are the dynamic descendants of this call.

The MPM (Reference Data section on input and output facilities) maintains an up-to-date list of all the DIMs that one can designate in an attach call. This reference also provides the subsystem writer a complete list of function calls besides attach, detach, read and/or write that are meaningful for each system-supplied DIM. The same reference supplies a list of the default *modes* that are set for use in package I/O read/write calls. The coding for modes recognized by the system-supplied DIMs is explained in the same reference. (Subsystem writers that must write their own DIMs are urged to follow this coding, although the particular code scheme that one devises is up to the DIM designer, since the I/O control module simply transmits this code to the target DIM and is otherwise oblivious to it.) The mode code for system-supplied DIMs is simply a character string of concatenated predefined code characters, one or more characters per each *use, access,* or *data* mode. For example, a mode code to attach a tape unit for reading only (use), forward only (access), and only logical, linear records (data) would be the concatenation, "RFGL" for *r*eadable, *f*orward, logical, *l*inear.

In the initial Multics implementation the mode argument may be null (i.e., "") because the I/O control module is not programmed to check the mode. Ultimately, however, it is planned that this module will check the *use code* portion of the mode argument (i.e., to see if codes R, for readable, and/or W for writable are compatible with the attached device) and will pass the remainder of the mode argument (access-mode and data-mode codes) to the DIM for further compatibility checks.

A complete explanation (interpretation) of the output argument called *status* is also maintained in the MPM, Reference Data section on input and

Table 8.1 The Most-Frequently Used I/O System Entry Points and Their Arguments

	Arguments					
Entry-point name	ioname	ioname1	type[a]	ioname2[a]	mode[a]	workspace
ios_$attach		√	√	√	√	
ios_$detach		√		√		
ios_$read	√					√
ios_$write	√					√

[a] For details, see MPM, Reference Data section on input and output facilities.

output facilities. Many of these error explanations should make more sense upon completing the reading of this section (8.4). Attempts to attach a device should fail if there is an incompatibility of the supplied arguments either with what is already recorded in the attach table for the process or with what is recorded in or known about the target DIM.

An attempt to attach a named segment for use as an *input* file will result in an error status return from ios_$attach if the specified segment cannot be found. An attempt to attach a specified segment for use as an *output* file will result in one of two actions. If the segment cannot be found, then one will be created and used (without comment). If the segment *is* found, writing into it will be by appending to the end of it.

In MPM parlance the I/O control module (which maintains the attach table) is referred to as the "I/O switch" because during function calls like ios_$read or ios_$write, the job of this module is to route or switch the incoming call not only to the appropriate DIM, but also to direct the call to the appropriate entry within the target DIM.

Each target DIM has an entry-point transfer vector, one entry per each of the functions supported by that DIM. The transfer vector is consulted when the DIM is called by the I/O switch for routing the call to the appropriate functional entry point, for example, read, write, backspace, rewind, and so forth. A call to a function that is not supported within the particular DIM (e.g., to read a printer) will reflect an error code when and if it is called. (Section 8.5 gives more details on the design of a DIM, including naming conventions for DIMs and for the calls the DIMs may receive.)

offset	nelem	nelemt (output)	disposal	status[a] (output)
				√
			√	√
√	√	√		√
√	√	√		√

By special design, a user that wishes to provide synonyms for a given stream name may do so by executing a call to ios_$attach in which the arguments take on their special meaning when the argument called *type* is supplied with the value "syn". For instance to assign the string "his_io" as a synonym for an already-attached stream named "her_io" one could write

call ios_$attach ("his_io", "syn", "her_io", mode, status);

8.4.2 ios_$detach

To detach or nullify a previous attachment, that is, delete the entire attach-table entry previously recorded for a given stream name—remember, there may be one and only one entry for each stream name—one calls ios_$detach and names the stream name and, as a redundancy check, the (presumed) device associated with that stream. A status return argument provides a report of the resulting action. Incompatibility (or invalidity) of the input arguments will result in an error message reflected from the I/O control module (I/O switch).

The input argument called *disposal* may be null (i.e.,"") for most applications. It is planted in this call for future use, to provide special instruction to the system or operator for the disposal of dedicated I/O devices such as tapes and/or magnetic tape drives. (Both tapes and drives can be considered as independent resources to be disposed of.)

When fully implemented, a *null* value for the disposal argument will mean: Take the default action and close out the device to allow future assignment to another user (e.g., dismount the tape). Alternatively, a value of "hold" for the disposal argument will mean: Keep the device active ("I will be back").

8.4.3 ios_$read

To execute a read the caller is obliged to name the input stream (source) and a pointer argument (workspace) that identifies the destination in the process's virtual memory where the input data is to be transmitted. Additional qualifying input arguments are the offset and the number of elements, nelem, that are to be read. The offset is from the beginning of the workspace in which to begin receiving the input data. (Offset is measured in elements where the element size is usually set by a default convention for each DIM.) Typical element sizes might be 9 bits for character-oriented streams or 36 bits for word-oriented streams. The number of elements specified is, of course, subject to the current upper-bound restraint imposed by the segment size of the workspace.

There are two output arguments, nelemt and status. The former provides a report on the actual number of elements read into the workspace, while status provides the normal advice on success, or degree of success, of the read operation. The report can reflect error reports transmitted from a variety of sources, including the GIM, or, in the case of the file devices, from file-system modules. (It may even reflect an error message that alerts the user to trouble caused during the preceding transaction—an indication of interest during certain asynchronous reading modes described later.)

8.4.4 ios_$write

As can be seen from Table 8.1, this call employs the same set of arguments. Their interpretation is what would be expected by symmetry with ios_$read. The workspace pointer and offset identify the place from which writing-out is to begin. The number of elements to be written out, nelem, and the number actually written out, nelemt, provide input instruction and output reporting, respectively. The argument status provides additional information to complete the reporting responsibility.

8.4.5 Other Calls

Several calls are available to provide the subsystem writer more flexibility or control of the use of I/O devices. For instance,

ios_$changemode

allows one to alter the current mode of a given attachment. Several calls deal with control over the *synchrony* of the read or write operations and/or of the workspaces employed in these operations. I won't burden the reader here with the actual names of these calls or their arguments. These can be found in the MPM. We will, however, digress here to discuss the subject of I/O synchronization control at a conceptual level.

Read/write synchrony refers to the type of coupling one wants [loose (asynchronous) or rigid (synchronous)] between the actual initiation of the I/O transfer and the corresponding read/write call in the user's program. *Workspace synchrony* refers to the type of coupling one wants (loose or rigid) between the point in time when the I/O workspace has been filled/emptied and the point in time when the program may resume execution beyond the read/write call (that would cause the work space to fill/empty.) These two types of synchronization are mutually orthogonal, so a user may wish to specify particular combinations for his subsystem application when other than the systemwide default selections are wanted. The next few paragraphs elaborate each type of synchronization control and suggest several applications.

Read (Synchronous or Asynchronous)

Shall "read-ahead" be permitted or not? That is the question. By read-ahead (*asynchronous*) I mean permitting the system to anticipate our program's read request by issuing an I/O order to read the attached device before our program actually executes the corresponding read call. Read-ahead is what is meant by read asynchrony and is precisely what is wanted in the typical console read operation. This allows the information that the user types ahead to be available in core when the program issues the read call. Hence, the system's default mode for typewriter input is *asynchronous*.

A *read synchronous* operation implies: Don't read a thing from the device until a call for it has been issued. This input mode locksteps a user to the program, thus in effect reversing the normal master/slave interactive relationship between them. Now the program is in control of the user rather than vice versa. Read synchronous might be useful in certain computer-assisted instruction applications or in situations where, say, no further requests may be accepted from an inquiry station that is attached to a subsystem.

Write (Synchronous or Asynchronous)

Shall "write-behind" be permitted or not? That is the question here. If so, then return is possible from the write call *before* all output information designated in the write call has been transferred to the device. In most applications write asynchronous is acceptable and in fact highly desirable for the sake of efficiency (so long as it is safe). Write asynchronous is the system's default decision. There are cases, however, where write synchronous operations are required. The system, for example, uses this mode of output during automatic logout of a user to be sure that all messages and other I/O transactions have been completed before taking subsequent action.

Workspace (Synchronous or Asynchronous)

Shall permission to return from a read/write call be permitted before the workspace designated in that call has been filled/emptied? That is the question asked here. The system's default decision is *workspace synchronous* (i.e., *no* return of control from the DIM until the workspace has been ascertained to be filled for the designated read or emptied for the designated write). Conceivably, some speedup of a read/write asynchronous action can be achieved by opting for workspace asynchronous, but this is risky practice because a succession of reads (or writes) could conceivably cause chaotic overlaps in the workspace areas; so, unless there is a special-purpose application where the user feels safe in doing so, workspace asynchronous is *not* recommended.

To summarize our foregoing discussions, the defaults for the synchronization options are as follows:

1. reading is *asynchronous*
2. writing is *asynchronous*
3. workspace use is *synchronous*

Still other calls provide the user an opportunity for such functions as abandoning data piled up as read-ahead in the input workspace so as to reuse this space for new reads. A symmetrical call aborts any, as yet physically unwritten, data that may be piled up as write-behind in the output workspace. These calls may be especially useful for designers of subsystems dealing with typewriterlike consoles where the read-ahead or write-behinds can become numerous in certain conversations. Often the need to reset the current pointers in the read or write workspace becomes essential to avoid frustrating the console user, for instance, by accepting previously typed but now-undesirable input or by typing out now-unwanted results.

Still other calls allow the user to control (or determine) the size of input or output elements for next (or current) reads or writes. These calls may be useful in certain applications where the device is the typewriter or a file.

In addition, there are ios_ calls to allow the user to control (or determine) the set of read delimiters and/or break characters in input streams. *Read delimiters* are used to condition read calls (e.g., the new line character for typewriter read calls) so they halt their scan of the input buffer after a read delimiter is seen (and transmit all characters seen up to that point, i.e., up to and including the read delimiter, to the user). *Break characters* are used to control the action of an "interactive" channel so that it will trigger a hardware interrupt (when such a character arrives over the channel), so as to make all data read since receiving the last break character available to the user. Break characters are useful to achieve a form of code conversion or editing known as "canonicalization" (see MPM, Reference Data section on typewriter character codes, for an orientation and a full explanation). They are also used to achieve erase and kill effects. These, too, are a form of immediate editing that has been found essential in the typing of input streams. (The section of the MPM just mentioned elaborates.) For typewriters, new-line is not only set as the read delimiter but is also set as a break character.

When segments are attached as pseudo input devices, say for absentee jobs, it would be nice if the file-system interface DIM could respond to both read delimiters and to break characters in input messages so as to fully simulate the action and effects of, say, reading typewriter input data. Although the file-system interface DIM *does* accept read delimiters (e.g., new-line), it does *not*, however, accept break characters, because it is not an interactive channel. Another point to note is that, as a result of a design decision, the file-system interface DIM supports (permits) no code conversion during input from a segment.

The default values of new-line for the read delimiter and nine (bits) for element size make it especially easy to have segments substitute for typewriter devices (that transmit ascii character strings). But the user may choose any read delimiter and/or any element size simply by executing appropriate calls to ios_$setdelim and ios_$setsize for the stream name in question.

The fact that the file-system interface DIM does not itself produce code conversion during input from a segment is no serious restriction either. The user's program that invokes the action of the file-system DIM is certainly free to perform the needed conversion steps either before or after the simulated input operation.

Finally, as if this portfolio of possible user-originated I/O control were not enough, the Multics designers have planned an open end to the list in the form of a special, catchall call,

ios_$order

This call permits the sophisticated subsystem writer to transmit special requests to the target DIM on subsequent read/write calls, such as the setting of hardware-device modes on typewriters or tape drives, for example, red or blue ribbon, high or low tape density.

8.5 Designing a Device Interface Module

Users may write nonprivileged Device Interface Modules[7] for a variety of purposes, usually to control a particular device or set of devices but occasionally to serve as an intermediate interface with existing DIMs. To construct a DIM that controls an actual device the subsystem designer must become thoroughly acquainted with the channel adapter that communicates with the device (or its controller). The channel adapter is connected to the GIOC. Additionally the programmer must become acquainted with the GIOC hardware, and with the software module that manages this hardware and that interfaces with the DIM on its outgoing end. He must also be familiar with the system-supplied I/O switch that must call the DIM.

The DIM is the only module in the chain of calls that knows about the I/O device being controlled. On the user's side of the DIM, the I/O switch routes the user's call to the proper DIM, checks for and transmits compatible sets of arguments, otherwise generating and returning appropriate error messages (status values). The switch also acts as a "reflector" of error messages generated as a result of the I/O action itself. On the device side of the DIM, the GIOC Interface Module (GIM) transmits control information to the GIOC, selects and reacts to interrupts received from the GIOC, and interprets and transmits status information to the DIM. The GIM also allocates and controls the use of channel buffers that must necessarily lie outside the user's virtual memory space. The GIM is designed so it need not care how the user makes use of a channel that it, as GIOC "manager," assigns to the user (through the DIM). Of the three modules in the chain, namely the I/O switch, the DIM, and the GIM, it is the GIM alone that provides for the system's safety in carrying out these various functions.

A user may also design a pseudo DIM that acts merely as an intermediate module between the I/O switch and one or more existing DIMs. To write a pseudo DIM one need know nothing about the GIM or the hardware it serves.

A "broadcaster" module would be an example of such a pseudo DIM. Its

7. The current implementation of Multics includes certain privileged (ring-0) system DIMs designed to satisfy certain high-performance requirements (e.g., typewriter response). The design details of these system DIMs are not considered in this book.

purpose might be to receive a single write call from the I/O switch and convert it to two or more ios_$write calls via the switch, this time to the actual DIM or DIMs that will in turn cause replication of the message on the devices in the "broadcast" set.

Schematically, this idea is easily displayed. For example, we may picture a call of the form

call ios_$attach ("A", "broadcast", "C, D, E", mode, status);

where we assume that "C", "D", and "E" are I/O stream names that are themselves already attached (to their respective devices).

The coding for the broadcast pseudo DIM would then be such as to anticipate and process a call of the form

call ios_$write ("A", workspace, offset, etc.);

so as to generate and execute the following three calls (and then return):

call ios_$write ("C", workspace, offset, etc.);

call ios_$write ("D", workspace, offset, etc.),

call ios_$write ("E", workspace, offset, etc.);

In the subsections that follow, a "checklist" of things a DIM writer needs to know is recited in a more systematic fashion.

8.5.1 Conformity with Other DIMs

There are some general rules of conformity that are worth reviewing when approaching the design of a DIM. These ideas are given here.

1. It goes without saying that a DIM or pseudo DIM designer must become acquainted with and try to adhere to all the ios_ conventions for communicating between the user and the I/O system. In this way the new DIM can be used interchangeably with other DIMs and thereby preserve the appearance of device independence.

Conventions that are enumerated in various sections of the MPM have to do with

a. interpretation of error codes,
b. attach modes,
c. treating default strategies re element size, read delimiters, and so forth.

2. In the same spirit of maximizing uniformity of application, calls to ios_ through the switch should be matched to the device's functions in a meaningful way, if necessary, using the many special calls already in use by

other system-supplied DIMs, for example, ios_$changemode, ios_$setsize, ios_$seek, ios_$tell, and as a last resort ios_$order.

Achieving this type of conformity can well have a high payoff during the debugging of a new subsystem that includes a new DIM. Remember that during early debugging of the subsystem the actual I/O device will probably not be physically connected to the system. So, the device will have to be simulated by using existing equipment, using the existing system-supplied DIM. (Letting the device be represented by a file and using the existing file DIM is regarded as the best choice.) Cutover to the actual DIM and the actual device should therefore present fewer problems if the new DIM presents an interface similar to the one used in the preliminary testing.

3. As a general rule of good design the DIM should be constructed to expect any reasonable ios_ call and do something sensible with it, that is, not reject it. For example, if a device has only one read delimiter, say the new line character, then a call transmitted via the I/O switch to set the delimiter to new line should be *accepted* (and of course ignored).

8.5.2 The DIM's Interface with the I/O Switch

When the call to ios_$attach is received by the I/O switch, it in turn calls the attach entry of the target DIM. The latter must be coded to return a device pointer that can be used as an argument during subsequent function calls transmitted through the switch.

The I/O switch employs a special naming convention in designating the appropriate entry point in the DIM target. The switch is coded to accept a call of the form

```
call ios_$attach (ioname1, type, etc.);
```

as signifying that there exists a transfer vector in the target DIM's linkage section whose elements point, via links, to the respective functional entry points in the target DIM. This transfer vector begins at type$type. For example, suppose one were writing a special DIM for the pdp7 computer regarded as a peripheral device. If the DIM is given the type name "pdp7", and if the call to attach were

```
call ios_$attach ("input7", "pdp7", etc . . . .);
```

then the I/O switch assumes that the segment <pdp7> has an entry point located at <pdp7>|[pdp7] at which there is to be found a vector of transfer instructions, one to each supported functional entry point in the DIM.

Since the order in which these entry-point transfer instructions is fixed by still another systemwide convention for all DIMS,[8] the I/O switch is able to execute a call to the desired point (offset) in the DIM's transfer vector so as to reach the desired functional entry point. Thus if the standard position for the read entry transfer is the third element in the vector, then a function call of the form

call ios_$read ("input7", workspace, offset, etc.);

would find the I/O switch transferring into the third element in the transfer vector of <pdp7>, that is, at <pdp7>|[pdp7]+2. Here it would be expected to find the assembled code for an instruction like

tra read–*, ic*

which transfers to the link named *read* whose contents, when completed, will be an its pair pointing to where the DIM designer has placed the DIM's read function.

The DIM must be written in such a way as to return an error indication when there is an attempt by the switch to transfer to an entry point that corresponds to an unsupported I/O function. Here again, status reporting of attempts to utilize an unsupported function of a DIM is to be handled in convention-set way. The transfer vector element that would correspond to an unsupported function, for example, ios_$seek for the typewriter DIM, is coded to send control to a small subroutine of fixed form[9] that fabricates the appropriate "entry-not-found" status word and returns to the I/O switch that called it.

By way of summary it is well to repeat that the DIM writer can only supply as entry points a subset of those that are in the "vocabulary" of the I/O switch (currently those twenty or so entry points given in the ios_ section of the MPM).

8.5.3 The DIM's Interface with the GIM

With each read/write function call, the DIM fabricates data control word lists (DCW lists) and passes these to the GIM for further modification and use. There is a series of calls, outlined in the MPM under "GIOC calls," which the DIM must make in order to give the GIM an opportunity to "set itself up" to receive and employ these DCW lists and to perform its various communi-

8. The particular order of these entries is to be found in a listing of the so-called *transfer vector template* that appears in the MSPM section that overviews the I/O system.

9. More details can be found in the same MSPM discussion that was cited in the preceding footnote.

cation tasks. To make much sense of these calls the reader must acquaint himself with the GIOC hardware system reference manual. It is beyond the scope of this guide to provide a sufficiently detailed explanation of the GIOC to make the DIM's calls to the GIM thoroughly meaningful.

A few general concepts can be conveyed here, however. First, it should be understood that the GIM's work areas and I/O buffers must be wired down, because they can only be referenced by the GIOC in an absolute addressing mode. The work areas are used for DCW lists that are compiled by the DIM and moved by the GIM from the virtual-memory work areas designated by the DIM in its principal call on the GIM (at the entry point hcs_$list_change). These transmitted lists are transformed by the GIM before being activated so that the address fields in the DCWs are in loaded-and-ready-to-use absolute form. The work areas are also used for holding status words received from each channel and periodically copied over to corresponding work areas in the DIM's (virtual memory) data base.

The I/O buffers are also necessarily wired down and are referenced by the GIOC in absolute mode. The output buffer holds the actual data to be written out onto the channels. These data are copied by the GIM into its buffer from a corresponding buffer previously established and filled by the DIM. Similarly, the GIM's input buffers are necessarily wired down and filled directly by action of the GIOC during input channel activity. These data are copied by the GIM from this buffer back onto the data array designated by the DIM. The GIM knows how to move data into its output buffer or out of its input buffer to/from the corresponding DIM data arrays because the call(s) made by the DIM to the GIM (at hcs_$list_change) provide the required pointers.

When the DIM is ready to ask the GIM to activate a DCW list, that is, actually start the I/O (physically), the former makes a call requesting the GIM to transmit a channel instruction word for processing by the GIOC's so-called *connect channel.*

Prior to transmitting a DCW list the DIM must issue two preliminary or "set up" calls to the GIM. The first call (to hcs_$assign) affords the user access to the desired channel; the DIM requests this access by supplying a symbolic name and receiving in return a uniquely generated device index (17 bits) to be used in all subsequent I/O calls to the GIM for service on this channel. In the same call the DIM transmits an event-channel name as an argument. This argument would be previously obtained from the interprocess communication facility (IPC) as a result of a call to ipc_$create_event_ channel. It is by this event-channel name that the process, when later blocked awaiting completion of a requested I/O operation, can be awakened by the GIM. The GIM acts as the interrupt handler for all I/O interrupts. It consults a privileged table that it maintains wherein are recorded the 4-tuples giving channel name, device index, process id, and event-channel name. The DIMs are normally programmed to call ipc_$block when processing reads or writes that are synchronous or when the read-ahead or write-behind buffers are filled.

Once the assign call has been successfully completed, the DIM, using the received device index as its key argument, can call the GIM again. This time the request is for the GIM to allocate sufficient wired-down workspace for the DCW list to be designated in subsequent calls that cause the DCW lists to be transmitted to that workspace and assembled into "loaded" form.

The reader has been treated to the promised sketch of the DIM/GIM interface and is now on his own, ready for independent study, except for a few final remarks in the next section.

8.6 Final Remarks

A tour through the I/O system design would not be complete without observing that the I/O switch → DIM → GIM → GIOC chain is not absolutely mandatory as the only path allowed by Multics for I/O. A sophisticated subsystem designer will be the first to recognize that the I/O switch → DIM portion of this chain is strictly for user convenience. In principle, because the GIM may be called directly by the user, there is no reason why a designer could not bypass the I/O switch and DIM altogether for I/O to some special-purpose or dedicated devices and/or communication channels. In essence the subsystem would be written with code that achieves the equivalent of many I/O switch and DIM functions but calls the GIM directly using calls such as those suggested in Section 8.5.3. At all events the subsystem designer that chooses to travel this route should profit by a careful inspection of the I/O switch and DIM functions before launching into his own design that would allow a bypass of these modules.

A Multics Bibliography

A. Reference Manuals That May Be Purchased from the Publications Office of the M.I.T. Information Processing Center

1.
M.I.T., Project MAC, "The Multiplexed Information and Computing Service: Programmers' Manual," Revision 7, April 5, 1971. Also called "Multics Programmers' Manual" or MPM. An updated reference manual giving calling sequences and reference information for all user callable subroutines and commands. Includes an introduction to the Multics programming environment and a guide to typical ways of using the system. approx. 800 pages.

2.
R. A. Freiburghouse, *A User's Guide to the Multics FORTRAN Implementation* (Cambridge, Mass.: Cambridge Information Systems Laboratory, General Electric Co., 1969). Subsequent printings will be issued by Honeywell. A document that provides the prospective Multics FORTRAN user with sufficient information to enable him to create and execute FORTRAN programs on Multics. It contains a complete definition of the Multics FORTRAN language as well as a description of the FORTRAN command and error messages. It also describes how to communicate with non-FORTRAN programs and discusses some of the fundamental characteristics of Multics that affect the FORTRAN user. 68 pages.

3.
The Multics PL/I Language Specification (Cambridge, Mass.: Cambridge Information Systems Laboratory, General Electric Co., n.d.). Subsequent printings will be issued by Honeywell. A reference manual that specifies precisely the subset of the PL/I language used on Multics. [It is a reprint of the appropriate sections of *PL/I Language Specifications*, IBM Reference Manual, Form Y33-6003-0 (Armonk, N.Y.: International Business Machines Corp., 1968).] 174 pages.

4.
R. A. Freiburghouse, J. D. Mills, and B. L. Wolman, *A User's Guide to the Multics PL/I Implementation* (Cambridge, Mass.: Cambridge Information Systems Laboratory, General Electric Co., 1969). Subsequent printings will be issued by Honeywell. Provides detailed information about how the PL/I language is embedded in the Multics programming environment. 53 pages.

B.

Manuals That May Be Examined in the Project MAC or Information Processing Center Document Rooms at M.I.T.

1.

"Multics System-Programmers' Manual." Also called MSPM. In principle, a complete reference manual describing how the system works inside. In fact, this document contains many sections that are inconsistent, inaccurate, or obsolete; it is in need of much upgrading. However, its overview sections are generally accurate and valuable if insight into the internal organization is desired. approx. 3,500 pages.

2.

M.I.T., Project MAC, "The Multics Programmers' Manual: System Programmers' Supplement," Revision 25, July 2, 1971. This updatable reference manual, in the same format as the "Multics Programmers' Manual," provides calling sequences of every system module. 850 pages.

3.

D. J. Riesenberg, *EPLBSA Programmers' Reference Handbook* (Cambridge, Mass.: Cambridge Information Systems Laboratory, 1968). A manual describing the assembly (machine) language for the GE 645 computer. The language has been renamed ALM since the publication of this manual. (Needed only by programmers with some special reason to use 645 machine language.) 85 pages.

4.

J. Andrews, M. L. Goudy, and J. E. Barnes, *Model 645 Processor Reference Manual*, Revision 4 (Cambridge, Mass.: Cambridge Information Systems Laboratory, Honeywell, 1971). A hardware description, including opcodes, addressing modifiers, etc. Of interest only to dedicated machine language programmers. 175 pages.

C.

Published Technical Papers about Multics Arranged Chronologically

1965

1.

F. J. Corbató and V. A. Vyssotsky, "Introduction and Overview of the Multics System," *AFIPS Conference Proceedings, Volume 27, Part 1, 1965 Fall Joint Computer Conference* (Washington, D. C.: Spartan Books, 1965), pp. 185–196.

2.
E. L. Glaser, et al., "System Design of a Computer for Time-Sharing Application," *AFIPS Conference Proceedings, Volume 27, Part 1, 1965 Fall Joint Computer Conference* (Washington, D. C.: Spartan Books, 1965), pp. 197–202.
3.
V. A. Vyssotsky, et al., "Structure of the Multics Supervisor," *AFIPS Conference Proceedings, Volume 27, Part 1, 1965 Fall Joint Computer Conference* (Washington, D. C.: Spartan Books, 1965), pp. 203–212.
4.
R. C. Daley and P. G. Newmann, "A General-Purpose File System for Secondary Storage," *AFIPS Conference Proceedings, Volume 27, Part 1, 1965 Fall Joint Computer Conference* (Washington, D. C.: Spartan Books, 1965), pp. 213–229.
5.
J. F. Ossanna, et al., "Communication and Input/Output Switching in a Multiplex Computing System," *AFIPS Conference Proceedings, Volume 27, Part 1, 1965 Fall Joint Computer Conference* (Washington, D. C.: Spartan Books, 1965), pp. 231–241.
6.
E. E. David, Jr. and R. M. Fano, "Some Thoughts About the Social Implications of Accessible Computing," *AFIPS Conference Proceedings, Volume 27, Part 1, 1965 Fall Joint Computer Conference* (Washington, D. C.: Spartan Books, 1965), pp. 243–247.

1968

7.
R. C. Daley and J. B. Dennis, "Virtual Memory, Processes, and Sharing in MULTICS," *Communications of the ACM* 11, no. 5 (1968): 306–312.
8.
R. M. Graham, "Protection in an Information Processing Utility," *Communications of the ACM* 11, no. 5 (1968): 365–369.
9.
F. J. Corbató and J. H. Saltzer, "Some Considerations of Supervisor Program Design for Multiplexed Computer Systems," in *Information Processing 68, Proceedings of IFIP Congress 1968*, edited by A. J. H. Morrell, vol. 1 (Amsterdam: North-Holland, 1969), pp. 315–321.

1969

10.

F. J. Corbató, "PL/I as a Tool for System Programming," *Datamation* 15, no. 5 (1969): 68–76.

11.

A. Bensoussan, C. T. Clingen, and R. C. Daley, "The Multics Virtual Memory," *Second Symposium on Operating Systems Principles, Princeton University, October 1969* (New York: Association for Computing Machinery, 1969), pp. 30–42.

12.

M. J. Spier and E. I. Organick, "The Multics Interprocess Communication Facility," *Second Symposium on Operating System Principles, Princeton University, October 1969* (New York: Association for Computing Machinery, 1969), pp. 83–91.

13.

J. H. Saltzer and J. W. Gintell, "The Instrumentation of Multics," *Second Symposium on Operating Systems Principles, Princeton University, October 1969* (New York: Association for Computing Machinery, 1969), pp. 167–174. Also in *Communications of the ACM* 13, no. 8 (1970): 495–500.

14.

F. J. Corbató, "A Paging Experiment with the Multics System," in *In Honor of Philip M. Morse*, edited by H. Feshbach and K. U. Ingard (Cambridge, Mass.: M.I.T. Press, 1969), pp. 217–228.

15.

R. A. Freiburghouse, "The Multics PL/I Compiler," *AFIPS Conference Proceedings, Volume 35, 1969 Fall Joint Computer Conference* (Montvale, N. J.: AFIPS Press, 1969), pp. 187–199.

16.

J. M. Grochow, "Real-Time Graphic Display of Time-Sharing System Operating Characteristics," *AFIPS Conference Proceedings, Volume 35, 1969 Fall Joint Computer Conference* (Montvale, N. J.: AFIPS Press, 1969), pp. 379–385.

1970

17.

J. H. Saltzer and J. F. Ossanna, "Remote Terminal Character Stream Processing in Multics," *AFIPS Conference Proceedings, Volume 36, 1970*

Spring Joint Computer Conference (Montvale, N. J.: AFIPS Press, 1970), pp. 621–627.

18.
J. F. Ossanna and J. H. Saltzer, "Technical and Human Engineering Problems in Connecting Terminals to a Time-Sharing System," *AFIPS Conference Proceedings, Volume 37, 1970 Fall Joint Computer Conference* (Montvale, N. J.: AFIPS Press, 1970), pp. 355–362.

1971

19.
D. D. Clark, R. M. Graham, J. H. Saltzer, and M. D. Schroeder, "The Classroom Information and Computing Service," M.I.T. Project MAC Technical Report TR–80, January 11, 1971.

20.
M. D. Schroeder, "Performance of the GE-645 Associative Memory While Multics Is in Operation," *ACM Workshop on System Performance Evaluation, April 1971* (New York: Association for Computing Machinery, 1971), pp. 227–245.

21.
M. D. Schroeder and J. H. Saltzer, "A Hardware Architecture for Implementing Protection Rings," *Third Symposium on Operating Systems Principles, Palo Alto, California, October 1971* (New York: Association for Computing Machinery, 1971), pp. 42–54.

22.
R. J. Feiertag and E. I. Organick, "The Multics Input-Output System," *Third Symposium on Operating Systems Principles, Palo Alto, California, October 1971* (New York: Association for Computing Machinery, 1971), pp. 35–41.

D.
M.I.T. Theses Related to Multics

1. J. H. Saltzer, "Traffic Control in a Multiplexed Computer System," Sc.D., 1966. MAC-TR-30.
2. H. Deitel, "Absentee Computations in a Multiple-Access Computer System," S.M., 1968. MAC-TR-52.
3. J. M. Grochow, "The Graphic Display as an Aid in the Monitoring of a Time-Shared Computer System," S.M., 1968. MAC-TR-54.

4. R. Rappaport, "Implementing Multi-Process Primitives in a Multiplexed Computer System," S.M., 1968. MAC-TR-55.

5. H. J. Greenbaum, "A Simulator of Multiple Interactive Users to Drive a Time-Shared Computer System," S.M., 1968. MAC-TR-58.

6. R. I. Ancona, "A Compiler for MAD-Based Language on Multics," S.M., 1968.

7. D. Clark, "A Reduction Analysis System for Parsing PL/I," S.M., 1968.

8. M. D. Schroeder, "Classroom Model of an Information and Computing Service," S.M., 1969.

9. C. M. Vogt, "Suspension of Processes in a Multiprocessing Computer System," S.M., 1970.

10. R. Frankston, "A Limited Service System on Multics," S.B., 1970.

11. R. R. Schell, "Dynamic Reconfiguration in a Modular Computer System," Ph.D., 1971.

Subject Index